"This is, I think, a unique book. It takes the deeply biblical identification with place and maps it onto our homogenized world to see what possibilities we have for new depth, new beauty, new meaning. I found it unrelentingly fascinating."

—**Bill McKibben**, author, *Eaarth: Making a Life on a Tough New Planet*

"In this ambitious new book Craig Bartholomew has assembled a remarkable range of ideas and resources for the work of making our world a place that glorifies God. Drawing on scholarship in biblical studies, theology, philosophy, and cultural studies, Bartholomew advances distinctly Christian thinking about place in a significant way."

—**Norman Wirzba**, Duke Divinity School

"Craig Bartholomew's *Where Mortals Dwell: A Christian View of Place for Today* is a stunning achievement. The book masterfully surveys the role of place in the Bible, helpfully looks at the role place has played in the Western philosophical tradition, and concludes with satisfying advice, both theoretical and practical, on how contemporary Christians should think about place as they engage in the crucial work of placemaking. It is rare to find an author with such command of biblical, theological, and philosophical issues, who provides original, powerful ideas delivered in clear, sparkling prose."

—**C. Stephen Evans**, Baylor University

"Ever since Walter Brueggemann's groundbreaking study *The Land* in 1977 we have been waiting for a comprehensive Christian theology of place. *Where Mortals Dwell* represents a significant step in that direction. In it, Bartholomew sets the agenda for Christians to think about both place and placemaking, shaping this long-overdue conversation for years to come."

—**Eric O. Jacobsen**, senior pastor, First Presbyterian Church, Tacoma, Washington; author, *Sidewalks in the Kingdom*

"This is a major work of theological rediscovery in which Craig Bartholomew imaginatively reconstructs a Christian view of human implacement. Bringing biblical, philosophical, and theological perspectives to bear, he explores unexpected aspects of implacement with ventures into ornithology, building, gardening, and the home. *Where Mortals Dwell* is an erudite, readable, original, and fascinating invitation to a theology and spirituality of place."

—**Gordon McConville**, University of Gloucestershire

"This study in theology that builds from a biblical base and moves to discussions of urban planning, biotic community, and pilgrimage—and even includes maps—may well be unprecedented. The very fact that this assemblage of concerns comes as a surprise to the reader points to the need for this study of what it means to come before God *in our places*."

—Ellen F. Davis, Duke Divinity School

"Place affects us all, but reflections about its significance are scarce—especially thoroughly Christian reflections. This outstanding book therefore deserves your attention. The entire teaching of the Bible about place is represented here in one fascinating overview followed by an intriguing confrontation with Western philosophical thought on matters of place. *Where Mortals Dwell* is a brilliant survey of the liberating Christian concept of placemaking."

—Bob Goudzwaard, Free University of Amsterdam

"In this comprehensive and detailed overview of scriptural, philosophical, and theological traditions, Craig Bartholomew offers a superb exploration and affirmation of the centrality of place in Christian thought and life. This book will be an important interdisciplinary resource wherever academic consideration is given to the art of human dwelling or implacement. *Where Mortals Dwell* is set to become the standard work in this emerging field."

—Peter Manley Scott, Lincoln Theological Institute, University of Manchester

Where Mortals Dwell

*A Christian View of Place
for Today*

Craig G. Bartholomew

Baker Academic

a division of Baker Publishing Group
Grand Rapids, Michigan

Published by Baker Academic
a division of Baker Publishing Group
P.O. Box 6287, Grand Rapids, MI 49516-6287
www.bakeracademic.com

Printed and bound by CPI Group (UK) Ltd, Croydon, CR0 4YY

Library of Congress Cataloging-in-Publication Data
Bartholomew, Craig G., 1961–
    Where mortals dwell : a Christian view of place for today / Craig G. Bartholomew.
        p.   cm.
    Includes bibliographical references (p.   ) and indexes.
    ISBN 978-0-8010-3637-8 (pbk.)
    1. Sacred space. 2. Place (Philosophy). I. Title.
BV895.B37 2011
231.7—dc22   2011016587

Dedicated to my sister Yvonne Laurel Bartholomew, who after the death of both of our parents in recent years has continued to maintain our family home in South Africa as a place to which it is wonderful to return

Contents

Illustrations

Preface

One of the glories of being human and creaturely is to be implaced. Sadly, this is threatened daily by the crisis of place in which we are immersed today. As I have discovered, the literature on place is vast, and there are many writers, teachers, and practitioners working to recover a human sense of place. Alas, with some notable exceptions the literature emerging from the Christian community in this respect is sparse, as though we are relatively unaware of the challenges facing us today. My hope is that this book will alert us to the importance of place, to the rich resources in the Bible for a Christian view of place today, and to the sheer joie de vivre—often amidst suffering—of placemaking, whether it be gardening, homemaking, urban development, or making place with and for the poor in our world.

By the concept of *placemaking* I aim to articulate a distinctively Christian view of place, but my hope is that it will be read well beyond the Christian community. We all participate in the contemporary crisis of place, and placemaking will require cooperation among diverse communities. My conviction is that it is only as we allow our different worldviews to come to fruition in a view of place that real dialogue and cooperation can begin, dialogue which does not seek a lowest common denominator, but rather enables cooperation which respects our differences and fundamental convictions.

I am grateful to my research assistants over the past three years, David Beldman, Sean Purcell, and James Sikkema, for their invaluable help in tracking down endless resources for this book. The support of Redeemer University College and The Paideia Center for Public Theology has been important in creating the space and providing a congenial place for this work. My colleagues Ryan O'Dowd, Calvin Seerveld, Edward Berkelaar, and an anonymous reviewer made helpful comments about the developing manuscript. My initial interest in place was sparked several years ago while I was assisting Canon Dr. Robert Llewellyn with his research on the anthropology of pilgrimage. That interest developed into a conference and consultation on pilgrimage, the results of which were eventually published by Ashgate as *Towards a Christian Theology of Pilgrimage* (C. G. Bartholomew and F. Hughes, eds.). Bob Walker repeatedly drew my attention to the importance of urban development in modernity and the possibility of geographical community, a long-standing interest of his. A special thanks goes to my good friend South African sculptor Gert Swart and his wife Istine, who have been unfailing in their support for this project from its inception. I have twice taught a course titled "A Christian View of Place" at Redeemer University College, and students have contributed to my thinking in all sorts of ways. I remain grateful to all those who have helped on my exhilarating journey in search of a theology and practice of place.

There is a great deal of work to be done by Christians in this area. As I have worked through as much of the vast literature as possible, I have been conscious that this work is far from the final word; my hope is that for many it will function as a first word and spur them on to do the hard thinking and practice that alone will enable us to recover a sense of place.

Finally, it remains to thank Jim Kinney and his colleagues at Baker Academic. It is a privilege to work with such a congenial and professional publisher.

Craig Bartholomew
Pentecost, 2010

Introduction

What Is Place?

Place is ubiquitous and yet always particular. Place is my backyard in Hamilton, Ontario, Canada, where the spring bulbs are now flowering and where a wild rabbit comes for a time to rest and graze, at peace amidst this busy city. Place is my office, painted a warm yellow by friends when I moved in here and where I sit to write this book. Place is the unutterable beauty of the Valley of a Thousand Hills, near where I grew up in KwaZulu-Natal in South Africa, the same context in which Alan Paton's classic novel, *Cry, the Beloved Country*,[1] is set.

Cry, the Beloved Country poured out of Paton while he was on a trip to Europe in 1946. Having just arrived in Norway and after visiting a cathedral, filled with intense homesickness, he returned to his hotel room, where he wrote the opening lines of what was to become a classic: "There is a lovely road that runs from Ixopo into the hills. These hills are grass-covered and rolling, and they are lovely beyond any singing of it."[2] That same beloved country is the scene of Nobel Prize–winning author J. M. Coetzee's *Disgrace*, with its almost unreadable accounts of rape and violence in postapartheid South Africa.

Place is the rich, African beauty of Rwanda and churches filled with human skulls from the genocide that still—how long?—indelibly marks the landscape

---

1. The title is drawn from a phrase that is used several times in the book. For example, from p. 80: "Cry, the beloved country, for the unborn child that is the inheritor of our fear. Let him not love the earth too deeply. Let him not laugh too gladly when the water runs through his fingers, nor stand too silent when the setting sun makes red the veld with fire. Let him not be too moved when the birds of his land are singing, nor give too much of his heart to a mountain or a valley. For fear will rob him of all if he gives too much."

2. See Paton, *Towards the Mountain*, 264–74.

1

of that country. Place is an Amish farm, and the animal factory, "which, like the concentration camp, is a vision of Hell."[3] Place is the home one retreats to for rest and nourishment, and place is the "homes" that are the scene of abuse. Place is Mother Teresa's home for the dying in Calcutta—"something beautiful for God"—with its translucent light caught on camera by Malcolm Muggeridge, and also Birkenau and Auschwitz. Place is gardens and parks, and millions of kilometers of road and millions of square acres of tarred parking lots. Place is my house, my garden, the university at which I teach, the city in which I live, the malls in which I shop, and the roads and trails on which I run. Place is where you are right now as you read this book.

Place is a rich, thick[4] concept which is notoriously difficult to define. As Aristotle rightly noted, "The question, what is place? presents many difficulties."[5] Place is real, but it is a complex creational structure. Place is so fundamental to human existence and so ubiquitous that, paradoxically, it is easy to miss.[6] Its reality and importance cannot be in doubt, but the neglect of it and its thickness make it hard to pin down conceptually. The result is that today many scholars write about place without attempting to define it. In part 2 and at the start of part 3 we will explore the structure of place in more detail. For now we will highlight some of the central elements that constitute place, elements that will guide us as we continue on our journey of exploration.

Firstly, place is a quintessentially *human* concept in that it is part of our creatureliness. E. Casey, who has done the most comprehensive work on the philosophy of place, notes that "to be in the world, to be situated at all, is to be in place. Place is the phenomenal particularization of 'being-in-the-world,' a phrase that in Heidegger's hands retains a certain formality and abstractness which only the concreteness of *being-in-place*, that is, being in the *place-world* itself, can mitigate."[7] Casey speaks in this respect of the human condition as one of *implacement*: "To exist at all . . . is to have a place—*to be implaced*, however minimally or temporarily."[8] Part of being embodied involves being in a particular place: "In my embodied being I am *just at* a place as its inner boundary; a surrounding landscape, on the other hand, is *just beyond* that place as its outer boundary. Between the two boundaries—and very much as a function of their different interplay—implacement occurs. Place is what takes place between body and landscape."[9]

3. W. Berry, *Way of Ignorance*, 99.

4. In Geertz's sense of the term as found in *Interpretation of Cultures*, 5–6, 9–10.

5. Aristotle, *Physics* 4.1.34.

6. Cf. Malpas, *Place and Experience*, 177–78.

7. Casey, *Getting Back into Place*, xv. Emphasis original. Casey notes that "Heidegger alone of postmodern thinkers has thematized place, albeit fragmentarily and inconsistently" (*Fate of Place*, 11). It is therefore not surprising that Casey uses Heidegger's terminology in defining place.

8. Casey, *Getting Back into Place*, 13. Emphasis original.

9. Ibid., 29. Emphasis original.

Secondly, since to be human is to be placed, it follows that place results from the *dynamic interaction* of humans and their particular locations. While human existence in the world is possible only in and through a particular place, place is also shaped and constituted by the activity of the humans who dwell in it. The interplay between humans and their contexts means that place has a developmental, *cultural* dimension.[10] Place is furthermore never individualistic; rather, it "insinuates itself into a collectivity."[11] There is inevitably a *social* dimension to place; humans are placed in relationship, and in relationship they form and fashion places. Implacement is an ongoing, dynamic process, and, being cultural and social, it is also *historical*. These dimensions contribute "to the felt density of a particular place, the sense that it has something lasting to it."[12] An exploration of place will thus attend to dimensions such as the natural landscape, flora and fauna, patterns of weather and sky, the human shaping of a place and its resources, the history of a place, memory, and the individual and communal narratives with which a place is imbued.[13]

Thirdly, although *space* and *place* are inseparable, place must be distinguished from space. As we will see in part 2, place is part of our lived, everyday experience, whereas space, especially in our modern world, is a theoretical concept and as such an abstraction *from* the lived experience of place. There has been a fatal tendency in modernity to privilege abstract, scientific knowledge over everyday experience as the path to the truth about the world. Such an approach sounds the death knell for place, since it fails to do justice to the thick, rich, holding action of local habitation.[14] Primacy must, we will argue, be given to lived, everyday experience in our knowledge of the world.

Why Does Place Matter?

We live amidst a crisis of place. In our late-modern age we have lost that very human sense of place amidst the time-space compression[15] characteristic of "postmodernity" and globalization. Place has become something that one moves through, preferably at great speed, and virtual reality is no re*place*-ment. As David Lyon perceptively notes of cyberspace, "There is no place to this space."[16] Casey describes our culture as *dromocratic*, that is, as a speed-bound era.[17] Indeed, the suffering of placelessness is not confined to refugees and those in exile, agonizing as their experiences are; in our dromocratic

10. Ibid.
11. Ibid., 31.
12. Ibid., 33.
13. Malpas, *Place and Experience*, 185.
14. Casey, *Fate of Place*, 20.
15. See Harvey, *Condition of Postmodernity*, 260–83, on this theme.
16. Lyon, *Jesus in Disneyland*, 124. Cf. Casey, *Fate of Place*, xiv; and Ward, *Cities of God*, 245.
17. Casey, *Getting Back into Place*, xiv.

society every person constantly "on the move" suffers from placelessness in one form or another.

In part 2 we will track how "space" won over "place" in modernity, leading to the neglect and suppression of place. According to Casey,

> In the past three centuries in the West—the period of "modernity"—place has come to be not only neglected but actively suppressed. Owing to the triumph of the natural and social sciences in this same period, any serious talk of place has been regarded as regressive or trivial. . . . For an entire epoch, place has been regarded as an impoverished second cousin of Time and Space, those two colossal cosmic partners towering over modernity.[18]

But place will not go away! One can ignore place, but it is unavoidable:

> We are immersed in it and could not do without it. To be at all—to exist in any way—is to be somewhere, and to be somewhere is to be in some kind of place. Place is as requisite as the air we breathe, the ground on which we stand, the bodies we have. We are surrounded by places. We walk over them and through them. We live in places, relate to others in them, die in them. Nothing we do is unplaced.[19]

The neglect of place has thus had devastating consequences. In our late-modern context we are witnessing the development of global cities in which "place no longer matters and . . . the only type of worker that matters is the highly educated professional."[20] The dehumanizing effect of Western urban sprawl is well documented. The crisis of city life is related to the concomitant crisis of rural and agrarian life. Problems in both areas are symptomatic of the larger crisis of place central to late-modernity.

Harvey Cox celebrates the gifts of the modern city as anonymity and mobility.[21] W. Brueggemann, however, perceptively notes that we suffer not so much from anomie but more foundationally from *atopia*, placelessness:[22]

> That promise concerned human persons who could lead detached, unrooted lives of endless choice and no commitment. It was glamorized around the virtues of mobility and anonymity that seemed so full of promise for freedom and self-actualization. But it has failed. . . . It is now clear that a *sense of place* is a human hunger that urban promise has not met. . . . It is *rootlessness* and not *meaninglessness* that characterizes the current crisis. There are no meanings apart from roots.[23]

18. Ibid., xiv.
19. Casey, *Fate of Place*, ix.
20. Saskia Sassen, quoted in Ward, *Cities of God*, 242.
21. Cox, *Secular City*, 33–51.
22. Terminology is from Casey, *Getting Back into Place*, xi.
23. Brueggemann, *The Land*, 3–4. Emphasis original.

Place is so constituent of human being that perhaps this is one reason why it is so easily overlooked. But we desperately need to recover a sense of place and placemaking. "The present moment is a propitious one for assessing the fate of place. This is so even though there is precious little talk of place in philosophy—or, for that matter, in psychology or sociology, literary theory or religious studies."[24] Theology and biblical studies suffer a similar neglect.[25] Emphases on an existentialist approach and a great-deeds approach resulted in the neglect of creation, nature, land, and place in most biblical theology. Brueggemann's *The Land* marked a significant reversal in this trend, and, encouragingly, an ecological biblical hermeneutic and theology are emerging with similar concerns. However, it is rare to find theologians and biblical exegetes working specifically with the concept of *place*. As we will see, "place" is particularly well suited to excavate key elements of the biblical message and to help us recover a robust practice of place today.

As part 3 of this book indicates, place has a very practical bent to it. Our concern is a recovery not just of a Christian view of place but of place*making*. It is here that the richness and sheer joie de vivre of place come firmly into view, as well as the agonizing ways in which place is misdirected in our day. However, there is no quick fix to such recovery; rigorous biblical work is required (part 1), as well as excavations into the Western philosophical and Christian traditions (part 2), so that we can see how we have arrived at *this* place, and how we can be reoriented by Scripture and the best of the Christian tradition toward a recovery of place today.

---

24. Casey, *Fate of Place*, xi–xii.
25. Inge, *Christian Theology of Place*, is an important exception.

Place in the Bible

For the Bible is *the* authority, insofar as any historical document is authoritative, for every kind of Christian theology. If we do not know what the Bible says about nature [place], therefore, the whole enterprise of historical exploration of the classical theological tradition could easily be questioned.[1]

Is the final aim of God, in his governance of all things, to bring into being at the very end a glorified kingdom of spirits alone who, thus united with God, may contemplate him in perfect bliss, while as a precondition of their ecstasy all the other creatures of nature must be left by God to fall away into eternal oblivion?

Or is the final aim of God, in his governance of all things, to communicate his life to another in a way that calls forth at the very end new heavens and a new earth in which righteousness dwells, a transfigured cosmos where peace is universally established between all creatures at last, in the midst of which is situated a glorious city of resurrected saints who dwell in justice, blessed with all the resplendent fullness of the earth, and who continually call upon all creatures to join with them in their joyful praise of the one who is all in all?[2]

As Santmire points out in the above quotes, Scripture is *the* authority for the church; thus, close attention to its teaching is crucial for any theology of place. As we will discover in this section, not only is "place" a fertile grid through which to approach the Bible, but the Bible also yields a staggering amount of data relating to place.

1. Santmire, *Travail of Nature*, 175. Emphasis original.
2. Ibid., 217–18.

1

The Theology of Place in Genesis 1–3

The world is the house where mortals dwell.[1]

Although most scholars nowadays consider the early chapters of Genesis to have been written later than much of the Old Testament, canonically they sit at the outset of the drama of Scripture and in this respect they are foundational. They contain the early acts in the great drama that unfolds, and without them the drama simply cannot be understood. As we will see, they are similarly foundational for a theology of place, and at the same time approaching them through the grid of place is revealing in terms of their theology.

Genesis 1:1–2:3

A Place Story

Genesis 1 is carefully crafted literature with a polemical dimension which sets it against alternative creation stories of the ancient Near East while articulating its own distinctive worldview. Ideological questions have been raised about Genesis 1, and particularly about humankind's relation to the earth.[2] Norman Habel's ecological reading of Genesis 1 is worth noting in this respect.

1. Heidegger, *Hebel der Hausfreund*, 13.
2. The most well-known critique is that by White, "Historical Roots of Our Ecological Crisis."

Habel rightly observes that while Genesis 1:1–2:3 is cosmic in its scope, its focus is clearly on the earth. According to Habel, "the earth story at the beginning of Genesis is a dramatic account that celebrates the wonder and worth of Earth as a geophany."[3] For Habel, earth is the primary character of the story, and the reader eagerly awaits her appearance and development. He finds this earth story, however, to be in stark contrast to the story of the creation of humans in 1:26–30: "The human story (Gen. 1:26–30) violates the spirit of the earth-oriented story that precedes it (Gen. 1:1–25)."[4] Genesis 1 moves from honoring earth to negating it as a force to be overcome by humanity.[5] In Habel's view it is time we restored the earth story to its rightful place as a genuine counterpart to the human story, with which the earth story interacts in subsequent narratives in Genesis.

There are several difficulties with Habel's discernment of conflicting narratives in Genesis 1, difficulties which I have discussed in detail elsewhere.[6] For our purposes it is important to note that the whole point of Genesis 1 is to present the earth as the context for human habitation, for implacement. The earth is one of the major actors in the narrative, but so too is the human, and one of the motifs of the narrative is how humans are to interact with the earth. Thus it is far better to see Genesis 1 as a *place* story than as an earth story. Place evokes human inhabitation of the earth, and in this respect it helps us to see what is going on in Genesis 1 far better than a renewed source criticism which uses ideological critique to discern conflicting stories. Genesis 1 portrays the earth as a *potential* place for human habitation and dwelling. As Heidegger notes, "The world is the house where mortals dwell."[7]

Differentiation of/and Place

Contra the *Enuma Elish* and other ancient Near Eastern creation stories, the differentiation of place that occurs during the six days of Genesis 1 is oriented toward creating a context suitable for human implacement and flourishing. The gradual differentiation of place that we find in Genesis 1 is, however, common to other creation stories. As Casey notes, "The cosmogonic gathering is in effect a formation of place. Thus, even if the beginning is characterized as a situation of no-place, the ineluctable nisus is towards place—and towards an ever increasing specificity of place, its laying out in the

---

3. Habel, "Geophany," 35.
4. Ibid., 47.
5. Ibid., 48.
6. Bartholomew, "Theology of Place in Genesis 1–3."
7. Casey notes, "If Bachelard is right in claiming that 'all really inhabited space bears the essence of the notion of home' and that home itself is 'a real cosmos in every sense of the word,' then home and cosmos alike—home *as* cosmos—result from practices of cultivation" (*Getting Back into Place*, 175).

right . . . order."[8] Creation involves differentiation, and this is progressively more determinate and leads toward human inhabitation. The differentiation of a variety of places is evident in Genesis 1 from the fivefold use of the Hebrew root *bdl* (divide, separate; vv. 4, 6, 7, 14, 18). "From the principle of separation, light; via something which separates, heaven; to something which is separated, earth and sea; to things which are productive of separated things, trees, for example; then things which can separate themselves from their places, heavenly bodies; and finally a being which can separate itself from its right way, the right way."[9] Clearly the separation in Genesis has more than place in view, but place is an essential element emerging from the differentiation process. Indeed, the placial ordering of the creation is already indicated in 1:1, in which the heavens and the earth are the objects of God's creative activity. By itself *haššāmayim* means "sky" or heaven as the abode of God, but here in 1:1 we have a spatial merism, according to which the totality of a thing is indicated by its two extremes, so that the reference is to the whole of the universe.

Central to the separation process and the repetitive "Let there be" is the introduction of time and thus history. Genesis 1:1–2:3 is structured around the seven days, and theologically it is vital to note that no tension is envisioned between this timedness of creation—including cyclical seasons (v. 14)—and the earth, the waters, plants, birds, animals, and humankind. As in the rest of the Bible, there is in Genesis 1 no dichotomy between "nature" and "history," though the finding there of such a dichotomy has bedeviled modern Old Testament scholarship, giving rise to a false dualism between creation and redemption and between history and nature.[10]

Genesis 1's theology of place is thus presented in the context of a complex, dynamic understanding of creation as ordered by God. The specific places mentioned are the earth (v. 10),[11] the seas (v. 10), and the sky (v. 8). The earth is "occupied" by vegetation and animals. Similarly, creatures are made to inhabit the seas and the sky. Humankind does not transcend this order but is part of it; as God's royal steward, humankind finds its place and flourishes through submission to this order:

> This network of structures and functions, governed by creational law, manifests his [God's] loving care *for all creatures. Every creature*, each in its own unique way, is subject to his constant yet dynamic ecosystem of creational laws. Compliance with it is not an odious burden. . . . The creation order is evidence of the

8. Casey, *Fate of Place*, 15–16.
9. Strauss, "On the Interpretation of Genesis," 12–13. Cf. Kass, *Beginning of Wisdom*, 31–36.
10. See Hiebert, *Yahwist's Landscape*, 3–22.
11. "Earth" ('*ereṣ*) is used in three different ways in Gen. 1: as part of the merism in v. 1, to refer to the whole of the planet in v. 2, and to refer to the dry land masses in vv. 9–10.

caring hand of the Creator reaching out to secure the well-being of his creatures, of a Father extending a universe full of blessings to his children.[12]

Insofar as Genesis 1 is concerned, the move toward place is particularly strong because, contra other ancient Near Eastern creation stories, Genesis 1 presents a picture of the earth being shaped into an environment that is very good for human habitation, rather than of humankind being created to make the lives of the gods easier.[13] As Barth notes, this is particularly true from the fourth day onward:

> The wisdom and goodness of the Creator abound in the fact that, following the creation, establishment and securing of a sphere of human life, He wills to fashion and does fashion it as a *dwelling-place* for the man who can recognize God and himself and his fellow-creatures, and who in the recognition of what is and occurs can be grateful and express his gratitude. . . . The office of these lights, the heavenly bodies, is to summon him in relation to his Maker to sight, consciousness and activity.[14]

Because day and night have already been created, there is a sense in which the luminaries are redundant, but not only are they not gods, they are given as signs *for humankind*, to demarcate seasons, days, and years (1:14).[15] In the surrounding cultures it was common practice to worship the star-studded heavens, but as Kass rightly notes, in Genesis 1 "not heaven, but man has the closest relation to God." In this sense 1:26–30 is indeed the high point of 1:1–2:3, since it involves the implacement of those earthly creatures made in God's image in the home he has prepared for them. As Heidegger notes, "The relationship between man and space is none other than dwelling, thought essentially."[16]

Thus, approaching Genesis 1 through the prism of place helps us to see that earth and humankind are both central characters in the narrative and that a central motif is their interrelationship. There remains the question of whether or not 1:26–30 affirms exploitation of the earth. Much has been written about this issue, and attention is focused on *wĕyirdû* in 1:26 ("let them have dominion") and *wĕkibšūhā* ("and subdue it") in 1:28.[17]

---

12. Spykman, *Reformational Theology*, 178. Emphasis added. On creation order see 178–94.

13. Cf. here sec. 6 of the *Enuma Elish*, where man is created: "He shall be charged with the service of the gods / That they might be at ease!" (in O'Brien and Major, *In the Beginning*, 25).

14. Barth, *Church Dogmatics*, vol. 3, pt. 1, p. 157. Emphasis added.

15. Ibid., 160.

16. Heidegger, "Building. Dwelling. Thinking." 359.

17. Jacob, for example, says of *kbš* in Gen. 1:28, "With this one word, echoed again in Psalms 115:16, humanity is granted unlimited sovereignty over the planet earth; therefore no work that is done on it, for example drilling or the levelling of mountains, drying up or diverting rivers, and similar things, can be regarded as a violent ravaging that is repugnant to God" (*Das Erste Buch der Tora Genesis*, 61).

Place and "Dominion"

Rdh, the root of *wĕyirdû*, can indeed have the connotation of brutal mastery, as for example in Leviticus 26:17, but it need not, and the context invariably determines its nuance. Thus in Leviticus 25:53 the resident alien who hires an Israelite as a laborer does indeed "rule" (*rdh*) over him, but is not to do so with harshness. Similarly in Ezekiel 34:4 the shepherds of Israel are castigated because they rule (*rdh*) over the Israelites with force and harshness. This section is followed in Ezekiel (34:31) by a wonderful vision of a very different type of rule, that of the LORD God, whose rule will result in the Israelites being "secure on their soil" (34:27). Ezekiel 34 is illuminating in terms of Genesis 1 because humankind's rule is a major way in which humankind images God. God, and not humankind, is the central character in the creation narrative, and dominion is best understood as a royal stewardship in which humankind's role is to serve, develop, and indwell the creation in such a way that it is enhanced and God is honored.[18] In my opinion the decisive key in this respect is that Genesis 1 envisages humans as herbivores; according to 1:29 the plants and the fruit of the trees are provided for food, not, by implication, the animals. Indeed, the same "table" is set for the animals!

Kbš, the root of *wĕkibšuhā*, is used of the conquest of Canaan by the Israelites (cf. Num. 32:22, 29), but, as N. Lohfink persuasively argues, it is best understood in these contexts as "to take possession of,"[19] so that in Genesis 1 *kbš* refers not to wanton destruction but to multiplication and expansion over the earth. E. F. Davis argues suggestively that *kbš* means "conquest" here but is used ironically; in the ears of landless exiles in Babylon it would evoke the land and the judgment that abuse of the land had resulted in, as well as hope of taking possession of the land once again.[20] Either way, wanton destruction of the earth and of animals is not in mind; humankind is viewed not only as vegetarian but as imaging God in his *good* creation. The occurrence of the seventh and final notice of fulfillment—"And it was so"—at the end of 1:30 follows God's provision of food for humans *and* animals, who are also referred to as having the breath of life. The elaborate stress on food for humans *and* animals in verses 29–30, which concludes the making of humans in God's image, suggests that an important way in which humans are to image God

18. Barth notes that "he [the man] thus appears as the being which must be able to and ready to serve in order to give meaning and purpose to the planting of the earth. . . . In view of his complete integration in the totality of the created world, there can be no question of a superiority of man supported by appeals to his special dignity, or of forgetfulness not merely of a general but of the very definite control of Yahweh Elohim over man. In spite of all the particular things that God may plan and do with him, in the first instance man can only serve the earth and will continually have to do so" (*Church Dogmatics*, vol. 3, pt. 1, p. 235).

19. N. Lohfink, *Theology of the Pentateuch*, 10.

20. E. F. Davis, *Scripture, Culture, and Agriculture*, 59–63.

is by perpetuating the abundant sufficiency God has built into his creation.[21] This is a far cry from brutal exploitation.

While the move in Genesis 1 *is* toward the creation of a perfect home for humankind, it is important to notice that the goodness of creation does not depend upon humankind but upon God. Prior to 1:26 some form of the phrase "And God saw that it was good" occurs six times, a reminder that the value of creation lies in its coming from the hand of God and not merely in its utilitarian value for humankind. Light, varieties of vegetation, seed, the sun and the moon, birds, animals, and sea creatures are all called "good"! And God's "very good" comes as he contemplates "*everything* that he had made" (1:31, emphasis added).

Wallace rightly notes the significance of Genesis 2:1–3 in this respect. Verse 1 stresses once again the interrelatedness and completeness of the creation. "Genesis 2.1–3 stands as a check against any interpretation of the role of humans in Genesis 1.28 that ignores the harmony and wholeness of all the work God has done in creation."[22] Polemically 2:1–3 establishes a calendar contrary to the Mesopotamian practice of a Sabbath related to the day of the full moon. The Israelite calendar is connected not to heavenly bodies but directly to the creator God. In contrast to the Akkadian and Ugaritic narratives, in which the god's rest is achieved at the expense of humankind, who are created to relieve the gods of manual labor, the Genesis account of creation represents humans as intended to participate in God's rest. Thus, "The seventh day is a recognition that the creation is held together by God and that God is the one on whom it is totally dependent."[23]

Being Human

The genre of Genesis 1:1–2:3 is contested; Blocher argues that it is wisdom literature,[24] whereas Davis and Brueggemann have suggested that it is a liturgical poem.[25] These proposals are not antithetical, and clearly God's contemplation of his creation and his declaration of it as good and very good encourage the reader to wonder at his handiwork and to explore its intricacy. At its best, the work of Christians in natural history has done and continues to do precisely this. Davis refers to Erazim Kohák's analysis of our need for a "contemplative strategy" that enables us to stand "in mute awe before the wonder of being."[26] Genesis 1 inducts us into a way of seeing the world such that we stand in awe before the creator and his marvelous handiwork, of which we ourselves are a part.

21. Cf. ibid., 58.
22. Wallace, "Rest for the Earth?," 53.
23. Ibid., 58.
24. Blocher, *In the Beginning*, 32.
25. Davis, *Scripture, Culture, and Agriculture*, 43; Brueggemann, *Genesis*, 26, 30.
26. Erazim Kohák, quoted in Davis, *Scripture, Culture, and Agriculture*, 46.

As part of its polemic Genesis 1 reminds its hearers, as noted above, that humankind has a closer relationship to God than any other creature. In this way Genesis 1 cuts through the Platonism and Neoplatonism that have so infected Christian theology through the centuries, hindering us from finding God *where* we are. B. Taylor observes that nowadays people will travel great distances searching for the divine and wisdom, but

> the last place most people look is right under their feet, in the everyday activities, accidents, and encounters of their lives. . . . My life depends on ignoring all touted distinctions between the secular and the sacred, the physical and the spiritual, the body and the soul. What is saving my life now is becoming more fully human, trusting that there is no way to God apart from real life in the real world.[27]

God is encountered by humankind in *this place* in which he has implaced us. And in this extraordinary creation humans are unique as image bearers; Genesis 1 clearly sets humankind apart from other creatures, giving us a unique role of dominion over them and charging us to "subdue" the earth. As G. Spykman so eloquently states,

> All creatures, great and small, are gifted—whether belonging to the kingdom of plants, animals or things—each true to its own nature: the lily as a lily, the lion as a lion; likewise the stars, the moon and the sun. . . . Those creatures also serve which can only stand and wait, willy-nilly, on the fixed laws of creation, complying without freedom of choice: falling rocks, shooting stars, budding trees, migrating birds, and hibernating animals. These creatures have been entrusted to our care to help make us, as earthkeepers, better servants of our Lord. . . . We, as responsible stewards, are free to domesticate their instincts, cultivate their use, and harness their powers, but always with tender, loving care. . . . With all our potentials—our rationality, imagination, feeling, culture-forming activity—we are called to play our servant roles in creation.[28]

It *is* an extraordinary vision of what it means to be human! One can only imagine what the Israelites, amidst their vulnerable existence, thought of this view of humanity. As a non-seafaring people, how would they have imagined exercising dominion over the sea creatures? Sadly, today we are at the other end of the spectrum, with the three great places of Genesis—land, sea,[29] and sky[30]—all under threat from humankind.

---

27. B. Taylor, *Altar in the World*, xiv–xv.
28. Spykman, *Reformational Theology*, 250.
29. On the current state of our oceans, see Safina, *Song for the Blue Ocean*.
30. Not only have we polluted the atmosphere, but outer space has become a new junkyard as satellites, rockets, and other debris are discarded.

When it comes to plants, fish, birds, and other animals, we are perennially tempted either to analyze them through a reductionistic scientific "objectivity" or to romanticize them by projecting human traits onto them. Neither approach is helpful, and, as we will see in part 2, both stem from the dominance of a reductionistic science which is incapable of doing justice to the full dimensions of human experience of the world. The elevation in the West of "rational empirical knowledge" has led to the "*disenchantment* of the world and its transformation into a causal mechanism."[31] For recovering a rich, holistic experience of "nature"—what is commonly called "reenchantment"[32]— while avoiding both of the dangers above, the doctrine of creation is crucial. As long as academic work remains in the grip of the modern subject-object dichotomy, we will never recover a rich view of place which avoids the dangers of both scientism and a New Age pantheism, which undermines the distinction between humans and the rest of creation.

The doctrine of creation alerts us to the interwoven coherence of the whole of creation as well as the ordered distinctions within it. Placially this is significant: the birds predominate in the sky, fish in the waters; animals and humankind live on the land and feed off the plants. But this does not imply a utilitarian ethic according to which the plants (or animals) are brought into existence only as food. The creation comes into existence progressively as a coherent whole, and part of humankind's stewardship will be to continue to ensure that the earth brings forth vegetation in a way that is "good," so that birds, fish, and animals are able to flourish in the environments designated for *them*.

Creation, Place, and Modern Science

Genesis 1:1–2:3 depicts progressive placial development and careful distinctions, as well as coherent wholeness. Humans alone are made in the *imago Dei* and in this respect are different from animals and birds and trees. But this difference calls for respect and not brutal mastery. The animals are indeed brought before Adam in Genesis 2 to be named by him, but the spirit of this naming is well captured in T. Herriot's experience of what awoke his interest in birds: "The thought of creatures being endemic to the place I lived stirred something to life in my brain. I began to see that learning the names of things mattered, not so much in the possession it afforded as in its capacity to call things forth from generality into a particularity that allowed for admiration, familiarity, even wonder."[33] Language and naming is a central element in attentiveness to, and the formation of, place, so that one way for us to recover a sense of place is to recover our rich heritage of placial language, even as it threatens

---

31. M. Weber, *Gesammelte Aufsätze zur Religionssoziologie*, 564. Emphasis added.
32. Berman, *Reenchantment of the World*.
33. Herriot, *Grass, Sky, Song*, 12.

to collapse into what B. Lopez calls "an attenuated list of almost nondescript words."[34] With an amazing group of writers, Lopez has edited *Home Ground: Language for an American Landscape*, an alphabetical resource aimed at just such a recovery. As he notes in his introduction, "We put a geometry to the land—backcountry, front range, high desert—and pick out patterns in it: pool and rifle, swale and riffle, swale and rise, basin and range. We make it remote (north forty), vivid (bird-foot delta), and humorous (Detroit riprap). It is a language that keeps us from slipping off into abstract space."[35]

Modern science, however, under the influence of the Enlightenment, has produced reductionistic models of inquiry which marginalize wonder and joy amidst the creation, which encourage mastery and marginalize the richness of the lived experience of place in favor of abstract space.[36] In contemporary natural history this problem is evident in the tension between writers' rich experience of place and the fear of unscientific anthropomorphism. Indeed, we urgently need an epistemology which can open up the richness and multifaceted dimensions of the world without collapsing important distinctions. Fortunately there is no shortage of scholars who have addressed these issues.

Martin Buber's work is important for our purposes; he distinguishes between "orientation," which is the "objective" attitude typical of so much science, and "realization," the approach which foregrounds the inner meaning of life. As is well known, Buber distinguished between the *I-it* and the *I-Thou* relationships. I-it is the attitude characteristic of science, whereas I-Thou evokes meeting and encounter. Significantly, Buber insisted that the I-Thou relationship should not be restricted to interpersonal relations but include nature and culture.[37]

The insights of the Dutch Christian philosopher H. Dooyeweerd are also helpful in developing a rich approach to creation while avoiding unhelpful anthropomorphism. Dooyeweerd's philosophy has three major building blocks: particular entities (this tree), fifteen modal aspects (how entities function), and individuality structures (God's order for entities). He argues that, as God has ordered the world, every entity functions in all fifteen modal aspects: Arithmetic—Spatial—Kinematic—Physical—Biotic—Sensitive—Logical—Historical—Lingual—Social—Economic—Aesthetic—Juridical—Ethical—Pistic. Thus, the aesthetic and spiritual dimensions of a butterfly are not imaginary but real, and are part of what it means for a butterfly to be a butterfly! V. Nabokov's description of standing among rare butterflies fits with reality: "This is ecstasy, and behind the ecstasy is something else, which

---

34. Lopez, *Home Ground*, xxiii.

35. Ibid., xxii–xxiii.

36. For the negative significance of Descartes's philosophy for animals, see Shevelow, *For the Love of Animals*, 27–32.

37. Buber, *I and Thou*.

is hard to explain. It is like a momentary vacuum into which rushes all that I love. A sense of oneness with sun and stone. A thrill of gratitude to whom it may concern—to the contrapuntal genius of human fate or to tender ghosts humouring a lucky mortal."[38]

Yet, Dooyeweerd explains, although entities function in all fifteen modes, they may not function as a *subject* in all modes; in some they may function *objectively*. Thus a plant functions as a subject in all modes up to and including the biotic and as an object in the remaining modes. Thus a tree is a living organism, and its qualifying mode—the biotic—gives it its distinctive character as a plant. A tree cannot speak or name other objects, but its function in the lingual mode means that part of creation is the capacity for humans to *name* trees. A tree will not admire the beauty of other trees, but its functioning in the aesthetic mode means that its beauty is not imaginary; it is real and able to be recognized and relished by humans.

This nonreductionistic approach is very helpful as we consider the role of plants and animals in place. Intriguingly, in volume 3 of his *New Critique of Theoretical Thought* Dooyeweerd discusses "this budding linden before my window,"[39] noting that by focusing his theoretical attention on the linden tree he is already engaged in abstraction, because things are never experienced—as opposed to being analyzed—in isolation, but are interlaced with everything else. Dooyeweerd notes that the tree functions as a subject in all modes up to and including the biotic, which is its qualifying mode. A purely mathematical-physical analysis would eliminate its typical structure as an individual whole and replace this whole with a system of interacting energy functions. Crucially for our purposes, Dooyeweerd insists that the reality of the linden tree is not completed in the biotic mode; it has object functions in the remaining modes, which are as real as the subject functions. So, for example, in the linguistic mode it has the potential for being symbolically signified. Aesthetically it has the potential for being appreciated as beautiful. Socially trees have amazing potential for providing the place for human interaction. And pistically we can see (or not) the tree as part of God's magnificent creation. Central to the opening up of these objective modes is the relationship of humans to the rest of the creation.

Creation and Natural History

The sheer goodness of birds, fish, animals, land, sky, and sea alerts us firstly to the respect owed them as part of the creation. Sadly much of human history is a record of cruelty and abuse toward animals. As early as AD 375 Basil of Caesarea could pray, "Oh, God, enlarge within us the sense of fellowship with all living things, our brothers the animals to whom Thou gavest the

38. Nabokov, *Speak, Memory*, quoted in Mynott, *Birdscapes*, 96.
39. Dooyeweerd, *New Critique*, 3, 54.

earth in common with us. We remember with shame that in the past we have exercised the high dominion of man with ruthless cruelty so that the voice of the earth, which should have gone up to thee in song, has been a groan of travail."[40] John Wesley found a "plausible objection against the justice of God, in suffering numberless creatures that had never sinned to be so severely punished." He speculates on whether "[God's] mercy might await mistreated animals on the other side."[41] It was nineteenth-century Christian reformers who founded the Royal Society for the Prevention of Cruelty to Animals (RSPCA) and its American counterpart,[42] but too many Christians appear to have lost such concern today. In his remarkable book *Dominion: The Power of Man, the Suffering of Animals, and the Call to Mercy*, M. Scully documents relentlessly the contemporary abuse of animals, in which they are reduced to units of consumption, and he does so within a rich Christian framework. It is chilling reading. The industrialization of the food system means that abuse of animals has multiplied exponentially.

Secondly, the goodness of God's creatures alerts us to the ways in which they reflect God's handiwork. This is expressed by Paul in 1 Corinthians 15:39: "God has provided variety in nature; *thus not every kind of flesh is the same flesh, but there is one kind for men, another for beasts, another for birds, and another for fish.*"[43] These creatures evoke respectful exploration by their fellow creature humankind. There is not space here to explore the comprehensive range of natural history, the usual name for such exploration. In what follows I have focused on the example of birds and place, but I could as easily have attended to the earth, the sky,[44] the sea,[45] fish,[46] animals other than birds,

40. Basil of Caesarea, quoted in Scully, *Dominion*, 13.

41. John Wesley, quoted in ibid., 14.

42. See Harwood, *Love for Animals and How It Developed in Great Britain*; Thomas, *Man and the Natural World*; Phelps, *The Longest Struggle*; Shevelow, *For the Love of Animals*.

43. Barrett, *Commentary on the First Epistle to the Corinthians*, 371. Emphasis original.

44. See Pretor-Pinney, *Cloudspotter's Guide*, for an intriguing recovery of cloud spotting and appreciation in the United Kingdom today.

45. The sea/oceans deserve mention, as they constitute 71 percent of the earth's surface and have only recently begun to be explored. The major figure behind exploration of the oceans was Jacques Cousteau (1910–97). In a chapter of *The Human, the Orchid, and the Octopus*, 116–29, Cousteau reflects on "the Holy Scriptures and the environment." A lifelong Roman Catholic, Cousteau defends Scripture against the charge that it supports brutal mastery of nature, but poignantly asks, "How many of these people rise to their feet or fall to their knees in cathedrals . . . all the while ignoring the living word of God just outside the window? . . . They choose to believe in a God who has issued divine commands; how many honor His divine commands to safeguard the environment?" (117).

46. One might think that fish are unable to develop relationships with humans. See in this respect the extraordinary story of Ulysses, a grouper of about sixty pounds who attached himself to Jacques Cousteau and his team of deep-sea divers. Cousteau notes that "Ulysses became our inseparable friend. He followed us everywhere, sometimes nibbling our fins" (*The Living Sea*, 157).

or plants. The story of human discovery in all these areas, and of wonder, shameful disrespect, use and abuse, is a fascinating and disconcerting story.[47]

Birds: "Let Birds Multiply on the Earth" (Genesis 1:22)

Bird-watchers are great at making lists, and intriguingly the earliest list of birds is found in an ancient Sumerian text, the *Nanše*, which uses one hundred different words for birds and from which some thirty-one varieties can be identified.[48] Perhaps this is the sort of thing Genesis 1 has in mind with Adam naming the animals? Part of Solomon's internationally renowned wisdom was that he was well informed about trees—from the cedars of Lebanon to the hyssop that grows in the wall!—and about animals, birds, reptiles, and fish (1 Kings 4:33).

Mynott notes that "any evocation of a place may miss a crucial aspect if it does not include in the account of its natural setting some reference to its characteristic bird life."[49] The Bible certainly does not fall short in this area. Multiple passages, especially in the Psalter, speak of God's concern for birds,[50] and significantly, a regular feature of judgment upon a place,[51] especially in Jeremiah, is the absence of birds and birdsong. In the New Testament, birds play a significant role. In his moving book on the grassland birds of North America and the threat they are under, Herriot observes,

> The summer-ending song of a bird that very likely failed to raise any young this year cries out to a more perfect fidelity dwelling in this land that marks the sparrow's fall. In the gospel . . . Jesus tells peasants of Galilee that not a single sparrow falls to the ground without God's knowing and caring. Our ancestors came to this land with that gospel and many others consoling them as they stripped the prairie of its sod, and fought against drought, grasshoppers, and early frosts. . . . God knows the sparrow. The land knows the sparrow. The trick of remaining here is to become a people who know the sparrow too, who will not give up on creatures who ask only for a place in the grass.[52]

In explaining to his disciples that the kingdom of God is present in his ministry, Jesus draws an analogy between that kingdom and the small black mustard seed, which becomes the greatest of shrubs and in whose branches the birds of the air can dwell (*kataskēnoun*).[53] The parable evokes the full manifesta-

47. Books I have found helpful include Gribbin and Gribbin, *Flower Hunters*; Stocks, *Forgotten Fruits*; Gollner, *Fruit Hunters*; Safina, *Song for the Blue Ocean*; Lopez, *Arctic Dreams*.

48. Veldhuis, *Religion, Literature, and Scholarship*.

49. Mynott, *Birdscapes*, 204. Hillel's useful *Natural History of the Bible* is an example in this respect; birds are not listed in his index.

50. Pss. 50:11; 104:12, 17; 148:10; Isa. 31:5; Ezek. 17:23; 31:6; Dan. 2:38; 4:21; Hosea 2:18.

51. Eccles. 12:4; Jer. 4:25; 9:10; 12:4; Hosea 4:3; Zeph. 1:3.

52. Herriot, *Grass, Sky, Song*, 69.

53. Matt. 13:31–32; Mark 4:30–32; Luke 13:18–19. On this parable see Snodgrass, *Stories with Intent*, 216–28.

tion of the kingdom in the creation; "birds" are often taken to represent the gentiles,[54] but a more literal interpretation is possible which does not minimize the metaphorical dimensions of the parable. The kingdom will ultimately bring harmony to the creation, in which even the birds of the sky will dwell at peace.

Creation evokes wonder and exploration, and it has been a pleasant surprise to discover the central role of Christians in natural history. In his enchanting *The Wisdom of Birds: An Illustrated History of Ornithology*, ornithologist T. Birkhead argues that the most influential ornithologist of all time was the Englishman John Ray (1627–1705).

> Ray spearheaded a new vision of the natural world, and he did so with a gentle modesty that belied a brilliant mind and wonderful clarity of vision. . . . Ray's God was responsible for the natural world in all its beauty and in particular the wonderful fit between an animal and its environment—something he called physico-theology (later known as natural theology) and what we today call adaptation. The culmination of his life's work, *The Wisdom of God*, published in 1691, laid out Ray's ideas in brilliant, readable style. In its day, physico-theology was as significant as Darwin's natural selection would be one hundred and fifty years later.[55]

A devout Christian, Ray, by developing a definition of what constitutes a species, initiated a nomenclature that inspired Carl Linnaeus sixty years later. His physico-theology provided a conceptual framework for ornithology, and his *Wisdom* initiated the study of birds in their natural environments. Although a less attractive character than John Ray, Linnaeus (1707–78) also "regarded the study of nature as God's work."[56]

Birds play a significant role in the fourth-most published book in English, Gilbert White's *The Natural History and Antiquities of Selborne, in the County of Southampton*, published in 1788.[57] White was a clergyman, and the book has been called "the journal of Adam in Paradise."[58] D. E. Allen says of it, "For it is, surely, the testament of Static Man: at peace with the world and with himself, content with deepening his knowledge of his one small corner of the earth, a being suspended in a perfect mental balance. Selborne is the secret, private parish inside each one of us."[59] White was fascinated by bird migration and loved swallows and martins in particular.

In a scientist like John Ray there was no contradiction between wonder and analysis. As science developed it became increasingly reductionistic, so that a tension developed between wonder and joy on the one hand and analysis on the

---

54. Snodgrass thinks this unlikely (*Stories with Intent*, 224).
55. Birkhead, *Wisdom of Birds*, 8–9.
56. Gribbin and Gribbin, *Flower Hunters*, 30. See also 29–66.
57. It is still in print, published by Thames and Hudson.
58. Mynott, *Birdscapes*, 191.
59. D. E. Allen, *The Naturalist in Britain*, quoted in Mynott, *Birdscapes*, 191.

other. Thus, in Mynott's wonderful *Birdscapes* one feels throughout the book a tension between his love of birds and the fear of anthropomorphism.[60] Above, we explained a way of resolving this issue without resorting to inappropriate anthropomorphism. In contemporary natural history there has developed, encouragingly, an openness to the transcendent in nature. In his acclaimed *Arctic Dreams*, Lopez describes the effect of his evening walks among the tundra birds while he was camped in the western Brooks Range of Alaska: "I took to bowing on these evening walks. I would bow slightly with my hands in my pockets, toward the birds and the evidence of life in their nests—because of their fecundity, unexpected in this remote region, and because of the serene arctic light that came down over the land like breath, like breathing."[61]

In terms of place, bird-watching and ornithology are significant because of the attentiveness to the particular that they require:

> Anyone who watches a particular patch regularly becomes very sensitive to all the gradual and small changes going on throughout the year. . . . Every bird has both its daily and seasonal rhythms and so therefore do the places they inhabit. . . . The whole country [the UK] is a mosaic of local patches that are watched intently, not for the great rarities that may occasionally turn up or for general scientific hypothesising but for the daily variations in the ordinary and the particular. . . . A good part of the pleasure comes from trying to ask the right questions of the place and starting to piece together the answers.[62]

Unsurprisingly, birders visit familiar places most of the time because "awareness depends on a prior sensitivity to place."[63] Local patches can be almost anywhere. What they have in common is that they are familiar to and known intimately by someone and that that person feels attached to them, all of which emerge from close observation over time. As Mynott notes, "The important point here, I think, . . . is the relish in the ordinary and the particular."[64] "In all these ways a bird may be the one thing we most associate with a place, the genius loci, and we can no longer think of either the bird or the place without the other."[65]

Suburban life discourages precisely such attentiveness, not to mention the effects of such a lifestyle on the plant, bird, and animal life.[66] Indeed the destructive effects of sprawl feed a growing inattentiveness and vice versa. Genesis 1 speaks of birds multiplying "on the earth," and in his *Grass, Sky, Song* T. Herriot focuses on grassland birds in North America, those that depend on grassy habitat

60. Mynott, *Birdscapes*, 23–27, 43, 112, 147, 180, 267, 289–96, 301–2.
61. Lopez, *Arctic Dreams*, xx.
62. Mynott, *Birdscapes*, 194–96.
63. Ibid., 197.
64. Ibid., 198.
65. Ibid., 206.
66. See Johnson and Klemens, *Nature in Fragments*, for the effects of sprawl and strategies to counteract them.

for their survival. They are declining faster than any other on the continent.[67] For Herriot, "It's a fool's dream, but a part of me can't stop imagining that if enough people would discover all that is good and holy in these birds, we might be able to turn things around before it's too late."[68] He says of his drawings and writing that "each story, argument, species profile, and drawing was conceived within a longing to reclaim the original spirit of grassland that survives yet in its birds. Beneath that longing lie the deeper human wish we all share: to find out how we might belong to a place, to find a way home."[69]

It is only through attentiveness that we will discover all that is good and holy in "these birds," and the place to start is where we are. Doing what we can to make our suburban plots attractive to birds would go a long way to recovering the good and holy in them. And as we make place for them, they will call us back into place. And in the process we may be surprised by the openness of wild animals to living in relationship with humans. Herriot describes Edgar's experience with chickadees in Central Butte, Saskatchewan:

> In the fall of '26 he got to know some chickadees on the property. One was cheekier than the rest, brave enough to come to his outstretched hand and get bread crumbs. Within a week he had five chickadees all over his head and shoulders. They'd ride to the barn with him and in the morning when he went out to do chores he'd give a whistle, imitating their song, and they would come to greet him.
>
> The birds disappeared for a spell, but the next fall he was out with a friend hunting rabbits and the friend said, "Edgar, there's a bird riding on your gun barrel." Edgar gave the whistle and four more chickadees came out of the bush to join the one on his rifle. He hadn't seen them for months and he was half a mile away from the yard where he'd been feeding them, but they still knew Edgar, and responded to this call.[70]

Genesis 2–3: Implacement and Displacement

Genesis 1 is universal in its scope, with a developing focus on the whole earth as humankind's home, whereas, as we will see, Genesis 2–3 is place specific in its focus.

Genesis 2: Implacement

The debate about the relationship between Genesis 1:1–2:4a and chapters 2–3 is well known. Source criticism has identified two different creation stories,

67. Herriot, *Grass, Sky, Song*, 2.
68. Ibid., 3.
69. Ibid., 4.
70. Ibid., 62–63.

with 1:1–2:3 identified as part of a tradition called P, for "priestly," after its supposed priestly redactors, and Genesis 2–3 as part of a tradition called J, for "Jahwist/Yahwist," because in that tradition God is referred to by the name Yahweh. Scholars continue to wrestle with the relationship between the two stories. Undoubtedly there are important differences between them; canonically, however, and in terms of the literary shape of Genesis 1–11, it is important to note the literary juxtaposition of these two narratives and the consequent relationship between them.[71]

The *toledoth* headings ("These are the generations of") structure Genesis as a literary unit, and it is significant that 1:1–2:3 stands outside this literary shaping, whereas 2–4 is the first major section under a toledoth heading.[72] Genesis 1:1–2:3, therefore, functions as an introduction to Genesis as a whole, whereas chapters 2–3 initiate the story that will lead on to Abraham and Israel. "The role of the toledoth formula in 2.4, which introduces the story of mankind, is to connect the creation of the world with the history which follows."[73] The genre of chapters 1–11 is much debated, but this much can surely be said: chapters 2–3 have more of a historical function within Genesis than does 1:1–2:3.[74]

In terms of the perplexing relationship between these creation stories, place is once again illuminating. We noted above that Genesis 1 presents the earth as a *potential* place for humans; it is depicted as an ideal home. We also noted the progressive placial differentiation. In Genesis 2 this differentiation is taken a step forward. Indeed 2:4b, with its inversion of "heavens and the earth"[75] to "earth and the heavens," signals the shift in focus to the earth.[76] Genesis 2 becomes far more placially specific with its focus on Eden as the garden in which Adam and Eve are to dwell. As Von Rad notes of J's account of creation, "It is altogether a much smaller area with which the narrator deals—not even the 'earth,' but the world that lies at man's own doorstep—garden, rivers, trees, language, animals, and woman."[77] "P is concerned with the 'world' and man within it, while J shows the construction of man's immediate environment and defines his relationship to it."[78] Yahweh Elohim plants a garden in Eden, and there he places the man he has formed

---

71. Cf. Childs, *Introduction to the Old Testament*, 149–50.

72. With G. J. Wenham (*Genesis 1–15*, 49, 55–56), I take 2:4 to be a heading for what follows in chaps. 2–4.

73. Childs, *Introduction to the Old Testament*, 146.

74. See G. J. Wenham, *Genesis 1–15*, 53–55. In the history of modern Old Testament scholarship the Old Testament emphasis on history has unhelpfully and wrongly been set against nature.

75. Cf. Gen. 1:1; 2:1; 2:4a.

76. As Barth notes, "The heavens are not overlooked or denied, but in this saga attention is focused on the earth" (*Church Dogmatics*, vol. 3, pt. 1, p. 234).

77. Rad, *Old Testament Theology*, 1:148.

78. Ibid., 150.

of dust from the ground. In this sense Genesis 2 represents a *continuation* of the place differentiation in Genesis 1.

Narratively, therefore, the move from Genesis 1 to 2, rather than indicating a juxtaposition of two unrelated sources, involves a movement of progressive implacement culminating in the planting of Eden as the specific place in which the earthlings Adam and Eve will dwell. It is important to note just how illuminating place is at this point. Genesis 1 presents the world as a *potential* place for human habitation, but the nature of Adam and Eve as embodied earthlings means that the human story itself must begin in a specific place, in this case Eden. As Casey notes, "Implacement itself, *being concretely placed*, is intrinsically particular."[79]

The Hebrew word for humankind in 1:26–28, namely '*ādām*, already creates the closest connection between humankind and the earth, with its association with '*ădāmâ* (= cultivable ground).[80] True, the word used for the earth as a whole in Genesis 1 is '*ereṣ*; in 2:7, however, Yahweh Elohim forms '*ādām* out of the '*ădāmâ*, and in Eden it is out of the '*ădāmâ* that Yahweh Elohim causes trees to grow which are aesthetically pleasing and nutritionally satisfying. Throughout 2:5–3:24 '*ădāmâ* is used for Eden and '*ereṣ* does not occur. "Earthling"[81] is therefore an apt description of human beings, since it points clearly to the embodied nature of human being. Hiebert notes, "Not only does '*ādām* cultivate '*ădāmâ*, he is fashioned by God out of the land he farms."[82] This link between '*ādām* and '*ădāmâ* alerts us to the fact that human embodiment and place are deeply interwoven and in practice inseparable.

The creaturely embodiment of human beings makes placement unavoidable. Embodied human life implies specific place, and the ordering of the content of Genesis 2 after that of chapter 1 exemplifies this. Human habitation can never straddle the whole earth; it is of necessity specific, and in Genesis 2 that means the garden which God plants, namely Eden. Place names begin to accumulate in Genesis 2—Eden, Pishon, Havilah, Gihon, Tigris, and Assyria—and this again indicates the differentiation toward a specific place: "Place-names embody this complex collective concreteness despite their considerable brevity."[83]

Genesis 2 thus begins the story of human history with the implacement of Adam and Eve in a specific place. "Here" and "there" are placial terms,[84] and in this respect the *šām* (there) of 2:8 is significant, carrying all the weight of implacement: "To dwell means to belong to a given place."[85] The place in mind is "a garden in Eden, in the east" (2:8). We are not told much about this

---

79. Casey, *Getting Back into Place*, 23. Emphasis original.
80. Hiebert, *Yahwist's Landscape*, 34–35.
81. Wurst, "'Beloved, Come Back to Me,'" 92, 106.
82. Hiebert, *Yahwist's Landscape*, 35.
83. Casey, *Getting Back into Place*, 23.
84. Ibid., 50–56.
85. Norberg-Schulz, *Concept of Dwelling*, quoted in Casey, *Getting Back into Place*, 109.

garden other than that it is fertile and has a variety of trees; aesthetically it is pleasing, and a river flows out of it so that it is well irrigated.[86] The result of this minimal information is that we easily read into Eden our own experience of gardens or the Romantic notion of untamed wilderness. What *should* we imagine when we think of Eden?

Firstly we should think of a specific place. As Barth notes, "The biblical witness is speaking of a definite place on earth."[87] Wenham explores the symbolic value of Eden as a place where God dwells; indeed several features of the garden liken it to a sanctuary. However, he rightly asserts that "the mention of the rivers and their location in vv 10–14 suggests that the final editor of Gen 2 thought of Eden as a real place, even if it is beyond the wit of modern writers to locate."[88] This assertion is strengthened by the toledoth context in which chapters 2–3 occur, signaling the unfolding *history* of humankind. Furthermore, as we have noted, the move in chapters 1–3 is from heavens and earth, to earth, to the garden. The setting in 2:5–8 suggests a Mesopotamian site for Eden.[89]

But what kind of garden is Eden? The details in chapter 2 are sparse. God plants the garden and makes all kinds of trees grow in it, trees for food and those that are aesthetically pleasing.[90] The garden is well irrigated, an attractive prospect in the arid East. The Hebrew word translated "Eden" probably derives from its homonym, a word meaning "pleasure, delight," indicating the abundance of provision and the fertility of the garden.[91]

D. C. Benjamin notes that the legacy of a Romantic perspective is the tendency to interpret Eden as an unspoiled wilderness.[92] In his view "it is more likely that the Eden in the story of Adam is a landscaped garden or urban masterpiece than an undeveloped wilderness or a geological wonder."[93] C. Tuplin, however, thinks the description of the garden of Eden is modest and in line with the other gardens mentioned in the Old Testament.[94] It is hard to be sure of the ancient Near Eastern background to chapter 2.[95] Gardens were an important part of the irrigation economies of Mesopotamia and Egypt; in the case of wealthy and influential persons the garden could be

---

86. The description of Eden, with its irrigation by river, is reminiscent of the river valley civilizations of Egypt and Mesopotamia, where agriculture depended on flooding by rivers and on irrigation systems connected to the rivers.

87. Barth, *Church Dogmatics*, vol. 3, pt. 1, p. 252.

88. G. J. Wenham, *Genesis 1–15*, 61–62.

89. Ibid., 66. Cf. Hiebert, who argues that the Yahwist has in mind the Jordan Valley oasis of the past (*Yahwist's Landscape*, 52–59).

90. Only three trees are specifically identified: the common fig (3:7) and the two special trees.

91. G. J. Wenham, *Genesis 1–15*, 61.

92. Benjamin, "Stories of Adam and Eve," 43.

93. Ibid., 43–44.

94. Tuplin, *Achaemenid Studies*, 81.

95. Cf. G. J. Wenham, *Genesis 1–15*, 51–53.

expansive and generally adjoined the residence. The ancient Egyptians also cultivated gardens, orchards, and parks, and wealthy families often maintained country estates where the owners could relax amidst flowers, fruit trees, and ponds.

Within the Old Testament, Yahweh Elohim's planting of a garden may be comparable with Qohelet's[96] planting vineyards, making gardens and parks, and making pools from which to water the forest of growing trees. This would fit with the imaginative portrayal of Qohelet as King Solomon in Ecclesiastes and the description of the projects of kings in the ancient Near East.[97] That it was generally the wealthier who owned gardens affirms the monarchical dimension, albeit democratized, of the *imago Dei* as presented in Genesis 1.

What is clear on all accounts is that a garden was an enclosed area designed for cultivation.[98] This background casts interesting light on Eden as a place for human habitation. What we have, then, rather than an image of primitivism, is one of an area that is bounded, probably by walls; carefully landscaped; and intensively cultivated with orchards and the like. In the light of its urban connotations in the ancient Near East, Eden may well have included buildings.[99] Thus God as King, a central image of God in Genesis 1, plants a garden, and as the under-kings, Adam and Eve dwell in the garden, which is their royal residence.[100]

And thus, secondly we should note that Eden is a garden characterized by cultivation.[101] This fits precisely with Yahweh Elohim putting Adam and Eve into Eden in order to "till it and keep it" (2:15). Hiebert suggests that the animals are created to help Adam with the challenging task of cultivation. Similarly he argues that the woman is created to be a helper *like Adam* so that the family unit, the very basis of agricultural society, can be set up.[102] A translation of ʿbd (NRSV = till) is "to serve,"[103] and this helpfully undermines any sense of brutal mastery over the garden. The verb šāmar (keep) is regularly used in the Old Testament for keeping God's laws; in Jeremiah 5:24 it refers to God's "keeping" of the weeks for the harvest. Thus it too evokes the sense of attentive, careful, obedient cultivation. "We get back into place—dwelling place—by the cultivation of built places. Such cultivation *localizes caring.* What is for Heidegger a global feature of existent human

---

96. *Qohelet* is the Hebrew word for "Teacher," used to refer to the writer of Ecclesiastes (1:1).

97. See Seow, *Ecclesiastes*, 151.

98. G. J. Wenham, *Genesis 1–15*, 61.

99. Contra the tendency to portray the narrative arc of Scripture as the move from a garden to a city.

100. For an alternate view see Hiebert, *Yahwist's Landscape*, 61.

101. Cf. Casey, *Getting Back into Place*, 155.

102. Hiebert, *Yahwist's Landscape*, 60.

103. G. J. Wenham, *Genesis 1–15*, 67.

being—namely, 'care' (*Sorge*)—is here given a local habitation and not just a name. We care about places as well as people so that we can say that *caring belongs to places*."[104]

Casey notes that the gardens he analyzes do not normally offer permanent dwellings,[105] but here the ancient Near Eastern background is instructive, since gardens in those cultures were linked to royal residences. Clearly in Eden the dwelling is *hestial*,[106] in the sense that Adam and Eve dwell there. Gardens evoke a mood that is peculiarly suited for sociality, contemplation, and reflection. This resonates with 3:8, where Adam and Eve "heard the sound of the LORD God walking in the garden at the time of the evening breeze." The garden is not just a place for the production of vegetables, fruits, and herbs; it is also a place of intimacy, contemplation, and familial solidarity.[107] Wenham has noted how Eden is depicted as a sanctuary,[108] and this fits with the intimate relationship pictured here with God. The unusual use of "Yahweh Elohim" as the name for God in chapters 2–3 alerts us to the relationship with God in which Adam and Eve participate.[109] It also—by juxtaposing *Yahweh*, God's name as redeemer, with *Elohim*, his name as creator—thoroughly undermines the dichotomies between creation and nature and between redemption and history that have prevented Old Testament scholars from excavating the powerful Old Testament vision of nature and place, and have opened the Bible to the charge that it is the cause of the modern environmental crisis.[110] "Yahweh," above all else the name of the God who redeems Israel (cf. Exod. 3; 6), is juxtaposed with "Elohim," the name for the creator God of Genesis 1, in order to alert the reader that *their* God is the creator of the heavens and the earth.

Thirdly we should note that we are presented in Genesis 2, as in chapter 1, with a *theology* of place. In the words of Genesis 13:10, this is "the garden of the LORD." The tree of life is at the center of the garden. In Scripture trees are a symbol of the life of God, and "the tree of life is an essential mark of a perfect garden in which God dwells."[111] The tree in the midst of the garden signifies that the garden is God's sanctuary: "While He gives man the enjoyment of the whole Garden and all its trees, by the planting of the tree of life in its midst God declares that his primary, central and decisive will is to give him Himself."[112] Significantly for place, Barth asserts that "God grants him

---

104. Casey, *Getting Back into Place*, 175. Emphasis original.
105. Ibid., 169.
106. Casey distinguishes between hermetic and hestial dwelling (*Getting Back into Place*, 2nd ed., 140–55). *Hestial* relates to the "intimacy and memorability of domestic space" (140).
107. Casey, *Getting Back into Place*, 158.
108. G. J. Wenham, "Sanctuary Symbolism."
109. L'Hour, "Yahweh Elohim."
110. See Hiebert, *Yahwist's Landscape*, 3–22.
111. G. J. Wenham, "Sanctuary Symbolism," 62.
112. Barth, *Church Dogmatics*, vol. 3, pt. 1, p. 282.

His own presence, i.e., Himself as the Co-inhabitant of *this place.*[113] From this perspective place is never fully place without God as a co-inhabitant.

Approaching Genesis 1 and 2 through the prism of place is fecund. It not only enables us to avoid some of the dualisms of contemporary readings but also illuminates the logical connection between Genesis 1 and 2, and in the process allows us to see the centrality of place for human identity and being.

Genesis 3: Displacement

Much has been written about Genesis 3. Suffice it to note here that place once again enables us to gain fresh insight into the condition of fallenness that Genesis 3 portrays. Note should be taken here of Robert Harrison's bizarre reading of Genesis 2–3 in his otherwise helpful book *Gardens.* He describes Eden as a "garden of ennui,"[114] a place of fruits without flowers and one in which a "frozen, temporally suspended nature reigned."[115] What Hannah Arendt called "natality"[116]—the initiation of new beginnings through human activity—was, according to Harrison, denied the first couple in Eden and only became possible as a result of Eve's transgression. Eve is the hero of the story; her "transgression was the first true instance of human action, properly understood."[117]

In the spirit of the post-Enlightenment this is truly a serpentine reading of Genesis 2–3. As we have seen, Eden was a garden of delight, the ideal home for the first couple, seasonal and full of potential for natality, albeit—and this is where it contradicts Harrison—subject to the winsome rule of the Creator. The fall is not a quest for natality and fecundity but for *autonomy*, and this death is not the condition of natality but its destruction.

Human identity is deeply bound up with place, and in Genesis 3 *displacement* is at the heart of God's judgment. Genesis 3 concludes with the damning indictment: "Therefore the LORD God sent him forth from the garden of Eden, to till the ground from which he was taken. He drove out the man" (vv. 23–24a). The prior judgment pronounced on the man in 3:17–19 also amounts to displacement: humankind's relationship to the ground, that is, his experience of place, will be transformed. Cultivation will be in danger of radical misdirection from care to abuse. The thorns and thistles which the ground will produce are indicative of ecological destruction: "With agriculture there begins the paradoxical history of human destruction of the Earth's fertility in the very search for productive land."[118]

---

113. Ibid. Emphasis added.
114. Harrison, *Gardens*, 15.
115. Ibid., 16.
116. Arendt, *The Human Condition*, 8–9, 177–78, 191, 247.
117. Ibid., 15.
118. Newsom, "Common Ground," 70.

With the modern suppression of place and our speed-driven societies, it is hard to grasp the horror of this judgment. However, in the Old Testament and ancient Near Eastern context there would have been a far greater sense of the angst associated with placelessness. If Genesis 2 and 3 were written around the time of the exile, then readers would have a keen sense of the pain of *this* exile, imaging as it does their being vomited out of the land. Casey observes that "landscape itself, usually a most accommodating presence, can alienate us. (Lyotard goes so far as to assert that 'estrangement (*dépaysement*) would appear to be a precondition for landscape.') Entire cultures can become profoundly averse to the places they inhabit, feeling atopic and displaced within their own implacement."[119] Genesis 1–3 alerts us to the fact that estrangement or displacement is not, as Lyotard suggests, a precondition for landscape. But what the above quote rightly notes is that in their fallen condition, not-being-at-home is a constant challenge for human beings. "Displacement within their own implacement" captures vividly the challenge that will now face humankind. Placement is unavoidable—it is part of the human condition—but to be at rest in their placement will from now on be an entirely different story.

However, among biblical scholars the relationship between chapters 2–3 and the rest of the Old Testament is disputed. C. Westermann concludes that there is no tradition of the narrative of Genesis 2–3 throughout the whole of the Old Testament. It is neither quoted nor mentioned.[120] Awareness of place is again revealing at this point. Contra Westermann, as a story of displacement, Genesis 2–3 is fundamental to the entire Old Testament and presupposed at every point. The quest for landedness will form the heart of the narrative that follows 2–3. Chapters 2–3 may not be quoted or "mentioned," but once we become aware of the centrality of place in the Old Testament, it becomes clear that Westermann's approach, which looks for quotes or specific mention, is inadequate. These two chapters may be of late origin and were perhaps crafted during the exile—this may be one reason for a lack of specific quotes and mention. However, in the context of the canon as a whole the connection between chapters 2–3 and what follows in the Old Testament is clear.

Conclusion

Approaching Genesis 1–3 through the prism of place is remarkably fertile both for solving long-standing problems in Old Testament criticism and for developing a theology of place. Genesis 1 is a *place* story, with all that that involves, and not just an earth story. And whereas Genesis 1 is universal in its scope, focusing increasingly on the earth as potential place, Genesis 2 begins the human story in a particular place, namely Eden.

119. Casey, *Getting Back into Place,* 34.
120. Westermann, *Genesis 1–11,* 276.

In terms of biblical theology, as Genesis 1–3 makes clear, for humans to say "God" is to be implaced, and insofar as *place* evokes—as it clearly does—the nexus God, place, and humankind, it would be quite right to see place as a major contender for the central theme of biblical faith, Scripture moving, as it does, from Eden (an urban-style garden) via the land of Israel and the cultic center of Jerusalem, to the incarnate Jesus, to the city of the new Jerusalem, which is central to the new heavens and earth. Redemption, examined through the prism of place, has the structure of implacement–displacement–(re)implacement.

In terms of a theology of place, Genesis 1–3 is rich and foundational. Its central insights are as follows:

1. Creation is the basis for place and not some neutral concept of nature.
2. As embodied creatures in the *imago Dei*, humans are always dated and *located*, that is, *placed*. As a metaphor the *imago Dei* alerts us to the similarities and differences between God and us, and our placedness is one of the differences.
3. Place is a rich, dense phenomenon. Among other things, Genesis 1–3 alerts us to its aesthetic, social, historical, agrarian, and urban dimensions.
4. God intends for humans to be at home in, to indwell, their places. Place and implacement is a gift and provides the possibility for imaging God in his creation. Place is thus a dynamic concept evoking the creative engagement of humans with their contexts.
5. Place is never fully place without God as co-inhabitant. Place is thus always, in one way or another, a theological concept.
6. After Eden the challenge of implacement and the danger of displacement are a constant part of the human condition. Humans remain placed, but displacement is a constant threat.

2

Outside Eden

Building Cities

Genesis 4–11

As is well known, in Genesis 4–11 the effects of sin gather momentum until they become a virtual tsunami in Genesis 6:5 and yet again in chapter 11. What is not so often noted is the central role of place in these chapters.

Cain and Abel

With the story of Cain and Abel (Gen. 4) we witness humankind's re-implacement after having been displaced from Eden. But their life is now lived outside of Eden, and it is the life of farmers involved in rain-fed agriculture, cultivating grain on fertile soil, and raising flocks,[1] typical of the highlands on the shores of the Mediterranean where Israel settled. The statement in 2:5 that "the LORD God had not caused it to rain upon the earth" is distinctive among ancient Near Eastern creation narratives, in which agriculture is usually said to depend upon the watering of lowlands by the flooding of rivers and related systems of irrigation. In contrast, Israel's land "drinks water by the rain from heaven" (ESV; cf. Deut. 11:10–11).

Cain is a farmer, Abel a shepherd: these activities of *cultivation* bespeak their recovery of a sense of implacement; indeed it is wrong to relate Cain and Abel to two distinct cultures as has often been done.[2] "Cain and Abel,

---

1. Hiebert, *Yahwist's Landscape*, 38.
2. Ibid., 39.

who live on this land, are typical sons of a highland farming family engaged in both cultivation and herding."[3] The mixed agricultural economy that their vocations reflect indicates the first family's re-implacement:

> This sharing of labor is characteristic of family life in a Mediterranean highland farming village in which subsistence is dependent both on the cultivation of fertile land and the raising of herds on less fertile pastures near the cultivated fields. Here, as is common in such families, the older son is primarily involved in cultivation, an activity related to his prestige as the primary heir to his father's estate. Meanwhile the younger son is delegated to caring for the flocks, a less esteemed role in such farming families.[4]

Arable land (*'ădāmâ*) is central to the narrative: Cain is a *tiller*—the noun is derived from the same verb (*'ābad*) used of Adam in 2:15—of the *'ădāmâ*, and he brings the LORD an offering from the *'ădāmâ*. The theme of implacement is strengthened by the first family's experience of the presence of the LORD; Genesis 4 repeatedly refers to the LORD. They may be outside of Eden, but their life east of Eden is still centered in the LORD. The phrase "In the course of time" (Gen. 4:3) indicates a sense of settledness and at-homeness.

But this recovery of implacement is short-lived. For whatever reason,[5] Cain's offering does not find favor with God, and Cain's anger festers into fratricide. "The field" which has been the *'ădāmâ* of cultivation becomes the scene of horrific murder. In response the LORD tells Cain that Abel's blood cries out from the *'ădāmâ* to him. Cain has polluted the *'ădāmâ*, and now the *'ădāmâ* will reject him: yields will be minimal for him, and he is condemned to be a wanderer. Cain is literally "cursed from the *'ădāmâ*" (4:11). "Like his father, he is an errant farmer, transgressing a divine command (2:16–17; 4:7). The result of disobedience is the same for both: the relationship between farmer and soil is imperiled. For *'ādām* the ground is cursed and yields its produce only to great labor (3:17–19); for *qayin* the ground refuses to produce at all (4:12)."[6] Cain's punishment thus includes the radical displacement of a vagrant as well as the more holistic punishment of separation from family and from God. Cain is condemned to permanent displacement.

This narrative introduces an important new concept into the pentateuchal vocabulary of place, namely *pollution*. As Wenham rightly notes of the words "your brother's blood is crying out to me": "Compressed into them is a whole theology whose principles inform much of the criminal and cultic law of Israel.

---

3. Ibid.

4. Ibid., 39–40.

5. G. J. Wenham lists five different explanations given for why Cain's offering is not accepted by God (*Genesis 1–15*, 104). The most common view, which Wenham espouses, is that it was the different approach to worship that counted. Abel offered his choicest animals, whereas Cain merely brought "some of the fruits of the soil" (4:3 NIV).

6. Hiebert, *Yahwist's Landscape*, 40.

Life is in the blood (Lev. 17:11), so shed blood is the most polluting of all substances. Consequently, unatoned-for murders pollute the holy land, making it unfit for the divine presence. To prevent such a catastrophe, the cities of refuge were established."[7] Notably this incident does not take place in "the land"; indeed the location is not specified. Cain is simply cursed from the 'ădāmâ, which has opened its mouth to receive Abel's blood. There is therefore a more universal perspective to this narrative and judgment than to later cultic laws, which are restricted to Israel, though instructive beyond Israel. An ethical perspective in relation to place is introduced, derived from the relationship between the presence of the LORD and place. Of course Genesis 1–3 is also ethically charged, but it does not contain this specific motif of pollution of the land. The field for cultivating crops has become a murder scene, and this pollution of the land is intolerable in God's presence.

We do not know what became of "the field" in which cultivation had turned to murder. Suffice it here to note that place is ethically charged and may be desecrated. One thinks, for example, of the effect on place of mass murder such as at Auschwitz and Birkenau, and more recently of Ground Zero in New York. Auschwitz has proved particularly controversial in recent years, as a result of John Paul II's celebrating mass there—thereby converting what was the SS commandant's office into a Catholic church—and the establishment of a Carmelite convent just outside the inner perimeter fence in 1984.[8] Auschwitz has become a contested place of memory, which raises the question as to whether such places can in any way be redeemed, or are best preserved as a type of museum. In this narrative there are also hints of the motif of creation's reaction to mistreatment. The voice of Abel's blood cries out to God from the 'ădāmâ. Place, we might say, will only take so much, and then there is a type of kickback effect with serious consequences for humans. As we will see in part 2, this is important to bear in mind in the context of globalization and climate change.

As we noted above, Cain and Abel's implacement outside of Eden involved them in cultivation. Cain's displacement following his murder of Abel leads to the building of a city, raising acutely the question of the norms for cultural development.

Building Cities

We shape the city, then it shapes us.[9]

Cain's displacement is connected with the building of the first city (4:17). This is ironic in terms of his being condemned to be a vagrant and could

7. G. J. Wenham, *Genesis 1–15*, 107.
8. See Charlesworth, "Contesting Places of Memory"; Bartoszewski, *Convent at Auschwitz*; Rittner and Roth, *Memory Offended*; Young, *The Texture of Memory*.
9. Reader, *Cities*, 1.

indicate that city building is a sign of his resistance to God's judgment. The Hebrew, however, is unclear at this point, and it is likely that it was Cain's son, Enoch, who built the first city and named it Irad, after his son.[10] The name Irad sounds like Eridu, the name of the city which Mesopotamian tradition held to be the oldest in the world. In terms of place we see here an important progression from Cain the farmer to Enoch the first city builder. The conciseness of the narrative at this point is notable, especially in comparison to origin narratives from Mesopotamian cultures, in which the founding of cities is central.[11]

The next builder of cities that we encounter in the Pentateuch is Nimrod (Gen. 10:8–12). Here we witness the building of cities and kingdoms on a grand scale. The four verses devoted to Nimrod occur as an expansion in the Table of Nations; more specifically, Nimrod is listed among the sons of Ham, whose names represent nations of great consequence to Israel. Amidst a concise genealogy, four verses indicate that the author regarded Nimrod as of particular importance. "Nimrod" could be translated "we shall rebel,"[12] possibly foreshadowing the rebellion in 11:1–9. His building achievements are extensive, including Babylon, which, if not the first city of Mesopotamia, was certainly the most prestigious; Erech, one of the earliest Sumerian cities; Nineveh, the most important city after Ashur in Assyria; and so on. Nimrod's achievements as a warrior, city builder, and hunter epitomize the ideal Mesopotamian hero, and the king in particular.

The next building of a city that we encounter in Genesis 1–11 is Babel. This is preceded by the flood narrative, which follows on from the marriage of the "sons of God" to the "daughters of humans." It is hard to know precisely what the marriage refers to; the sons of God are most probably heavenly, angelic creatures.[13] But clearly these marriages represent a catastrophic breakdown of God's order for creation. Like Abel's murder, this incident, which alerts God to just how wicked mankind has become (6:5–6), pollutes the earth and is incompatible with God's presence. The occurrence of 'ereṣ—here translated "earth" and also the main word for "earth" in Genesis 1—three times in 6:5–7 indicates the universal, placial significance of sin.

When Noah and his family emerge from the ark, the initial command to Adam and Eve to fill the earth is reissued to them, and they receive God's blessing; both are signs of a new beginning, a new creation. Never again will God destroy the earth with a flood, and the seasonal cycle fundamental to agriculture is assured. Genesis 8:22 lists all the major seasons of the agricultural year: sowing of grain in the fall, harvesting in the spring, the harvest of summer[14]

10. See G. J. Wenham, *Genesis 1–15*, 111; Westermann, *Genesis 1–11*, 326–27.

11. Hiebert, *Yahwist's Landscape*, 43.

12. G. J. Wenham, *Genesis 1–15*, 222.

13. See G. J. Wenham, *Genesis 1–15*, for the different views.

14. *Qayiṣ* is used in the Old Testament for the season of summer and for summer fruit (cf. Amos 3:15; 8:1–2).

fruit, and the autumn[15] harvest of olives.[16] But humankind's relation to the animals is changed; the animals will now fear humankind, and they will now be available as food to humans. Furthermore, the complexity of humankind's relationship to the earth soon manifests itself again.

Noah is a man of the soil (*'ădāmâ*), a farmer, and the first to plant a vineyard. "This seems to mark a step forward in agriculture. Whereas Noah's ancestors raised only the most basic foodstuffs (cf. 3:18–19; 4:2), Noah introduces the cultivation of luxury items so that he can produce 'wine that maketh glad the heart of man.'"[17] Noah's relationship to the cleansed earth does represent an advance, but it is not without complications: he gets drunk from the wine, and again God's order for familial relationships is somehow transgressed.[18] As with Cain and Abel, humankind's cultivation of the land is bound up with the breakdown in relationship with the LORD. Implacement remains complex.

The Table of Nations, listing the sons of Japheth, Ham, and Shem, follows this incident, a vision, as we will see in the next chapter, of all the nations of the world with Israel at the center. The descendants of these sons of Noah fill the known earth, forming nations, each with its own language. Juxtaposed with this is the story of the building of another city, Babel/Babylon, with a different angle on the development of separate languages, or so it would seem. Genesis 11 opens with the whole world having one language and a common speech. Humans journey east, find a plain in Shinar, and settle there. A plain is here a broad, flat area ideal for settlement and agriculture, and "'they found' probably expresses their relief that they can now settle down."[19] Implacement beckons and is here accompanied with building on a major scale. They rouse each other to the communal task: "And they said to one another" (11:3). The exhortation "Come" occurs twice in verses 3–4 and is followed by four exhortations: let us make bricks and let us burn them; let us build a city and let us make a name for ourselves. "Hortatory speech is the herald of craft. And craft enables man to play creator: God, too, had said, 'Let us make.'"[20] Using bricks, typical of Mesopotamian culture as opposed to the use of stone by Israelites, they build a city and a tower that reaches to the heavens. "Imitating God's creation of man out of the dust of the ground, the human race begins its own project of creation by firing and transforming portions of the earth."[21]

15. *Ḥōrep* is often used in the Old Testament to refer to winter as opposed to summer, but in Prov. 20:4 it refers, as probably here in Gen. 8:22, to the autumn harvest.

16. Hiebert, *Yahwist's Landscape*, 45.

17. G. J. Wenham, *Genesis 1–15*, 198.

18. The sin could be that of voyeurism; Ham should have covered his father and not publicized it to his brothers. See ibid., 198–99.

19. Ibid., 239.

20. Kass, *Beginning of Wisdom*, 225.

21. Ibid., 226.

The tower is that most distinctive style of Babylonian architecture, the zig-gurat.[22] The Babylonians regarded E-temem-an-ki, the temple of the foundation of heaven and earth, as the great tower of their ancient city. This tower was dedicated to Marduk, Babylon's chief deity. It is likely that it is this tower that the Babel narrative refers to. It consisted of six square stages built upon a platform, topped with a small sanctuary. The base was 185 m square, and at the top of the last tower there was a cell in which a large couch was laid, and by it a golden table; the cell was reserved for the god, who came and rested on the couch. The total height of the tower was 85 m. "The House of the Foundation of Heaven and Earth thus sought to link the city with the cosmos, and to bring the city into line with the heavenly powers that be, or—perhaps, conversely—to bring the powers that be into line with the goals of the city. In more ways than one, the towered city is, in principle, 'cosmopolis.'"[23]

The aim of this massive building project is to "make a name for ourselves" (11:4). Prior to Genesis 11 the verb "make" (*'āśâ*) is used only of God. "Name" is also used in a new sense here:

> To *make* a name for oneself is, most radically, to "make that which requires a name." To make a new name for oneself is to remake the meaning of one's life so that it deserves a new name. . . . At once makers and made, the founders of Babel aspire to nothing less than self-*re*-creation—through the arts and crafts, customs and mores of their city. . . . The children of man (*'adam*) remake themselves and, thus, their name, in every respect taking the place of God.[24]

This major effort at implacement evokes God's wrath and judgment. Once again the judgment involves displacement: "So the LORD *scattered them* abroad from there over the face of all the earth, and they left off building the city" (11:8, emphasis added). The judgment is also linguistic, for "the LORD confused [their] language" (11:9; cf. v. 7). This confusion is often assumed to be the multiplicity of languages, but in context it is more likely that the punishment refers to a breakdown in communication.[25]

Ironically, considering the humans' intention to build a tower up to heaven, the LORD has to come down to see what the children of *'ādām* built (11:5; NRSV "mortals"; cf. ESV "children of man"). The reference to Adam is deliberate: Adam sinned in his quest for autonomy, and so too do the city builders. The sin involved is their hubris, shown in their saying, "Let us make a name for ourselves"; their idolatry, implied by the tower associated with Marduk; and their resistance to filling the earth, to being "scattered abroad." The LORD's

22. Wiseman, "Babylonia," 402.
23. Kass, *Beginning of Wisdom*, 230.
24. Ibid., 231. Emphasis original.
25. See V. P. Hamilton, *Book of Genesis, Chapters 1–17*, 350; Wolters, "Creation, Worldview and Foundations."

rejection of this tower of ascent is also a reminder that God is not to be found in nature worship of the sky:

> The most striking characteristic of J's cosmology is the insignificance of these other spheres and the significance of the terrestrial sphere as the realm of divine activity. . . . It is the Yahwist's concrete, agricultural terrain that J's deity inhabits and in which he appears to be largely at home. J's God . . . lives a very earthly life. He plants the Garden of Eden, walks in it, and talks to its residents. . . . He meets Cain in the field, closes the door of the ark behind Noah, smells the fragrance of his offering, and eats dinner with Abraham.[26]

In Genesis 1–11, then, cities do not appear favorably, to put it mildly. It is this type of material which leads scholars such as J. Ellul to conclude that Scripture is hostile to cities, because "the city is a phenomenon absolutely removed from man's power, a phenomenon which he is fundamentally incapable of affecting."[27] Ellul is right to recognize that the city has a profound spiritual influence,[28] but it is quite another thing to assert that the spiritual influence of the city is always negative, that by its very origin and structure the city is cursed. This is a strong statement with significant implications for placemaking and calls for careful evaluation.[29]

Cultural Development in Genesis 1–11 and the City

The building of cities must be seen as part of the cultural development in Genesis 1–11. Abel kept flocks, while Cain worked the soil (4:2). Jabal lived in tents with herds (4:20):

> Yabal is thus the father of the Bedouin lifestyle. He did not merely reestablish Abel's pastoral work. Abel shepherded צֹאן [ṣōʾn] "sheep and goats," but Yabal tended מקנה [miqneh] "herds": that term covers all animals that are herded—sheep, goats, cattle, asses, or camels. . . . Whereas Abel merely lived off his flocks, Yabal could trade with his beasts of burden, and this represents cultural advance.[30]

Prior to this mention of Jabal we have the reference to Enoch building Irad, which we discussed above. Jabal's brother Jubal is described as the father or originator of all who play the harp and flute.[31] Here we see the origin of

---

26. Hiebert, *Yahwist's Landscape*, 64.

27. Ellul, *Meaning of the City*, 47 (cf. 60).

28. Ibid., 9.

29. It should be noted that for Ellul the city is a symbol of politics, commerce, and autonomy. His dialectical method means that we should not understand him to be rejecting urbanization as such.

30. G. J. Wenham, *Genesis 1–15*, 113.

31. On music and the Old Testament see Borowski, *Daily Life in Biblical Times*, 87–93.

music, which will form part of culture and cultus. In Genesis 4:22 the origin of metalworking is described: "Tubal-Cain, father of all who sharpen copper and iron."[32] If Hiebert is correct that we should translate this phrase as "the blacksmith for all who plow with bronze and iron,"[33] then Tubal-Cain is the ancestor of the village blacksmith, who sharpened the metal plow points used by farmers.

Music included poetry and song, and in 4:23–24 we have the first poem or song from Lameck, an example of early Hebrew poetry using a variety of literary devices to maximum effect.[34] There is parallelism and rhyme; many words end with or include *î* (my, me), indicating Lameck's egoism; and metrically there are three bicola.[35] The content of the poem, however, is utterly vindictive, the disciplined form accentuating the barbarity of the message: Lameck is more depraved than Cain.[36]

Genesis 4:26 relates the origin of regular worship, namely prayer and sacrifice—"At that time people began to invoke the name of the LORD"—just as preceding verses have noted the development of farming, music, and metallurgy. This verse is best read as a record of the start of public worship, comparable to the record, in the Sumerian flood story, of the establishment of worship in the pre-flood era. It is significant that the start of worship is linked with the line of Seth, the line out of which Abraham and Israel will emerge.

Scholars debate whether these cultural developments reflect a desert-nomadic context[37] or an urban one,[38] in which cattle breeders, metalworkers, and musicians are three guilds of urbanites.[39] To debate such matters is, however—apart from their relevance for source criticism of the Pentateuch—to miss the point that such development opens up the route toward urban life, albeit via the village settlement. Although the narratives in Genesis 1–11 are well known to be related to the ancient Near Eastern narratives of the time, the former present a significantly different perspective on nomadism than the latter. In the Sumerian flood story, for example, nomadism is something from which the gods rescue man, whereas with Cain it is a judgment imposed, and with Jabal nomadism—living in tents—would seem to be a positive development. Wenham notes, "This contrast [on nomadism] fits in with the overall optimism of Mesopotamia which believes in human progress over against the biblical picture of the inexorable advance of sin. . . . It would seem likely

---

32. This is G. J. Wenham's translation (*Genesis 1–15*, 93).

33. Hiebert, *Yahwist's Landscape*, 44.

34. Wenham, *Genesis 1–15*, 114.

35. A bicolon is a verse structure of poetry with two cola (lines) that are related rhythmically and thematically.

36. G. J. Wenham, *Genesis 1–15*, 114.

37. Gunkel, *Genesis*, 51; idem, *Folktale*, 51–52; Rad, *Genesis*, 110–11.

38. Wallis, "Die Stadt," 133–35; Coote and Ord, *The Bible's First History*, 66–73; Frick, *The City in Ancient Israel*, 205–6.

39. Hiebert, *Yahwist's Landscape*, 42.

that the other human achievements listed here—farming, metalwork, and music—are also seen by Genesis as *somehow* under the shadow of Cain's sin."[40]

The key question is *how* Cain's sin overshadows these developments. On the one hand, there is something insightful about Wenham's notion. As we saw above, the building of cities is related as taking place among the descendants of Japheth and Ham as well as among those of Cain, whereas nothing is said of such developments in the elect line of Shem. This might incline one toward a secular-sacred dichotomy, or what Niebuhr calls a *Christ against culture* position.[41] However, the situation is more complex than this. In Eden the serving of the garden is the task divinely given to Adam and Eve. Abel and Cain's activities are described positively; there is a problem with Cain's attitude, but not with his vocation as a worker of the soil. And it would surely be quite ridiculous to suggest that the invention of instrumental music, song, and poetry is somehow evil, considering their positive role in the Psalter and in the entire Old Testament. Would anyone seriously argue that this is a negative development?

The case is similar with Lameck's poem. It is the first in the Bible, and it reeks of vengeance and hatred. But this does not make poetry bad; it merely indicates the misuse of poetry. Although poetry is a wonderful gift of God, and its appearance here indicates an important cultural development signifying the origin of literature in its great variety, it can, like all the cultural developments named in this passage, be radically *misdirected*. Thus the shadow over these developments is not that they are intrinsically bad, but that in human hands they are only too capable of misdirection.

And so too it is with the city. While it is true that thus far cities are not looking good in Genesis, cities are part of this pattern of cultural development and should not be seen as intrinsically evil. Eden is an urban garden—this in itself indicates that we are not to see Genesis as siding with rural life against urban life. This perspective is confirmed by a philosophical and cultural examination of that very human action of building and cultivation, and not least, of building cities. This is one of those places where a dialogue between Scripture and philosophy proves illuminating. Building is an inescapable part of human implacement, as is cultural development. Once again a consideration of place is insightful.

Building as Part of Cultural Development: A Philosophical and Theological Analysis

> It is hardly an exaggeration to say that the city is the defining artifact of civilization.[42]

40. G. J. Wenham, *Genesis 1–15*, 98–99. Emphasis added.
41. Niebuhr, *Christ and Culture*, 45–82.
42. Reader, *Cities*, 7.

The first reference to *building* in the Bible is to Enoch son of Cain building Irad. For a city to be built, however humble, the art of building must be already advanced. After that the next reference is to Noah building an ark, a great mobile home. The fact that Jabal built tents would seem to imply that others built houses. Van Selms notes, "Throughout the whole of biblical times the common man built his own house, perhaps with the help of his family and neighbors."[43]

Cities are an extension of the development of building, and an examination of the philosophy of building in relation to place is revealing in this respect. There is an inevitable logic between embodiment, implacement, and building. To be stable and inhabit a place, humans must build to make sure of stable inhabitation. Casey sets out this logic: "When we cannot find a habitable place, we must set about *making* or *building* such a place to ensure stable inhabitation. The place made, a 'built place,' occurs in a distinctly limited sphere of space. We gain thereby not just a measure of security but a basis for dwelling *somewhere in particular*."[44] Casey perceptively notes that building is not only a logical development of embodiment but also a response to the home of the universe in which we find ourselves: "As 'our first universe,' home has already been cultivated within and without."[45] Building is thus a profound response to God and our imaging of him in his world. Similarly, E. Levinas comments, "The somewhere of dwelling is produced as a primordial event relative to which the event of the unfolding of physico-geometrical extension must be understood—and not the reverse."[46]

The capacity to build is woven into the fabric of our being and is an important part of the dynamic of imaging God in his good creation. Where and how we dwell are not marginal elements of human existence; they affect us deeply: "A dwelling where we reside comes to exist in our image, but *we*, the residents, also take on certain of *its* properties."[47] There is also an inevitable social dimension to building. "In becoming implaced, we emerge into a larger world of burgeoning experience, not only by ourselves but with others."[48]

The sociality of building means that building would inevitably carry with it the development of collectives of buildings, from villages, to towns and cities, to larger regions, all of which we see in the texts we have examined in Genesis. Communal implacement in cities brought a range of advantages: the stability, the nurturing environment of a home, the capacity to wage war and defend oneself, education, contemplation, conviviality, lingerings and

---

43. Van Selms, "Build, Building," 553.
44. Casey, *Getting Back into Place*, 109. Emphasis original.
45. Ibid., 175.
46. Levinas, *Totality and Infinity*, 168.
47. Casey, *Getting Back into Place*, 120. Emphasis original.
48. Ibid., 111.

durations,[49] commemoration, art, athletic contests.[50] "Moving about in a city draws us away from the interior depth of a home into the exterior breadth of a wider urban world."[51]

Any theological assessment of the city must take account of the variety of functions a city enables and not just the negative possibilities, real as they are. Indeed, just as there are different ways of directing culture, so there are different ways of building. Casey is at pains to explore how we can build in order to inhabit and indwell our buildings. Similarly, in his remarkable work on pattern language and building, C. Alexander insists that we can build in a way that is life-giving or in a way that is dead: "The specific patterns out of which a building or a town is made may be alive or dead. To the extent they are alive, they let our inner forces loose, and set us free; but when they are dead they keep us locked in inner conflict."[52] Casey notes that "every built structure takes up a stand" in relation to the natural world.[53] But this stand varies, and

> we must question the presumption that building is an exclusively Promethean activity of brawny aggression and forceful imposition. . . . Building is also, and just as crucially, *Epimethean*. . . . In this latter capacity building is most effectively cultivational in character, for it seeks not to exploit materials but to care for them. In building-as-cultivating, the builder respects the already present properties of that from which building begins.[54]

Casey's distinction here between different types of building is deeply insightful. In terms of the biblical material it alerts us to the possibility that the account of Nimrod's cities and that of the Tower of Babel may not damn cities but that those cities are examples of a radical misdirection of building. Just as homes can become places of oppression and terror, so too can cities, but, as with homes, cities are not inherently evil. They too can be places for dwelling, with all the positive connotations of this word.

Casey's distinction between Promethean and Epimethean types of building alerts us to the ecological issues involved in building, and that has a resonance with the command for Adam and Eve to serve the garden, which evokes Epimethean building-as-cultivating rather than Promethean mastery. Casey elaborates on the Epimethean approach as follows:

> Cultivation construed as caring-for thus includes all of the following: matching precise grains of wood, finding that a certain column goes well with a given balustrade, realizing that one building design suits the location better than another,

49. Ibid., 112.
50. Ibid., 114.
51. Ibid., 180.
52. C. Alexander, *Timeless Way of Building*, 101.
53. Casey, *Getting Back into Place*, 152.
54. Ibid., 173.

discovering that the same design also opens up a dialogue among those who are going to reside in the building it projects, as well as among friends, neighbors, and others who will be affected by this eventual building in some significant way.[55]

The biblical accounts, however, introduce an overt theological dimension as well, a dimension implicit but undeveloped in Casey's philosophy. The problem with Babel would not appear to be brutal mastery; indeed the plain of Shinar would seem to fit with the requirement that "building calls for heeding the parameters of the natural setting."[56] Rather, the problem is idolatry—Babylon is the city of Marduk—and a quest for control and autonomy rather than a submission to God and his call to spread out around the earth. Needless to say, this theological dimension does not supersede Casey's useful distinction but complements it and, theologically speaking, grounds it. To allude to George Steiner's *Real Presences*, the *real presence* of place requires a grammar of creation.

Conclusion

Genesis 11 leaves us with the great building project of Babel in ruins. What is to become of implacement now? In Genesis 12 God starts afresh with Abraham by commanding him to leave his place of abode and go to *the land* that God will show him. From this point onward in the biblical story "the land" will become the central focus. In the next chapter we turn to the commission of Abraham, with its implications for the geographical horizon evoked in the seventy nations of Genesis 10,[57] and to the journeying of Abraham and his immediate descendants from place to place.

55. Ibid., 174. Elsewhere (149), Casey distinguishes between contentious and contented building.

56. Ibid., 149.

57. See Bauckham, "Geography—Sacred and Symbolic," in *Bible and Mission*, 55–81.

3

The Nations, Abraham, and Journeying to the Land

From Genesis 12 onward the focus of the biblical narrative narrows to Abraham and his descendants, from whom Israel will emerge. However, even as the story narrows, it never loses touch with its creation-wide concern. A key element of the promise to Abraham is "the land," which will provide both background and focus to the narrative from this point onward. Indeed it is implicit in Genesis 10.

The Table of Nations: Genesis 10

Robert Gordon makes much of the fact that neither Jerusalem nor mountains are mentioned in Genesis 1–11. He relates this to historical veracity—Jerusalem was not part of the world's earliest history—and to the Old Testament's concern for the whole of creation.[1] This is true and insightful, but Israel's presence is implicit in Genesis 10, the Table of Nations.

Prior to the particularity of God's call to Abram in response to the Tower of Babel episode, we have the Table of Nations with its universal concern for nations and territories. "This is the known world from Israel's perspective in the Old Testament period."[2] Not many of the peoples mentioned in the Old Testament are excluded from this list. Thus the list is historically particular but

1. Gordon, *Holy Land, Holy City*, 4–16.
2. Bauckham, *Bible and Mission*, 56.

also symbolically comprehensive—the number of descendants listed is seventy, suggesting completeness, so that the seventy nations listed symbolize the nations of the earth. Reflecting the "inner map" of the author,[3] the list orders the names in terms of their relation to Israel, suggesting that Israel is at the center of the inhabited world, and the nations most distant from Israel at the edges of the world. The vision is not an ethnocentric one, but, as is typical of the biblical story, one in which particularity (Israel) is always connected with universality (the nations) in God's purposes of redemption.

Abraham and the Nations

From now on the land is the focus; this is clear from the brief description of Abraham's long journey from Ur—probably the well-known Ur in southern Iraq[4]—to Haran and, by contrast, from the way the narrative slows down to describe his journey from Haran to and in Canaan. Abraham's call is a radical one: he is to go "by himself" (*lk*, lit. "by yourself") to the land that he is promised. As T. Muraoka observes, the prepositional phrase *lk* evokes "the impression . . . that the subject establishes his own identity, recovering or finding *his own place* by determinedly dissociating himself from his familiar surrounding. Notions of isolation, loneliness, parting, seclusion or withdrawal are often recognizable."[5] This impression is strengthened by what we know of immigration around this time; many Amorites settled in Mesopotamia before and after 2000 BC, and it is possible that Terah's family was among them. However, Abraham's journey from Ur to Haran to Canaan would have taken him *against* the mainstream of Amorite migration.[6]

One is reminded of Thoreau's suggestion that when one leaves for the wilderness one should leave as though never to return.[7] This was not true of Thoreau, who did return home, but it is of Abraham. Genesis 12:1 makes clear that, contra Westermann, we should not think of Abraham as a nomad for whom departure would be easy; he is called to abandon his old life in order to find a new one in a new place.[8] As B. Jacob says of 12:7, "This monumental statement, the shortest of all promises, yet names both people and land and unites them by the verb give, here uttered for the first time."[9]

---

3. Work on people's mental maps took off in the light of Lynch's 1960 book *The Image of the City*. For a sense of how geography has developed since then, see Gould and White, *Mental Maps*. I am using the expression "inner map" for the way in which a view of the world is constructed/represented by the author.

4. G. J. Wenham, *Genesis 1–15*, 272.

5. Muraoka, *Emphatic Words and Structures in Biblical Hebrew*, 122. Emphasis added.

6. G. J. Wenham, *Genesis 1–15*, 272–73.

7. Thoreau, "Walking," in *Wild Apples*, 94.

8. For evidence that Abraham was not a nomad see Wiseman, "Abraham Reassessed," 139–54.

9. Jacob, *Das Erste Buch der Tora Genesis*, 344.

Abraham is called to embark on a journey that will result in his becoming a great nation[10] and in all nations of the world being blessed through him. Muraoka's point about *lk* is pertinent in terms of the fivefold recurrence of the root "bless" in 12:1–13. Some form of the root "curse" occurs five times in Genesis 1–11 (3:14, 17; 4:11; 5:29; 9:25), whereas "bless" occurs five times in these three verses: "This fivefold repetition answers to the fivefold reference to 'curse' in chapters 1–11, signalling that the agenda of salvation history is to counteract the workings of evil in the world and to restore the world to its divinely intended blessedness."[11] By separating himself from his past, Abraham will journey toward such implacement and make re-implacement possible for the nations of the world.

This particular yet universal setting of the covenant with Abraham surfaces as well in the descriptions of the land. In Genesis 15:18–21, "this land" is followed by a spatial merism: from the river of Egypt to the Euphrates. As scholars have noted, this depiction is different from the precise delineation of the land in Numbers 34. On the other hand, depictions similar to that in Genesis 15 are found in Exodus 23:31; Deuteronomy 11:24; Joshua 1:3–4; and 1 Chronicles 13:5. Weinfeld thus discerns two conceptions of the extent of the land in the Old Testament: first, the priestly depiction found in Numbers 34 and repeated in Ezekiel 47–48, and second, the broader one represented by Genesis 15 and related texts.[12] Weinfeld argues that this broader conception reflects the military gains of the united monarchy (cf. 1 Kings 4:21), which was later adopted as an ideal by Deuteronomistic theology.

This view, however, fails to distinguish the spatial merisms in the broader texts, which evoke general, vast, often undetermined regions, from the clearly defined boundaries in the narrower texts. N. Wazana thus rightly notes, "The differences in form and context reveal that these are two separate genres that convey two different *conceptions* of the Promised Land, but not two different *territorial units*."[13] The concept and literary form of these spatial merisms have a compelling background in Neo-Assyrian imperial claims, in which they evoke world rule.[14] Thus, in the Old Testament "the spatial merisms in promise terminology reflect a land that has no borders at all, only ever-expanding frontiers; they are referring to universal rule, using stock terminology typical of Neo-Assyrian royal inscriptions."[15] They embody God's promise that through Abraham he would bring blessing to all nations, to every place.

10. The use of *gôy* is significant in that it has a political dimension that *'am* lacks, indicating "the status and stability of nationhood in a land designated for that purpose" (Speiser, "'People' and 'Nation' of Israel," 162–63).

11. Janzen, *Abraham*, 5, 15; Borgman, *Genesis*, 109.

12. Weinfeld, "Covenant of Grant"; idem, "Covenantal Aspect of the Promise."

13. Wazana, "From Dan to Beer-Sheba," 63–64. See also idem, *All the Boundaries*.

14. Wazana, "From Dan to Beer-Sheba," 67–71. Cf. Deut. 11:25.

15. Ibid., 71.

Abraham: Journeying

> A gift that has the power to change us awakens a part of the soul.
> But we cannot receive the gift until we can meet it as an equal. We
> therefore submit ourselves to the labor of becoming like the gift.[16]

> I can here only advert to the need for fresh explorations to, for
> example, the role of travel as a device for composing a dissenting
> world-view that places alienation at the center of originality—for
> example, Abram's journey through Genesis, from chs. 12 to 22.[17]

The theme of journeying holds the rest of the Pentateuch together. Abraham
and the other patriarchs travel down and up the land of Canaan, and sometimes in and out of Egypt. Joseph and his descendants settle in Egypt, and
then their descendants journey to the promised land. Deuteronomy's context
is that of Moses's speeches to the Israelites as they are about to enter the land.

The land as it lay before Abraham contained a diversity of topography, landscape, and environmental conditions. From Dan to Elath—north to south—the
land measures only 254 miles (410 km), but only 136 miles (220 km) of this area,
namely that from Dan to Beersheba, is suitable for permanent settlement. The
distance from the Mediterranean Sea to the Jordan River[18] is on average 50 miles
(80 km), and the inhabited land of the Transjordan is no more than 25 miles (40
km) in width, so that Canaan lies compressed between the Mediterranean Sea
and desert. In total the fertile land approximates 780 square miles (2,000 km²).

Canaan was situated like a bridge between the two ends of the Fertile
Crescent: Egypt in the south and Syria and Mesopotamia in the north. The
result was that, "more than any other country in the ancient world, Palestine
was always directly or indirectly connected with other parts of the Near East
and the eastern Mediterranean."[19] Geographically, Canaan divides into seven
longitudinal strips from west to east: the coastal plain, the Shephelah foothills,
the central mountain ridges, the Judean desert, the Rift Valley, mountains or
plateaus to the east of the Rift Valley, and the eastern desert. East-west valleys
transect these strips, creating communication lines between the coastal plain
and the inner parts of Canaan.[20]

16. Hyde, *The Gift*, 65.
17. A. Gibson, *Text and Tablet*, 101. Gibson points to Hacking's *Mad Travellers* as a good
starting point.
18. As a narrow, winding body of water, the Jordan is never in the Old Testament called
"river" (*nāhār*), a name reserved for the large rivers of Egypt, Syria, and Mesopotamia (Wazana,
"From Dan to Beer-Sheba," 46). On rivers in the OT and the ancient Near East see Wazana,
"Water Division in Border Agreements"; Reymond, *L'eau, sa vie, et sa signification dans l'ancien
testament*.
19. Mazar, *Archaeology*, 1.
20. See ibid., 1–9, for more detail.

Casey notes that even journeys harbor a commitment to place, and this is certainly true of a journey as significant as that of Abraham. Journeys are place bound and place specific,[21] so that place names are no contingent matter; they are the locatory units of everyday journeys.[22] Places are far more than mere backdrops; they provide the changing but indispensable material medium of journeys, furnishing way stations as well as origins and destinations of the journey.[23]

The journeys of Abraham, Isaac, and Jacob in the land of Canaan were primarily along what has come to be called the Beersheba-Jerusalem-Jenin Highway, or the National Highway.[24] This famous north-south route, already well known in the biblical period, connected prominent cities such as Beersheba, Hebron, Jerusalem, Gibeah, Ramah, Bethel, Shechem, Ibleam, and Jezreel. Y. Aharoni provides the most detailed and current reconstruction of the route, as follows:

> One longitudinal road of some importance is that through the hill country ... which runs along the length of the north-south mountain ridge. In this section between Hebron and Shechem it follows a single track corresponding approximately to the watershed, and the deep wadis on both sides prevent any deviation to the right or left. The main cities in the hill country are situated near or on this route, e.g. Debir, Hebron, Bethlehem, Jerusalem, Mizpah and Bethel. ... From Shechem the road forks out into two branches: the western one passes through Samaria, Dothan, Ibleam and Beth-haggan via Tirzah and Bezek. ... South of Hebron the road also forks to form additional branches: the westernmost descends via Debir and Madmannah to Beer-sheba, whence it continues southward past Nissana towards the "Way of Shur" which leads to Egypt. The eastern branch turns from Hebron towards Juttah and Eshtemoa and descends towards Arad and Hormah. From here it extends southward through the heart of the Negeb past Aroer, Oboda and Bir-Hafir to Kadesh-barnea.[25]

In 12:4–9 Abraham journeys across the land of Canaan from north to south along this route. He travels south from Haran to Shechem to a place where the only distinguishing feature in the landscape is "the oak of Moreh" (12:6). The LORD appears to him and promises to give the land to Abraham's offspring (12:7). The accompanying reference to the Canaanites still being in the land (12:6) makes it likely that the tree is a sacred one associated with Canaanite worship. Abraham faces a choice of adopting local worship or worshiping the LORD; he chooses the latter: "Abram chooses to open up

---

21. Casey, *Getting Back into Place*, 274.
22. Ibid., 280.
23. Ibid., 274.
24. Dorsey, *Roads and Highways*, 117.
25. Aharoni, *Land of the Bible*, 57–58.

within himself a significant space for the God of what-is-to-come, the God who is promising."[26]

Casey notes that one can come to a place never before visited, and yet feel one knows it for a second time; he calls this re-inhabiting.[27] With its overarching motif of re-implacement, Abraham's journey into the land contains something of this. However, according to Casey, re-inhabiting means that one must take up life in the region in a way that echoes the placeways of the original occupants; what is vital is the adoption of the appropriate habitat and the right set of local practices. This is precisely what re-inhabiting must not involve for Abraham; Eden, and not Canaan, is the model, and while sensitivity to the land and its ecology is crucial, Abraham is to follow the LORD and not to adopt the local practices to the extent that they are religiously shaped. In this respect it is significant that Abraham and his extended family, apart from Lot, who ends up in Sodom, tend to set their tents up outside the major Canaanite cities rather than in them. This is not an antiurban motif but an anti-idolatry one.

Genesis 12:5–9 takes Abraham from the northern to the southern border of the land; he sees it, walks through it, and lives and worships in it: "Symbolically he has taken possession of it."[28] Casey notes that "journeys thus not only take us to places but embroil us in them."[29] This is certainly true of Abraham, as his adventures in Egypt indicate. In 13:17 God tells Abraham to "rise up, walk through the length and the breadth of the land, for I will give it to you." As Casey observes, "Journeying adds to our understanding of place,"[30] and God appears determined that Abraham will understand the whole land.

In his *The Land Is Mine: Six Biblical Land Ideologies*, N. Habel deals with Abraham under the heading "Land as Host Country." Habel makes much of the fact that "the ideology of the Abraham cycle has Abraham formally recognizing the rights of the host peoples to their various territories. . . . Abraham's rights and responsibilities are not those of a monarch or conqueror, but those of the head of an ancestral household."[31] On the whole this is correct. For example, after moving south to the region between Kadesh and Shur in the Negeb (20:1), Abraham enters into a covenant with Abimelech not to deal falsely with him or his descendants (21:22–34). Abraham remains a resident alien (21:34) in Canaan.

Yet even while he lives as such he receives repeated promises that the whole land will be given to his descendants. Indeed the Abraham narrative (chaps. 12–22) moves forward on the basis of promise and covenant. The threefold

---

26. Borgman, *Genesis*, 62.
27. Casey, *Getting Back into Place*, 295.
28. G. J. Wenham, *Genesis 1–15*, 281.
29. Casey, *Getting Back into Place*, 276.
30. Ibid., 275.
31. Habel, *The Land Is Mine*, 133.

promise to Abraham—of being a landed nation, a dynasty, and a blessing to the nations—is followed by three grant-type covenants (chaps. 15; 17; 22) that climax in the third one with its emphasis on the third promise (22:16–18).[32] The gift of the land is central to the covenant in Genesis 15, and in 15:19–20 the present inhabitants of the land are specifically mentioned. Thus, if these covenant passages are read canonically, Habel is wrong to assert that in comparison to the other five land ideologies he finds in the Old Testament, "the image of the land of Canaan in the immigrant ideology of the Abraham narratives is markedly different."[33] Abraham's status as a resident alien is different, but the land theology is the same as found elsewhere in the Old Testament, as we will see.

God's formation of Abraham amidst his journeying, as evidenced in the promise and threefold covenant making, is typical of the Pentateuch as a whole. God will work *through* Abraham and his descendants to bring blessing to the whole of his creation, but first he has to work *in* Abraham and his descendants to make them truly a people of the blessing. As L. Hyde notes, "A gift that has the power to change us awakens a part of the soul. But we cannot receive the gift until we can meet it as an equal. We therefore submit ourselves to the labor of becoming like the gift."[34] This is the labor to which Abraham is called as he journeys through the land which God will give to his descendants. "To be a blessing requires a journey within, a reorientation."[35]

Nowhere is this clearer than in Genesis 22. Abraham and Sarah finally have their son, Isaac, but now Abraham faces by far the biggest challenge of his life, the seventh station on his journey, according to Buber: "The revelations appear as stations in a progress from trial to trial and from blessing to blessing."[36] God *asks* him—note the "please" (*nā'*) in 22:2[37]—to take Isaac and offer him as a burnt offering on Mount Moriah. A great deal has been written about this episode in Abraham's life;[38] suffice it to note here that in my opinion the sort of reading offered by Kass is by far the most convincing.

The agonizing, mysterious nature of Genesis 22 is inescapable. However, a canonical interpretation must take the note from the narrator in 22:1 seriously; God is testing Abraham, and this is the final stage—the seventh—in his formation as carrier of the blessing. Abraham is called to go on a journey, a pilgrimage, but it is the accompanying inner journey that is most significant: "Abraham must show that he understands that one's *spiritual* orientation is

32. See Hahn, "Kinship by Covenant," 168–211.
33. Habel, *The Land Is Mine*, 136.
34. Hyde, *The Gift*, 65.
35. Borgman, *Genesis*, 108.
36. Buber, "Abraham the Seer," 36. Buber stresses the unity of the Abraham narrative (36–37).
37. See G. J. Wenham, *Genesis 16–50*, 97, 104.
38. See, e.g., G. J. Wenham, *Genesis 16–50*; Moberly, *Bible, Theology, and Faith*, 71–183.

decisive also for *all human relations*, both personal and political."[39] This terrible test will also be the final stage in his education as the one through whom blessing will come to the nations. The cosmic implications of this test are evident already in the change of the divine name back to "Elohim"—echoing Genesis 1—whereas it has been "Yahweh" in the previous six visits of God to Abraham.

The nature of the test must be sought in the context of the ongoing formation of Abraham, and as Kass notes, "Horrible though it is to say so, the test God devises is perfect: for only if Abraham is willing to do without the covenant . . . out of awe-reverence for the Covenantor, can he demonstrate that he merits the covenant and its promised blessings."[40] I would stress merit less than Kass, but I think he is right that this awful test goes for the bull's-eye in Abraham's experience as to whether or not he really has become *like the gift*.

The structure of 22:2 mirrors that of 12:1. As is the beginning so is the end. At the beginning Abraham is called to relinquish all his family and placial ties. Now it would appear that he is called to relinquish the very covenant itself! And the letting go is performed on a slow, three-day journey, an excruciating pilgrimage to Mount Moriah.[41] Four set out on the journey; when Abraham sees Mount Moriah, he reduces the party to two—himself and his son; but once the son is bound, it is Abraham by himself. The outcome of the story is well known. It concludes with the strongest of the three grant covenants, one emphasizing that through Abraham's offspring the nations of the world will be blessed (22:15–18).

Central to the Abrahamic narratives is the land. Abraham symbolically possesses the land even as God forms him and enacts grant-type covenants with him, swearing an oath that he will give the land to Abraham's descendants and that through him all nations will be blessed. Genesis 22 in particular reminds us that the view of place implied in these narratives is a theology of place. Contra Kass, the land is not first holy because it is where Abraham and Sarah are buried,[42] but because it is the place where God keeps revealing himself to Abraham and the place which he bequeaths as a gift to Abraham and his descendants. It is the particular presence and work of God in and through Abraham that makes the land holy.

Isaac and Jacob: The Challenge of Implacement

Although the patriarchal narratives are full of fascinating placial details which we lack space to explore, two deserve our attention in the Isaac and Jacob

39. Kass, *Beginning of Wisdom*, 333. Emphasis original.
40. Ibid., 337.
41. Traditionally associated with Jerusalem.
42. Kass, *Beginning of Wisdom*, 348.

stories. The first is Isaac's blessing of Jacob and Esau, because in this episode the agrarian nature of the Hebrews is clear. Although it is by deceit that Jacob obtains Isaac's blessing, the terms of the blessing illuminate what is valuable in this family: the smell of Jacob (posing as Esau) is like "the smell of a field that the LORD has blessed" (27:27), and Isaac requests God to bless his son with rain ("the dew of heaven") and "the fatness of the earth, and plenty of grain and wine" (27:28). For farmers like Isaac who were vulnerable in Canaan, fertile land and a guaranteed water supply (dew) were indispensable to their survival and flourishing.

Yet we find repeatedly that these seminomadic pastoralists face difficulty in settling in the land (cf. Gen. 26:12–14). As D. Hillel notes,

> Isaac's engagement in farming as well as grazing expressed the natural desire of pastoralists to attain a more secure mode of subsistence or even to make the transition from nomadic herding to sedentary farming. Alas, that opportunistic attempt, although it may be successful in favorable years, is certain to encounter the resistance of the native agriculturalists, who perceive it as an encroachment on their own fragile domain.[43]

The second detail we should note appears in the account of Jacob's flight to Haran to escape Esau's revenge. En route, he sleeps with a stone for a pillow and dreams of a ladder reaching from earth to heaven, with angels ascending and descending on it.[44] Appropriately, he calls the place Bethel (the house of God). "Looking back at it as he walked away, he saw a stone finger rooted in the earth, pointing straight up through the sky."[45] In her reflections on this story, quoted earlier (p. 15), B. Taylor notes that nowadays people will go to great lengths in search of spiritual experience: "The last place most people look is right under their feet, in the everyday activities, accidents, and encounters of their lives."[46] Jacob's experience calls us to look for God right under our feet:

> *This is wonderful news.* I do not have to choose between the Sermon on the Mount and the magnolia trees. God can come to me by a still pool on the big island of Hawaii as well as at the altar of the Washington National Cathedral. The House of God stretches from one corner of the universe to the other. Sea monsters and ostriches live in it, along with people who pray in languages I do not speak, whose name I will never know.[47]

As the accompanying maps reveal, apart from journeys back in the direction of Haran to find wives and Jacob's flight east away from Esau, the patriarchs

---

43. Hillel, *Natural History of the Bible*, 65.
44. In John 1:51 Jesus equates the Son of Man with the ladder.
45. B. Taylor, *Altar in the World*, 4.
46. Ibid., xiv.
47. Ibid., 13. Emphasis original.

remain in the middle and southern parts of the land, pursuing with difficulty an agrarian way of life. They are unable to settle down and become truly implaced in the land, living on the whole in arid regions on the margins of Canaanite society. The insufficiency of agricultural land and the tensions to which this gives rise are a recurring motif (Gen. 26; 36). Genesis culminates in Jacob and his sons and their families moving down to Egypt to be with Joseph and escape the famine in the land. Here again their lifestyle is presented as agrarian, as is evident from Joseph's instruction to his brothers to tell Pharaoh that they are shepherds (46:32). Jacob's "Bethel" experience evokes the possibility of implacement in the land. However, this is never achieved and the move to Egypt appears to take the patriarchs in a very different direction.

Joseph: Implacement in Egypt

As with the other patriarchs, Joseph's remarkable journeying is paralleled by an equally remarkable inner journey, from spoiled youth to mature, forgiving leader. Joseph's rise to power and his capacity to forgive his brothers, as well as Pharaoh's remarkable hospitality,[48] enable his family to survive the famine, and they settle in Goshen, in the East Nile Delta. The Hebrews remain pastoralists and on the margins of Egyptian society, as if ready for the move back to the land. However, their stay in Egypt was long and formative; during this time their numbers grew to form the basis of the nation Israel (Exod. 1:7).

Historical-critical studies downplay the biblical indications that the Israelites spent some four hundred years in Egypt before they were liberated and, much more numerous and wealthy, journeyed to Sinai. Clearly the developing nation was influenced by Mesopotamian and Canaanite as well as Egyptian culture. Moreover, the Bible itself glosses over the effect of these four hundred years, focusing always on the land. Nevertheless, it is a mistake to ignore the potentially profound influence of this long sojourn. Hillel, who in his focus on the "natural history" of Israel recognizes that four hundred years would entail substantial implacement, devotes significant attention to this period. Referring to the Joseph narratives, Hillel notes that "whoever wrote this account obviously had a profound knowledge of Egypt and of its mostly regular but occasionally anomalous water supply, as well as of its cultural traditions."[49] Read in this light, the Joseph narratives, and later the story of the plagues, illuminate who the people of Israel will become.

Joseph enables the Israelites, the Egyptians, and others to survive the severe famine, but his practice of enslaving the entire people of Egypt (47:21), although it fits well with the Egyptian view of Pharaoh as divine, forms a stark contrast with the polity God will foster among his people in the land.

48. Hillel, *Natural History of the Bible*, 104.
49. Ibid., 99–100.

Salvation via Joseph involves highly effective drought contingency planning,[50] but it leads to slavery; salvation via the LORD is from slavery and will lead to a very different polity. No Egyptian law code has ever been found; probably, because of Pharaoh's divine status, one was not regarded as necessary. In Israel, however, law will be vital as a means for the people to live under the Lord's reign.

Exodus, Sinai, and Journeying to the Land

As J. Levenson points out, Exodus in general contains two parts, divided geographically: Egypt, the land of Pharaoh, is the setting for the first half (1:1–15:21), and Sinai, the realm of Yahweh, dominates part two (15:22–40:38).[51] In the two halves the lives of Moses and the Israelites mirror each other: both flee from Egypt, and both encounter God at Mount Sinai. The conflict between the two domains is resolved through Yahweh's clash with Pharaoh, which culminates at the sea, where the LORD "gained glory for [him]self over Pharaoh, his chariots, and his chariot drivers" (14:18). Exodus is arranged as "a double journey to, and sojourning at, the holy place of Sinai. In this way, pilgrimage constitutes the basic pattern of the book."[52] Indeed in 5:1 the verb used for "celebrate a festival" is *hgg*, more accurately translated as "make a pilgrimage." It is the same verb that is later used of the three compulsory pilgrimages for Israelites to Jerusalem each year.

Building emerges as a theme in Exodus when the new ruler presses the Israelites into forced labor to build the supply cities of Pithom and Rameses for food storage. Like Goshen, these cities were in the delta region and were part of the great building projects of the Nineteenth Dynasty. "Building is, of course, the essential Egyptian project. The lives of individual slaves have a merely instrumental, quantifiable value."[53] Egypt, formerly the place of exceptional hospitality, has become the place of terrible oppression. Ironically, the descendants of Joseph, whose drought management plan saved Egypt from catastrophe, now become enslaved in the food management plans of the new pharaoh. "In Egypt, work is alienated and, far from building a just society, contributes rather to increasing injustice and to widening the gap between exploiters and exploited."[54]

Because of his precipitate action in murdering an Egyptian, Moses is forced to flee into the desert and settle in Midian. The geographical location of Midian is uncertain, possibly because the Midianites were nomads. Moses is well

50. Ibid., 100.
51. Levenson, *The Hebrew Bible*, 127–59.
52. M. Smith, *Pilgrimage Pattern in Exodus*, 191.
53. Zornberg, *Particulars of Rapture*, 37.
54. Gutiérrez, *Theology of Liberation*, 159.

received by the Midianites, finds a wife, and settles with them; among the Midianites he finds temporary implacement, as the name of his son, *Gershom*, indicates. Although Gershom is probably derived from *gr* (drive, cast out), the narrator relates it to "stranger" (*gēr*) and "there" (*šām*). As J. Durham notes, *Gershom* evokes Moses's "most complete integration into his Midianite family. . . . Moses, who had been all his life a stranger there [in Egypt], was here a stranger no longer. . . . Moses has come to a people who not only worship the God of the fathers, but are free to do so. Thus he is at home, because this God is his God."[55] Moses's new occupation reconnects him placially with his ancestors. He assumes his role as liberator after leaving the riverine domain of Egypt and experiencing life as a shepherd in the semiarid pastoral domain. This experience enables him to identify with the journeys of his ancestors and prepares him for the exodus from Egypt.[56]

In Old Testament and Christian spirituality the desert has played a central role. Thomas Merton says of the desert fathers that in order to escape the decadence of their culture they had to jump off the shipwreck, as it were, and swim for their lives. Once, however, they had found firm footing in Christ, they were obliged to pull their culture with them to safety.[57] Moses's experience is similar; he has to get out of Egypt to find himself, and once he is re-implaced he can help his people find a similar freedom.

But the desert by itself is insufficient; Moses must be formed by God in the desert before he can lead Israel to liberation. Shepherding in arid regions sometimes required traveling far distances to find grazing, and on such an occasion Moses found himself in new territory by Horeb, the mountain of God. "The whole impression is of a completely new and strange and distant place, one outside familiar Midianite territory."[58] It is here that the LORD appears to Moses in a burning bush. What intrigues Moses and catches his attention is that the bush is burning but it is not consumed! Such a blaze of fire is a recurring symbol of God's approach;[59] it is intriguing, however, to note the contrast with God's judgment of Sodom and Gomorrah, where even "what grew on the ground" (Gen. 19:25) is destroyed.

Moses approaches the bush but is told to come no closer and to remove his sandals, for he is standing on holy ground.[60] The soil is rendered holy by theophany. Moses is commissioned by God to go to Pharaoh to liberate his people, and the sign he is given is that the people will worship here at this mountain. S. Terrien insists in relation to the burning bush that the holy "obtains its significance not from geography but from the intervention of the

---

55. Durham, *Exodus*, 23–24. On Jethro and his relationship to the Israelites see Exod. 18.
56. Hillel, *Natural History of the Bible*, 86; cf. 108.
57. Merton, *Wisdom of the Desert*, 3–24.
58. Durham, *Exodus*, 30.
59. Jeremias, *Theophanie*, 56–66; Kuntz, *Self-Revelation of God*, 138–47.
60. Cf. Josh. 5:15.

Deity, and it is reduced to the temporal dimensions of the theophany."[61] There is truth to this, but it ignores the effect theophany can have on a place as well as the hints in the narrative that this mountain and precinct is special. The Hebrew for "bush" is *sĕneh*; it occurs three times in 3:2–4 and sounds like the Hebrew for "Sinai," although "Sinai" is used only once the nation reaches the mountain (16:1). Moses experiences a blazing bush; when he returns with the Israelites, the whole mountain will be on fire, and in Exodus 15:17 the entire land is referred to as the mountain of God's abode. Like fire, holiness is contagious; it spreads from place to place!

Moses's call is to confront Pharaoh and to lead the Israelites out of Egypt. "Sent by Yahweh, Moses began a long, hard struggle for the liberation of his people."[62] But the struggle is not ultimately that of Moses but one between Yahweh and Pharaoh. An account of the Egyptian view of the pharaoh illuminates what is at stake in this context. The title *pharaoh* comes from the Egyptian *per aa*, or "great house," a reference to the palace "towards which all people turn."[63] The pharaoh was understood to literally become a god through his coronation. Thus he was seen as "the greatest of all gods, or at least their equal, the master of men and objects, the master too of the waters of the Nile, of the land and even of the growing harvest."[64] It is possible that this high view of the pharaoh was gradually diminished, but even in the twelfth century BC, around the time of the Exodus, Rameses II could still assert, "Listen . . . for I am Râ, lord of heaven, come to earth."[65] As god, the pharaoh was responsible for the maintenance of *ma'at*, that is, truth, justice, and the natural order of the world. Not surprisingly, this related in particular to the Nile and its annual flooding, which was indispensable to the existence and survival of Egypt.

This context explains why much of the action revolves, especially initially, around the Nile. The plagues address head-on whether Pharaoh or Yahweh is the true source of *ma'at*. The plagues involve the Nile, fish, insects, livestock, human health, the elements, crops, light and darkness, and finally the first-born sons of Egypt. "What the plagues of Egypt show is the inability of the obstinate king to maintain [*ma'at*]. Rather, it is Yahweh and his agents Moses and Aaron who overcome in the cosmic struggle, demonstrating who really controls the forces of nature."[66] Thus Gutiérrez sets up a false dichotomy, one that has dogged the footsteps of modern Old Testament scholarship, when he asserts in relation to the exodus that "the God of Exodus is the God of history and of political liberation *more* than he is the God of nature."[67]

---

61. Terrien, *Elusive Presence*, 111.
62. Gutiérrez, *Theology of Liberation*, 156.
63. Braudel, *Mediterranean in the Ancient World*, 83.
64. Ibid.
65. Ibid. Cf. Exod. 3:8, where God says he has "come down" to deliver the Israelites.
66. Hoffmeier, *Israel in Egypt*, 153.
67. Gutiérrez, *Theology of Liberation*, 157. Emphasis added.

The route taken by the Israelites out of Egypt and to Sinai is contested. Whichever route they took, it meant entering the desert, and the difficult and vulnerable reality of this context soon hits home. What turns out, for the generation of Israelites leaving Egypt, to be forty years of wandering in the desert is a time of profound formation of God's people: "A gradual pedagogy of successes and failures would be necessary for the Jewish people to become aware of the roots of their oppression, to struggle against it, and to perceive the profound sense of the liberation to which they were called. The Creator of the world is the Creator and Liberator of Israel, to whom he entrusts the mission of establishing justice."[68] The pedagogy, like their complaints, begins immediately. Exodus 15:26 makes an intriguing reference to God as the Lord who *heals* Israel. N. Lohfink notes that

> we have already seen that here a kind of opposition is being constructed. Now the narrative of the events in Egypt is finished. It was a story of a sick society in which human beings were enslaved and exploited, where those in positions of authority did not listen to YHWH's voice, and where, as a result, plague after plague erupted—a society that must ultimately sink down into sickness and death. Now there begins . . . the story that can be told about the proper society, the one in which people do listen to YHWH's voice and in which, as a result, no diseases break out; where, instead, is realized what the prophets have promised as the salvation that YHWH will create in Israel: Israel as a healthy, living people. . . . everything depends on listening to YHWH's voice and living according to YHWH's order for society.[69]

It is in the desert en route to Sinai that this healing and formation begins.

This healing is holistic, and E. Davis helpfully suggests that the manna story (Exod. 16) is a counternarrative establishing an alternative to the agricultural economy Israel experienced in Egypt.[70] Egypt is the archetype of the industrial society (cf. Deut. 4:20), and its centralized grain economy enabled it not only to distribute food to its citizens but to export it. Egyptian food production is akin to what is nowadays called "agribusiness." The desert economy does not appeal to the Israelites, and perversely they long for the days when they "sat by the fleshpots and ate [their] fill of bread" (Exod. 16:3). "God responds to their sick hunger by initiating a different mode of food production."[71] God provides abundant meat (quail) and daily manna, and remarkably they are all able to gather as much as they need (16:18). This is a powerful reminder that food is a gracious provision of Yahweh and that it is to be received with restraint, to be equitably distributed, and not to be sought on the Sabbath.

68. Ibid., 156.
69. N. Lohfink, *Theology of the Pentateuch*, 93–94.
70. E. Davis, *Scripture, Culture, and Agriculture*, 69–79.
71. Ibid., 70.

Exodus 16:35 notes that the Israelites ate manna for forty years, the entire time they were in the wilderness.

The references in the manna narrative to "evening" and "morning" (16:6, 7, 8, 12, 13) and to the Sabbath connect this story with the creation narrative in Genesis 1, a reminder that Israel is being formed according to the Creator's order for his creation and not Pharaoh's *ma'at*. Lest this lesson in the economy of food be forgotten—"Eating is the most basic of all cultural and economic acts"[72]—a jar containing an omer of manna is placed "before the LORD" (16:33; cf. 16:34), that is, in the tabernacle, as a reminder.

Three months after leaving Egypt the Israelites arrive at Mount Sinai (19:1). They camp in front of it, and Moses goes up to God. Three days later, after the Israelites have consecrated themselves, God reveals himself to them on the mountain in fire, smoke, thunder, lightning, and earthquake. He summarizes what he has done for the Israelites and what they will be if they obey his voice and keep his covenant, namely his treasured possession, a royal priesthood, and a holy nation (Exod. 19:4–6). The imagery of being borne on eagles' wings, of a "treasured possession," and of priestly royalty all evokes notions of royal treatment and status. "The eagle or vulture is a symbol of transcendence over the earthly sphere of events, and applied to royalty, an indication that the king is invited to participate in a dominion normally beyond the level of human capacity."[73] *Sglh* (possession) is a commercial/legal term applied to royalty to express their relationship to a higher royal power.[74]

As a priestly royalty, "Israel is assured of the privilege of royal status, a royalty characterized by the essence of priesthood, namely, access to divine presence. Israel's corporate priesthood is pre-eminently that which is exercised towards God, not other nations."[75] Durham, however, argues that as a kingdom of priests Israel is committed as a servant people to spreading Yahweh's presence throughout the world. They are "a display-people, a showcase to the world of how being in covenant with Yahweh changes a people."[76] Yet the difference between these two views does not make them antithetical; Israel *will* experience Yahweh's presence in a unique way, and all the earth will know about Yahweh, to whom the whole earth belongs (19:5).

If the image of God in Genesis 1 is a mirroring of God's kingship, then what we have here is a recapitulation of Eden, but now with a nation rather than a first couple. Redemption is portrayed as re-creation, though not in the sense of a return to Eden. As Casalis notes, "The heart of the Old Testament is the Exodus from the servitude of Egypt and the journey towards the promised land. . . . The hope of the people of God is not to return to the mythological

72. Ibid.
73. J. A. Davies, *Royal Priesthood*, 39.
74. Ibid., 60.
75. Ibid., 102.
76. Durham, *Exodus*, 263.

primitive garden, but to march forward towards a new city, a human and brotherly city whose heart is Christ."[77]

At Sinai, in the giving of the Ten Commandments, we learn how the Israelites must be formed in order to fulfill their calling: they must be reduced to trembling (19:16); intriguingly, the same verb for "tremble" (*ḥārad*) is also used of the mountain when the Lord descends upon it (19:18), although this is intensified by the addition of *mĕ'ōd* (exceedingly). "Both people and nature (specifically, the sacred space of the covenant-making ritual) tremble equally before YHWH."[78] A. Zornberg refers evocatively to the Israelites' "volatile standing at Sinai."[79]

> A certain human standing (*ma'amad*), an existential posture is disrupted at the very moment that is called *ma'amad har Sinai*: the Standing at Sinai. This becomes stance as oscillation, a motion that rocks them to the very roots of being. . . . What is enacted at Sinai is the revelation of the human being in larger range and strength. A new consciousness is born in this revelation; the Israelites endure an initiation that ensures them against the extremities of history. God comes at Sinai, so that the human may come fully into its own.[80]

Exodus 19–40 deals with the establishment of the Israelites in a covenant relationship with God, with the laws governing that relationship, and with the instructions for and building of the tabernacle, God's house in their midst. This leads us to the subject of the next chapter, namely the role of place in law and ritual.

77. Cited in Gutiérrez, *Theology of Liberation*, 157.
78. Klingbeil, *Bridging the Gap*, 184.
79. Zornberg, *Particulars of Rapture*, 264.
80. Ibid.

4

Place, Law, and Ritual

To know who I am is a species of knowing where I stand.[1]

From Narrative to Law

In a chapter entitled "The Self in Moral Space," C. Taylor insists, against the rampant individualism of Western culture, that we cannot do without "frameworks," or what I prefer to call a worldview.[2]

> To know who you are is to be oriented in moral space, a space in which questions arise about what is good or bad, what is worth doing and what not, what has meaning and importance for you and what is trivial and secondary. I feel myself drawn here to use a spatial metaphor; but I believe this to be more than personal predilection. There are signs that the link with spatial orientation lies very deep in the human psyche.[3]

For Taylor we can learn about anger, anxiety, love, and the move toward wholeness only through experiencing these as objects for us "in some common space."[4] This space is shared by a "defining community."[5] "Orientation in moral space turns out to be similar to orientation in physical space. We know

1. C. Taylor, *Sources of the Self*, 27.
2. See Goheen and Bartholomew, *Living at the Crossroads*.
3. C. Taylor, *Sources of the Self*, 28.
4. Ibid., 35.
5. Ibid., 36.

where we are through a mixture of recognition of landmarks before us and a sense of how we have traveled to get here."[6]

Narrative, community, moral space—all three of these elements are clearly present in the Sinai narratives in Exodus and in the legal literature of the Old Testament. Old Testament law is always embedded in narrative, and for good reason; it draws its validity from the narrative of God's having brought Israel "out of *the land* of Egypt, out of *the house* of slavery" (Exod. 20:1, emphasis added). At Sinai God legally establishes the Israelites as the covenant people of this story; communally they assent to living as God's people. Torah flows from this communal narrative with the intention of redefining the moral space of the Israelites as they move toward the land that God will give them. Four hundred years in Egypt is not easily shaken off, and considerable formation, including torah, "instruction," will be required to redefine Israel as the people of God. "Out of the land . . . out of the house" tells us that from now on the new land, the new house, is in view.

The Ten Words

Place functions literally and metaphorically in the ten words[7] that are at the heart of the Sinai covenant. The Sinaitic law is given to a particular people who have come out of Egypt, and though it bears the marks of typical ancient Near Eastern law,[8] the differences between it and other law codes of the region are often the most significant. There is nothing among those codes, for example, comparable to the ten words,[9] and as C. J. H. Wright[10] and others have noted, Old Testament law differs from other ancient Near Eastern law in valuing people over property.

In the first of the ten words Yahweh commands his people that they are to have no other gods *'al-pānāya*, literally, "before my face." "Face" refers to God's presence, and thus "before my face" should firstly be understood to refer to the possibility of placing other gods in Yahweh's shrine. "Thus Israel was to acknowledge no other gods in her cult, and as worship outside the cult was not envisaged, this meant that for her there could be no contact with any other deity."[11] A. Phillips notes that the first commandment transfers the concept of political suzerainty to the religious sphere and thus establishes God's exclusive covenant relationship with Israel. In this way it ensures Israel's independence of other political powers because submission to another polity would involve

6. Ibid., 48.
7. This is a common phrasing for the ten commandments.
8. G. J. Wenham, "Structure and Date of Deuteronomy," 290–96, documents thirty-two thematic parallels between ancient Near Eastern laws and those of Deuteronomy.
9. A. Gibson, *Text and Tablet*, 168.
10. C. J. H. Wright, *Living as the People of God*, 163–64.
11. Phillips, *Ancient Israel's Criminal Law*, 38–39.

adopting their gods.[12] The first word thus gives us a powerful sense of the way in which torah establishes the moral space for Israel to inhabit in order to become a royal priesthood.

Yahweh will be truly present in Israel's cult, as the building and consecration of the tabernacle will make clear, but the second word guards against any view that he will be able to be controlled or confined to the cultus. "Yahweh was a free agent and could never be contained by men for their own purposes, nor confined to a particular place."[13] Thus the second word establishes the cult of the imageless Yahweh![14] At the heart of the most holy place there is to be . . . nothing, because Yahweh is truly and uncontrollably present.

In Exodus 20:8–11 the Sabbath is specifically connected to the creation narrative of Genesis 1. As B. Childs notes, "it is built into the very structure of the universe."[15] By comparison, in Deuteronomy 5 the Sabbath commandment is connected to the exodus from Egypt, an important difference between the two versions.[16] "Two such different applications of the fourth commandment have often been thought to be contradictory. They are in fact complementary, since it is the Exodus redemption which makes the new life in the land, and thus the Edenic values recaptured, possible. Israel in Canaan is a microcosm of mankind as blessed, an illustration of what is intended for the whole world."[17]

The fifth commandment ties parental respect to the rich blessing of the society in harmony with the divine order.[18] "It is in the commandment regarding the honor of parents that the community hears that its life is in a gifted place, 'the land that the Lord your God is giving you.' This order of space is marked not so much by substantive freedom as it is by substantive goodness."[19]

The tenth commandment is intriguing in terms of the light it casts on property rights in Israel. Durham observes that this commandment is a fitting conclusion to the ten words: "covet" (ḥmd) evokes an obsessive covetousness which could be the gateway for the breaking of all the other commandments.[20] "House" (byt) refers to the neighbor's family and entire property. Implicit in the tenth commandment is the importance of the inalienable holding of land by kin groups in Old Testament law. As C. J. H. Wright explains, "That the land should be held in the form of patrimonies which should not pass out of

12. Ibid., 39.
13. Ibid., 49.
14. Ibid., 50.
15. Childs, *Exodus*, 416.
16. See Stamm and Andrew, *Ten Commandments*, 13–18, for the twenty points at which the two versions of the Decalogue differ.
17. Dumbrell, *Covenant and Creation*, 122–23.
18. Childs, *Exodus*, 419.
19. P. D. Miller, *Way of the Lord*, 62.
20. Durham, *Exodus*, 298.

the family was a cherished ideal in Israel that was protected by legislation and theologically justified and sanctioned."[21] Leviticus 25:23 asserts that the land belongs to Yahweh, and T. Mettinger rightly notes that "the proper concept of this divine ownership appears to be that every Israelite was to regard his holding as deriving from God himself. . . . There existed the consciousness of an intrinsic equality among the Hebrews before God . . . which was expressed . . . by each head of a family holding his land as from God."[22] One's land was a symbol of one's share in the inheritance of Israel and the means of economic survival for one's family.

The tenth commandment also presupposes that the Israelites settled in houses and thus assumes the existence of towns and cities. So too does the ninth commandment with its background of lawsuits in the city gates. Much Old Testament law is agrarian, but much too relates to town and city life, as one would expect for a nation in a land. The Old Testament never suggests that either city life or life in the countryside is better than the other.

The ten words thus literally refer to place in multiple ways but also function metaphorically *par excellence* for the creation of Israel's moral space. P. D. Miller describes the moral space defined by the ten words as "the good neighborhood":

> What the commandments do, therefore, is to chart the moral topography of the Christian life, a topography that, because of the other images and metaphors I have called upon is found to be diverse and detailed, a map that takes one in many directions and charts windy paths, straight and highly visible routes, places to settle in, hills to be climbed, home territory and foreign territory, and the like. . . . The Commandments create a structure in which one is at home.[23]

Old Testament Law and Place

> The most detailed scriptural witness regarding how we might live within the intended harmony of God's creation is to be found especially in that part of the Bible that Christians to this day dismiss most readily . . . the legal codes of Exodus, Leviticus, and Deuteronomy. Here in the heart of the Torah lies a vision of what I am calling a "wholesome materiality."[24]

For our purposes the complex relationship between the legal codes is not crucial; more important is how place functions in Old Testament law. Old Testament law is strongly connected back into creation and God's order for creation,

21. C. J. H. Wright, *God's People in God's Land*, 55–56.
22. Mettinger, *Solomonic State Officials*, 109.
23. P. D. Miller, *Way of the Lord*, 49.
24. E. F. Davis, *Scripture, Culture, and Agriculture*, 82.

an insight that historical criticism has often obscured.[25] Law is always embedded in narrative, and both the narrative framework and the laws themselves connect life in the land to a recovery of God's Edenic intentions. Leaning on Jewish tradition, S. McBride has evocatively argued that the ten archetypal injunctions in Genesis 1, each introduced by "and God said," which "invoke structural cosmos out of chaos," should be compared to the ten words that constitute the covenantal society of Israel by calling forth community from the chaos of slavery.[26] "The words of creation and the words of commandment echo each other as parts of God's creation of order in the world and in human society."[27]

Deuteronomy, too, reflects a connection between law and the creation. R. O'Dowd notes that "the laws for the land in Deuteronomy reflect God's primordial intention for humanity (all nations) to live before him in a re-created garden."[28] The universal dimensions of what God is doing with Israel come to the fore in passages such as Deuteronomy 4:5–8;[29] 4:32–39 (cf. v. 32: "ever since the day that God created human beings on the earth"); and 8:1–10. In 8:3 that which comes from the mouth of God is referred to as sufficient for *'ādām*. "It is striking that the lesson on dependence concerns not only Israel alone but humanity (*hā'ādām*). This universal dimension has been met before in connection with Yahweh's universal rule (4:32–40). . . . Here Israel's experience is explicitly made a paradigm of human experience in general, and there is an echo of the Genesis creation narratives' assertion of the divine interest in all humanity (Gen. 1–3)."[30] Of 8:11–20 Brueggemann observes that "this is 'creation theology'; Deuteronomy anticipates that a land rightly ordered by Torah will become fruitful, blessed by the *shalom* anticipated already in the doxologies of creation."[31] And so we could continue. The point to note is that "torah places Yahweh at the center of Israel's world and therefore conditions her knowledge by the cosmic structure and stability of the created order. By obeying the torah, Israel conforms to the universal created order as an expression of her love for Yahweh; her participation in creation enables her to know Yahweh through imitation."[32]

The laws in the Pentateuch look not only backward to the creation but also forward to the land for which the laws are given, including evocative descriptions of the goodness of the land (cf. Deut. 8:7–10). Place surfaces in a variety of ways in particular laws. The place of worship is, for example, a major theme,

25. It is encouraging to see, for example, how Davis's dialogue between the Old Testament and the new agrarianism repeatedly surfaces the issue of creation order.

26. McBride, "Divine Protocol," 10 and note 16.

27. P. D. Miller, *Way of the Lord*, 33. See Braude, *Pesikta Rabbati*, 444: "The Ten Commandments were meant to be paired off with the ten words whereby the world was created."

28. O'Dowd, *Wisdom of Torah*, 27; cf. Brueggemann, *Deuteronomy*, 104.

29. O'Dowd, *Wisdom of Torah*, 39–41.

30. McConville, *Deuteronomy*, 170.

31. Brueggemann, *Deuteronomy*, 104.

32. O'Dowd, *Wisdom of Torah*, 48–49.

ranging from the altar law at the outset of the Book of the Covenant (Exod. 20:22–26) to the law of the place which *Yahweh will choose* in Deuteronomy 12 (12:5, 11, 14, 18, 21, 26). Place is often evident in small details, such as the ritual in the slavery law in Exodus 21:1–11: if a slave does not wish to be freed after six years, his master brings him before God to the door or doorpost (of the house or sanctuary?), where the slave's ear is pierced with an awl. Presumably, the doorway, if the house is being referred to, functions as a symbol of the home as well as a public place for such a ritual. The laws about open pits relate to civil responsibility in terms of place (21:33–35). The Sabbath is developed into a seven-year cycle as well, so that in the seventh year the land too is allowed to rest (23:10–11)! In today's context of topsoil destruction and overuse and abuse of land, the importance of giving land rest is easily recognizable as of fundamental importance. Such ecological practice also helps the poor and wild animals to find the food they need. When juxtaposed, Exodus 23:11 and 23:29 evoke an intriguing ecological balance: there must be food for the wild animals, but they must also not be allowed to "multiply against you." Exodus 23:29–30 gives an often-unnoticed reason for the manner of the conquest. The Canaanites will be expelled gradually to prevent the land from becoming desolate, and so that the wild animals will not multiply beyond control. Hidden in the mysterious purge of the land is a concern for the land itself!

For us today one of the most difficult elements of Old Testament law to relate to is the instruction to destroy the inhabitants of Canaan (Exod. 23:23–33) and conquer the land, led by Yahweh himself (Josh. 5:3–15). If one understands Jesus and the New Testament to advocate pacifism, then that becomes a canon within the canon for handling these parts of the Old Testament. I do not think this is true to Jesus or the New Testament as a whole, and while these texts are hard to come to grips with, they do give us some clues—however unacceptable to us today—as to how to understand these laws and the conquest.

Genesis 15:16 tells Abraham that his ancestors will return to the land only in the fourth generation, because the iniquity (*ʿāwōn*) of the Amorites—who stand here for all the inhabitants of Canaan—is not yet complete (cf. Lev. 18:24–27; Deut. 9:4–5; Amos 2:9–16). V. P. Hamilton says of this verse that "this commentary on the immorality of the indigenous population of Canaan also establishes Joshua's invasion as an act of justice rather than aggression."[33] Leviticus 18:24–30 notes in cultic language that the land became defiled—18:1–23 indicates the defiling practices in view—so that the land vomited out its inhabitants; importantly, it alerts the Israelites that the same fate awaits them if they do not keep God's commandments. The personification of the land in this text is intriguing (cf. 26:35; Num. 13:32). As J. Joosten notes, "In these verses the land is clearly pictured as an entity distinct from its inhabitants. Moreover, it is represented as an independent agent. While it

33. V. P. Hamilton, *Book of Genesis, Chapters 1–17*, 436.

is stated in the same context that YHWH will cast out the nations dwelling in the land (18:24; 20:23), in the present verses the casting out is done by the land itself."[34] Leviticus 18 is framed by the repeated "I am the LORD your God" (18:2, 30). Behind the conquest of the land lies the holiness of the LORD and his intolerance for that which defiles the land and violates his nature. A holy God, the notion of sin and judgment; these are extremely unpopular in Western culture nowadays. But perhaps that, rather than a supposed conflict between the Old and New Testaments, is our problem, for the Gospels are just as full of teaching about judgment.[35]

Intriguingly, pilgrimage is rarely mentioned in ancient Near Eastern sources outside the Bible,[36] but it is mandatory in Exodus 23:14–17; 34:18–26; Leviticus 23; Numbers 28–29; and Deuteronomy 16:1–17.[37] The technical term for making a pilgrimage is *ḥāgag*. Apart from Deuteronomy 16, in all these texts the Sabbath law either prefaces the laws about pilgrimage or, as in Exodus 34, occurs in the midst of them.[38] This links the pilgrimages back into Genesis 1 and God's order for creation and serves to remind the Israelites that in making these pilgrimages they are imitating God, the creator. This is confirmed by the number of annual festivals: seven (Passover, unleavened bread, weeks, solemn rest day, Day of Atonement, booths, day after booths); during these festivals there were seven days of rest; most of the festivals occur in the seventh month of the year; every seventh year is a sabbatical; and after 7 × 7 years there was the year of Jubilee.[39]

Exodus 23 mentions three festivals: unleavened bread, harvest, and ingathering. All reflect the agricultural year: the first harvest of grain, the harvest of other cereal crops seven weeks later, and the final harvest of all crops in the autumn. Among other Old Testament references to pilgrimage, Psalms 120–34 are particularly significant; every one is titled "A Song of Ascent," presumably because they were used on the pilgrimages to Jerusalem. Zion is the focus of these psalms,[40] yet they clearly articulate that Zion's God is the creator of heaven and earth (Pss. 121:2; 124:8; 134:3). It is fascinating to read these psalms, imagining Israelites singing them as they processed toward and into Jerusalem.

Amidst the challenges of daily life it was too easy for the Israelites to forget their story and their responsibility to embody it in the land. The pilgrimages

34. Joosten, *People and Land in the Holiness Code*, 152.
35. See J. W. Wenham, *Goodness of God*, which remains a useful book on this whole subject.
36. Cf. Postgate, "In Search of the First Empires," 8; M. S. Smith, *Pilgrimage Pattern in Exodus*, 52.
37. The interrelationship between these law complexes is challenging.
38. A point picked up by Keil, *Manual of Biblical Archaeology*, 1:469–82.
39. G. J. Wenham, *Book of Leviticus*, 301–2.
40. In the following chapter we will explore in more detail the establishment of Jerusalem as the city of God.

are a break in daily routine and involve a journey to Zion, to the place where Yahweh dwells in their midst. The intention is that through the journey they reconnect with Yahweh and recontextualize their lives in the story of redemption. Psalm 50, possibly a festival psalm—note the admonition, "Gather to me my faithful ones, who made a covenant with me by sacrifice!" (50:5)—evokes God as creator (vv. 1, 11, 12) and redeemer (vv. 2, 5, 7) and rebukes the Israelites on the basis of the seventh, eighth, and ninth commandments (vv. 18–20). Thus recentered, the Israelites will return to their daily lives to incarnate the redemption and covenant life they are part of.

The curses of Deuteronomy 27:11–26 are to be proclaimed in a ceremony once Israel has entered the land. The laws are to be inscribed on large stones covered in plaster.[41] Six tribes will stand on Mount Gerizim and six on the adjacent Mount Ebal, both in the vicinity of Shechem. Then in a responsive liturgy the Levites are to pronounce each of the twelve curses, with the people responding "Amen." In Joshua 8:30–35 this ceremony is reported as having been performed. It is unclear whether it was to be repeated, but as C. J. H. Wright notes, "Certainly, the mere identification of the two mountains with curse and blessing would remind Israelites, every time they passed through that valley, of the straightforward choice that faced them day by day—loyalty and obedience or disloyalty and disobedience—and of the serious consequences of the choice."[42]

Deuteronomy 28 and 29 contain a further series of blessings and curses. They have a strong agrarian nature, but significantly, the opening blessing and curse declare: "Blessed shall you be in the city, and blessed shall you be in the field" (28:3); "Cursed shall you be in the city, and cursed shall you be in the field" (28:16). Covenant life encompasses *both* city and field, and neither is better than the other; both are potential contexts for obedience and thus blessing as well as disobedience and thus curse. It is this potential that the prophets will repeatedly invoke until both northern and southern kingdoms are carried off into exile.

The Cultus

As we have seen, the first commandment refers directly to the cultus, and the fourth commandment, "the sanctification—making holy—of a day to the Lord, is the *opening* of a trajectory of holy times, holy places, holy lives, and holy things."[43] The tabernacle is one of those holy places, and both the command to build it and the building of it follow on from the establishment of the Sinai covenant (Exod. 25–40). Yahweh is now going to set up his portable home in

41. A. E. Hill, "The Ebal Ceremony," relates this event to a land grant ceremony.
42. C. J. H. Wright, *Deuteronomy*, 277.
43. P. D. Miller, *Way of the Lord*, 32. Emphasis original.

the midst of the Israelites. This is accomplished at the end of Exodus when the cloud covers the tabernacle and the glory of the LORD fills it. Bearing in mind the fearful reaction of the Israelites to Yahweh's self-revelation at Mount Sinai, one wonders how on earth this is going to work. A diplomatic protocol will be required to maintain Israel in an appropriate relationship with Yahweh, and this is indeed what we find in Leviticus. Unsurprisingly, both tabernacle and protocol evoke implicitly and explicitly a vision of God's intention for Israel and of her connection to his purposes with his whole creation. This vision illumines the theme of place, and simultaneously place functions in myriad formative ways in the protocol.

The Place of the Tabernacle

We have already witnessed how, after the expulsion from Eden, places where Yahweh appears to Abraham and his descendants tend to be regarded as special and to have memorials set up and/or altars built in them. Whereas all of Eden was holy and pervaded by the presence of God, the effect of sin is that certain places become special because of God's appearance there. This tendency becomes institutionalized with the establishment of the tabernacle.

The instructions for building the tabernacle follow the legal establishment of the covenant in Exodus 24. At this point Mount Sinai is *the* place where God is present in a dynamic way to his people, who are encamped around the mountain. Strict limits are set around the mountain on pain of death. Here we see clear spatial boundaries separating the holy Yahweh from his people. These characteristics of holiness and boundaries and cleanness will become institutionalized in the cultus which is set up en route to the promised land. In the process the notion of sacred or holy place becomes central.

The importance of the sanctuary is clear from the slowing down of the narrative and the almost painful repetition of 25:1–31:11 in 35:1–40:33. At this stage the Israelites are en route, living in tents, and so the LORD will dwell with them in a tent. However, as the list of offerings required from the Israelites makes clear (cf. Exod. 25:3–7), this will be no ordinary tent. The fine metals gold, silver, and bronze; the blue, purple, and crimson yarns and fine linen; the skins, leather, oil, spices, and gemstones all indicate that this is a royal tent.

Figure 4.1 indicates the shape and furnishing of the LORD's tent. Around the tent a courtyard was constructed by erecting a curtain fence. The rectangular sanctuary was divided into two sections by a curtain, one room being twice the size of the other. The first, larger room, called "the Holy Place," was furnished with a golden table, a lampstand, and an incense altar. The curtain separating the Holy Place from the Most Holy Place (or Holy of Holies) was decorated with cherubim as a reminder to sinful human beings that entrance into the immediate presence of the LORD was barred (cf. Gen. 3:24).

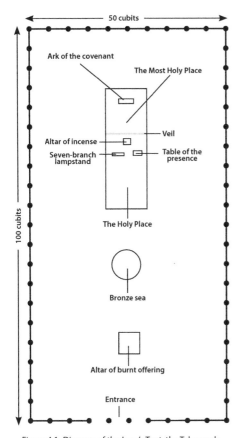

50 cubits

Ark of the covenant

The Most Holy Place

Veil

Altar of incense

Seven-branch lampstand

Table of the presence

The Holy Place

100 cubits

Bronze sea

Altar of burnt offering

Entrance

Figure 4.1 Diagram of the Lord's Tent, the Tabernacle

The Most Holy Place contained a rectangular wooden chest covered inside and out with gold. For ease of journeying and so none would have to defile it by touching it, like Uzzah (2 Sam. 6:3–7), this "ark" was constructed with gold rings and poles. Two golden cherubim were attached to the ends of the lid of the chest, facing one another with wings outspread. The place between the cherubim was where God would meet with Moses to convey his torah (instruction) to his people (Exod. 25:22). The chest functioned both as a container (the tablets of the covenant would be placed in it [Exod. 25:21]) and as a seat or throne (1 Sam. 4:4, for example, speaks of the Lord as "enthroned on the cherubim").

In the Holy Place was a wooden table overlaid with gold and fitted as well with rings and poles. Plates, dishes, flagons, and bowls, all of gold, were provided for the table. And as the Lord commanded, the "bread of the Presence" was to be on the table "before me always" (Exod. 25:30). Additionally, the Holy Place contained a gold lampstand with seven lamps; the lampstand was constructed like a tree and provided light (Exod. 25:37). In an ancient home the table, lampstand, and chair were the main items of furniture, and thus in the tabernacle they indicated that the Lord lived within the tent.[44] Yahweh's dwelling place is established while the Israelites are en route to the land, that is, as part of their journeying. As Casey notes, "If human beings may peregrinate in place, so they may also dwell stably even as they move from place to place."[45]

Casey distinguishes two ways of dwelling, namely *hestial* dwelling and *hermetic* dwelling (see also p. 28). The former is centered and self-enclosed; its directionality is from the center toward the periphery.[46] Hermetic place,

44. T. Alexander, *From Paradise to the Promised Land*, 196.
45. Casey, *Getting Back into Place*, 133.
46. Ibid.

by contrast, is about motion and the public spheres of society. As is apparent in the setting up of the sanctuary, the type of society envisaged in the priestly literature is relentlessly *hestial*. Just as Israel is the center of the nations in Genesis 10, so Yahweh, living in the tabernacle, is the center of Israel's life, and the camp boundaries mark the limit of life under his reign and the wilderness and chaos that threatens outside (see figure 4.1). This is not to say that the hestial and the hermetic are mutually exclusive categories; while Deuteronomy, for example, maintains unequivocally the hestial center of the life of Israel, it strongly emphasizes the public, hermetic dimension of life as well.

By establishing the sanctuary at the heart of the Israelite camp, the LORD emphasizes the special nature of the place of the sanctuary. The sanctuary embodies and establishes *gradations of holiness*. The Most Holy Place is where the LORD dwells above the cherubim. He further exalts the sanctuary's place by establishing a special priesthood and a gradation among the high priest, the priests, and the Levites. Ordinary Israelites could enter the outer court and view the bronze altar and basin; only priests could enter the Holy Place and view its gold furnishings; however, only the high priest could enter the Most Holy Place, and even then he probably used smoke from incense to conceal the top of the ark (Lev. 16:12–13).[47] The different metals used in the furnishing of the sanctuary distinguished it from the courtyard. Bronze and silver, not as valuable as gold, were used in the courtyard furnishings.

The gradations of holiness thus result from the actual presence of the LORD among his people; the sanctuary embodies the real presence of the royal, holy Yahweh. The sanctuary is also the place of meeting between the LORD and his people, indicating the centrality of communion to the covenant.[48] But this immediately raises the question of how a holy God is to dwell among and commune with a sinful people. Hence the gradations of holiness and the extensive cultus set up in Leviticus to manage the relationship with the LORD. Although the camp is marked above all by hestial dwelling, the LORD intends always that the center of the camp should affect every aspect of the life of the camp, so that it too is maintained in a state of holiness. Thus the hestial focus has an inevitable hermetic consequence. As such it hearkens back to Genesis 1 and 2 with their concern for a creation ordered with participation in the life of God at its heart.

Several scholars have noted the link between the order of the cultus and the order of creation. F. Gorman notes, "A central feature of the Priestly world view is the belief that the world order is a created order, brought into being by Yahweh."[49] "Creation serves as context for cult; cult serves as one means of actualizing creation."[50] J. Blenkinsopp argues that the completion for-

---

47. T. Alexander, *From Paradise to the Promised Land*, 208.
48. As Vriezen, *Outline of Old Testament Theology*, in particular has noted.
49. Gorman, *Ideology of Ritual*, 39.
50. Ibid., 104.

mula found in Exodus 39:32; 40:33 (and Josh. 19:51) deliberately evokes the
completion formulae in Genesis 1.[51] R. Kearney notes that the phrase "and
the LORD said" occurs seven times in Exodus 25–31 and argues that this corresponds to the seven speeches of God in Genesis 1.[52] Indeed groups of seven
loom large in Exodus 20–40 and in Leviticus 1–9. Gorman thus rightly notes
that "cosmos provides the necessary context for correct enactment of ritual;
ritual only has meaning within a specific cosmos."[53]

The link between cultus and creation is not surprising because cultus, with
its ritualized acts, reinforces a way of viewing one's society and the world. In
Genesis 1–2 we noted the move from the world as the home of humans to the
particularity of Eden; in reverse fashion the particularity of Israel's cultus
opens out on a *world*view. Ritual as an accompaniment to place establishes
and reestablishes such a perspective, as we will see in our discussion of ritual
and place below. As a way into this discussion we will focus on the consecration of the priesthood in Leviticus 8 and 9.

Although our discussion of the tabernacle depends upon a canonical reading
of the final form of the text, a word about its historicity is appropriate. The
work of K. Graf and J. Wellhausen has led many to see the tabernacle as a
postexilic invention to support the fiction of a period of desert wanderings.[54]
Homan, in his rigorous study of tents in the ancient Near East, found his view
changing as he studied the evidence: "Although I began this enterprise as a
skeptic, the many parallels collected to the Tabernacle's form and function
have convinced me that an elaborate tent served as the focal point for Israelite
religion until the completion of Solomon's temple. If this tent-shrine did not
correspond exactly to the description in Exodus 25–27, it came very close."[55]
We cannot here engage this debate in detail; suffice it to note that attention
to place renders an imaginary tabernacle docetic.[56]

Ritual and Place

> The primary function or metafunction of liturgical performances is
> not to control behavior directly, but rather to establish conventional
> understandings, rules and norms in accordance with which everyday
> behavior is *supposed* to proceed.[57]

51. Blenkinsopp, "The Structure of P."
52. Kearney, "Creation and Liturgy."
53. Gorman, *Ideology of Ritual*, 47.
54. Cross, "The Tabernacle," published in 1947, remains the most influential rebuttal to
Wellhausen.
55. Homan, *To Your Tents, O Israel!*, 5.
56. Docetism was a heresy in the early church that argued that Christ was not fully human,
he merely appeared so.
57. Rappaport, *Ritual and Religion*, 123. Emphasis original.

> There is in ritual not only a representation of creation, but a re-
> creation of the primordial order, the primordial union of form and
> substance which forever comes apart as the usages of life depart
> from the Order that should be.[58]

From anthropologists we know that ritual is a crucial and powerful means whereby humans enter into the world as a habitable and hospitable place. Rituals provide the place, time, symbols, and bodily involvement that enable us to recenter ourselves in the large story of which we are part and connect it to the individual and communal stories we inhabit. Some ritual theory stresses that it is through ritual that we construct meaning. This is not true for Israel; her large story is provided by Yahweh and his acts on her behalf. Yet she is challenged to remain embedded in that story and to keep on indwelling it. As Israel's experience testifies, this order "forever comes apart" in her hands, and Old Testament ritual is the indispensable means for restoring her relationship with Yahweh, for recentering her in the biblical story, and for providing resources for maintaining her in that center which is Yahweh himself.

We cannot examine the multitude of rituals found in the Old Testament, but in order to demonstrate the role of place in such rituals and their illumination of place we will attend to the ordination of the priests and the vision of Leviticus and the cultus as a whole.

The Consecration of the Priesthood: Leviticus 8–9

Leviticus 8 and 9 recount the fulfillment of Exodus 29, namely the consecration of "my priesthood" (Exod. 28:3; cf. 29:1). The ritual consecrates Aaron and his sons as the priests who will serve in the cultus and mediate between God and his people. In preparation for the priestly ordination "the whole congregation" is assembled at the doorway to the sanctuary (8:3).[59] "The whole congregation" is probably not the entire camp of Israelites but the representative heads.[60] The establishment of the priesthood is of great significance for the Israelites, and the ritual is enacted publicly. "The cult is founded in the context of the community and the community is defined, in large part, by its orientation with reference to the cult."[61] The doorway thus

---

58. Ibid., 164.

59. Gorman, *Ideology of Ritual*, 112, notes that if Lev. 8 is read as a continuation of Exod. 40:2, which tells Moses to erect the tabernacle on the first day of the first month, then the priesthood would begin its consecration on that day. Blenkinsopp, "Structure of P," 283–84, suggests that this date corresponds to the day the world emerged from the flood (Gen. 8:13) and corresponds to the first week of creation in Gen. 1:1–2:4a. Gorman, *Ideology of Ritual*, 112–13, thus notes that "a larger temporal framework may be operative in this ritual which serves to connect the establishment of the wilderness cult with the creation of the world and thereby present the ordination of the priesthood in that same context."

60. G. J. Wenham, *Book of Leviticus*, 98; Keil, *Manual of Biblical Archaeology*, 2:316.

61. Gorman, *Ideology of Ritual*, 115.

symbolizes the convergence of cult and community as well as establishing a boundary between community and cult.

Moses separates Aaron and his sons from the Israelites (8:6) and washes them with water, an outward act symbolic of inner purity. The anointing ceremony (8:10–12) delineates the primary places of Aaron's service.[62] The change of clothes indicates the ritually constituted change of status of Aaron and his sons. The ceremonies involve three offerings: the purification offering (vv. 14–17), the burnt offering (18–21), and the peace offering (22–30). The first offering is that of purification because if God is to be present amidst the priests presiding at his sanctuary, then the sanctuary must be first of all purged from sin's pollution, specifically that introduced by Aaron and his sons; *they* put *their* hands on the head of the bull. As Gorman notes, "The defilement of the sanctuary represents the gravest threat to the community in that a breakdown in the cultic order would entail a breakdown in the created order. Thus, the structures that serve to order life are first established."[63] Placially an intriguing aspect of the consecration is that Aaron and his sons are commanded to remain at the entrance of the tabernacle for seven days (8:33). Seven days is the typical number for rituals of major purification, and this camping by the priests also establishes for them and the Israelites their institutional association with the sanctuary. Significantly, the ritual begins and ends at the doorway to the tabernacle.

An advantage of the historical-critical linking of Leviticus with Genesis 1— both are regarded as from the Priestly writer—is that a number of scholars have noted the creational resonances in the cultus and its laws.[64] Anthropological insight has further confirmed this perspective. For example, although many different explanations have been offered for the division between clean and unclean animals in Leviticus 11, M. Douglas argues in *Leviticus as Literature* that the dietary laws of Leviticus are not firstly instrumental—their aim is not hygienic—but constitute a symbolic system evoking holiness and the order of creation.[65] In this work Douglas, unlike in her earlier *Purity and Danger*, appropriates J. Milgrom's ethical view that the dietary laws establish that "animal life is inviolable except for a few edible animals, provided they are slaughtered properly (i.e., painlessly, Lev. 11) and their blood (i.e., their life) is drained and thereby returned to God."[66] "On the earth" occurs seven times in Leviticus 11, evoking Genesis 1 and reminding us that "we eat only in the context of

62. Ibid., 119.

63. Ibid., 127.

64. In his discussion of the laws of leprosy (Lev. 14:1–20) Gorman notes that "the physical body is symbolic of the social body, and, it should be added, the 'cosmological' body" (Ibid., 151).

65. Douglas, *Leviticus as Literature*, 134–51.

66. Milgrom, *Leviticus*, 12.

creation."[67] Thus, as E. F. Davis notes, "the dietary regulations as formulated here make it the special obligation of Israelites, specifically as flesh eaters, to observe and protect the fruitfulness of creation. The work of the Priestly legists reflects careful study of the created order."[68] Douglas asserts, similarly, "The idea of goodness in Leviticus is encompassed in the idea of right ordering. Being moral would mean being in alignment with the universe, working with the laws of creation, which manifest the mind of God."[69]

In Leviticus 17–26, the holiness code, land is central (cf. 18:3). "YHWH's land and Israel's land, . . . the people of Israel have no other title to the land than the religious one: they are represented in the image of asylants granted the right to settle on temple lands. The land is Israel's because its owner and lord is YHWH. . . . The entire territory settled by the Israelites . . . stands under the influence of the divine presence in the earthly sanctuary."[70] Perhaps the text in Leviticus that most clearly evokes its vision is that of the law of Jubilee in 25:8–55, a law that overrides other legislation to ensure that the poor Israelite retains his freedom and original land.[71] The law evokes the image "of the land of Israel as a huge temple estate, worked by people who are in the simultaneously exalted and humble role of slaves consecrated to their God, humble because they are only slaves, exalted because they have been chosen for service to the lord of the universe."[72] Levenson follows Daube in seeing the Jubilee law against the background of Israel's slavery in Egypt and perceptively comments:

> If, as I think highly likely, laws like this one do underlie the depiction of Israel's servitude in Egypt, then the effect is to make pharaoh into a Simon Legree: he becomes the archetype of the impious slave-driver, and his dehumanizing regime becomes the foil for God's liberated kingdom. The implication of this, in turn, is that pharaoh's deepest problem is his refusal to conform to the laws decreed by the real master of the universe, the God of Israel, whom he brusquely and arrogantly dismisses (Exod. 5:1–2). Pharaoh's refusal to acknowledge his own creaturely subjugation to God seals his doom.[73]

Ritual and Place Today

Nowadays we tend to think of ritual in relationship to church services, with Catholics, Orthodox, and some Anglicans being "into ritual" and Protestants not. It is true that, as O. O'Donovan points out, Catholics read Old Testament ritual through a cataphatic hermeneutic, whereas Protestants read it

67. E. F. Davis, *Scripture, Culture, and Agriculture*, 95.
68. Ibid., 96.
69. Douglas, *Leviticus as Literature*, 44.
70. Joosten, *People and Land in the Holiness Code*, 189–90.
71. C. J. H. Wright, *God's People in God's Land*, 124.
72. Levenson, *The Hebrew Bible*, 144.
73. Ibid., 151.

apophatically, believing that Old Testament ritual has been fulfilled in Christ and thus terminated.[74] Yet in the institutional church some form of ritual is unavoidable, and the more unconscious we are of the rituals we practice, the more impoverished they are likely to be. Protestants and evangelicals would be wise, in my view, to cease reacting against Catholic ritualism and concentrate on honing rituals that reflect their own traditions. Ritual and place are interconnected, and attention to ritual will make one aware of the kind of places we build and in which we worship. Rituals embody our most cherished values, and we need to find ways to use ritual in our churches to evoke and reinforce the importance of what we do when we gather there. We will say more about this in part 3 in our discussion of the church and place.

Ritual is not, however, restricted to church life, but pervades all of culture. The opening of parliament is ritualized because it is of fundamental importance to a democracy and the well being of its citizens. The opening of a new academic year is marked by the ritual of the opening convocation. Birth, death, coming of age, and marriage are usually marked by some form of ritual. Sadly, in our consumer culture, our rituals are generally unconscious, and this says much about what we really value. Coming of age in North America is often marked by the acquisition of a car by a young adult. In public, the predictable behavior of the thousands who gather at sports events is ritual.

To have any hope of resisting the worst elements of Western consumer culture, we Christians will need an arsenal of rituals to keep us alert to the story of the world that really matters. North American culture has a monochrome, dumbed-down character in which every event is much the same as any other. In my experience of the opening convocation of the academic year at Christian colleges, for example, attendance is not compulsory, and while faculty robe, students attend in jeans and T-shirts. The result is a nearly vacuous ritual. Imagine if, instead, the opening convocation were taken seriously as the entry into a vibrant Christian learning community, in which one will be shaped for a lifetime of service of the LORD Christ. Attendance would be compulsory, dress would be appropriately formal, and we would be far more aware of what is at stake in Christian education.

Ritual played a crucial role in all areas of the Israelites' lives as a means to continually call them back to who they really were. It is the same with us. We need appropriate rituals scattered through our lives to draw us back to our center in Christ and to remind us that every place belongs to him. We ought also to have a vested interest in shaping public rituals that will call our culture back to its best values.

74. O'Donovan, "Loss of a Sense of Place."

5

Place in the Historical Books, the Prophets, and the Wisdom Literature

The Historical Books

Joshua to Kings tells the story from the conquest of the land to the exile, first of the northern kingdom and then of the southern kingdom. Chronicles covers the same ground with its own emphases, extending the story back to Adam. As P. D. Miller points out rightly,

> One might argue that from Exodus through the book of Kings, the First Commandment is a sort of touchstone and that much of the narrative and legal materials serve to develop a sense of the force and significance of this primary covenantal stipulation in the life of the community, whether familial, official, cultic, or political. In short, there is a sense in which these books of the Old Testament tell the story of the First Commandment, and, in so doing, teach and instruct the community that lives by these scriptures about what it means to keep the covenant, that is, the commandments.[1]

Place in Joshua and Judges

The Pentateuch builds toward the fulfillment of the promise of the land, a promise which the LORD declares to have been fulfilled by the end of Joshua: "I gave you a land on which you had not labored, and towns that you had not built, and you live in them; you eat the fruit of vineyards and oliveyards that you did not

---

1. P. D. Miller, *Way of the Lord*, 81.

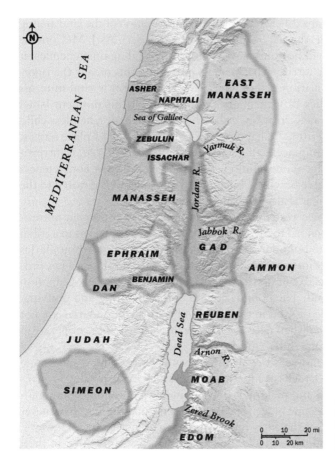

Figure 5.1 Map of the Areas Occupied by the Twelve Tribes of Israel (based on an original by International Mapping)

plant" (Josh. 24:13). Throughout Joshua the land is clearly portrayed as Yahweh's *gift* to the Israelites (1:3–6, 13, 15). The conquest is perilous for the Canaanites, but it is also dangerous for the Israelites, since they are dealing with Yahweh.

Joshua is rigorous in its insistence that the Canaanites must be eradicated from the land, but, as Miller notes, this depends upon the Canaanites' response to Yahweh. The prostitute Rahab's response is exemplary; she acknowledges that Yahweh is indeed God in heaven and on earth (2:11). Thus she and her extended family are spared. "The story of the taking of the land begins with the conversion of one of the Canaanites to the true worship of the Lord. In other words, the opening to the land is through an act of obedience to the First Commandment."[2] The rulers of Canaan face a challenge similar to that faced by Pharaoh: how will they respond to the claim of Yahweh? Joshua stresses their resistance and consequent destruction (9:1, 2; 11:19).

2. Ibid.

Much of Joshua (chaps. 13–22) deals with the distribution of the land among the twelve tribes by lot, that is, by Yahweh (see figure 5.1). As J. McConville notes, "Tribal Israel will not only have to hold this land against enemies, it will have to demarcate territory between its parts, and this means the rigorous, painstaking delineation of boundaries."[3] This section is vital in terms of the land; it embodies Brueggemann's point that "at this moment Israel does indeed become a new creation, a slave becomes an heir, a helpless child becomes a mature inheritor."[4] Chapters 15–21 are chock-full of place names, and, as Casey notes, "Implacement itself, *being concretely placed*, is intrinsically particular. . . . Place-names embody this complex collective concreteness despite their considerable brevity."[5] Intriguingly, most detail is devoted to the territory of Judah, which is also dealt with first (Josh. 15).

Chapters 15–21 have a vested interest in boundaries, a topic that anthropologists have long attended to.[6] Even where a detailed list of towns in a tribal territory is lacking, the boundaries are emphasized. Clearly the boundaries portrayed in Joshua are intended to be understood as geographical. They provide the tribes with social cohesion as well as responsibility for full occupation of their part of the land. The boundaries are both separating and unifying. Israel is the one people of God in the land, and thus the boundaries are not absolute but permeable; when necessary, for example, the tribes cooperate in clearing the land of Canaanites (Judg. 1:3–7).

Both of the placial moves Casey distinguishes as homecoming and homesteading are present in Israel's occupation of the land. Homesteading involves coming to a new place and making it one's home, whereas homecoming involves returning to the same place. The Israelites entering the land have never been there before, so that the entry into the land is a homesteading. However, as the place names indicate, this land is already deeply embedded in their collective memory, so that the conquest also has an element of homecoming. Ending places exhibit, according to Casey, that structure of habitat whereby they become familiar so that we are at home in them. We achieve this when a place attains the "requisite density" for ending a journey.[7] The extensive lists of place names and boundaries in chapters 15–21 evoke precisely this density. Some town names we recognize from the patriarchal narratives, but many are unknown to us. The patriarchs remained marginal to the urban life of the land, but the Israelites will take possession of the cities and towns, as the references to the number of towns allotted indicate (15:32, 36, 41, 44, 50, 54, 57, 59, 60, 62). Israel has come home. The occupation of the land clearly

---

3. McConville and Williams, *Joshua*, 8.
4. Brueggemann, *The Land*, 45–46.
5. Casey, *Getting Back into Place*, 23. Emphasis original.
6. See Donnan and Wilson, *Border Approaches*; Eliade, *Forge and the Crucible*; Roof, "Religious Borderlands"; Turner, *Dramas, Fields, and Metaphors*; Van Gennep, *Rites of Passage*.
7. Casey, *Getting Back into Place*, 292.

involves both city and rural life, and there is no indication that one is better than the other; in both Israel is called to obey the Lord.

The double challenge of the Canaanites' resistance and Israel's own proneness to wander soon appears, as is clear from Judges. As Page notes, "In its canonical form, Judges could also be characterized as a *Deuteronomic Casebook* that illustrates the transgressive nature of the pre-monarchic era, a time when virtually no boundaries were inviolable."[8] The first commandment continues to hover over Judges, so that the boundary between the Israelites and the Canaanites is clearly established in 2:1–3:6. Judges 3:4 notes that the LORD left Canaanites in the land to test the Israelites' fidelity to him. Ideally the judges played a crucial role in restoring this boundary (2:18–19). Yet Judges depicts not only a repeated pattern of sin, subjection, and deliverance but also a spiral down until the final judge, Samson, becomes a bizarre image of what Israel has become. The places of Israel's troubles are spread across the entire land. Judges is full of placial references, and like the list of town names in Joshua, these names alert us to the density associated with implacement, but it is a disturbing density. Indeed, as Page notes, the narratives contained within the "when there was no king in Israel" sayings (17:6; 18:1; 19:1; 21:25) embody multiple transgressions of varieties of boundaries.[9]

Monarchy and the Temple

With the emergence of dynastic monarchy (2 Sam. 6–7), the Old Testament view of place develops significantly, for during the monarchy the temple is built on Mount Zion and the Zion tradition emerges. Israel's request for a king is granted, and the Davidic covenant in 2 Samuel 7 establishes dynastic monarchy in Israel and grafts the Davidic covenant onto the Sinaitic covenant. David establishes Jerusalem as the capital of the united kingdom, his palace is built there, and the tabernacle is brought into Jerusalem. The Solomon narratives are structured chiastically in 1 Kings to highlight his building of the temple.[10]

In the detailed description of the temple in 1 Kings 6, we see that it is more than a "restoration" of the tabernacle; Yahweh's position among the Israelites is now permanent, and the temple is far larger than the tabernacle.[11] As Yahweh's son, Solomon builds his palace adjacent to the temple, so that "during the period of the monarchy, Yahweh's house extended to the palace of the king and other public buildings of the monarchy."[12] Like the tabernacle, the temple evokes Eden: the wood covering the interior is carved with fruits,

---

8. Page, "Boundaries," 43. Emphasis original.
9. Ibid., 48–49.
10. Frisch, "Structure and Its Significance."
11. Leithart, *1 & 2 Kings*, 55.
12. Japhet, *I & II Chronicles*, 55.

vegetables, and flowers (6:14–18);[13] cherubim guard the inner sanctuary as they defended the return route to Eden; the verb "finish" (*klh*) is used repeatedly in chapters 6–7, evoking Genesis 2:1 and Exodus 40:33. The temple is pyramid shaped, a stylized mountain.[14] "Tabernacle and temple are both 'world models,' and Moses and Solomon are 'creators' who imitate the divine creator."[15] The temple is a microcosm of the primal creation and of the new creation. In both we see God dwelling in the earth as his temple, with humans serving him and it as his priesthood.[16]

When the temple is consecrated, the glory of Yahweh fills it (1 Kings 8:11). Yahweh now has an address on earth! Yahweh's fixed address changes nothing about his demands upon his people, as Kings makes quite clear. Yet it does shift focus from the tabernacle to the temple and the city of Jerusalem. Geographically Jerusalem held several advantages: it was situated on the major north-south route and also on the east-west route that connected the Jordan Valley to the districts to the east. Thirdly it had a guaranteed supply of water through the Gihon spring. However, it was vulnerable to attack from the higher areas nearby.

The history of monarchy in Israel has some high points but is on the whole a tragic one, ending with first the northern and then the southern kingdom being taken off into exile primarily because of their violation of the first commandment (cf. 2 Kings 17:5–23).

Mount Zion

With the establishment of the temple and the palace of the king on Mount Zion, Zion develops as a powerful symbol of God's presence in the midst of his people. Through the Davidic covenant, monarchy is grafted onto the Sinaitic covenant, and once the temple is set up permanently on Zion, it is entirely understandable that Zion would develop as a multivocal iconic symbol,[17] closely connected with Davidic kingship. "The ark serves as the transportable throne of Yahweh until he takes his rest in the temple, but once there the temple itself is seen as the 'throne' of Yahweh."[18]

---

13. The pillars Jachin and Boaz (1 Kings 7:15–22) resemble cherubim guarding the Holy Place and contain garden images.

14. Wiseman, *1 and 2 Kings*, 108.

15. Leithart, *1 & 2 Kings*, 56. Leithart follows Jordan, *Through New Eyes* (197–240), in finding added symbolism in the amount of water contained in the temple (56–57). This and the four bulls, one facing each point of the compass, lead Leithart to assert that, "contrary to all appearance, the restless sea of Gentiles is supported by the obscure priestly nation living on a small seaside corner of the world" (57).

16. C. J. H. Wright, *Mission of God*, 415.

17. See Ollenburger, *Zion, the City of the Great King*.

18. Leithart, *1 & 2 Kings*, 67.

The theology of Zion is found in the Psalms[19] and is also a major motif in the prophets. In the Psalter we see this theology already in Psalms 1 and 2, which are deliberately placed as the introduction to the book. Psalm 1 deals with the individual Israelite, but Psalm 2 deals with the nations, indicating that the torah of the LORD is relevant to both the individual and the world of politics and nations.[20] The LORD's reassuring laugh at the antics of the nations (2:4) is followed in verse 6 by Yahweh's assertion, "I have set my king on Zion, my holy hill." As Psalm 9:11 notes, Yahweh dwells in Zion. Psalm 2 is a royal psalm, possibly with a coronation ceremony in the background, but for our purposes the important point is that Yahweh identifies Zion as his holy hill. It is the place where he lives and from which he reigns. God's rule is at the very heart of the Psalter, and as J. Mays notes, "The LORD's rule is first of all the double work of creation and salvation. . . . Israel is the people in whom the LORD's dominion takes shape in the world. *The place* that represents the LORD's kingship in the world is Zion, the city of God."[21]

As a symbol, Zion thus evokes God's real presence amidst his people, so that Jerusalem now becomes the focus of pilgrimage (cf. Pss. 122; 125–26; 128–29; 132–34). All that we have learned of Yahweh thus far becomes associated with Zion; his prerogative over Israel, for example, is exclusive.[22] Placially, therefore, Mount Zion is asserted as God's address on earth; it further casts its wing over the Davidic king as Yahweh's son. Its influence extends to the whole of Israel as the place of Yahweh's people, in whose midst he dwells. However, as in Psalm 2, the vision is much wider than Israel; the nations come regularly into view, and indeed, as in the quotation from Mays above, the redeemer Yahweh is clearly portrayed as the creator of heaven and earth. B. Ollenburger rightly notes that Zion symbolism is "fundamentally a theology of creation"; "it is preeminently through creation, rather than nature or history, that God is related to the world."[23]

Significantly, the psalmists are not reluctant to identify Jerusalem as the "*city* of our God" (Ps. 48:1, emphasis added). Here we see the potential for urban life to be the very place where Yahweh is enthroned. God is actually at home in Jerusalem, and adjacent to his home is that of the king and the administrative offices of Israel. His rule extends literally over Israel, but Zion is simultaneously an evocative symbol of his reign over his whole creation, over all the nations. To argue that urban life, politics, and nationhood are somehow alien to the Old Testament is a violation of the comprehensive vision of the Psalter. As P. D. Miller notes of Psalm 2,

19. Relevant psalms are 18; 24; 46; 47; 68; 89; 93–99; 118.
20. See P. D. Miller, *Interpreting the Psalms*, 81–99.
21. Mays, *Psalms*, 31. Emphasis added.
22. See Ollenburger, *Zion, the City of the Great King*, chap. 3.
23. Ibid., 61.

In the move from Psalm 1 to Psalm 2 the human plane is greatly expanded. . . . the reader of the Psalter is led to understand that it speaks about individual piety and ethics and also about the larger horizon of world affairs, foreign policy, human government, and international alliances, about the rule of God over nations and parliaments, kings and presidents, as well as the individual life of faith. The way of the Lord's instruction and the rule of the Lord's anointed are the chief clues to what matters in all of this.[24]

If Zion evokes the sheer potential of life with God, it simultaneously evokes the danger of disobedience. And indeed, Israel's persistent rebellion led to her being exiled from the land.

Place in/and the Prophets

Brueggemann rightly notes that "the land creates a situation in which the new decisive word of Yahweh must be made visible to Israel. It is the condition of being in the land which creates a prophetic situation."[25] The land is the place of blessing but also the potential place of curse, as Deuteronomy makes clear. Betrayal of the covenant by king and people remained a constant danger for Israel; hence the crucial role of the prophet: "His view is oblique. God is the focal point of his thought, and the world is seen as reflected in God. Indeed the main task of prophetic thinking is to bring the world into divine focus."[26]

The prophets above all others insist that place must be characterized theologically. "A clean house or a city architecturally distinguished may yet fill the prophet with distress."[27] In the books of Kings some kings who achieved much in terms of building projects and development are glossed over as kings who "did evil in the sight of the LORD." Omri, for example, who we know from archaeology achieved a great deal,[28] establishing Samaria as the new capital of the northern kingdom, is given a short, negative six verses (1 Kings 16:23–28).

In the prophetic books of the Old Testament the two major themes are judgment and hope. On the basis of the Sinaitic covenant the prophets continually warn the northern and the southern kingdoms that if they persist in disobedience then judgment in the form of exile lies ahead (cf. Amos 4:2–3; 6:7). Amos 1:2–2:16 is a classic declaration through Amos of God's judgment.

Amos came from the southern kingdom, from Tekoa, a few kilometers south of Bethlehem (Amos 1:1). Amos 1:1 describes him as a "shepherd," but the word used here, *nōqēd*, is an unusual word for a shepherd in the Old

24. P. D. Miller, *Interpreting the Psalms*, 91.
25. Brueggemann, *The Land*, 91.
26. Heschel, *The Prophets*, 24.
27. Ibid., 7.
28. Mazar, *Archaeology*, 406. See also 406–10.

Testament, which normally uses *rō'eh*, the word used in 1:2. Ugaritic parallels suggest that as a *nōqēd*, Amos

> probably owned, or managed, large herds of sheep and was engaged in the marketing of their products. Indeed, it was probably his marketing duties that took him north from his home state of Judah to the market towns of Israel, there to sell his goods. Taken together, the evidence indicates that Amos was engaged extensively in agricultural business, being involved in cattle and fruit-farming, in addition to sheep. And it was from this large and responsible position that Amos was called to be a prophet, a vocation to which he responded willingly.[29]

Amos's vocation is primarily to the north, but he is clear that judgment comes from the temple, that is, Zion (1:2). His imagery is evocative: Yahweh roars like a lion[30] about to spring on its prey, and the effect is felt on the land; the pastures of the shepherds mourn,[31] and the top of Mount Carmel dries up.

Amos's rhetorical strategy is devastating; he declares Yahweh's judgment on the surrounding nations, then Judah and then the northern kingdom. The oracles proceed from foreign nations to blood relations and are also arranged geographically, so that they slowly but steadily close in on the northern kingdom. "The geographical orientation thus moves from the northeast (Aram) to the southwest (Philistia), the northwest (Phoenicia), the southeast (Edom, Ammon, Moab) and finally to Judah and Israel" (see figure 5.2).[32] As C. J. H. Wright notes, the effect is "to throw a kind of geographical noose around Israel and thus to make the climactic accusation against her even more devastatingly powerful."[33]

The oracles of judgment (and salvation) directed at nations other than Israel are a powerful reminder to the Israelites—for whose hearing the oracles are declared—that Yahweh, who dwells in Zion, is indeed the Lord of all nations, of the whole creation. In Amos creation is implicit in phrases like "of all the families of the earth," but explicit in the so-called hymn fragments, namely 4:13; 5:8–9; 9:5–6. In the hymn fragments, creation serves to remind the Israelites just who this Yahweh is that they are going to encounter in judgment; he is the creator God. Amos's longest and final oracle of judgment is reserved for Israel; she will be pressed down in her place, as a cart is pressed down when heavily loaded (2:13).

Amos does not have a lot to say about the effect of the coming judgment on the land itself—a motif which is particularly clear in Joel—but it is clear from

29. Craigie, *Ugarit and the Old Testament*, 73–74. Cf. Amos 7:14.
30. Möller, *Prophet in Debate*, 160–64. The terrifying image of Yahweh as a lion is common in the minor prophets; cf. Hosea 5:14; 11:10; 13:7; Joel 3:16.
31. Ibid., 163–64.
32. Ibid., 195.
33. C. J. H. Wright, *Living as the People of God*, 123.

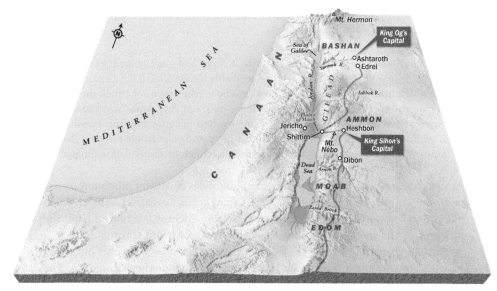

Figure 5.2 Map of Israel and Surrounding Countries (based on an original by International Mapping)

1:2 that conquest would be devastating for the land, and in his major oracle of hope (9:11–15) he articulates a vision of a renewed land, a new house of David whose reign will extend to all the nations (9:12), a time of agricultural abundance and thriving urbanism. The building of cities, viticulture, gardening, and farming will flourish!

Although each prophet's message is unique, Zion is a central motif in many of the prophetic books (e.g., Isa. 1:27; Jer. 3:14; 4:6; Ezek. 10; 40–48; Joel 2:1, 15; 3:16; Obad. 17, 21; Jon. 2:4, 7; Mic. 1:2; 3:10, 12; 4:7; Hab. 2:20; Zeph. 3:5; Hag. 1–2; Zech. 2:12, 13; 8:3). So too is the motif of creation and its connection with judgment and redemption (cf. Jon. 1:9; Mic. 4; Nah. 1:5; Hab. 2:14; Zeph. 3:9, 19).

This is particularly true of Isaiah. Without bypassing the question of its complex history, there has been a welcome and creative rediscovery of Isaiah as a book as a whole in recent decades.[34] Seitz argues that chapter 1 of Isaiah provides us with a lens through which to read the book as a whole, and that

> central to understanding Isaiah is God's dealing with Israel within the destinies of the nations at large. . . . The final two chapters of the book appear in many ways to reiterate the message of chapter 1. Where we began is where we leave this book, with the testimony behind us of God's will to deal with Israel and the nations already clearly manifested on the canvas of human time and space. . . . The Zion with evil offspring is replaced by a Zion who delivers children without

34. See, for example, Childs, *Isaiah*; Seitz, *Word without End*, 113–228.

travail, who nurse and are satisfied at her consoling breast. These are joined by the nations at the farthest extremes of God's creation, reassembling the table of nations of Genesis 10.[35]

This lens is clearly in place in 2:1–4, showing a marvelous vision of the mountain of the LORD being established as the highest of all mountains—symbolizing Yahweh's universal kingdom[36]—and one to which all nations stream[37] in search of instruction by the LORD. As throughout Isaiah, Zion remains central,[38] but the canvas is clearly that of all the nations. Childs notes that 2:1–4 picks up the theme of the faithful city in 1:21 and that the exaltation of Zion "reflects the theme of a new creation, but one that bears the marks of God's original intention of primordial harmony of the universe (Gen. 2:10ff.). Jerusalem as the seat of the house of God now exerts an overwhelming attraction for the nations, which stream to it."[39] The full explication of the new heavens and new earth comes in Isaiah 65 and 66, but as Childs notes, "The hope of a radical new world order apart from evil and sickness has been adumbrated throughout the entire Isaianic corpus."[40]

The judgment against the nations is set out clearly in chapters 13–23, but this section is not all about judgment. Isaiah 19:18–24 contains a remarkable vision of Egypt and Assyria being included among God's people. Five cities in Egypt will speak the language of Canaan, and there will be an altar to the LORD in the center of Egypt and a pillar to the LORD at its border (19:18–19). The pillar will be a sign of Egypt experiencing the same salvation that Israel did through the exodus (19:20). There will be a highway from Egypt to Assyria, and it will be used by both Egyptians en route to Assyria and Assyrians en route to Egypt; indeed they will worship together! That highway, as we noted in our discussion of Abraham, already existed. Indeed Israel had been perched precariously on it for centuries. But now it will function as highways should, not as a contested focus of power games but as a means for celebrating before Yahweh the wonderful diversity of his creation. Places and nations will not be obliterated, but will become what Yahweh always intended them to be. "On that day Israel will be the third with Egypt and Assyria, a blessing in the midst of the earth, whom the LORD of hosts has blessed, saying, 'Blessed be Egypt my people, and Assyria the work of my hands, and Israel my heritage'" (19:24–25). Little wonder that Brueggemann describes the book of Isaiah as

---

35. Seitz, *Word without End*, 210.

36. Cf. Micah 4:1–5 and see Waltke, *Commentary on Micah*, 191–220.

37. The same verb (*nhr*) is used in Micah 4:1. Waltke notes that worshipers "flowed" by boat on the Euphrates to worship in Babylon (*Commentary on Micah*, 196), so that this motif of flowing to Mt. Zion may be a polemical motif against such pilgrimages (cf. Jer. 51:44).

38. Intriguingly, the Davidic emphasis of chaps. 1–39 is missing in chaps. 40–66, where the overwhelming emphasis is on Yahweh as King. See Seitz, *Word without End*, 150–67.

39. Childs, *Isaiah*, 30.

40. Ibid., 185.

"the great urban document of the Bible."[41] The vision of the new heavens and new earth comes to full expression in Isaiah 65:17–66:24, and 66:18–23 "is a succinct summary of eschatological themes that occur throughout the entire book of Isaiah. . . . What is new in the passage is the joining of them together in one concluding oracle. The radical formulation of 65:17–18 is repeated, but now in such a way as to provide an interpretation of the earlier promises as part of the one eschatological goal: the creation of new heavens and new earth."[42]

From 593 BC to about 586 BC Ezekiel ministered to some upper-class Judeans who had been deported by Nebuchadnezzar to a labor camp in Babylon. Ezekiel's prophecies interpret the horror of exile so that the survivors understand that it is not outside of Yahweh's control but firmly within it. It is hard to imagine the pathos evoked by the exile from the land. A. Heschel asserts, "With Israel's distress came the affliction of God, His displacement, His homelessness in the land, in the world. . . . Should Israel cease to be home, then God, we might say, would be without a home in the world."[43] Prophets such as Ezekiel play a crucial role in keeping alive the hope that exile is not the end, but that Israel and the world still have a future with God. The prophets, as we have seen, use different imagery in setting out this future. In Ezekiel temple imagery dominates the hopeful note sounded in chapters 40–48.

The very high mountain to which Ezekiel is brought symbolizes the sovereignty of Yahweh over all nations (40:2). In contrast to other ancient Near Eastern accounts of the revelation of temple designs, Ezekiel, a prophet, is shown a "blueprint"[44] and thus participates in "the very process of world-creation."[45] The depiction of the new temple in chapters 40–48 is visionary (40:2). Stevenson helpfully describes it as "territorial rhetoric, produced in the context of the Babylonian exile to restructure the society of Israel by reasserting YHWH's territorial claim as the only king of Israel."[46] The account of the temple is complex, and the reader is referred to the major commentaries for the details.[47]

In chapter 43 the glory of the LORD enters the temple via the east gate. Yahweh says, "Mortal, this is the place of my throne and the place for the soles of my feet, where I will reside among the people of Israel forever" (43:7). Ezekiel 43:12 indicates that the temple alone will now dominate Mount Zion; no longer will the palace of the king stand adjacent to it, nor will the city include the temple in its boundaries. The temple complex itself takes over the

41. Brueggemann, *Using God's Resources Wisely*, 3.

42. Childs, *Isaiah*, 542.

43. Herschel, *The Prophets*, 112.

44. The two-dimensional nature of Ezekiel's description of the temple has given rise to the term *blueprint*.

45. Niditch, "Ezekiel 40–48," 215.

46. Stevenson, *Vision of Transformation*, 163.

47. Block, *Book of Ezekiel, Chapters 25–48*, is particularly helpful.

function of a city. "The restructuring of space in the new society will make Israel ashamed of her past iniquities which have necessitated the stricter regulations concerning areas, boundaries and access to territory."[48] Nevertheless, the special place of the priests and the prince is acknowledged in the territories allotted to them on either side of the temple (45:1–8).

Chapters 47–48 deal with the relationship between the temple and the land. In 47 a river flows from the temple, giving life wherever it flows. The tribes are assigned new boundaries in latitudinal strips from north to south. Each strip includes coastal plain, highlands, and the Jordan Valley.[49] The large tribes are never again to dominate the interests of the smaller tribes. Intriguingly the aliens residing among the Israelites are also to be allotted land: "They are to be to you as citizens of Israel; with you they shall be allotted an inheritance among the tribes of Israel" (47:22). The territorial rhetoric establishes the land unequivocally as Yahweh's possession.

What is clear from our all too brief examination of the prophets is the centrality of Zion and the clear teaching that God's salvation will extend to all nations, to every place. W. Zimmerli is thus quite right when he notes, referring particularly to the prophets, that "Old Testament hope is hope for the world."[50]

The Wisdom of Place and the Place of Wisdom

Place is a fundamental element in human experience. Von Rad appropriately begins his classic on Old Testament wisdom with a discussion of experience: "man must know his way about in the world in which he finds himself in order to be able to hold his own in it."[51] In common with ancient Near Eastern and other traditions of wisdom, the Old Testament aims at discerning order amidst experience. There is thus a deeply experiential dimension to Proverbs, Job, and Ecclesiastes, but as Von Rad rightly notes, many of the experiences of Israel seemed to her quite different from those of her neighbors, "because she set them in a quite specific spiritual and religious context of understanding."[52]

Human wisdom is a correlate of the wisdom by which the world has been made; Lady Wisdom, whom I take in Proverbs 8:27–31 to be a personification of Yahweh's wisdom as his architect associate,[53] "dances" before Yahweh at the creation of the world in Proverbs 8. The multiple placial expressions in 8:23–31—earth, depths, springs, mountains, hills, earth and fields, heavens,

48. Renz, *Rhetorical Function of the Book of Ezekiel*, 98.
49. See M. Greenberg, "Idealism and Practicality in Numbers 35:4–5 and Ezekiel 48," 64–66.
50. Zimmerli, *Old Testament and the World*, 136.
51. Rad, *Wisdom in Israel*, 4.
52. Ibid., 5.
53. Van Leeuwen, "Book of Proverbs," 94.

skies, fountains of the deep, sea, foundations of the earth—evoke the order of
creation and the comprehensive range of wisdom. These realms—sky, waters,
and land—comprised all of reality for the ancients. Wisdom embraces not just
placial differentiation but human activity in these contexts, as Lady Wisdom's
call in the public places of Israel implies.[54] Proverbs 8:1–5 "presents Wisdom
as virtually omnipresent in the human city."[55] She calls out on the heights, in
the streets, at the crossroads, and in particular at the gates, where business is
conducted and legal cases are settled. "In God's economy, all things, including
human beings and their various activities, have their proper place and limits."[56]
Thus there is no nature-culture dichotomy in wisdom; both are subject to
God's creation order.

Old Testament wisdom is thus above all else a theology of creation. Proverbs, Job, and Ecclesiastes are also equally in touch with what we might call
the "fallenness of the world." They lack, of course, a speculative doctrine of
what went wrong, but they are intensely aware that believers face *two ways*
in God's world, a way of wisdom and a way of folly, the same theme we find
in Genesis 3, for example, and in Psalms 1 and 2.

While Proverbs lacks a major focus on place per se, it is full of placial
metaphors for wise living: the way, two ways, two houses, the paths, walking,
dwelling, and so on. In terms of the distinction Al Wolters makes between
structure and direction,[57] in Proverbs placial metaphors play a central role in
pinpointing the issue of direction.

Proverbs clearly teaches that wisdom literally enriches place, declaring,
for example: "the upright will abide in the land" (2:21); "then your barns
will be filled with plenty, and your vats will be bursting with wine" (3:10);
and "he [the LORD] blesses the abode of the righteous" (3:33). Proverbs
1–9 teaches the character-consequence structure to life in the vision of
the world it evokes: living wisely, choosing the way of wisdom rather than
folly; eating at Lady Wisdom's house, leading to blessing. However, the
overall picture in Proverbs is more complex than this; especially in the
later chapters, Proverbs is well aware that life may involve exceptions to
the character-consequence motif.[58]

Wisdom can and does lead to implacement and placial flourishing. Proverbs
climaxes in chapter 31 with the Song of the Valiant Woman, who embodies
holistic implacement.[59] In the history of interpretation readers have struggled

54. See Prov. 8:15–16 for the relevance of wisdom to politics. For a more detailed discussion
see Bartholomew, "A Time for War and a Time for Peace."
55. Van Leeuwen, "Book of Proverbs," 88.
56. Ibid., 93.
57. Wolters, *Creation Regained*, 72–95.
58. See Van Leeuwen, "Wealth and Poverty."
59. See Wolters, *Song of the Valiant Woman*, 13.

with this passage because her activities appear to be so worldly,[60] but this is precisely the point: it is in and through her rich implacement that she manifests wisdom (31:30). Snow (31:21) was rare in Israel, and the mention of it here indicates that she lived in the Judean hill country.[61] She is the quintessential homemaker, who creatively attends to food (31:14–15) and clothing (31:21). Her grain probably came from the fertile Jezreel Valley, Israel's breadbasket.[62] "The woman's scope of action encompasses the entire creation: Both land and sea provide resources for her house as she brings goods from near and far (v. 14)."[63] The comparison of this woman with the ships of the merchants and the fact that she brings her food from far away (v. 14) imply international as well as local knowledge. Indeed, to turn a field in the Judean highlands into a vineyard as the basis for viticulture would require intimate local knowledge (v. 16). Not surprisingly, she also contributes to local and possibly international knowledge: she opens her mouth with wisdom (v. 26). "As wisdom builds and supplies her house, so also the capable wife builds and fills her house with good."[64] And she is generous with what she obtains: she has "hands that grasp to produce open wide to provide."[65] In sum, the Proverbs 31 woman is a marvelous example of what W. Berry calls husbandry and housewifery:

> Husbandry pertains first to the household; it connects the farm to the household. It is an art wedded to the art of housewifery. To husband is to use with care, to keep, to save, to make last, to conserve. . . . Husbandry is the name of all the practices that sustain life by connecting us conservingly to our places and our world; it is the art of keeping tied all the strands in the living network that sustains us.[66]

---

60. See ibid., 15–29, 59–154.
61. Van Leeuwen, "Book of Proverbs," 262.
62. Ibid., 261.
63. Ibid.
64. Ibid.
65. Ibid., 262.
66. W. Berry, *Way of Ignorance*, 96–97.

6

Place in the Gospels

Although the Old Testament is not often approached through the grid of place, it is clear how land and thus place are central to it. The Gospels appear, however, to present an entirely different challenge. While there is a growing discussion about Galilee, Samaria, and Jerusalem in relation to Jesus's ministry, it is commonly assumed that with the new era instituted by Jesus the importance of land and thus place recedes into insignificance. Jesus is rightly seen by many to fulfill the great Old Testament places of land, temple, and Jerusalem, but the inference is then drawn (or not) that place no longer really matters. As G. Lilburne notes, "The problem appears to be that while the Hebrew Scriptures speak centrally of the land, its preservation and proper use, this concern is entirely lost in the New Testament. By universalizing the scope of God's reign, the New Testament appears to trivialize the concern with place and locality and to move its spirituality beyond issues of land."[1]

In the last major work on the gospel and the land, W. D. Davies articulates what many take to be the view of the land and thus place in the New Testament. "In sum, for the holiness of place, Christianity has fundamentally, though not consistently, substituted the holiness of the Person; it has Christified holy space."[2]

1. Lilburne, *Sense of Place*, 10.
2. W. D. Davies, *Gospel and the Land*, 368.

Davies on Jesus and the Land

In discussing the relationship between Jesus and the land in the final chapter of his book, W. D. Davies rejects the suggestion that Jesus was a Zealot and is convinced neither by Bornkamm's portrait of Jesus as apolitical[3] nor by Caird's portrait of Jesus as highly political.[4] For Davies, Jesus's challenge was religious, since he sought to form a new community; his cleansing of the temple, for example, was a religious and not a political challenge. "The aim of Jesus was neither non-political nor directly political: rather it was focused on the creation of a community worthy of the name of the people of God within Israel."[5]

Davies examines four Gospel texts in his attempt to discern Jesus's approach to the land, namely the parable of the barren fig tree (Luke 13:6–9), the parable of the hidden talents (Matt. 25:14–30), the beatitude of Matthew 5:5, and the *palingenesia* (the new world, ESV) of Matthew 19:28. As regards the parable of the barren fig tree, Davies focuses on the words in verse 7, "Cut it down! Why should it be wasting the soil?" This phrase is unique to Luke, and "the soil" could refer to the land of Israel or to the whole earth, the implication being that Israel has polluted the land. Davies argues, however, that the phrase remains ambiguous and sheds little light on Jesus's view of the land.

Davies discerns the focus of the parable of the talents in the one talent that was hidden "in the ground." "Ground" could be translated as "land," and thus Jesus could be rebuking the Jews for hiding away what has been entrusted to them. However, as Davies notes, one cannot push the details of parables too far, and hiding a treasure in the ground was the safest way to protect it from theft.

The same Greek word for "ground, earth" (*gē*) appears in the beatitude in Matthew 5, "Blessed are the meek, for they will inherit *the earth*" (v. 5; emphasis added). Davies is doubtful that Jesus actually uttered this beatitude, and as regards its meaning he concludes that

> there are two possibilities, either to combine the two alternatives referred to above and hold that Matthew 5:5 refers to inheriting, not the earth, but the land of Israel in a transformed world, in the Messianic Age or the Age to Come, or to recognize that for Matthew "inheriting the land" is synonymous with entering the Kingdom and that this Kingdom transcends all geographical dimensions and is spiritualized. Despite the use of the term "earth," we need not be removed from such spiritualization in Matthew 5:5, because we have previously recognized that in Judaism itself, as elsewhere in the New Testament, the notion of "entering the land" has been spiritualized.[6]

3. Bornkamm, *Jesus of Nazareth*.
4. Caird, *Jesus and the Jewish Nation*.
5. W. D. Davies, *Gospel and the Land*, 352.
6. Ibid., 362.

In the context of his discussion of this beatitude Davies asserts that "certainly the 'inheritance' of Christians in other parts of the New Testament is supra-terrestrial."[7]

According to Davies, for Luke, verse 30 of chapter 22 is symbolic—the disciples are to rule with Jesus "in a new kind of kingdom—in another dimension of existence."[8] Matthew 19:28, however, speaks of "the new world" (*palingenesia*). Davies thinks that this saying may be authentically from Jesus, but argues that it does not refer to the land of Israel but evokes a cosmic renewal, so that in 19:28 the restored twelve tribes are probably also to be understood not so much as a restored land of Israel as a renewed cosmos.[9]

Davies concludes from his analysis of Jesus and the land that

> one thing only emerges from all the above. Jesus, as far as we can gather, paid little attention to the relationship between Yahweh, and Israel and the land. But we have seen indications that the Early Church was so concerned. This concern was part of the matrix which led to that process, often treated, whereby Jesus was increasingly draped in an apocalyptic mantle and specifically Jewish expectations developed in the Church in a form highly enhanced from that which they had assumed in Jesus' own teaching. Where were these expectations to be fulfilled? Judaism had given its answer in terms of the centrality of the land and the indestructible connection between it and Yahweh and Israel. The Church came both to reject and to transmute this answer in various ways. After struggles which we can now only glimpse with difficulty, she remained true to the intent of her Lord.[10]

In analyzing the approach of the New Testament overall to the land, Davies discerns different strata. In one stratum (e.g., Acts 7) the land, Jerusalem, and the temple are rejected outright. However, in other strata they become "symbols especially of eternal life, of the eschatological society in time and eternity, beyond space and sense. In such strata the physical entities as such—land, Jerusalem, temple—cease to be significant, except as types of realities which are not in essence physical. It is justifiable to speak of the *realia* of Judaism as being 'spiritualized' in the Christian dispensation."[11]

For Davies, therefore, the Gospels and the other literature of the New Testament are in continuity with the historical Jesus in spiritualizing the land. It is not hard to see the implications of such an approach for a theology of place—it becomes negated and marginalized by the vision of a spiritual kingdom that transcends this creation.

New Testament studies have moved on in a variety of ways since Davies wrote, and the time is ripe to reevaluate the data of the Gospels in relation to

7. Ibid.
8. Ibid., 363.
9. Ibid., 365.
10. Ibid.
11. Ibid., 366.

land, to place, and thus to creation. The data is far more extensive than what Davies examines, and in what follows we will consider it more thoroughly, first briefly surveying contemporary studies of Jesus, then discussing the central theme of his teaching, namely the kingdom, and finally examining particular elements of the Gospel traditions.

Jesus: The Third Quest

Albert Schweitzer, with his stress on seeing Jesus in the context of first-century Judaism, apocalyptic, and the expectation of the imminent end of the world, profoundly influenced studies of Jesus, and his influence continues today. Schweitzer bequeathed two alternative approaches to Jesus studies: his own thoroughgoing eschatology and the skepticism of Wilhelm Wrede. "As we turn to the current scene in Jesus-studies," observes N. T. Wright, "we discover that these two streets have become broad highways, with a good deal of traffic all trying to use them at once."[12] On the *Wredebahn* are, for example, the Jesus Seminar: B. Mack, J. Crossan, F. Downing, and M. Borg.[13] Wright positions himself among those pursuing the alternative, "third-quest" approach,[14] which attempts to take history and the Jesus of history seriously. For our purposes a historical, eschatological framework within which to understand Jesus's ministry is crucial for grasping his theology of the kingdom of God, and thus for opening up his, and the Gospels', view of place.

Place in Contemporary Gospel Studies

Social-scientific readings of the Gospels have called forth renewed attention to place as a constituent element in understanding Jesus and the Gospels.[15] Scholars have, for example, become aware of the significance of Galilee as the context of much of Jesus's ministry. H. Moxnes's work has shifted attention from Jesus's conception of time to the role of place in relation to his identity and ministry.[16] S. Freyne, in his *Jesus, a Jewish Galilean*, asks, "In a word, what were the most likely wellsprings that Jesus could draw on in order to challenge the prevailing sense of place that was Herodian Galilee, and how might he have sought to legitimate for his followers his particular strategy to

12. N. T. Wright, *Jesus and the Victory of God*, 28.
13. Ibid., 28–82.
14. See ibid., 84, for a list of scholars pursuing this approach.
15. This renewed attention can be traced back to R. Lightfoot's *Locality and Doctrine in the Gospels* and to H. Conzelmann's influential *Theology of St. Luke*, the first part of which (pp. 18–94) is entitled "Geographical Elements in the Composition of Luke's Gospel."
16. Moxnes, *Putting Jesus in His Place*.

realize his vision?"[17] Yet Freyne notes a lacuna in social-scientific readings of the Gospels: they are alert to economic and social factors but still tend to ignore place. "This calls for an exploration of the extent to which Jesus is indebted to those aspects of his inherited tradition that include an understanding of the earth as God's creation, and the implications of such a perspective for human interaction in his view."[18]

This re-implacement of Jesus yields important insights. Freyne, for example, explores the significance of the placial shift in Jesus's ministry from his baptism by John in the Judean wilderness to the fertility of Lower Galilee. In the Old Testament Israel's sojourn in the wilderness is portrayed as both a time when Israel tested Yahweh with their unbelief and a time of dependence and closeness to him. In John's baptism, therefore, the wilderness functions as a constituent part of his message; it is a call to Israel to rediscover her vocation as the people of God. Freyne suggests, somewhat reductively, that one reason why Jesus's ministry took on an approach so different from that of John once he arrived in Galilee is the shift in environment. The contrast between the arid wilderness and the fertile land must have been "blindingly obvious."[19] "It seems altogether plausible to suggest that the contrasting experience of the *potential blessedness* of life in the land, must have touched him to the point of re-evaluating the present as a graced moment rather than one of awaiting God's imminent judgment, cathartic though the desert environment had been viewed by various Jewish reformers, before and after him."[20]

The "potential" of "potential blessedness" must be stressed. The effect of Herod's rule was such that the Old Testament vision of the land as Yahweh's and for the benefit of all Israelites was increasingly undermined by greed and exploitation. Much of Jesus's teaching reflects the village economy of the day, and in the context of exploitation, teachings like his beatitudes would have resonated deeply with his hearers. To call poverty and hunger blessed "and not a curse, as the Deuteronomic theology would have suggested, called for a bold religious imagination."[21]

While Jesus's ministry was directed primarily toward the Jews, geography reveals a broader orientation of his ministry. The Gospels do not mention Jesus visiting the Herodian centers of Sepphoris and Tiberias; however, "when one holds up a map of Jesus's movements in Galilee, against the template of a more detailed description of the region indicating known places of Jewish observance, he is frequently to be found in the environs of, if not actually within, pagan cities, than he is in recognizably Jewish locations."[22] The rab-

17. Freyne, *Jesus, a Jewish Galilean*, 19.
18. Ibid., 26.
19. Ibid., 42.
20. Ibid., 42–43. Emphasis original.
21. Ibid., 47.
22. Ibid., 83.

bis, furthermore, carefully defined the borders between Tyre and Israel, but according to Mark, Jesus went to the region of Tyre, where Mark locates his encounter with the Syrophoenician woman, and to the cities of the Decapolis.

Intriguingly, Mark's Gospel ends with the young man, dressed in a white robe, sitting in the tomb, telling the visitors to "go, tell his disciples and Peter that he is going ahead of you to *Galilee*; there you will see him, just as he told you" (Mark 16:7; emphasis added). Going back to Galilee "was neither an exercise of nostalgia nor a return to the everyday of their past lives, but a recalling of the mission and ministry that had challenged them initially in Galilee, and that was now about to make new and dangerous demands if they were to be true to the call of the rejected servant whom they believed had been exalted by God."[23]

Clearly this attention to the place of Jesus is fecund. Place is also particular and therefore historical, so that this recovery of Jesus "in place" connects with the rediscovery of Jesus as a Jew, whose message must be read against the background of the Old Testament and first-century Jewish expectations. However, encouraging as this recovery of the implacement of Jesus is, we still lack an analysis of the significance of Jesus's ministry as a whole for our view of place.

The Kingdom of God/Heaven

Most remarkably, the kingdom of God is not indexed in Davies's work *The Gospel and the Land*, and the entire volume contains no discussion of the kingdom in any detail. This is a major lacuna, since Jesus's heralding of the kingdom bears directly on his view of place. It is clear, at least according to the Synoptics,[24] that the kingdom of God/heaven was the major theme of Jesus's teaching, and other New Testament scholarship, as well as missiology,[25] over the last century has recovered this understanding.[26] The evidence for this is overwhelming; suffice it here to note Mark's summary of Jesus's teaching in Mark 1:14: "Now after John was arrested, Jesus came to Galilee, proclaiming the good news of God, and saying, 'The time is fulfilled, and *the kingdom of God* has come near; repent, and believe in the good news'" (emphasis added). As N. T. Wright notes, "We may therefore safely conclude that Jesus habitu-

23. Ibid., 174.

24. In John's Gospel "the kingdom of God" occurs only twice, in 3:3, 15. John's equivalent phrase to "the kingdom of God" in the Synoptics is "eternal life." Wilder notes of John that "with his categories of eternal life, light, and truth, this evangelist does not forfeit in any way the celebration of the New Age and the travail of its advent" (Wilder, "Preface," in Willis, *Kingdom of God*, ix).

25. See Newbigin, *Sign of the Kingdom*.

26. The major works on the kingdom list the extensive literature on the subject in their bibliographies, and I will not duplicate that information here.

ally went about from village to village, speaking of the kingdom of the god of Israel, and celebrating this kingdom in various ways, not least in sharing meals with all and sundry."[27]

But what did Jesus mean by "the kingdom of God"? He never defines it, but appears to assume an understanding on the part of his audience, so that we are compelled to explore the Old Testament background, the background in the Judaism of Jesus's day, and most importantly the variety of ways in which Jesus explains the kingdom.

The Kingdom in the Old Testament

In the Old Testament the language of the kingdom (Hebrew *malkût*) of God is found notably in Psalms 103:19; 145:11–13; Daniel 2; 7; 1 Chronicles 28:5; and 2 Chronicles 13:8.[28] Mays notes, "The Psalms are the liturgy of the kingdom of God. . . . The Psalter as a whole composes a language world in which God and world and human life are understood in terms of the reign of the Lord."[29] D. Wenham argues that the full significance of Daniel as background to the New Testament concept of the kingdom has yet to be realized and that "in fact *the book of Daniel may be the primary background to the Gospels' teaching about the Kingdom.*"[30] This is particularly true of Daniel 2–7, a chiastically arranged section containing the most extensive exploration of heaven, earth, and kingdom themes found anywhere in Jewish literature.[31] Central to Daniel 7 is the figure of one like a son of man, the major source for Jesus's preferred self-designation, the Son of Man.[32] As Goldingay notes, "The theme that is central to Daniel as it is to no other book in the Old Testament is the kingdom of God."[33] Daniel makes clear that final authority rests with God, and the book looks toward the coming of his reign on earth.[34]

The references to the kingdom of God in Daniel and Chronicles represent the later parts of the Old Testament corpus, and most Old Testament scholars nowadays see the idea of God's kingdom as a late development in the life of Israel.[35] Certainly the idea of God as king who reigns over Israel and the

27. N. T. Wright, *Jesus and the Victory of God*, 150.
28. See Patrick, "Kingdom of God in the Old Testament."
29. Mays, "Language of the Reign of God," 121. On the centrality of God's kingship for the Psalter see McCann, *Theological Introduction to the Book of Psalms*.
30. D. Wenham, "Kingdom of God and Daniel," 132. Emphasis original. See also Evans, "Daniel in the New Testament"; Pennington, *Heaven and Earth*, 268–78.
31. Pennington, *Heaven and Earth*, 271.
32. Moule, *Origins of Christology*.
33. Goldingay, *Daniel*, 330.
34. Wilson, "Creation and New Creation," perceptively suggests that behind the imagery of Dan. 7 lies the creation story of Genesis.
35. Pennington, *Heaven and Earth*, 255.

world developed between the time it appeared and the time of Jesus, though historically we cannot be sure when it surfaced in the life of the nation. Undoubtedly it was formed through Israel's own experience of monarchy, and especially of the Davidic covenant, as well as through the prophetic eschatology of a coming Son of David. Canonically, however, it is there from the very beginning and appears throughout the Old Testament.

Genesis 1 portrays God as a great king, with humans as his royal stewards. Genesis 3 represents rebellion against this rule, and Genesis 12:1–3 indicates his plans to recover his purposes for his world through the line of Abraham. Thus kingdom theology is written deeply into the narrative of the Old Testament; as creator, God is king over all. After the fall he rules in particular over his people, Israel, who are called to be a *royal* priesthood, explicitly acknowledging his reign and demonstrating to the world what normative creaturely life looks like. As Israel slides down toward exile, the prophets look toward the time when God will act decisively to fulfill his purposes with Israel and his creation. Buber rightly notes that "this is what it comes to: the realization of the all-embracing rulership of God is the Proton and Eschaton of Israel."[36] "The messianic faith of Israel is . . . according to its central content the being-oriented-toward the fulfillment of the relation between God and world in a consummated kingly rule of God."[37]

Jesus's Redefinition of the Kingdom

In the intertestamental Jewish literature we do find the expression "kingdom of God," and "kingdom of heaven" occurs twice in the Mishnah.[38] In Jewish literature this phrase denotes firstly the rule of God over all creation, but secondly the hope for God's coming world-dominion, which will free Israel from pagan rule and subject the nations to God. Thus, as N. T. Wright notes,

> But at least we can be sure of this: anyone who was heard talking about the reign of Israel's god would be assumed to be referring to the fulfillment of Israel's long-held hope. The covenant god would act to reconstitute his people, to end their exile, to forgive their sins. When that happened, Israel would no longer be dominated by the pagans. She would be free. The means of liberation were no doubt open to debate. The goal was not.[39]

Wright correctly suggests that in relation to this expectation we should primarily see Jesus as a prophet in continuity with and bringing to a climax the work of the great Old Testament prophets, culminating in John the Baptist,

36. Buber, *Kingship of God*, 58.
37. Ibid., 14–15.
38. See N. T. Wright, *New Testament and the People of God*, 302–7; Pennington, *Heaven and Earth*, 258–68.
39. N. T. Wright, *Jesus and the Victory of God*, 151.

whose ministry Jesus used to launch his own. Jesus was a "leadership prophet" in the sense that he gathered disciples around himself and explained this as the reconstitution of Israel. As he traveled from village to village, Jesus heralded the message of the kingdom; he should be imagined more like a politician on the campaign trail than a schoolteacher, more like a herald of urgent news than a teller of timeless truths. The proclamation of the kingdom was a warning of imminent catastrophe, a summons to repentance, a call to Israel to rediscover her true vocation.

Wright observes that while Jesus assumes the basic Jewish framework, in his proclamation of the kingdom he nevertheless consistently redefines the contours of the fulfillment of the reign of God. The phrase "kingdom of God" was not, Wright points out, radically new, and it did indeed evoke the new covenant foretold by Jeremiah, the restoration of creation, the liberation of Israel, and Yahweh returning.[40] Jesus assumes the Old Testament and the Jewish story line. But through his teaching[41] and actions he gives it a radically new twist, while inviting his hearers to make it their own.

Jesus's proclamation of the kingdom was thus eschatological and apocalyptic: "The expression 'The time is fulfilled' will thus have to be understood as the indication that the threshold of the great future has been reached, that the door has been opened, and that the prerequisites of the realization of the divine work of consummation are present; so that now the concluding divine drama can start."[42] Jesus saw his arrival as signifying the climax of Israel's history, involving events which only the metaphors of end-of-the-world language are adequate to express, but resulting in a new phase within history. "Kingdom is a social word first of all. 'Kingdom' indicates that God is about to do a big world event and not just a big *individual* event—a cosmic thing and not just a heart thing. What happens when *God* comes is not going to be grapeshot; it is going to be nuclear, a kind of explosion, a reshaping of the earth."[43]

Jesus proclaimed the arrival of the kingdom and its future consummation. This tension between the presence and the future of the kingdom involves the reworking of Jewish apocalyptic, but decidedly not by substituting the vertical eschatology of private devotion for the horizontal eschatology of Jewish thought. "The point of the present kingdom is that it is the firstfruits of the future kingdom; and the future kingdom involves the abolition, not of space, time, or the cosmos itself, but rather of that which threatens space, time, and creation, namely, sin and death."[44]

---

40. Ibid.
41. Wright says of the parables that "they seem designed, within the worldview of the Jewish village population of the time, as tools to break open the prevailing worldview and replace it with one that was closely related but significantly adjusted at every point" (ibid., 173).
42. H. Ridderbos, *Coming of the Kingdom*, 48.
43. Bruner, *The Christbook: Matthew 1–12*, 87. Emphasis original.
44. N. T. Wright, *Jesus and the Victory of God*, 218.

Wright notes that in Jesus's reworking of the eschatology of the Jewish story the typical Jewish symbols are missing.[45] Jesus tells the story without a focus on the national, geographical liberation of Israel; he articulates the life of the kingdom without close reference to the Torah. Whereas till now the temple has been the locus for remission of sins, Jesus radically usurps the temple's place by claiming he can forgive wherever he chooses.[46] "The answers to the worldview *questions* can be given in terms of a redeemed humanity and cosmos, rather than in terms simply of Israel and her national hope."[47] In Acts 1:8 Luke reveals that "the newly inaugurated kingdom claims as its sacred turf, not a single piece of territory, but the entire globe."[48]

This reworking of the symbols of Israel raises acutely the question of place. If the holy land is no longer the center of God's purposes, how does place function in the context of the new story told by Jesus? Recent scholarship rightly stresses the social and political implications of following Jesus; because his agenda was theological, it was inevitably social and political, indeed dangerously so.[49] But society and politics are unthinkable without place, so why has so much biblical and theological scholarship continually neglected place?

Kingdom: Reign or Realm?

There are several possible reasons. One is the long-standing tendency to define the kingdom in terms of God's *reign* rather than his *realm*. This view can be traced back to G. Dalman,[50] and J. O'Neill asserts that "in New Testament studies, perhaps the most influential sentence ever written has come from Gustaf Dalman: 'There can be no doubt whatever that in the Old Testament and in Jewish Literature the word [*malkût*] when applied to God always means "kingly rule" and never means "kingdom," as if to suggest the territory ruled by him.'"[51] Indeed it has become common to assert that the focus of kingdom is reign and *not* realm.[52]

Within twentieth-century evangelical circles no one did more to rehabilitate the theme of the kingdom of God than G. E. Ladd. In *Jesus and the Kingdom* Ladd argues that "the interpretation of the Kingdom of God as God's *reign or rule* is to be understood as the correct historical meaning of Jesus's

45. Ibid.

46. Ibid., 257–58, 271–72.

47. Ibid., 218. Emphasis original.

48. Ibid.

49. Ibid., 297.

50. Dalman, *Words of Jesus*, 94.

51. O'Neill, "Kingdom of God," 130.

52. Bultmann notes that the kingdom of heaven is "the future which God will bring about— though not, of course, a worldly future. . . . No, something quite different, something which transcends the things of this world" (*This World and the Beyond*), 204–5.

proclamation."[53] As R. Brown notes, "But most of all, Dalman's view was propagated in the Evangelical community by G. E. Ladd."[54] In the footnotes to his discussion Ladd finds a long list of supporters for this view, and indeed it is pervasive.

Even such careful scholars as Wright and Ridderbos favor the emphasis on reign rather than realm. On the one hand Wright notes that "when Israel was restored, the whole creation would be restored,"[55] yet on the other he diminishes place by asserting that "although 'kingdom of god' referred more to the *fact* of Israel's god becoming king than to a localized *place*, the sense of Holy Land was evoked by the phrase as well, since YHWH had promised this country to his people."[56] Similarly, Ridderbos, for all his insight into the comprehensive nature of the kingdom, is in no doubt that "dominion" is the dominant sense of *kingdom*; the spatial meaning is secondary.[57]

Of course, as a tensive symbol,[58] *kingdom* evokes different aspects of its meaning in different contexts, and justice must be done to the resulting variety. However, in the Old Testament and in the intertestamental Jewish literature it is simply not the case that *malkût* evokes the idea of reign and not realm. Within creation reign will always be placially situated, whether in terms of the nation Israel or the creation in its entirety. Dalman's interpretation is woefully reductive, and it has been encouraging to see more holistic, linguistically sensitive readings appear in recent years. R. Brown, for example, rightly argues that the kingdom of God is a complex, multistage concept with many components of meaning.[59] Realm *is* one component of the meaning of the kingdom, so that Bruner is right to note that "the word 'kingdom' denotes both a *place* (the king's *dominion*) and a *power* (the *king's* dominion); it is both a space-word horizontally and a time-word vertically. The idea of space is by no means secondary."[60]

Matthew, as is well known, mainly uses the expression "kingdom of heaven." Since Dalman's discussion of this[61] at the end of the nineteenth century, it has been assumed that "kingdom of heaven" is a Jewish circumlocution for "kingdom of God." However, Pennington has reopened the debate on this issue, and argues that the kingdom of heaven is not a circumlocution, but an integral part of Matthew's theology and closely connected to his "heaven and

53. Ladd, *Jesus and the Kingdom*, 144. Emphasis added.

54. R. Brown, "A Brief History of Interpretation of 'The Kingdom of God' and Some Consequences for Translation," 16.

55. N. T. Wright, *Jesus and the Victory of God*, 193.

56. Ibid., 206. Emphasis original.

57. H. Ridderbos, *Coming of the Kingdom*, 24–25.

58. Ott describes the kingdom as a metaphor which projects a variety of images ("New Look at the Concept of the Kingdom of God"), 3.

59. R. Brown, "Translating the Whole Concept of the Kingdom," 43–44.

60. Bruner, *The Christbook: Matthew 1–12*, 140. Emphasis original.

61. Dalman, *Words of Jesus*.

earth" language. Matthew's primary source for his concept of the "kingdom of heaven" is Daniel 2–7.[62] Matthew may not have coined the phrase,[63] but, according to Pennington, he developed it through reflection on Daniel.

Matthew's "kingdom of heaven" upholds the Old Testament duality between heaven and earth, critiques first-century Jewish expectations of the overthrow of Roman dominion, insists on the inclusion of gentiles in the new people of God, and potentially extends sacred space to the whole world. "Sacred space is no longer defined simply in terms of the Land of Israel, in which the Davidic kingdom is to be inaugurated and the temple restored to its former glory. . . . The whole world is now a mission field. . . . Sacred space is wherever Jesus is present with his followers (Matt. 28:20 [cf. 1:23])."[64]

Holy Place or Holy Person?

Davies, as noted above, suggests that Jesus and the early church replaced Israel's notion of holy place with that of a holy person, namely Jesus. While a case can be made for seeing Jesus as the fulfillment of the land (see below), Davies sets up a false dichotomy in this contrast. The land is holy precisely because of Israel's relationship to Yahweh and because it is owned by him and given to Israel as the place where they are to live in communion with him as his people. C. J. H. Wright, for example, notes that

> the theology of the land, with its twin themes of divine ownership and divine gift . . . is inseparable from Israel's consciousness of their unique covenant relationship with Yahweh. . . . Because of its explicit links with the land traditions, the relationship between God and Israel was thoroughly "earthed" in the socio-economic facts of life—shaping and being shaped by them, and at times threatened by developments in that relation.[65]

Land in the Old Testament is therefore just as much relationally focused as is kingdom in the New Testament, and to suggest otherwise is to succumb to the idolatry of land that the Old Testament prophets warned against repeatedly.

If one takes the canonical shape of Scripture seriously, leading from creation through fall and redemption to new creation, as well as the embeddedness of Jesus in first-century Judaism, then the realm of the king's reign in the kingdom of God is obvious; it is the entire creation. Let us explore some of the new creation motifs in the Gospels.

---

62. See D. Wenham, "Kingdom of God and Daniel"; Evans, "Daniel in the New Testament"; Pennington, *Heaven and Earth*, 285–93.

63. Of course, it is possible that Jesus used both phrases.

64. Riches, *Conflicting Mythologies*, 292–93.

65. C. J. H. Wright, *God's People in God's Land*, 22–23.

New Creation Motifs in the Gospels

The Introductions to the Gospels

The title of Matthew's Gospel is revealing: "An account of the genealogy of Jesus the Messiah, the son of David, the son of Abraham." The first two words, *biblos geneseōs*, would remind Jewish readers of Genesis 2:4 and 5:1, where the same expression occurs in the Septuagint (hereafter LXX). Thus W. Davies and A. Allison translate the first part of Matthew 1:1 as "*Book of the New Genesis wrought by Jesus Christ. . . .*"[66] C. Keener suggests that Matthew's first words may project an arc which extends to the Gospel's final words in 28:20c, "to the end of the age," so that the trajectory of Matthew is from Genesis to final consummation.[67] Thus the first two words of Matthew already alert us that with Jesus's arrival we are in the midst of the new creation.

The carefully crafted genealogy that follows 1:1 demonstrates that Jesus is indeed the Son of David and thus the promised Messiah in David's line, as well as the son of Abraham. Bruner perceptively notes that "the two great baskets of promise in the Hebrew Scriptures are the promise to *David . . .* and the promise to *Abraham . . .* that is to say, a *temporal* promise to David ('forever') and a *spatial* promise to Abraham ('for everyone')."[68] The spatial dimension in the promise to Abraham means that although sin has brought God's judgment on the good creation, through Abraham God will reverse this judgment and recover his original purpose of blessing all the families of the earth, by blessing them and the places that sustain them. The title and genealogy in Matthew thus tie Jesus into the redemptive history of the Old Testament and indicate that his coming ushers in the new creation.

Mark's Gospel begins with a title (1:1) and a prologue (1:2–13). *Euangeliou* is significant for our purposes. In classical Greek, in which it was normally plural, *euangelion* originally referred to the reward for the bearer of good news, and then came to refer to the good news itself. In the Hellenistic period it is sometimes used in a more religious context such as the cult of the emperor, whose birth, accession to the throne, and so on were each hailed as *euangelion*. In the LXX the singular noun is not used, but the verbal form is somewhat common, being used in the Psalms (e.g., 40:9; 96:2) and in the prophets, most notably in Isaiah 40:9; 52:7; and 61:1.

As R. Watts argues, Jesus's proclamation of the kingdom appears to have been understood in the light of the *mĕbaśśēr* tradition of Isaiah (cf. 40:9; 52:7; 61:1).[69] The context of Isaiah 40:9 is important, with its strong theology of

---

66. Davies and Allison, *Matthew 1–7*, 153. Emphasis added.

67. Keener, *Commentary on the Gospel of Matthew*, 77n17.

68. Bruner, *The Christbook: Matthew 1–12*, 5. Emphasis original. Boring notes that every reference to Abraham in Matthew relates to the promises of God for all humanity ("Gospel of Matthew"), 126.

69. R. Watts, *Isaiah's New Exodus*, 96–99.

redemption and creation. If this is the primary background of *euangelion,* then clearly the title of Mark's Gospel alerts us that the *euangelion* "of Jesus Christ"—that is, the news about Jesus as well as the news Jesus proclaimed— has significance for all nations and thus the whole creation.

Mark 1:4–11 makes it clear that John the Baptist is the herald of Isaiah 40, and that in Jesus the LORD has arrived. The noun *hē hodos* (the way) occurs twice in verses 2–3. Several scholars have noted that *hē hodos* is a central motif in Mark's Gospel, and particularly in the section 8:27–10:52, in which Mark uses *hē hodos* seven times (8:27; 9:33, 34; 10:17, 32, 46, 52).[70] In both Exodus 23:20 and Isaiah 40:3 "the way" is that which leads to the promised land. Thus, as W. Swartley notes, "For Mark, the promised land is the kingdom of God."[71]

Luke's Gospel begins by telling of the preparations for the births of John the Baptist and Jesus. P. Minear notes that Zechariah's song previews all that follows. There is a return to this beginning at the end of the Gospel, forming an inclusio.[72] The initial assurance of forgiveness of sins (1:77) is repeated in Jesus's commission to the apostles (24:47). Zechariah's anticipation of peace (1:79) is fulfilled in Jesus's greeting to his disciples (24:36).[73] As we will see when we look at Jesus's relationship to the temple, the emphasis on forgiveness is significant, as is the dominance of the temple motif in the early chapters of Luke. For Jews forgiveness was available, but only through the temple cultus. Jesus's radicality was to assume the authority to pronounce forgiveness wherever he chose to do so. Jesus's statement at the end of Luke that, in fulfillment of the Old Testament, repentance and *forgiveness* of sins are to be proclaimed to all nations is tantamount, therefore, to a move in the Gospel from temple to new temple.[74]

John's prologue emphasizes Jesus as the *Logos* (1:1) who "became flesh" (1:14), thus adapting to his missional purpose a word[75] which in Greek philosophy commonly referred, especially among the Stoics, to the rational principle of the universe. The tremendous scandal for Greeks comes of course in verse 14— it would be inconceivable for a Greek that the Logos should become *flesh*. It was this sort of radical contrast with Greek philosophy that led Tertullian to confess that he believed because it was absurd! By this assertion and by his opening phrase *en archē,* "In [the] beginning," John clearly and unequivocally connects the story of Jesus with creation. "All that now follows in the Gospel

---

70. See R. Watts, *Isaiah's New Exodus*, 123–32, for a review of the debate in this respect.

71. Swartley, "Structural Function of the Term 'Way' (*Hodos*) in Mark's Gospel," 81.

72. Inclusio is "A literary construction in which the discourse boundaries are marked off by a similar word, clause, or phrase." T. J. Murphy, *Pocket Dictionary for the Study of Biblical Hebrew*, 90.

73. Minear, *Christians and the New Creation*, 8–9.

74. Minear discerns significant new creation motifs in the story of the shepherds (2:8–20) and in Luke's story of Mary (ibid., 17–19). Minear locates the Old Testament background to the story of the shepherds in Ezekiel (particularly Ezek. 34:25–31).

75. Several backgrounds to John's use of *logos* are possible. See Barrett, *Gospel according to St. John*, 2nd ed., 151–56.

has to be understood from the perspective of that 'beginning': It arises from that beginning, and that beginning is its deepest and most essential *Sitz im Leben.*"[76] Verses 3, 10, and 11 elaborate on the Word as the creator: everything came into being through him (vv. 3, 10); he came to *what was his own* (v. 11).

Jesus's Baptism

John the Baptist[77] was a controversial figure in the late 20s, an oracular prophet who gathered disciples around him. With his appearance prophecy returned to Israel.[78] He warned Israel of coming judgment if she did not repent and offered water baptism in the Jordan for forgiveness of sins. The latter activity provoked controversy because forgiveness was thought to be available only through the temple cultus. John's family was priestly, which serves further to foreground his radicality. He also proclaimed that he was preparing for the coming one who would baptize with the Holy Spirit. In several ways John's ministry and Jesus's baptism help us understand the role of place in the New Testament.

1. John was a desert or wilderness figure, ministering along the Jordan, at Aenon near Salim, or more generally in Perea (John 3:22–24; 10:40–42), that is, in the barren region from east of Jerusalem down to the Dead Sea. Meyer notes that "if judgment be taken as the matrix of John's field of meaning, the probable nexus binding all the motifs of his preaching together was the well-established conception of Israel in the wilderness (Exodus to Deuteronomy) as the type of eschatological Israel."[79] In the Old Testament traditions the desert evokes not only testing and judgment but also intimacy and hope. John certainly pronounces judgment on Israel, but he also announces the coming one and thus the restoration or reconstitution of Israel. In all the Gospels Jesus's public ministry starts with his baptism by John.

2. The association of John with the messenger preparing the LORD's way and the events surrounding Jesus's baptism all speak of this as the time when Old Testament expectations would be fulfilled. The open or rent (Mark 1:10) heavens evoke Isaiah 64:1a, "O that you would tear open the heavens and come down." The voice from heaven evokes Psalm 2:7, where the LORD says to his anointed that he will make the nations his heritage and the ends of the earth his possession, and Isaiah 42:1, "Here is my servant, whom I uphold, my chosen, in whom my soul delights; I have put my spirit upon him." Genesis 22:2 may also be part of the background. The precise intertextual allusions

---

76. H. Ridderbos, *Gospel of John*, 23.

77. John's ministry has been studied in depth in recent years. See Webb, *John the Baptizer and Prophet*; Scobie, *John the Baptist*; Wink, *John the Baptist in the Gospel Tradition*; Meyer, *Aims of Jesus*, chap. 6; and Hollenbach, "John the Baptist."

78. Meyer, *Christus Faber*, 29; but cf. N. T. Wright, *Jesus and the Victory of God*, 150–55.

79. Meyer, *Christus Faber*, 29.

are debated, but the overall picture is clear: Jesus is the Servant of God, the Son of God, the Son of David, the Spirit-Bearer, the Christ. All this is simply a way of portraying the kingdom of God as having come in Jesus.

3. Most importantly, Jesus's baptism indicates that his presence and purpose have "cosmic significance . . . indicated by the vision of the rending of the heavens, the descent of the Spirit and the testimony of the voice from heaven."[80] The open heaven has its background in Isaiah 64:1 with the plea (cf. Isa. 64:2) that God would make known his name to his adversaries so that the nations will tremble at his presence. The vision is creation-wide. Mark's (1:10) use of *schizō* ("tear apart") is unique among the Gospels and probably connects with his use of the same word in Mark 15:38 to refer to the rending of the temple curtain. This too has creation-wide implications: God no longer dwells in the tabernacle but is present and available to his entire creation in Jesus. "What was once a wide gulf between two realms has now been bridged; the heavenly and the earthly are as close as parent and child."[81]

4. Jesus's intention to "fulfill all righteousness" in his baptism (Matt. 3:15) enhances its cosmic significance. J. Ratzinger, the current pope of the Roman Catholic Church, notes that Luke says Jesus was praying while being baptized (Luke 3:21), and asserts, "Looking at the events in light of the Cross and Resurrection, the Christian people realized what had happened: Jesus loaded the burden of all mankind's guilt upon his shoulders; he bore it down into the depths of the Jordan. He inaugurated his public activity by stepping into the place of sinners."[82] Ratzinger argues that Jesus's baptism is a "repetition of the whole of history." Throughout history the world was powerless to defeat the "strong man," but Jesus's "struggle is the 'conversion' of being that brings it into a new condition, that prepares a new heaven and a new earth."[83]

The Temptation in the Wilderness

In the Synoptics, after Jesus's baptism he is immediately led by the Spirit into the wilderness, where he is tempted by Satan. Though brief, Mark includes a detail that the others do not: "*he was with the wild beasts*; and the angels waited on him" (1:13; emphasis added). Although the reference to the wild beasts has been interpreted variously, Jeremias, and more recently Bauckham,[84] intriguingly see this image as indicating that Jesus is presented here as the second Adam, through whom "Satan has been vanquished, the gate to paradise is again opened."[85] Bauckham presents a modified restoration-of-paradise proposal, appealing to

80. W. L. Lane, *Gospel of Mark*, 55.
81. Malbon, *Narrative Space and Mythic Meaning in Mark*, 82.
82. Ratzinger, *Jesus of Nazareth*, 18.
83. Ibid., 20.
84. Bauckham, "Jesus and the Wild Animals."
85. Jeremias, *New Testament Theology*, 70.

Isaiah 11:6–9 and 65:25 for background and stressing that *meta* (with) indicates not a hostile but a positive association between Jesus and the animals. We may add that the reference to harmony among the animals in 11:6–9 concludes, "The earth will be full of the knowledge of the LORD as the waters cover the sea."

The temptations as elaborated by Matthew and Luke relate to how Jesus will use his power, whether he will embody Israel's vocation as the Isaianic servant or follow Satan's way. The devil offers him all the kingdoms of the world, so that realm is clearly in view, but Jesus rejects the satanic route to such authority.

> Notice that the devil leads Jesus higher and higher: first from the wilderness and its rocks to the top of the temple and now, explicitly, to "a *very* high mountain." The Holy Spirit led Jesus *down*—into the easily misunderstood baptism of John, and then down still further into the wilderness of temptation. The Holy Spirit's way is not so much up into the fascinatingly great as it is down into the ordinarily mundane and into the way of the cross and of suffering.[86]

Jesus's battle with Satan begins with the temptations in the wilderness;[87] they "sound the dominant note of his entire ministry."[88] In Satan's offer of all the kingdoms of the world, he rightly recognizes the realm that is at stake in Jesus's ministry. Wright perceptively comments, "The struggle that was coming to a head was therefore cosmic, not merely martial (just as the temple was the focal point not merely of Israel but of the cosmos)."[89] Jesus's exorcisms are more than the liberation of individual tormented souls; they are central to Jesus's mission and indicate the real enemy, not Rome, but Satan. Wright argues that the success of the exorcisms means a prior battle had already been won, and this happened in Jesus's temptation in the wilderness.[90]

Jesus's so-called nature miracles had a similarly universal meaning: "They symbolize the creator god reclaiming the natural order, defeating the forces of chaos."[91] The temptations in the wilderness have already led us into Jesus's public ministry, and to this we now turn.

Jesus's Public Ministry

The Synoptics all have Jesus beginning his public ministry in Galilee.[92] Already here we begin to see its eschatological and creation-wide dimen-

---

86. Bruner, *The Christbook: Matthew 1–12*, 131. Emphasis original.
87. N. T. Wright, *Jesus and the Victory of God*, 453.
88. W. L. Lane, *Gospel of Mark*, 60.
89. N. T. Wright, *Jesus and the Victory of God*, 451.
90. Ibid., 543.
91. Ibid., 454.
92. We have already explored the great theme of Jesus's teaching, namely the kingdom of God/heaven. Needless to say, it is not possible to examine Jesus's teaching in detail. Readers are referred to ibid., chaps. 6–8.

sions. In a passage unique to Luke that has become known as the *Nazareth Manifesto* (Luke 4:16–30), Jesus quotes from Isaiah 61:1–2a, with a phrase from Isaiah 58:6, "to let the oppressed go free," inserted before the quote from Isaiah 61:2, "to proclaim the year of the Lᴏʀᴅ's favor." The year of the Lord's favor is generally read as the year of Jubilee; with Isaiah, Jesus appropriates this imagery[93] from Leviticus 25 to proclaim that with his arrival the kingdom has come. The context in Isaiah 61 has creation-wide implications: 61:11 indicates that the "Lᴏʀᴅ God will cause righteousness and praise to spring up before all nations." Furthermore, as D. Bosch rightly notes in his examination of Luke's approach to mission, "One could say that, for Luke, salvation actually had *six* dimensions: economic, social, political, physical, psychological, and spiritual."[94]

In Matthew's Gospel, too, in the Sermon on the Mount, Jesus gives a significant role to place. The sermon, whose theme is the kingdom of heaven, portrays Jesus as a second Moses, who goes up the mountain to teach his disciples. In 5:3, 10 "the kingdom of heaven" functions as an inclusio for the beatitudes, the characteristics of the citizens of the kingdom and thus of the King himself, who forms his disciples in his image. But the third beatitude is most interesting: "Blessed are the meek, for *they will inherit the earth.*" This placial reward clearly contradicts the notion that the kingdom of God always refers to the reign of Israel's God and never to his realm.

Hill says of this beatitude, "The spatial reference in 'land' ought not to be pressed; it is those who do the will of God that matter, not the place where it is done."[95] However, the clear placial referent in this beatitude will not go away, and in the context of Jesus's preaching it must be read as a reference to the earth as a whole. Bruner is thus right to note that "the promise of the *earth* in this Beatitude points to one of the most breath-taking facts in Scripture: that *this earth* is to be the scene of the coming kingdom of God, this renewed earth, but *this* earth (like our renewed bodies at the resurrection)."[96]

Matthew 5:13–16 articulates the influence disciples are to have as they manifest the character of the beatitudes. Bruner entitles this section, "The Ordination of Disciples to World Service."[97] Jesus's disciples are called to be the salt (preservative, flavor) of *the earth* and the light of *the world.* It is

---

93. See ibid., 295.

94. Bosch, *Transforming Mission*, 117. Emphasis original.

95. D. Hill, *Gospel of Matthew*, 112.

96. Bruner, *The Christbook: Matthew 1–12*, 166. Emphasis original. See H. Ridderbos's insightful comments on the beatitude (*Coming of the Kingdom*, 274). He argues that "earth" refers to the new earth to which the kingdom of heaven will descend at the end of the world. "Thus the deliverance of the kingdom consists in the subjection of the whole earth to God's perfect dominion."

97. Bruner, *The Christbook: Matthew 1–12*, 187.

not surprising that twentieth-century evangelicals have recovered a cultural concern particularly through this text.[98]

The Lord's Prayer portrays the realm of the kingdom poignantly. It is addressed to "our Father" who is *in heaven* and whose name we long to see treated as special. But how might his name be treated thus? Through the coming of his kingdom. And what will this look like? In it his will will be done *on earth* as it is in heaven. As Bruner notes, "'On *earth* as in heaven' girdles the globe; it reminds us again that the Lord's Prayer is cosmic."[99] Bruner argues that the phrase "on earth as it is in heaven" applies to all three preceding petitions: as our Father's name is hallowed in heaven, may it be hallowed on earth; as his kingdom is fully present in heaven, may it be present on earth; as his will is practiced in heaven, may it be practiced on earth. The petition has a clear future, eschatological reference, but this does not conflict with a desire to see signs of the kingdom now.[100] The central point is that "the scope of our Lord's Prayer is nothing less than the whole earth."[101]

Jesus's appointment of the Twelve also evokes the earth, here in the sense of the land of Israel. His appointing of twelve alludes to the twelve tribes of Israel and thus involves the reconstitution of the true Israel (Mark 3:13–16; Matt. 10:1–4; Luke 6:12–16). The sayings in Matthew (19:28) and Luke (22:30) about the Twelve sitting on thrones to rule over the tribes point to the same restoration, which according to Matthew will take place at the "*renewal of all things* [*palingenesia*], when the Son of Man is seated on the throne of his glory." Thus Wenell, in *Jesus and Land*, asserts that "the action of calling twelve disciples evokes a new spatial vision which includes the land. And yet, we have not seen a particular focus on the boundaries of sacred space for Jesus, either through a positive interest in the temple, or by an emphasis on ritual purity. What is the significance of the Twelve for the theme of the land?"[102] Wenell is right in recognizing that the appointment of the Twelve evokes the land. As Ezekiel looked forward to the day of the LORD, he spoke of a reallotment of the land to the twelve tribes (45:8; 47:13).[103] Thus there is a placial resonance to the gathering of the Twelve as the nucleus of the new Israel. But what realm is in mind?

From diverse parts of the Gospels it is clear that Jesus envisages the new Israel as extending way beyond ethnic Israel. In Matthew 8:10–13, for example,

98. See Greenman, "John R. W. Stott," 266–73. N. T. Wright notes that "we have seen that Jesus was challenging Israel to be Israel; that is, to be the light of the world, the salt of the earth. He was, that is, criticizing his contemporaries for being more concerned for victory over the gentile world than for bringing YHWH's healing and salvation to it" (*Jesus and the Victory of God*, 308).

99. Bruner, *The Christbook: Matthew 1–12*, 304. Emphasis original.

100. See Trilling, *Das wahre Israel*, 134, for the argument that the petition for God's kingdom to come involves asking for "the gradual penetration on earth" of the kingdom.

101. Bruner, *The Christbook: Matthew 1–12*, 301.

102. Wenell, *Jesus and Land*, 106.

103. Wilken, *Land Called Holy*, 13.

he speaks of many coming from east and west to eat with Abraham and Isaac and Jacob in the kingdom. N. T. Wright is therefore correct, contra Wenell, in noting that Jesus's redefined family "was in principle open to all, beyond the borders of Israel. Land and family were simultaneously rethought in the promise that the eschatological blessing would reach beyond the traditional confines."[104] Jesus "had not come to rehabilitate the symbol of the holy land, but to subsume it within a different fulfillment of the kingdom, which would embrace the whole creation."[105]

But what of the image of the Twelve ruling on their thrones and (in Matthew) of the renewal of all things? *Palingenesia* is used once by Josephus to refer to the recovery of the land of Israel,[106] and the word also has a Hellenistic background; in Philo it is used to refer to the soul's journey toward immortality.[107] As we noted earlier, according to W. D. Davies, for Luke, verse 30 of chapter 22 is symbolic—the disciples are to rule with Jesus "in a new kind of kingdom—in another dimension of existence."[108] Matthew 19:28, however, speaks of "the new world" (*palingenesia*). Davies thinks that this saying may be authentically from Jesus but argues that it does not refer to the land of Israel but "evokes a cosmic renewal, so that in 19:28 also probably the restoration of the twelve tribes is understood not so much in terms of a restored land of Israel as of a renewed cosmos."[109]

How we understand "my kingdom" in Luke 22:30 will depend on how we understand *kingdom* in Luke as a whole, and as we have argued above, in its Jewish context *kingdom* never refers to a new kind of kingdom in another realm of existence. Yet Davies's interpretation of Matthew 19:28 is preferred by most scholars, both for Matthew 19:28 and as the key to Luke 22:30. Matthew's use of "Son of Man," Jesus's preferred self-designation, can help us respond to this interpretation. The main background to this somewhat enigmatic title is Daniel 7:12–14. Verse 14 states,

> To him was given dominion
>   and glory and kingship,
> that all peoples, nations, and languages
>   should serve him.
> His dominion is an everlasting dominion
>   that shall not pass away,
> and his kingship is one
>   that shall never be destroyed.

104. N. T. Wright, *Jesus and the Victory of God*, 431.
105. Ibid., 446.
106. Josephus, *Jewish Antiquities* 11.66.
107. Burnett, "Philo on Immortality."
108. W. D. Davies, *Gospel and the Land*, 363.
109. Ibid., 365.

Thus the description of the Son of Man and of the Twelve on their thrones refers to the final consummation of the kingdom. Among the various interpretations of this promise, Bruner's captures its essence:

> Jesus' phrase points simply and soberly . . . to a wonderful vindication of God's flock at the end of the age . . . as well as a splendid vindication of creation in its magnificent totality. Then, along with a thrilling transformation of Israel and of the whole world, breathtaking responsibilities will be given to God's people, a teaching corroborated often in Jesus' eschatological teaching. . . . The future holds exciting responsibilities for those who live their discipleships responsibly now.[110]

Palingenesia in this context must therefore be understood to refer to the end-time renewal of all things: "The word also means that not only *individual souls* but, indeed, the *whole cosmic order*—creation, the world, and all their structures and components—will be renewed, reestablished, and finally, put in good working order again. Jesus's future teaching does not depict 'heaven'; it depicts a new heaven *and a new earth!* ('The meek shall inherit *the earth*,' 5:5)."[111]

New creation motifs also develop in the Gospels' treatment of the temple, a major institution and symbol of Israel. In Luke 2:49 Jesus describes it as "my Father's house," but on the whole his attitude toward the temple is decidedly negative. We have already noted his controversial claim to be able to forgive *wherever* he chose to.[112] In the context of his lament over Jerusalem in Matthew 23:37–39, Jesus tells his disciples that the temple will be destroyed (24:1–2; cf. Luke 19:39–44). In his ministry Jesus was inviting his hearers to participate in the establishment of the true temple; the temple in Jerusalem was under judgment, historically a judgment which would fall before too long. The cleansing of the temple should be understood in this context; it is an "acted parable of judgment, of destruction."[113] "In that temple, in which all the privileges and pretensions of the religion they [the Jewish leaders] represented were concentrated, Jesus set himself as the Son of the Father with full power and authority over his house. And there he pronounced a devastating judgment over the havoc that the people had wreaked there."[114]

The identification of Jesus and his kingdom with the true temple is clear from the sayings in Mark 14:58, Matthew 26:61, and John 2:19. The temple will be destroyed, but in three days Jesus will raise it up. The glory of the indwelling of God in Jesus creates the new temple; this, according to John,

110. Bruner, *The Churchbook: Matthew 13–28*, 312.
111. Ibid. Emphasis original.
112. Beale makes the same point (*Temple and the Church's Mission*, 177). It was this that led Jesus's opponents to accuse him of blasphemy. On the temple in the Gospels see ibid., 169–200.
113. N. T. Wright, *Jesus and the Victory of God*, 334. See also 413–28.
114. H. Ridderbos, *Gospel of John*, 120.

was manifest in his earthly life but was only understood by the disciples after his resurrection (John 2:22). In Matthew 27:40 those who mock Jesus on the cross shout to him, "You who would destroy the temple and build it in three days, save yourself!" Ironically, when Jesus breathes his last (Matt. 27:50), the curtain of the temple is torn from top to bottom. The embroidery on the curtain was of the starry heavens, so that the tearing of the curtain is a sign of the new openness of heaven.[115] This eschatological dimension is confirmed by the earthquake, the splitting of rocks, and the remarkable opening of tombs and the resultant rising of many saints (Matt. 27:51–54).

C. Meyers shows how Jesus's identification of himself as the true temple points to a new creation: "The symbolic nature of the Jerusalem temple . . . depended upon a series of features that, taken together, established the sacred precinct as being located at the cosmic center of the universe, as the place where heaven and earth converge and thus from where God's control over the universe is effected."[116] Significantly, only the high priest could pass through the veil, and that only once a year; but now the curtain is rent asunder, because the risen Holy One is present and available to all. Thus, like the Jerusalem temple, the true temple has a place, but now it is the entire creation.

Jesus communicates a similar message through his parables, which were a major component of his teaching. These are miniature stories which evoke the story of Israel and show how it is being fulfilled.[117] The parables are speech acts, as N. T. Wright points out; they inaugurate the kingdom by inviting hearers to enter it and make its story their own.[118] He offers the parable of the sower as his main example, explaining that Isaiah 55:10–13 is a key background. Verses 10–11 closely link the utterance and fulfillment of God's word to his creative activity, and that fulfillment is the celebration of the creation (vv. 12–13). Thus the parable clearly bespeaks the power of the word and "the Word's own ability to bring the kingdom into the world."[119]

Scholars debate whether or not Jesus intended to found a church. However, as G. Lohfink notes, he did not, because there already was one, namely Israel.[120] Jesus reformed Israel by calling the Twelve and by calling numerous followers who were to remain in their villages and practice the life of the kingdom *there*. In Jesus's day the household defined one's identity.[121] It is significant, then, as Moxnes points out, that Jesus left his home in Nazareth and began an itiner-

---

115. Beale, *Temple and the Church's Mission*, 189.

116. Meyers, "Temple, Jerusalem," 359.

117. J. Michaels notes that "together with the Old Testament background, Jesus's parables define for us the kingdom he proclaimed and bring it to life. They flesh out the skeletal framework and impart to it color and depth" (*Servant and Son*, 85).

118. N. T. Wright, *Jesus and the Victory of God*, 229.

119. Bruner, *The Churchbook: Matthew 13–28*, 3. See Luz, *Matthäus 8–17*, 298–305, for the variety of interpretations of this parable.

120. G. Lohfink, *Jesus and Community*.

121. Moxnes, *Putting Jesus in His Place*, 43.

ant ministry; and Jesus himself observes that whereas foxes have holes and the birds of the air nests, the Son of Man has nowhere to lay his head (Matt. 8:20; Luke 9:58). In opposition to the skewed implacement of Israel, Jesus's ministry involves challenging, personal displacement. His rejection in his home village of Nazareth (Mark 6:1–4) must have been terribly painful, but his retort that "prophets are not without honor, except in their hometown, and among their own kin, and in their own house"—note the thick placial terms—alerts us to his sense of a new implacement, namely as that of a prophet of the kingdom.[122]

In the social context of his day Jesus's remarks to the crowds around him when his mother and brothers came to see him, namely, "Here are my mother and my brothers! Whoever does the will of God is my brother and sister and mother,"[123] would have been truly shocking. "He confronts the household of origin: those who do the will of God are his household. . . . He establishes a new household. Jesus is placed in a house, and this house becomes a center for Jesus in his wanderings. Moreover 'house' becomes an important architectural metaphor in Mark for the new community in conflict with other 'houses,' the synagogues and the temple."[124]

The kingdom evokes a vision for imagining place differently.[125] Thus the parable of the mustard seed becoming the "greatest of all shrubs . . . so that the birds of the air can make nests in its shade" imaginatively juxtaposes the sowing of a small seed with the emergence of a world tree symbolizing the nations of the earth.[126] Bauckham rightly notes of this parable:

> Here it is the spatial aspect that is stressed, in the contrast between the smallest of all seeds and the greatest of all shrubs into which it grows. The sizeable shrub is so described as to evoke the image of the mythological world tree, which overshadows the whole world with its branches. In Daniel (4:10–12) and Ezekiel (17:22–23) this was already an image of God's universal kingdom, the birds in its branches representing the nations that enjoy the blessings of God's rule.[127]

Moxnes argues that the household is the central image that informs Jesus's explication of the kingdom and that in this respect the kingdom was countercultural. Jews spoke much about God as king but said little about kingdom

---

122. Moxnes notes that Jesus, "by presenting himself as a prophet, had rejected the order and structure of that place. . . . Jesus breaks out of the mold and will not be limited by the place defined by his lineage and household. . . . By refusing to give him honor, the village has also removed him from their place" (ibid., 53). Cf. N. T. Wright, *Jesus and the Victory of God*, 145–474.
123. Mark 3:31–35; see also Matt. 12:46–50; Luke 8:19–21.
124. Moxnes, *Putting Jesus in His Place*, 61.
125. Ibid., 109.
126. See ibid., 111–13.
127. Bauckham, *Bible and Mission*, 17–18. Bauckham also argues that the parabolic story of the miraculous catch of fish (Luke 5:1–11 and John 21:2–11) suggests the incorporation of all nations in the church (ibid., 18–19).

or about God as Father. Thus Jesus's exhortation to seek first the kingdom in Matthew 6:25–33 takes its images from nature (God is the creator and sustainer) and from the household (God is our Father).

> There can be no doubt that the kingdom of God was the driving force in Jesus' life, and that this spatial metaphor was, so to speak, the central code for Jesus in his activity. . . . Jesus speaks of the kingdom of God not in imperial pictures, but with images from households, with God as a housefather. But this is not a way to "scale down" the ambitions of Jesus' proclamation of the kingdom. It is to make the place of the household, with generalized reciprocity as the form of householding, to be the model for politics. It represents a turning away from domination and control of place, as typical of politics over a place, into appropriation and use of place.[128]

Jesus's new household clearly has particular as well as creation-wide connotations. In Mark 10:28–31 those who follow Jesus are promised houses, families, and fields, plus persecutions, *in this age*. The creation-wide dimension is apparent in the link of the new community to the new covenant. The word *covenant* is used sparingly in the Gospels, but its imagery is pervasive; indeed kingdom is but the opposite side of the coin to covenant. However, it is in the Last Supper that the word *covenant* itself is found. The saying about the cup of the new covenant is found in all the Synoptics (Mark 14:24; Matt. 26:28; Luke 22:20). As Tan observes, this saying connects Jesus with the Zion traditions of the Old Testament.[129] However, as I have argued elsewhere,[130] covenant also roots us back into creation, so that the Lord's Supper must be read with creational overtones. S. Hahn rightly notes that "the covenant represents the formal structure of divine revelation, that is, the redemption of all creation by Christ in the New Covenant."[131]

In Jesus's teaching on *judgment*, a theme far more pervasive than is popularly recognized, we encounter some texts that appear to argue against new creation as the goal of the kingdom. One such text is the "little apocalypse" of Mark 13 with its parallels in Matthew 24 and Luke 21. According to Mark 13, Jesus, when emerging from the temple with his disciples, prophesied the destruction of the temple. Later, when he is sitting on the Mount of Olives looking across at the temple, the disciples ask what will be the sign of all these things being accomplished. The so-called little apocalypse follows, with its language of wars and earthquakes, persecutions and betrayal, the setting up of the desolating sacrifice in the temple, the darkening of sun and moon, and then the Son of Man coming in the clouds.

---

128. Moxnes, *Putting Jesus in His Place*, 157.
129. Tan, *Zion Traditions and the Aims of Jesus*, 217–18.
130. Bartholomew, "Covenant and Creation."
131. Hahn, "Kinship by Covenant," 656.

Albert Schweitzer has influenced many in arguing from this story that the early Christians, including Jesus, expected the imminent destruction of the physical world, but that they were of course mistaken in this belief. Evangelicals, on the other hand, have seen the references to the Son of Man coming in the clouds as a reference to the second coming, and some have seen the dissolution of the cosmic structure as an indication that this world will be destroyed.

N. T. Wright argues persuasively that the whole of Mark 13 deals with the destruction of the temple, and that a proper understanding of Jewish apocalyptic leads us in the right direction. The focus throughout is on the coming destruction of Jerusalem and the temple in particular—which took place in AD 70—and the apocalyptic language invests this judgment with its theological significance and Jesus's vindication, as the one who is setting up the new temple.[132] The apocalyptic language of Jesus, then, in line with that of the Old Testament and of intertestamental Judaism, "has nothing to do with the world itself coming to an end. This makes no sense either of the basic Jewish worldview or of the texts in which the Jewish hope is expressed. It was after all the Stoics, not the first-century Jews, who characteristically believed that the world would be dissolved in fire."[133] Similarly, W. L. Lane says of Mark 13:24–25 that "no other section of the eschatological discourse is more indebted to scriptural imagery and language. . . . In the prophets and later Jewish apocalyptic writings the dissolution of the cosmic structure frequently orchestrates the intervention of God *in history*."[134]

Crucifixion

Much of the Gospel material is concerned with Jesus's passion, about which the central question is "Why did he die?" This question can be answered on at least three levels. He died, firstly, because he was crucified as a rebel against Rome;[135] secondly, because of the charge made by the Jewish leaders against him;[136] thirdly and most significantly, because he saw it as his vocation to do so. We have already noted Jesus's reference to "the blood of the covenant" at the Last Supper. This implies that he saw his death as effecting the renewal of the covenant. This reference also alerts us to the fundamental significance of the Old Testament in understanding Jesus's death. Daniel (especially chap. 7), Zechariah (especially chaps. 9–14), the Psalms, and especially Isaiah 40–55 are the central background for understanding Jesus's death. By taking on

132. For the details of N. T. Wright's case see *Jesus and the Victory of God*, 339–65.

133. N. T. Wright, *The New Testament and the People of God*, 285. On apocalyptic see ibid., 280–99.

134. W. L. Lane, *Gospel of Mark*, 474–75. Emphasis added.

135. As N. T. Wright points out, crucifixion "insisted, coldly and brutally, on the absolute sovereignty of Rome, and of Caesar" (*Jesus and the Victory of God*, 543).

136. Chilton suggests that what Judas betrayed to the Jews was Jesus's scandalous counter-temple celebration of his own supper as a new alternative (*Temple of Jesus*, 151).

himself the wrath of Rome, the Jews, and God, Jesus believed that "he himself would be vindicated . . . and Israel's destiny, to save the world, would thereby be accomplished."[137]

Resurrection

All the Gospels narrate the story of the empty tomb. N. T. Wright articulates two major meanings of the resurrection. Firstly, Jesus's resurrection indicated that the eschaton had indeed arrived. Israel's God had acted definitively in defeating evil and death. Secondly, by its demonstration that Jesus is the Son of God, the resurrection resulted in the Christians launching

> a claim on the world: a claim at once absurd . . . and very serious, so serious that within a couple of generations the might of Rome was trying, and failing, to stamp it out. It grew from an essentially positive view of the world, of creation. It refused to relinquish the world to the principalities and powers, but claimed even them for allegiance to the Messiah who was now the lord, the *kyrios*. . . . The early Christians saw Jesus' resurrection as the action of the creator god to reaffirm the essential goodness of creation and, in an initial and representative act of new creation, to establish a bridgehead within the present world of space, time and matter . . . through which the whole new creation could now come to birth. . . . The resurrection, in the full Jewish and early Christian sense, is the ultimate affirmation that creation matters, that embodied human beings matter.[138]

The Great Commission

In Matthew 28:18 Jesus tells his disciples, "All authority on heaven and on earth has been given to me." N. T. Wright perceptively notes that this is an answer to the Lord's Prayer; the wording is almost identical to the kingdom clause in Matthew's version of the Prayer.[139] As Chris Wright notes,

> The whole earth, then, belongs to Jesus. It belongs to him by right of creation, by right of redemption and by right of future inheritance—as Paul affirms in the magnificent cosmic declaration of Colossians 1:15–20. So wherever we go in his name, we are walking on his property. There is not an inch of the planet that does not belong to Christ. Mission then is an authorized activity carried out by tenants on the instructions of the owner of the property.[140]

Beale discerns the background to Matthew's Great Commission in Daniel 7; Genesis 18:18; 22:18; and 2 Chronicles 36:23. He suggests that Matthew

---

137. N. T. Wright, *Jesus and the Victory of God*, 610. On the whole issue of Jesus's death see ibid., 540–611.
138. N. T. Wright, *Resurrection of the Son of God*, 729–30.
139. Ibid., 643.
140. C. J. H. Wright, *Mission of God*, 403–4.

shapes his Gospel to reflect the beginning and ending of Chronicles, but with Jesus as the goal of the genealogy. The temple is a major theme in Chronicles, and Beale sees Jesus here depicted as the new temple and thus the new creation. "The New Testament pictures Christ and the church as finally having done what Adam, Noah, and Israel has [sic] failed to do in extending the temple of God's presence throughout the world."[141] "If the temple construction of 2 Chronicles is in mind, then this is an implicit commission for the disciples to fulfill the Genesis 1:26–28 mandate by rebuilding the new temple, composed of worshippers throughout the earth."[142]

Conclusion

S. Caldecott says that in the Gospels "words shift their meanings: indeed often new meanings for words are forged in the heat of the Gospel paradox itself, and the very light that shines from this 'furnace of meaning' reveals a deeper level of reality."[143] Our examination of the Gospels reveals that they are a furnace of meaning that does indeed shed light on the deeper level of reality embodied by place.

We conclude this chapter with a story from the Gospels that thus far has not caught our attention, namely that of Peter's denial of Jesus after his arrest. In his extraordinary *Mimesis: The Representation of Reality in Western Literature*, E. Auerbach focuses on this story to articulate the unique achievement of the Gospels among ancient literature. This story, says Auerbach,

> portrays something which neither the poets nor the historians of antiquity ever set out to portray: the birth of a spiritual movement in the depths of the common people, from within the everyday occurrences of contemporary life, which thus assumes an importance it could never have assumed in antique literature. What we witness is the awakening of "a new heart and a new spirit." All this applies . . . to every other occurrence which is related in the New Testament.[144]

Auerbach argues that in the story of Peter's denial, and in the New Testament as a whole, we see a world which is real, "identifiable as to place, time, and circumstances, but which on the other hand is shaken in its very foundations, is transforming and renewing itself before our eyes. . . . For the New Testament authors . . . these occurrences on the plane of everyday life assume the importance of world-revolutionary events, as later on they will be for everyone."[145]

141. Beale, *The Temple and the Church's Mission*, 169.
142. Ibid., 177.
143. Caldecott, "Zeal in Detachment," 228.
144. Auerbach, *Mimesis*, 42–43.
145. Ibid., 43.

I am not competent to assess Auerbach's comparison of the Gospels with ancient literature, but his insight into the furnace of the Gospels and how they shed new light on ordinary life caught up in world-transformation is most perceptive, and not least in regard to place. For, as this chapter shows, while the Jesus event is rooted in very particular places, its significance is creation-wide. The arrival of Jesus means the kingdom has come and is still to come. As the promises to Abraham always anticipated, through the son of Abraham blessing would come to all nations, thereby removing the effect of the curse upon the creation. *The kingdom of God* clearly refers not just to reign but also to realm, and the realm in view is nothing less than the creation as a whole.

What Auerbach recognizes, which is crucial for a theology of place, is that the universal perspective of the kingdom is precisely what gives poignance and density to the local and the particular. Bauckham notes that for mission, and I would say for a theology of place, we need a hermeneutic of the kingdom which does justice to its particularity and universality.[146] Such a hermeneutic will take account of

1. the temporal movement of the biblical story from creation through fall to redemption and consummation;
2. the placial movement of the biblical story from "one place to every place, from the center to the periphery, from Jerusalem to the ends of the earth."[147]

Just as the presence of the Holy One among the Israelites was to permeate every aspect of their lives, so now this is how it is to be throughout the creation, as groups of followers live the life of the kingdom in their particular places.

> And did those feet in ancient time
> Walk upon England's mountains green?
> And was the holy Lamb of God
> On England's pleasant pastures seen?
>
> And did the Countenance Divine
> Shine forth upon our clouded hills?
> And was Jerusalem builded here,
> Among these dark Satanic Mills?
>
> . . . .
> I will not cease from Mental Fight,
> Nor shall my Sword sleep in my hand,
> Till we have built Jerusalem
> In England's green and pleasant Land.
>
> William Blake, "Jerusalem"

146. Bauckham, *Bible and Mission*, 1–26.
147. Ibid., 14. Bauckham adds a third dimension, noting that movement in time and place is also a movement of people, so that human sociality is a crucial component (ibid., 15).

7

Place in Paul

Paul's letters are the earliest extant Christian documents. It is generally recognized that 1 Thessalonians is Paul's first letter, and if the Pastoral Epistles were written by Paul,[1] then 2 Timothy was his final letter, written around AD 64–67. His letters were written in a fifteen- or seventeen-year period between AD 49 and AD 64/67. It might be thought, therefore, that we should first examine Paul's view of place before that of the Gospels. However, for all his distinctiveness, Paul is a follower of Jesus rather than the founder of Christianity,[2] and for theological interpretation, it makes sense to follow the canonical shape of the New Testament in our exploration.

W. D. Davies, with whom we began our exploration of place in the Gospels, makes a useful starting point for our examination of place in Paul. Davies played a major, largely positive role in redirecting Pauline studies to the Jewish background of Paul.[3] As a Jew and a Pharisee, "Paul, we can be sure, would have *felt* the full force of the doctrine of the land, Jerusalem, and the temple."[4] According to Davies, Paul reinterpreted his Jewish background, not least in respect of land. Thus in relation to the promise to Abraham, which for Jews of Paul's day was inseparable from national Israel, "for Paul the promise did

---

1. For a useful discussion concluding that they are indeed Pauline see Knight, *Pastoral Epistles*, 21–52.
2. See in particular D. Wenham, *Paul: Follower of Jesus or Founder of Christianity?*
3. See in particular W. D. Davies, *Jewish and Pauline Studies*.
4. W. D. Davies, *Gospel and the Land*, 166.

not so much confirm status as require faith."[5] The aim of Paul's mission was to build the body of Christ:

> To build the body of Christ in places mean and not mean, among Jews first and, when they rejected his message, among the Greeks—this was his aim, to create a body wherein was neither Jew nor Greek, bond nor free, male nor female "in Christ." What is noteworthy is that that body knew no geographic limitation or even concentration: Pauline ecclesiology is *a-territorial*.[6]

Davies concludes his analysis of Paul and the land, which is significantly more nuanced than this brief summary, as follows:

> For Paul, the Lord and the Spirit were almost exchangeable. And once Paul has made the Living Lord rather than the Torah the center in life and in death, once he had seen in Jesus his Torah, he had in principle broken with the land. "In Christ" Paul was free from the Law and, therefore, from the land. . . . Theologically he had no longer any need of it: his geographical identity was subordinated to that of being "in Christ," in whom was neither Jew nor Greek.[7]

Davies's emphasis on Paul's concern to build the body of Christ in "places mean and not mean" is helpful, but his emphasis on Paul's ecclesiology as *a-territorial* is not. It is not hard to see at work here Davies's unhelpful dichotomy between Land and Person, as if Paul, like the Gospels, shifts the focus from the Jewish centrality of the land or Torah to the centrality of a person, Jesus. However, in order to examine just what is going on in Paul's theology with respect to place, we will need to examine the shape of his theology, and then see where place fits into it.

Pauline Studies Today[8]

As with Jesus, studies of Paul in the twentieth century go back to Schweitzer as the determinative figure.[9] In his *Geschichte der Paulinischen Forschung*,[10] published in 1912, Schweitzer poses two questions: Is Paul a Jewish or a Greek thinker? And, What is the center of Paul's theology? To the first, Schweitzer responds adamantly: "Paulinism and Hellenism have in common their religious terminology, but in respect of ideas, nothing. The Apostle did not Hellenise

5. Ibid., 178.
6. Ibid., 182. Emphasis added.
7. Ibid., 220.
8. For a useful assessment of Pauline studies see Neill and Wright, *Interpretation of the New Testament, 1861–1986*, 403–30. For a good introduction to Paul see Thiselton, *The Living Paul*.
9. Schweitzer, *Paul and His Interpreters*.
10. Literally "History of Pauline Research."

Christianity."[11] Paul's teaching is rather to be regarded as a primitive Christianity which shared Jewish eschatological expectations or Jewish apocalyptic. To the second question Schweitzer answered that justification was not, as many thought, the center of Paul's thought; that doctrine, rather, was a polemical argument related to the admission of uncircumcised gentiles into the church. The center, Schweitzer said, is to be found in what he called "Christ mysticism," by which he referred to Paul's concept of "being in Christ," a doctrine which he understood sacramentally and against the background of apocalyptic Judaism.

To W. D. Davies, on the other hand, Paul was a Jewish rabbi who believed that Jesus was the Jewish Messiah, and he derives point after Pauline point from rabbinic sources. Käsemann agreed with Schweitzer that the background to Paul was to be found in apocalyptic Judaism; by recognizing that Paul developed a critique of Judaism from the inside, Käsemann contributed significantly to Pauline studies.[12]

E. Sanders's *Paul and Palestinian Judaism* (1977) ushered in a veritable revolution in Pauline studies. Against a broader canvas of the Palestinian Judaism of Paul's day than that of Davies, Sanders argued that first-century Judaism was not a religion of legalistic works righteousness, as Protestantism thought. Rather, it espoused what Sanders calls "covenantal nomism"; keeping the law is always a response to God's grace in bringing his people into covenant relationship with himself. Paul's only substantial critique of Judaism was that it was insufficient; more was required. The center of Paul's thought was "participation," a reference to Paul's doctrine of "being in Christ."[13] Today almost all scholars regard Paul as a very Jewish thinker, although there is no agreement on the center of his theology.

The Contours of Paul's Thought

There is no debate about Romans being written by Paul, and it remains a very useful entry point into Paul's theology. There is much debate about the center of Romans, but for a long time it has seemed clear to me that the center of Romans, and indeed of Paul's theology as a whole, is demarcated in 1:1–6.[14] The center of Romans and of Paul's theology is "the gospel of God" (1:1). As we noted in the previous chapter, *euangelion* has a double background, namely Isaiah and the Greco-Roman context in which *euangelion* was a technical

11. Ibid., 238.

12. W. D. Davies, *Jewish and Pauline Studies*; Käsemann, *Perspectives on Paul*.

13. Sanders, *Paul and Palestinian Judaism*.

14. N. T. Wright correctly asserts, "This short passage, which has often been allowed to fall off the front of the letter, is in fact intended as every bit as much a thematic introduction as 1.16–17" (*Resurrection of the Son of God*), 242.

term for the announcement of the birth or enthronement of an emperor or of a great victory. These meanings are complementary and should not be set against each other: "The Isaianic message always was about the enthronement of YHWH and the dethronement of pagan gods; about the victory of Israel and the fall of Babylon; about the arrival of the Servant King and the consequent coming of justice and peace. . . . As far as first-century Jews were concerned, the 'secular' claims of the imperial cult were in fact profoundly 'religious.'"[15] *Euangelion* is thus an inherently eschatological term. It is the "gospel *of God.*" "God" is Israel's God, the God of the Old Testament as he is rendered in that corpus of literature. "God" alerts us to the fact that it is the one true God, the creator Elohim and the redeemer Yahweh, who has acted in Jesus of Nazareth to bring his purposes to fruition.

In verses 2–5 Paul unpacks the central content of this *euangelion.* The gospel was promised beforehand through God's prophets in the Old Testament (v. 2). Paul refers to the Old Testament by the term "prophets" rather than "the law and the prophets" (cf. 3:21) in order to evoke the notion of promise and fulfillment.[16] The gospel concerns God's Son, who was the son of David (v. 3). Jesus's Davidic lineage plus the reference to "Jesus *Christ*" in verse 1 alerts us unequivocally to the messiahship of Jesus.[17] Davidic sonship is a common quality of the Messiah in the Old Testament as well as in Jewish sources, not least the Qumran manuscript.[18] Thus *euangelion* for Paul means that the messianic promises of salvation have come true in Jesus. The primary referent of "Christ" (= anointed one, = Messiah) in first-century Judaism was the coming king. For Paul the one God has revealed himself definitively in Jesus, the true king, the true son of David. This royal theology is further evoked in verse 4 in the phrase "Jesus Christ our Lord." *Kyrios,* which is Paul's favorite designation for Jesus, also has a double background; in the LXX it is used to translate "Yahweh" some five thousand times, but it also has a first-century Greco-Roman background in the acknowledgment that Caesar is *kyrios.* Thus for Paul, the gospel is the announcement of the story of Jesus, who is heir and king of and over all.

Central to the *euangelion* is the resurrection: it was through the resurrection from the dead that Jesus was declared to be the Son of God with power. As a Jew and a Pharisee,[19] Paul understood resurrection to mean *bodily* resurrec-

15. N. T. Wright, *What Saint Paul Really Said,* 44.

16. Dunn, *Romans 1–8,* 10–11.

17. Cranfield argues that the correct word order is likely "Christ Jesus" (*Romans,* 1:51). That Paul often puts "Christ" before "Jesus" supports the view that he understood "Christ" not just as a proper name but as a title.

18. Cf. Cranfield, *Romans,* 1:58–59.

19. The Sadducees denied the resurrection from the dead, unlike the Pharisees. On the views of the Pharisees see N. T. Wright, *Resurrection of the Son of God,* 190–200. On the Sadducees and resurrection see ibid., 131–40.

tion; hence "from the dead." Resurrection comes into focus only late in the Old Testament, where hope generally remains focused on God's faithfulness to his creation and his covenant. In Isaiah, and Daniel in particular, we find the belief that God's faithfulness would include even bodily life beyond death for his faithful ones: "The biblical language of resurrection . . . when it emerges, is simple and direct; the belief, though infrequent, is clear. It involves, not a *reconstrual* of life after death, but the *reversal* of death itself. . . . It is a way of saying that a time will come when sleepers will sleep no more. Creation itself, celebrated throughout the Hebrew scriptures, will be reaffirmed, remade."[20]

In Second Temple Judaism resurrection possessed two basic meanings:[21] firstly it was a metaphor for the restoration of Israel, and secondly it referred literally to the reembodiment of human bodies. It was "about *the restoration of Israel* on the one hand and *the newly embodied life of all YHWH's people* on the other . . . and that it was thought of as the great event that YHWH would accomplish at the very end of 'the present age,' the event which would constitute the 'age to come.'"[22]

In verse 3 and verse 4 Jesus is described as "God's Son." Although this description has ontological implications,[23] it primarily refers to Jesus as the son of David, the Messiah.[24] But why is it that the resurrection declared Jesus to be the Son of God with power according to the Spirit (v. 4)? The answer is that in Second Temple Judaism it never entered the mind of anyone that the Messiah would die a shameful death as a criminal, let alone be raised from the dead:[25] "The resurrection of the person who had done and said these things, and who had been put to death as a messianic pretender, said it all. Israel's God, the creator, had reversed the verdict of the court, in reversing the death sentence it carried out. Jesus really was the king of the Jews; and, if he was the Messiah, he really was the lord of the world, as the psalms had long ago insisted."[26]

The resurrection thus affirms the centrality of the cross in the gospel. The cross is implied but not mentioned here, but it is central to Paul's theology as the means by which God asserts his control, his power over the entire

---

20. Ibid., 127–28. Emphasis original.

21. For the details of Second Temple views see ibid., 129–206.

22. Ibid., 205. Emphasis original.

23. Cranfield, *Romans*, 1:58, asserts that "the designation 'Son of God' expresses nothing less than a relationship to God which is 'personal, ethical and inherent,' involving a real community of nature between Christ and God."

24. N. T. Wright, "Romans," 416–19. Wright correctly notes that "Paul builds in other meanings to this phrase in, e.g. 5.10 and 8.3; but these, though rich and dense, have not left behind the home base of 'Messiah,' which is indicated here not least by the reference to David and by the 'royal' overtones of his worldwide rule in 1.5" (*Resurrection of the Son of God*, 242n74).

25. Meyer asks, "Where in the orthodoxy of the Torah was there room for a crucified Christ?" He answers, "Nowhere" (*The Early Christians*, 162).

26. N. T. Wright, *Resurrection of the Son of God*, 244.

creation: "Contrary to what casual onlookers might have thought, when Jesus was crucified it was he who was leading the principalities and powers in his triumphal procession, celebrating his victory over them, instead of the other way around (Colossians 2:14–15)."[27]

"According to the spirit of holiness" has occasioned much debate. It is best understood as referring to the Holy Spirit as the agent of the resurrection. The Old Testament clearly documents the role of the Spirit in the consummation of the ages, as the agent of new creation. Thus Michel is correct in characterizing Jesus's resurrection as an eschatological event, the start of the new creation.[28] That the Spirit is "the Spirit of holiness" reminds us that the eschatological role of the Spirit is to cleanse the creation of sin and death.[29]

The significance of the gospel for the whole creation is further indicated by the reference to Jesus as Lord, as well as by the resulting apostleship "to bring about the obedience of faith among all the Gentiles for the sake of his name" (1:5). The genitive in the "obedience of faith" probably implies both the response of faith to the message of the gospel and the obedience issuing from such faith.[30] However, in this context it seems to me that the latter meaning is primary. This becomes apparent once one unpacks obedience in its eschatological context:

> The one who is obedient is the eschatological counterpart of the one who out of disobedience surrendered his creatureliness. He is hence the beginning of the new world, the manifestation of that freedom of the children of God for which earth cries out from its self-imprisonment—cries out without clearly understanding the meaning of its cry. Obedience is the sign of regained creatureliness; it is man's condition before the face of God in that it is simultaneously his condition when he ceases to reach out beyond himself.[31]

The "obedience of faith" has in view the restoration of the whole of human life. H. Ridderbos calls this "totalitarian character of the new obedience . . . the most essential and characteristic feature" of Paul's theology.[32]

An important clue to just what "obedience" involves for Paul is given in his description of himself as a *doulos Christou*, a slave of Christ. The background here is that of the Old Testament rather than Hellenism, and in the LXX the

---

27. N. T. Wright, *What Saint Paul Really Said*, 47.

28. Michel, *Brief an die Römer*, 38.

29. According to Käsemann, Paul's unusual expression *pneuma hagiōsynē* meant "not moral holiness (Kuss) but originally cultic, and then (as often) holiness transposed into the eschatological sphere . . . which finally overcomes what is profane and secular and opens access to God" (*Commentary on Romans*, 11).

30. Dunn, *Romans 1–8*, 17; H. Ridderbos, *Paul and Jesus*, 237. On the latter meaning cf. 2 Cor. 7:15.

31. Käsemann, *Perspectives on Paul*, 41.

32. H. Ridderbos, *Paul: An Outline*, 265.

verbal form of *doulos* "is in fact the commonest expression for the service of God in the sense of total allegiance and not just isolated acts of worship."[33] Of course, what is radical here is that the obedience the Old Testament understood as rightly owed to Yahweh is here directed to Jesus. This alerts us that for all his Jewishness, Paul has come to understand the biblical story and its fulfillment in a very different way from that of his contemporaries. As several scholars have pointed out, the only adequate explanation for this is Paul's conversion experience.[34] Paul's encounter with the risen Jesus[35] convinced him that the end time had broken in to the present age in Jesus and that the final consummation was inevitable. Paul's mission theology, although it never forsakes its basic Jewish framework, is "an analysis of reality triggered by an initial experience that gave Paul a new world-view."[36] "This means that Paul's theology is not unifocal, but bi-focal; coming from God's past act in Christ it moves towards God's future act. Indeed, both events stand or fall together, and both converge on Christian life in the present: 'For as often as you eat this bread and drink the cup, you proclaim the Lord's death until he comes.'"[37] The implicit acknowledgment of Jesus's deity in 1:1 is made explicit by a comparison with Romans 12:1–2, where Paul argues that the only adequate response to the gospel is slavelike obedience to *God*.[38]

According to Paul, it is this sort of absolute obedience that faith facilitates which the church is called upon to bring about among all the nations! There is some debate about how to translate *ethnesin* in this verse, whether, with most scholars, as "gentiles" or as "nations." The plural "we" of verse 5a, and the universal dimensions in mind here, incline me toward the view that "nations" is the more appropriate translation. "All the nations" has clear eschatological overtones; it is the same phrase Paul uses in his quotation of Genesis 12:3 in Galatians 3:8, thus evoking the fulfillment of God's promise to Abraham of blessing for the nations. Significantly, Paul begins and ends Romans with a reference to this great task of bringing about the obedience of the nations (16:26; cf. 15:18). "His task was not merely to bring the nations to worship the right God and find salvation through faith in the gospel of Jesus Christ. He aimed at ethical transformation as well—a massive challenge in the degraded world of Greco-Roman culture, as his epistles bear witness."[39] "The ethical dimension of the task actually forms an envelope around the whole letter, as Paul twice gives it as his life's work to bring about 'obedience of faith among the nations.'"[40]

33. Cranfield, *Romans*, 1:50.
34. See, e.g., Bosch, *Transforming Mission*, 125–29.
35. See N. T. Wright, *Resurrection of the Son of God*, 375–98.
36. Senior and Stuhlmueller, *Biblical Foundations for Mission*, 171.
37. Bosch, *Transforming Mission*, 143.
38. See N. T. Wright, *Resurrection of the Son of God*, 263–64.
39. C. J. H. Wright, *Mission of God*, 526–27.
40. Ibid., 333.

As is clear from our discussion above, for Paul the gospel has creation-wide implications. In at least four Pauline texts this implicit dimension becomes explicit, namely Romans 8:18–25; Colossians 1:15–20; Ephesians 1:10; and Philippians 2:5–11.[41] In Romans 8, Paul speaks of the creation itself waiting with eager longing for its liberation. "It is a picture in which the corruption and futility of creation itself, created good but doomed to decay, is seen as a kind of slavery, so that creation too, needs to experience its exodus, its liberation."[42] This makes it quite clear that the sphere of redemption is creation-wide. Similarly, in Colossians 1:15–16, the Christ who is the head of the body, the church, is the one in whom, through whom, and for whom all things were created! The telos of the Jesus story enshrined in the marvelous christological hymn of Philippians 2 is that "at the name of Jesus every knee should bend, in heaven and *on earth* and under the earth, and every tongue confess that Jesus is Lord, to the glory of God the Father" (vv. 10–11; emphasis added). In the long, grammatically challenging sentence of Ephesians 1:3–14, Paul notes that the mystery of God's will has been revealed, and that that will is to "gather up all things in him [Christ], things in heaven and things on earth" (v. 10).

Of course this summary of Pauline theology through the grid of the few opening verses of Romans needs to be worked out in detail in relation to the whole Pauline corpus. In a chapter of this nature such a task is not possible, and the reader is referred to the sources in the footnotes for further substantiation of this approach. Suffice it to note that we are in full agreement with H. Ridderbos, in what remains a masterly exposition of Paul, when he asserts:

> The whole content of Paul's preaching can be summarized as the proclamation and explication of the eschatological day of salvation inaugurated with Christ's advent, death, and resurrection. It is from this principal point of view and under this denominator that all the separate themes of Paul's preaching can be understood and penetrated in their unity and relation to each other.[43]

For our exploration of place in Paul this conjunction of the eschatological, the universal, and the ethical is most important. As our discussion above makes clear, it is precisely Paul's eschatology that makes the particular and thus the ethical so significant. Few have picked up on the significance of the eschatological or apocalyptic for everyday life as has C. Beker. He notes rightly that the abandonment of apocalyptic in theologies of Paul's thought has a major impact on Christian thought. Among other things, it "produced a spiritualistic interpretation of the gospel. The message of the gospel came to focus almost exclusively on the topic of God and the individual soul—at least in the West—so that it had no relevant word to say about the relation of

---

41. This is a minimal list of major texts, but countless others come to mind.
42. N. T. Wright, *Resurrection of the Son of God*, 258.
43. H. Ridderbos, *Paul and Jesus*, 73.

the gospel to nature and to the structures of this world."[44] However, as Beker further observes, the cosmic implications of Paul's apocalyptic gospel "drive us out of our cultural ghettos—to the larger concerns of our interdependent and pluralistic world."[45] "And so both God's *past* act in Christ and his *future* act in the resurrection of the dead converge on Christian life in the present."[46] As Bosch observes,

> Paul perceives the church in a way that fundamentally modifies standard apocalyptic thinking. The church already belongs to the redeemed world; it is that segment of the world that is obedient to God. . . . As such, it strains itself in all its activities to prepare the world for its coming destiny. Precisely because of this the church is not preoccupied with self-preservation; it serves the world in the sure hope of the world's transformation at the time of God's final triumph. The small Pauline churches are so many "pockets" of an alternative lifestyle that penetrates the mores of society around them. . . . The life and work of the Christian community are intimately bound up with God's cosmic-historical plan for the redemption of the universe.[47]

A major obstacle to an eschatological/apocalyptic understanding of Paul's theology has been the view that he anticipated the imminent return of Christ, about which history has shown him to be quite wrong. The answer to this would appear to be that if we take Jesus's prophecy of the destruction of the temple seriously, and understand the language associated with it as typical of apocalyptic discourse, then this problem is defused. Many of the texts typically associated with the return of Christ, such as 2 Thessalonians 2:2, simply do not refer to the second coming. Second Thessalonians envisages that the Thessalonians might hear of the day of the Lord by letter, clearly indicating that the second coming is not in view![48] M. Hengel speaks of the widespread notion of the delay of the parousia as a "tired cliché,"[49] and as Wright notes, "This means, of course, that the old scholarly warhorse of the 'delay of the parousia' has had its day at last, and can be put out to grass once and for all."[50]

Thus, as we noted concerning Auerbach's comments about the Gospels in the previous chapter, Paul's gospel, with its theocentric, eschatological bent, makes every place-in-time significant precisely in relation to the epochal Christ event. Beker rightly notes, "What is truly amazing in Paul is that he is able to correlate a profound analysis of an individual's existence before God (Rom. 7:7–25) with a cosmic-universal view of humanity in all its social and

44. Beker, *Paul's Apocalyptic Gospel*, 108.
45. Ibid., 120.
46. Ibid., 87. Emphasis original.
47. Bosch, *Transforming Mission*, 150.
48. N. T. Wright, *New Testament and the People of God*, 460.
49. Hengel, *Between Jesus and Paul*, 184. See also Bauckham, "Delay of the Parousia."
50. N. T. Wright, *New Testament and the People of God*, 462.

biological dimensions (Rom. 8:18–30). In other words, Paul's cosmic anthropology enables him to overcome a bifurcation between the personal and social aspects of the gospel."[51] Davies is thus quite wrong in suggesting that Paul's gospel is a-territorial; his shift in focus is not from the land to nowhere, but from the land to the whole of creation, to all nations, and it is precisely this creation-wide shift that gives particular places importance.

Paul's Mission

As W. Meeks rightly notes in his seminal analysis of the social makeup of Paul's churches, Paul was a city person,[52] and his remarkable amount of travel was made possible by the mobility facilitated by the Roman Empire. "Ronald Hock has calculated that Paul traveled nearly ten thousand miles during his reported career, which put him on the roads busy with 'government officials, traders, pilgrims, the sick, letter-carriers, sightseers, runaway slaves, fugitives, prisoners, athletes, artisans, teachers, and students.'"[53] The century and a quarter of relative peace and of support for urbanization following Octavian's victory at Actium enabled the cities of Asia to enjoy unprecedented prosperity.

The Pauline communities in Asia were all centers of trade and benefited from that prosperity.[54] This is particularly true of Colossae, Laodicea, and Hierapolis, a cluster of cities in the Lycus valley, whose claim to fame was their wool industry. The governmental center of the province, Ephesus, was a free city with home rule and a Greek constitution and was the home of the huge temple to Artemis. Possessing a harbor, it benefited from trade most of all. Jewish communities were active in Ephesus and in most of the remaining cities of the province. Philippi was colonized twice in a short time, and this plus the constant passage of troops through it gave it a more Roman character. It was also distinct in being primarily an agricultural rather than commercial center. Thessalonica had an excellent, strategically placed harbor and, with Corinth, became one of the two premier trading centers in Roman-occupied Greece.

Corinth's refounding by Julius Caesar in 44 BC transformed the city; Caesar refounded it mainly with freedmen, his veterans and urban tradespeople and laborers. Its distinctive geographical position at the crossroads between east and west and north and south brought it much trade and commerce and ensured that it would prosper. While the north-south axis was less significant commercially, it was strategic politically and culturally. Like Philippi, Corinth

51. Beker, *Paul's Apocalyptic Gospel*, 36–37.

52. Meeks, *First Urban Christians*, 9.

53. Ibid., 16. The reference in Hock is *Social Context of Paul's Ministry*, 27. See also Casson, *Travel in the Ancient World*, 128–37.

54. See Meeks, *First Urban Christians*, 40–50, for more detailed discussion of the summary below.

was a Roman *colonia*, governed by an assembly of citizen voters, a city council, and annual magistrates. Abundant soil and clay facilitated a thriving manufacture of pottery, roof tiles, and terra-cotta objects. Water from the Peirene Springs was readily available.

Engels evokes the first-century experience of Corinth when he describes how the traveler approaching Corinth would pass

> through the mercantile suburb, beneath colonnaded side-walks that protected from sun and weather. Ascending the terraces upon which the central city was located, he would see the Asklepieion, with its temple, colonnades and bath-houses, and the Old Gymnasium on his right. Nearby he might have stopped to refresh himself at the beautiful Fountain of Lerna. . . . Moving closer to the Forum . . . large market buildings, basilicas and the law courts would line the colonnaded street. On his left would be the Baths of Eurycles, public latrines, and the periobolos of Apollo with its famous works of art, and next the great Fountain of Peirene. . . . He would pass beneath the majestic triumphal arch surmounted by two gilded, horse-drawn chariots. . . . The Forum itself was a vast open space thronged with merchants, street-hawkers, travelers, and local residents. Varicoloured tents covered the market stalls. . . . He would see . . . works of public art: paintings, marble sculpture and works of bronze . . . shrines, sanctuaries and temples . . . shops, stoas, and the administrative offices in the imposing South Stoa . . . dazzling colours.[55]

This gripping description evokes the density of places: as Casey notes, "The cultural dimension of place—along with affiliated historical, social and political aspects and avatars . . . contributes to the felt density of a particular place, the sense that it has something lasting in it."[56]

There is no doubt that Paul focused his ministry on cities, and largely on ones at the heart of trade routes and intense travel, perfect vehicles for the spread of the gospel.[57] It is easy to forget how the individual city names evoke a powerful view of place and its significance. As befits mission, Paul's theology embodies a hermeneutic of time—"the fullness of time"—and of place, the planting of gospel communities in city after city, from place to place. Indeed the very occasional nature of Paul's letters—"Paul . . . to all God's beloved in *Rome*," "Paul . . . to the church of God that is in *Corinth*," "Paul . . . to the churches of *Galatia*," "Paul . . . to all the saints in Christ Jesus who are in *Philippi*," and so on—implies a powerful theology of place with all its particularity. As Casey observes, "Implacement itself, being concretely particular,

55. Engels, *Roman Corinth*, 13.

56. Casey, *Getting Back into Place*, 33.

57. W. D. Davies notes that Paul also visited less significant places, such as Antioch in Pisidia, Lystra, Iconium, and Derbe (*Gospel and the Land*, 181). In terms of Paul's ambition to go to Spain, Davies notes that "Paul was thinking not of capturing the Empire but the whole known world" (ibid., 181–82).

is intrinsically particular. . . . Place-names embody this complex collective concreteness despite their considerable brevity."[58] The "obedience of faith" has to spread to every place, starting with the population centers, the cities. And Paul's letters engage the particular struggles of Christians in particular places as they seek to live under Christ's rule.

Even the common name appropriated for these communities, namely *ekklēsia*, alerts us to the universal-particular dynamic in Paul's theology. *Ekklēsia* must have struck many as a strange name, referring, as it usually did, to the adult male assembly in a town or city. For our purposes two points are significant about the appellation *ekklēsia*: firstly it could refer to the church in one place as well as the universal people of God.[59] Secondly *ekklēsia* has strong public connotations: "The early Church did not see itself as a private religious society competing with others to offer personal salvation to its members; it saw itself as a movement launched into the public life of the world, challenging the *cultus publicus* of the Empire, claiming the allegiance of all without exception."[60] Newbigin rightly makes much of the hermeneutic of the local *ekklēsia*; as part of the catholic people of God, the local congregation is to be a sign of the kingdom in its particular place:

> The question which has to be put to every local congregation is the question whether it is a credible sign of God's reign in justice and mercy over the whole of life, whether it cares for its neighbours in a way which reflects and springs out of God's care for them, whether its common life is recognizable as a foretaste of the blessing which God intends for the whole human family.[61]

Significantly, however, city names occur almost entirely in the addresses of Paul's letters. He says virtually nothing of his sea travel, an important theme in Acts.[62] Indeed, apart from the addresses and apart from his references to Jerusalem, Paul refers to regions rather than cities, which suggests that he sees his own world almost in entirely regional terms.[63] "Paul's mental map is totally lacking in sentimentality: his mission is set very firmly in the contemporary

58. Casey, *Getting Back into Place*, 23.
59. See Meeks, *First Urban Christians*, 108.
60. Newbigin, *Sign of the Kingdom*, 46.
61. Ibid., 63–64.
62. Sleeman's *Geography and the Ascension Narrative in Acts* is an important contribution to a theology of place. Utilizing Soja's concept of thirdspace to examine ascension geography in Acts 1–11, he notes that "Jesus' ascension casts all places as non-neutral, either conforming to, or resisting, his ordering of spaces. . . . All earthly places, with their associated spatialities ever generating a thousand new and sinuous places, remain—for believers—subject to the continuous Christofocal assessment critique of Acts" (ibid., 261). "The narrative's relentless optimism that the unconstrained word will reach all spaces . . . seeks to overflow into auditors' understanding of every place" (ibid., 262).
63. L. Alexander, *Acts in Its Ancient Literary Context*, 100–101.

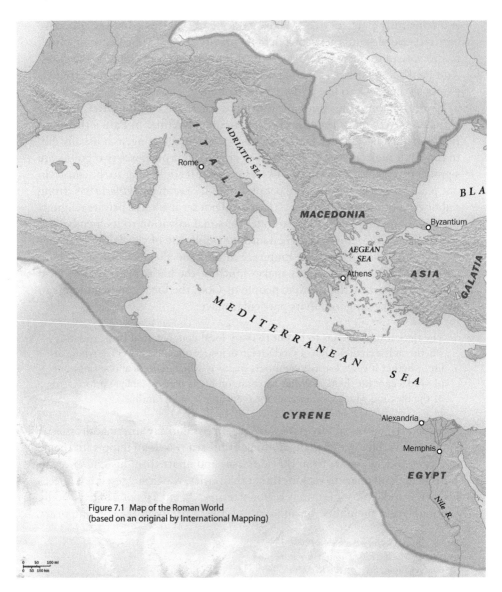

Figure 7.1 Map of the Roman World
(based on an original by International Mapping)

political scene, and he has no qualm about a strategic approach which mirrors the Roman attitude to its conquered territories"[64] (see figure 7.1).

The role of the cities as nodes of travel, trade, and communication and the leading of the Spirit both no doubt played a role in Paul's missionary strategy. However, in choosing which areas to focus on, Paul may have been motivated

64. Ibid.

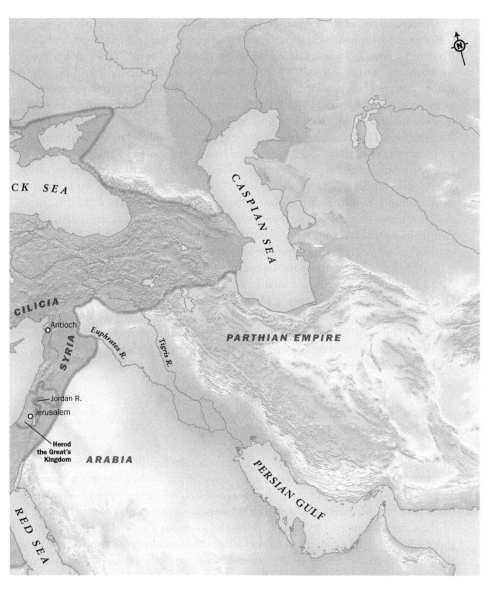

more deeply by his awareness of the Old Testament motif of the Table of Nations. In our examination of place in Genesis 4–11 we noted the significance of that list, with its universal, geographical perspective. In his *Paul and the Nations*, J. Scott examines this motif in early Judaism, in the Gospels—note the evocation of the table in Jesus's sending out of *seventy* disciples—and its appropriation by Paul. The reference in Romans 11:25 to the "full number of the Gentiles" probably alludes to the Table of Nations and to verses such

as Deuteronomy 32:8.[65] However, the most significant verse in this respect
is Romans 15:19, in which Paul says, "From Jerusalem and as far around as
Illyricum I have fully proclaimed the good news of Christ." Scott proposes
we translate "from Jerusalem—and in a circle—to Illyricum," and argues
that underlying this description is the Table of Nations' notion of Jerusalem
as the center of the world, with Paul assigned the Japhethite nations as his
sphere of mission, which includes all of Asia Minor and Europe as far as the
Adriatic Sea. This is what Paul is referring to, for example, in 2 Corinthians
10:13 by "the field that God has assigned to us." In Romans Paul already has
his eye on Spain (15:24), which was regarded as the westernmost part of the
territory of Japheth. When Paul says that "from Jerusalem and as far around
as Illyricum I have fully proclaimed the good news of Christ" (15:19), he
does not mean that the whole territory has been thoroughly evangelized, but
that he has preached to a representative number of the sons of Japheth and
established churches in their countries. Scott suggests that this strategy of Paul
unfolded through the apostolic council referred to in Galatians 2:1–10 and
Acts 15. The textual evidence focuses on the circumcised and uncircumcised
(cf. Gal. 2:1–10), but, especially in the light of Paul's missionary practice,
Scott suggests that the apostolic council agreed to divide the world according to the Table of Nations, with Peter assigned to the territory of Shem and
another apostle to the territory of Ham. Indeed, Scott suggests that Acts can
be divided into three sections:

1. The Mission to Shem (2:1–8:25)
2. The Mission to Ham (8:26–40)
3. The Mission to Japheth (9:1–28:31)

The evidence for Scott's interpretation is suggestive rather than compelling,
but it confirms what is clear from Paul's gospel, namely that, far from having
an a-territorial perspective, he was concerned to have the gospel embodied in
every place in the creation. As with the Gospels, so for Paul, the universality
of the Christ event had tremendous implications for particular places, and
indeed Paul's epistles witness to this eloquently, dealing, as they do, with
the practical challenges of living under Christ's reign in Philippi, Colossae,
Rome, and so on.

Paul's theology, then, takes place seriously. But is this explicit in his ethical
formation of the communities he founded? As regards the social composition
of the Pauline churches, Meeks concludes that they reflected a cross section
of urban society. He suggests that the most active and prominent members
were people of high status inconsistency; they were upwardly mobile people

---

65. On Deuteronomy 32 and Romans see Hays, *Echoes of Scripture in the Letters of Paul*,
163–64. Hays argues that "Deuteronomy 32 contains Romans in nuce" (ibid., 164).

whose achieved status was higher than their attributed status. If the creation-wide dimension is as central to Paul as we have suggested, then one would expect to find ample indications of cultural engagement and transformation in Paul's letters, but do we?

The Life of Paul's Churches

Paul's churches, and probably most of the early churches, met in private houses (Rom. 16:15; 1 Cor. 1:16; 16:19; Col. 4:15; Philem. 2). In Paul's letters, groups are regularly identified by the households to which their members belong, and even the saints "of the emperor's household" are mentioned (Phil. 4:22). In this way the local structure of the Pauline churches was superimposed on the household, the basic unity of Greco-Roman society. The household was, of course, much larger than the modern family and would have included relatives, slaves, freedmen, hired workers, and sometimes tenants, as well as colleagues in trade and crafts.[66] Ordinarily there would be several such house groups in one place. "The house as meeting place afforded some privacy, a degree of intimacy, and stability of place."[67] In the Pastorals (1 Tim. 2:1–6:2; Titus 2:1–10; 1 Pet. 5:1–5) the whole church is described as the household of God, but this metaphorical use should not detract from the household as the central *place* of the early Pauline churches.

Despite this grafting on of the churches to the household structure of the day, Paul's churches cannot simply be defined by this model. The paterfamilias hierarchical structure was challenged in several ways by the governance structures of the churches and the ritual processes of baptism and Eucharist, and the beliefs of the early churches define their identity as something other than a household. The identity of the early churches has also been sought in parallels with the voluntary associations of the day, the synagogues, and the philosophical schools, but

> the fact is that none of these models captures the whole of the Pauline *ekklēsia*, although all offer significant analogies. At the least, the household remains the basic context within which most if not all the local Pauline groups established themselves, and the manifold life of voluntary associations, the special adaptation of the synagogue to urban life, and the organization of the instruction and exhortation in philosophical schools all provide examples of groups solving certain problems that the Christians too had to face. For the structures worked out by the Pauline movement itself, however, which may after all have been unique, we must turn to the primary sources it has left us.[68]

66. Meeks, *First Urban Christians*, 75–76.
67. Ibid., 76.
68. Ibid., 84.

According to Bosch, the *ekklēsia* simply was a community in a class by itself.[69]

The early Christians faced a major challenge in establishing their identity as the people of God amidst the powerful Greco-Roman culture, and in his letters Paul was concerned to help them meet this challenge. Meeks helpfully draws on Turner's anthropological concepts of *liminality* and *communitas* in this respect.[70] *Liminality* refers to the transitional stage between two different modes of integration into a society, and *communitas* to the close social relationships between initiates.[71] Not surprisingly, Paul's letters and churches manifest a strong sense of belonging and a clear sense of boundaries between the churches and their contexts. They are part of the family of God, brothers in Christ; the rite of baptism in particular initiated a process of resocialization. "Thus the dialectic between 'structure' and 'anti-structure' that Turner describes appears again and again in the tensions addressed by the Pauline letters."[72]

Meeks notes that a major service that groups perform for their members in our modern, differentiated society is "provision of a limited social space within which a consensus may be attained about a perceived reality and its requirements."[73] In a variety of ways the members of Paul's churches would have experienced this need in a culture hardly less complex than ours. The result is that

> Paul and the other founders and leaders of those groups engaged aggressively in the business of creating a new social reality. They held and elaborated a distinctive set of beliefs. . . . They developed norms and patterns of moral admonition and social control. . . . They received, practiced, and explicated distinctive ritual actions. . . . The resultant, nevertheless, was an evolving definition of a new, visibly different subculture.[74]

Undeniably, then, Paul and his churches considered the establishment of boundaries a major task. Yet the extent of their ethical engagement with their surrounding culture is debatable. The church was a "fledgling Christian movement . . . peripheral to society, a totally negligible entity as far as size was concerned, and its survival—humanly speaking—in jeopardy."[75] Thus we should not expect a major social critique from Paul and his churches, though they could not avoid engagement with their culture. Meeks speaks in this respect of "*Gates in the Boundaries*"[76] and argues that "there is a self-conscious

---

69. Bosch, *Transforming Mission*, 166.
70. Turner, *The Ritual Process*; idem., *Dramas, Fields, and Metaphors*.
71. Meeks, *First Urban Christians*, 88–89.
72. Ibid., 89.
73. Ibid., 104.
74. Ibid., 104–5.
75. Bosch, *Transforming Mission*, 175.
76. Meeks, *First Urban Christians*, 105. Emphasis original.

communal dimension of the sect's ethic which is far removed from the civic mindedness of Greek ethics."[77]

To assess the relationship of the Pauline churches to their culture, we must also consider the role of Torah in Paul's thought. We have seen in our examination of the Old Testament just how comprehensive Torah is and how unavoidable, therefore, is its concern with place. What does Paul think about the Old Testament law in his refigured Jewish theology, now centered in Christ? Many argue nowadays that Paul rejects the law. H. Räisänen, for example, argues that "Paul states in unambiguous terms that the law has been abolished. In his actual teaching he ignores it, the ritual and moral side alike."[78] If this is correct, then J. Ziesler's question is poignant: "The Law gave Israel divine guidance for the whole of life. If for Christians it is no longer the key authority, then where do they look for guidance?"[79]

Sanders's work has raised the question of the Law in Paul's thought acutely, emphasizing that contemporary Judaism was not a works religion, but always understood law as a response to covenantal grace.[80] Sanders argues that as regards the Law Paul is a coherent but not a systematic thinker, and that for different questions he gives different answers. For Sanders, "the sequence of themes in Galatians (the law does not lead to righteousness *since* righteousness is by faith; God gave the law in order to lead up to salvation by faith in a negative way; Christians fulfill the law, summarized by Lev. 19:18) shows the way in which Paul actually thought."[81] For all its revolutionary impact, Sanders's "covenantal nomism" has not been universally accepted.[82] Nevertheless, we must grasp the role of Torah in Paul's refigured theology. Of the many treatments of this topic, I prefer that of N. T. Wright, who discerns that *covenant* is the clue for understanding the diversity of Paul's statements about the law. Wright speaks of his "growing conviction that covenant theology is one of the main clues, usually neglected, for understanding Paul, and that at many points in his writings . . . what he says about Jesus and about the Law reflects his belief that the covenant purposes of Israel's God had reached their climactic moment in the events of Jesus's death and resurrection."[83] Wright asserts that "covenant

77. Meeks, *Moral World of the First Christians*, 130.
78. Räisänen, *Paul and the Law*, 199. See ibid., 199–202, for a summary of his conclusions. Räisänen's position is self-contradictory in that while declaring that Paul abolishes the Law he nevertheless maintains that "Paul also makes positive statements which imply that the law is still valid" (ibid., 199).
79. Ziesler, *Pauline Christianity*, 116.
80. See Sanders, *Paul, the Law, and the Jewish People*.
81. Ibid., 152. See ibid., 143–67, for his conclusions.
82. See Carson, O'Brien, and Seifrid, eds., *Justification and Variegated Nomism*; Watson, *Paul and the Hermeneutics of Faith*.
83. N. T. Wright, *Climax of the Covenant*, xi. See also ibid., 137–267.

theology is characteristic not only of Jewish thinking in this period, but also of Paul's whole worldview."[84]

Wright's argument proceeds through close readings of central Pauline texts. Thus he finds the crucial background to Galatians 3:10–14 in Genesis 15 and Deuteronomy 27–28. For Paul covenantal curse reached its climax in the cross, and thereby the door was opened for covenant renewal—now, in Abraham's terms, for all nations—to be realized. The covenantal background reminds us that in Galatians 3:10 Paul has the nation of Israel as a whole in mind, not the solitary individual. The verse thus argues logically that those who embrace Torah embrace Israel's national ways of life; as a nation Israel has suffered covenantal curse, so that all who embrace Torah are now under this curse, as 3:10 states. In verses 11–14 Paul ties in Habakkuk's redefinition of the covenant community in terms of faith with the promise to Abraham (v. 14), so that now (v. 11a) no one is justified—becomes part of the covenant community—by Law.

Leviticus 18:5 is quoted in Galatians 3:12b and in Romans 10:5 but it appears to function very differently in these contexts. In Romans, Leviticus 18:5 is related to doing the Law, whereas here doing is not the answer. Wright argues that in Romans 10 Paul is saying that in the new covenant even the doing of the Law is appropriated and fulfilled in faith.[85] However, in Galatians the issue is membership of the covenant people; if the doing of the Law were the boundary marker, then the covenant would be determined by race and the blessing promised to Abraham would be unfulfilled. "This is not then to say that the Torah is bad; merely that, in the face of divine covenantal judgment on Israel, one cannot say that the Torah, and the attempt to keep it, provide the way to life."[86]

The problem which Galatians 3:13–14 addresses is, taking into account the promises to Abraham, what happens to those promises as regards the Law? The death of the Messiah resolves this problem: "Because the Messiah represents Israel, he is able to take on himself Israel's curse and exhaust it."[87] The coming of the Spirit (v. 14) indicates the end of exile and the renewal of the covenant: "The death of Jesus finally exhausts the curse which stood over the covenant people, so that the blessing of Abraham might after all come upon the Gentiles."[88]

Galatians 3:15–20 deals with membership of the covenant people. The problem Paul is dealing with is not, as so often suggested, legalism, but whether or not one must become a Jew in order to join the people of God. The "law" in verse 18 is not law in general but the Mosaic law given to the Jewish people

84. Ibid., 156.
85. Ibid., 149.
86. Ibid., 150.
87. Ibid., 151.
88. Ibid., 156.

and to them alone. In Christ God has fulfilled his Old Testament purposes and is making one new family and not two; thus keeping the Law cannot be the entry requirement into the new people of God. Central to Wright's argument is that Christ has ushered in a new stage in the drama of salvation, a stage in which the promise to Abraham of blessing to the nations is now being fulfilled. Clearly the Mosaic law, with its national and ethnic links to Israel, cannot continue to function as it had done.

As regards the land, Wright notes that "in interpreting the promises to Abraham, Paul quietly passes over the concept of the land. What has happened to it? It has been transformed: Abraham, as in Romans 4.13, is to inherit the *world*."[89] W. D. Davies notes with respect to the promise to Abraham that among Jews, "The universal dimension of the promise was often neglected or transformed. . . . The exigencies of Jewish history—not surprisingly—had pressed upon the Abrahamic promise a 'national,' territorial stamp which often tended to obliterate its universal range."[90] Even proselytes were not allowed to call Abraham "our father."[91] There can be no doubt that one of the things Paul is reacting against in his treatment of the Law is "the law taken over too completely by Israel, the law misunderstood by a misplaced emphasis on boundary-marking ritual, the law became a tool of sin in its too close a focus for nationalistic zeal. Freed from that too narrowly Jewish perspective, the law still has an important part to play in 'the obedience of faith.'"[92]

Romans 7 and 8 are two further crucial passages in Paul's discussion of the Law.[93] The husband in 7:1–3 is not the Law, as often thought, but the "old you," over which the Law exercised a hold in its condemnation of the sons of Adam.[94] The Law is not evil, but its effect was the same as God's instruction to Adam and Eve, namely to exacerbate the plight of those who received it once sin set in. Through baptism into Christ, the resurrected one (7:4–6), believers are liberated from the stranglehold of the Law. In 7:7–25 Paul goes to great lengths to explain that it is not the Law which is the problem, but sin. "The paradox of 8.1–11 is that God does, by the Spirit, what the law intended but could not do of itself."[95]

N. T. Wright sums up his analysis of Paul's view of the Law as follows:

His view of Torah . . . is that it was God's law, holy and good; that it could not give the life it promised; and therefore, if absolutized, it became a demonic gaoler [jailer]; that precisely in its negative mode it remained the agent of the

89. Ibid., 174. Emphasis original.
90. W. D. Davies, *Gospel and the Land*, 177.
91. Ibid., 177.
92. Dunn, *Romans 1–8*, lxxii.
93. See N. T. Wright, *Climax of the Covenant*, 193–225.
94. Ibid., 196.
95. Ibid., 204.

divine saving purpose, drawing sin on to Israel in order to deal with it in the Messiah; that what it itself could not do God had done by Christ and the Spirit, so that Torah was both reaffirmed and relativized, and all within the unifying framework of the covenant story. . . . Jesus therefore properly (from Paul's point of view) takes on the role of Torah, relativising Torah in the process by setting aside the temporary dispensations of land, circumcision, and food laws, whose tasks are now complete.[96]

If this analysis is correct, then the Torah, with its comprehensive concerns—albeit reworked in relation to the new act in the drama of Scripture—remained a major source of ethics for the early church. Dunn perceptively notes that,

> freed from that too narrowly Jewish perspective, the law still has an important part to play in "the obedience of faith." And the parenetic section ([Romans] 12:1–15:6) can then be seen as Paul's attempt to provide a basic guideline for social living, the law redefined for the eschatological people of God in place of the law misunderstood in too distinctively Jewish terms. . . . It is my contention that only with such an understanding can we do justice to both the positive and the negative thrusts of Paul's treatment of law in Romans, and that failure to appreciate "the social function" of the law . . . is a fatal weakness both of alternative attempts (e.g., Cranfield, Hahn and Hübner) and of Räisänen's critique.[97]

In his creative exegesis of Romans 13:1–7, Dunn offers an example of this new role of Law in the new age. The Old Testament people of God had been a state with a national religion, but in the light of the new age inaugurated by Christ this is no longer possible, and Paul redraws the boundaries of the redefined people of God in relation to the state.[98] The new boundaries leave no room for a social or sacred/secular dualism.[99] With regard to the government, 13:1–7 is clearly linked to chapter 12, whose exhortations closely resemble Jesus's teaching in the Sermon on the Mount and are often used to argue for pacifism. Christians (12:19) are never to take revenge, but are to leave room for the wrath of God. But this is no call for pacifism; 13:4 is clear that the governing authorities are God's intended instrument for executing his wrath. Commenting on Romans 12:9–21, Dunn notes that "all in all Paul had no thought of the Roman Christians as compartmentalizing their lives (into spiritual and ordinary affairs) or of living their lives cut off from contact with the wider community. He takes it for granted that Christians will live out their daily lives and wider relationships motivated by the same love as in their relationships with fellow believers."[100]

96. Ibid., 265–66.
97. Dunn, *Romans 1–8*, lxxii.
98. Dunn, *Romans 9–16*, 771.
99. Ibid., 773.
100. Ibid., 756.

Early believers faced their greatest challenge in regard to the role of the Law, however, in considering how it applied to gentiles. M. Bockmuehl probes this topic in his *Jewish Law in Gentile Churches*. He rightly acknowledges the formative role of the Jewish tradition; the *form* of Christian ethics with its focus on Christ may be a radical innovation, but in *content* Christian ethics is less radically changed.[101] Clearly, the Law could not as such function as law for gentiles, but what were the criteria by which its relevance was determined? Bockmuehl finds the traditional distinction between moral, civil, and ritual law unhelpful; it is unknown in the Old Testament and New Testament and is "legally unworkable and practically awkward."[102] Bockmuehl nuances the discussion through an examination of the Jewish tradition of moral teaching for gentiles and argues that this tradition, rooted in the Torah, determined much of the substance of early Christian ethics. He finds evidence that the early Christians looked at the pre-Sinaitic torah and the wisdom tradition[103] for guidance as to how the Law might continue to inform Christian ethics.

Scholars continue to debate the extent to which early Christians were actively involved as citizens in their societies. In his *Seek the Welfare of the City: Christians as Benefactors and Citizens*, B. Winter has argued that Christians were far more actively involved than is often realized and that the church taught a civic consciousness among its members. Winter argues that the approval of rulers in Romans 13:3 and 1 Peter 2:14 is related to public benefactions: "Public benefactors of a city were duly recognized by its rulers. This also applied to the Christian who acted as a public benefactor. . . . These verses confirm the Christian's involvement in civic life in the first century A.D. and the warrant for it."[104] Bockmuehl disputes Winter's view of New Testament benefactors, agreeing with Meeks that the vast majority of early Christians were in no position to play such a role. We need not resolve this debate, but only recognize that for the early Christians the lordship of Christ over all of life was nonnegotiable and that it relativized all other standards. It is often suggested nowadays that in an attempt to gain recognition Paul simply appropriated much of the value systems of his context. His treatment of slavery is a leading example, but as N. Petersen demonstrates in his masterly sociological and narratival study of Philemon,

> Paul's thinly veiled command that Philemon receive back his runaway but now converted slave as a brother, and indeed that he do more even than this, represents an intentional confrontation between Paul and Philemon, but also between Paul and the church that meets at Philemon's house, for the church itself will also have to receive the converted slave as a brother and deal with Philemon should

---

101. Bockmuehl, *Jewish Law in Gentile Churches*, 148.
102. Ibid., 149.
103. Ibid., 113–43.
104. Winter, *Seek the Welfare of the City*, 39–40.

he fail to obey Paul. . . . Significantly, he [Paul] does not attack the institution of slavery as such, nor even the participation of a believer in it. Rather, he attacks only the participation of a believing master and his believing slave. . . . *Being* in Christ or *being* in the Lord is a state of social being that governs the relationship between believers even outside the spatial and temporal boundaries of the church. . . . Paul's line of argument strongly suggests that the only acceptable action would be for Philemon to free his slave.[105]

In terms of the life of the early Pauline churches, and what is vitally important for our exploration of place is that, as Bockmuehl notes,

the New Testament authors' description of the created order is invariably underwritten by the incarnation and resurrection of Christ; it can never be considered other than *ex post facto*. Christ is both its source and destiny. . . . And yet, from this vantage point, it is all the more remarkable that the early Christian focus of attention still always remains the created *universe* and all its citizens. The moral theatre of redemption is nothing less than *the world* that God has loved. Creational givens are at once relativized, embraced and redeemed in the light of Christ's resurrection, and of the renewal of creation that he promises and we await.[106]

---

105. Petersen, *Rediscovering Paul*, 288–90.
106. Bockmuehl, *Jewish Law in Gentile Churches*, 143. Emphasis original.

8

Place in the General Epistles

Hebrews

The Epistle to the Hebrews provides a paradigm for W. D. Davies of what he sees as the New Testament tendency to transfer Christian hope from the earthly Jerusalem to the heavenly Jerusalem. Referring to 12:18–24, Davies argues, "It is because God has his seat there that Zion is the city with foundations. But God's habitat is not on earth: he is in heaven, and Zion, therefore, must be a heavenly reality. . . . Christians . . . have no permanent home on earth but are seekers for a city to come . . . a city that cannot be touched, eternal in the heavens."[1]

L. Hurst notes, "The Epistle to the Hebrews continues to be a storm-center of debate in New Testament study,"[2] and this is certainly the case for our examination of place in the New Testament. If there is one New Testament book which might appear to be a firewall against the idea of a new creation, Hebrews is that book. In his major commentary on Hebrews, Spicq finds the background in Philo and Platonism; if this is so, clearly one will be inclined to read "the heavenly Jerusalem" (12:22) as referring to the realm above, in line with Davies's argument. Perhaps no one articulates the implications of such an approach for a theology of place as clearly as does G. Josipovici, when he comments on the author of Hebrews' use of Jeremiah 31:

1. W. D. Davies, *Gospel and the Land*, 162.
2. Hurst, *Epistle to the Hebrews*, 2.

141

The law may be inscribed in the hearts of men, but here [in Jer. 31] a real Jerusalem and real fields and farms are being referred to. It is not simply that the author of Hebrews has given the passage a meaning which the original did not have, but that by so doing he has *obscured the meaning it did have*. The concreteness of God's dealings with Israel, his concern not with an abstract entity but with animals and trees and buildings, has completely vanished from Hebrews. It is not that an old meaning has been subsumed into a new one but that a new meaning has blotted out the old.[3]

However, much in our interpretation of Hebrews, and especially of its eschatology, depends on the worldview background against which one reads it. Already in 1950 K. Schmidt recognized the significance of whether one reads "the heavenly city" against a Platonic or apocalyptic background.[4] More recently, a Platonic and a gnostic background have been subjected to major critique. Hurst, for example, argues that while Philo and the author of Hebrews share a common conceptual background in the Old Greek version of the Old Testament, Philo developed these concepts platonically, while the author of Hebrews did so eschatologically. From this perspective the background to Hebrews is to be located in Jewish apocalyptic and early Christian tradition. That the primary background to Hebrews is to be found in *Jewish* apocalyptic is vitally important for its interpretation, since, as N. T. Wright has shown, "*there is virtually no evidence that Jews were expecting the end of the space-time universe.*"[5] Such a view would flatly contradict Israel's creational monotheism.[6]

The authorship, date, and setting of Hebrews are notoriously difficult to ascertain. It was written for a specific local group, a house church, in an urban setting, whose theological vocabulary was informed by the rich legacy of Hellenistic Judaism.[7] Most likely they were located in or near Rome. W. L. Lane suggests that Hebrews be dated between the aftermath of the great fire in Rome in AD 64 and Nero's suicide in AD 68.[8] Some members of this Jewish church had defected because of the pressure on them, and in the context of growing persecution the author writes to encourage the Christians to remain faithful to Christ. Not surprisingly, eschatology looms large in this call to hope and faith, and it is precisely the nature of Hebrews' eschatology that is disputed.

Hebrews manifests a strong doctrine of creation as well as a sense that the age to come is breaking in to the present. Both these themes appear in the opening statement (1:1–4), which is "programmatic for the entire discourse."[9]

---

3. Josipovici, *The Book of God*, 266–67. Emphasis original.
4. Schmidt, "Jerusalem als Urbild und Abbild."
5. N. T. Wright, *New Testament and the People of God*, 333. Emphasis original.
6. Ibid., 286.
7. W. L. Lane, *Hebrews 1–8*, lv.
8. Ibid., lviii–lx.
9. Ibid., 17.

Here as elsewhere in Hebrews, the Son is described in the language of divine Wisdom.[10] In 1:2 the Son is "heir of all things, through whom he [God] also created the worlds." "Heir of all things" is an allusion to Psalm 2:8, in which God's anointed is promised the nations as his inheritance. Although appointed heir, he is the preexistent Wisdom through whom all things were created. In 1:3 the Son "sustains all things by his powerful word."

> The new clause ascribes to the Son the providential government of all created existence, which is the function of God himself. As the pre-creational Wisdom of God, the Son not only embodies God's glory but also reveals this to the universe as he sustains all things and bears them to their appointed end by his omnipotent word. The ascription of cosmic dimensions to the work of the Son was prompted by the total estimate which the writer had formed of his transcendent dignity.[11]

In 1:10–12 the writer affirms the traditional belief in God as creator, describing the heavens and the earth as God's creation—they will "perish" and "wear out," but like clothing they will "be changed." In 2:10 he describes God as the one "for whom and through whom all things exist." Creation is understood by faith: "By faith we understand that the worlds were prepared by the word of God, so that what is seen was made from things that are not visible" (11:3).

In 1:1–4 not only is the doctrine of creation strongly present but so too is the eschatological doctrine of the two ages that was common to Jewish and Christian thought. The typically New Testament distinctive, of course, is that with Jesus the new age has already broken in upon the old age. So 1:2 states that "in these last days" or "in this final age"[12] God has spoken in his Son; this is his final and climactic word, which fulfills the words formerly spoken through the prophets. We have already come to Mount Zion and to the city of the living God, the heavenly Jerusalem (12:22). Nevertheless, a Sabbath rest still remains for the people of God (4:9); we still look for "the Day approaching" (10:25); we still await "the one who is coming" (10:36), and we still look forward to the city whose builder is God (11:10). As Lane rightly notes, "Apocalyptic eschatology provided him [the author] the categories with which to interpret the entire history of God's redemptive action."[13] The new age has broken in, but we await its final consummation, "the coming world" (2:5).

In Hebrews 4 the concepts of Sabbath and rest are metaphors for the salvation already available in Jesus and to be finally consummated when he returns. H. Montefiore notes that "this 'rest,' like everything else God has made, was

10. On the chiastic structure of 1:1–4 see ibid., 5–9. The references to creation in vv. 2c and 3a–b stand at the center of the chiasm.
11. Ibid., 14.
12. Ibid., 10.
13. Ibid.

created when the universe came into being. . . . That which was created at the beginning is reserved for the end."[14] That the writer's theology of rest does not deny the doctrine of a new creation is also apparent from Psalm 95, which the author is expounding in this section and which celebrates God as our creator (cf. vv. 4–7). Thus Hurst is unhelpful when he comments, "The 'rest' of God in Acts 7:49 is, fittingly, something entirely independent of any earthly fixture or particularity, an idea perhaps closer to the general argument of Hebrews than anything else in the Christian tradition."[15]

In 8:1–9:28 the new covenant comes into clear view. However, as J. Dunnhill rightly notes, covenant imagery and allusions appear throughout the book.[16] The author uses Jeremiah 31:31–34[17] as his Old Testament basis for asserting that Christ has inaugurated the new covenant, which is superior to the old. The new covenant enables believers to receive the "promised eternal inheritance" (9:15). In verse 15 the discussion of Christ's heavenly redemptive ministry reaches its climax. The expression "eternal salvation" occurs elsewhere in Hebrews only in 5:9. As elsewhere in the New Testament, "eternal" (*aiōniou*) does not mean "heavenly," but "of the age to come"; it is an eschatological term for the renewed creation.

The author of Hebrews does, however, strongly emphasize heaven as the place of God, and in chapters 8 and 9 the earthly tabernacle is contrasted with the heavenly Holy Place. In line with his typological reading of the Old Testament, the author focuses on the Israelites en route to the promised land, and thus, cultically, his focus is on the tabernacle rather than the temple. Christ enters the greater and perfect tent "not made with hands, that is, not of this creation" (9:11). οὐ ταύτης τῆς κτίσεως is generally taken to refer to heaven as the dwelling place of God and angels, and thus Lane translates the phrase "not of ordinary building."[18] However, intriguingly, in 12:25–29 the one who speaks "from heaven" (v. 25) will shake the earth and *the heaven*! In this section "heaven" is part of what is created (v. 27), and, relating this section intertextually to 9:11, one wonders if ταύτης τῆς κτίσεως should not be translated as "this creation" including "heaven," so that the heavenly tabernacle refers to entering the very presence and life of God itself.

In 1:10–12 the author quotes from Psalm 102:26–27 in order to demonstrate that the Son is superior to the creation. Through quoting a version of the LXX the author is able to take these verses as addressed by the Father to the Son.[19] For our purposes the key question is the eschatology in view in verses 11–12. Of the earth and the heavens it is said that they will

14. Montefiore, *Epistle to the Hebrews*, 83–84.
15. Hurst, *Epistle to the Hebrews*, 102.
16. See Dunnhill, *Covenant and Sacrifice in the Letter to the Hebrews*, 149–87.
17. Hebrews 8:8–12 is in substantial agreement with the LXX[A] text.
18. W. L. Lane, *Hebrews 9–13*, 238.
19. W. L. Lane, *Hebrews 1–8*, 30.

- perish;
- wear out like clothing;
- be rolled up like clothing;
- be changed like clothing.

W. L. Lane, E. Adams, J. W. Thompson,[20] and others insist that the author here teaches the dissolution, the perishability of the cosmos. In Adams's words:

> The statements of vv. 11a–12b express, as much as they do in their original psalmic context, the destructibility of the natural world. Heaven and earth had a beginning, they will grow old and they will eventually be dissolved. The cosmic order is viewed as "naturally" perishable: it deteriorates with age. It was not created to be everlasting, but with the propensity to decay. When the time comes, the creator himself . . . will dissolve the works of his hands; he will actively "roll them up."[21]

There can be no question that through this quote the writer clearly asserts the sovereignty of the Son over the creation—indeed in verses 13–14 he draws precisely this point from the previous verses; the Son will have his enemies made a footstool for his feet, whereas the angels are "merely" spirits in God's service. However, it is indeed questionable whether these verses teach, as Adams and Thompson argue, the destruction of the cosmos. Commenting on *apolountai* ("they will perish"), B. Westcott argues, "The idea, as it is afterwards developed (xii. 26ff.), is of change, transfiguration, and not of annihilation."[22]

Clearly what is said about the earth and the heavens is highly metaphorical, and right interpretation of the passage will depend on right interpretations of the metaphors. Verse 11b and verse 12a elaborate what it means for the earth and the heavens to "perish," using the imagery of clothing. The verb *apolountai* by itself does not make this clear; it can mean "to die" or, as in Luke, "to be broken." Like clothing, the earth and the heavens will wear out, like a cloak they will be rolled up, and like clothing they will be changed. Nothing, it should be noted, in this imagery of clothing suggests annihilation. If Adams is correct in seeing the image of rolling up (v. 12a) as evoking Isaiah 34:4, according to which "the sky will be rolled up like a scroll," then it is likely that we have here, as in Isaiah, the apocalyptic language of judgment, and as in Isaiah this should not be taken literally but as the use of cosmic catastrophic language to evoke the notion of judgment. Indeed in verse 13 the writer picks up on this very theme, with its evocation of Isaiah 66:1 and Psalm 2:13, verses

---

20. J. W. Thompson, *Beginnings of Christian Philosophy*, 137–38.

21. Adams, *Stars Will Fall from Heaven*, 184–85.

22. Westcott, *Epistle to the Hebrews*, 28. Similarly, Montefiore comments that "the Psalmist looks forward to a new heaven and a new earth. . . . It will be as though God were to give them a new suit of clothes" (*Epistle to the Hebrews*, 48).

which refer not to the annihilation of creation but to the eradication of evil and revolt against the Son from his creation.

And verse 12 does speak of transformation: "they will be changed." The problem in view is not that of a mutable creation but of a creation cursed with death as a result of sin. Thus the contrast being drawn in Hebrews 1:10–14 is not between the imperishable Son and the perishable creation but between the perfect Son and a creation in dire need of redemption and transformation! The Son remains (v. 11) in the sense, as verse 12 puts it, that he is "the same" and his years never end.

So far so good. The writer's eschatology is basically the same as that of Jesus and Paul. Particularly interesting is the use Hebrews makes of Psalm 8.[23] In Hebrews 2, Psalm 8 is used in relation to "the coming world" (2:5). Psalm 8 intertextually evokes Genesis 1:26–28 and is read this way by the author of Hebrews: the doctrine of royal stewardship is stated unequivocally in 2:8, but it is noted that we do not yet see all things subject to human beings. However, Jesus has already achieved this role, since he is now crowned with glory and honor. Jesus has achieved the state for which Adam was created, namely "crowned with *glory*" (cf. 2:9 with 2:7). Jesus is enthroned as the representative of humanity, and his crowning anticipates ours![24] The context of Psalm 8 is crucial in understanding the author's use of "glory." "Glory" refers to the dignity of being royal stewards over the creation, and while humans do not yet have everything in subjection to themselves (2:8), Jesus is already crowned with "glory" (2:9). Verse 10, therefore, when it speaks of the creator God as "bringing many children to glory," is not talking about taking them to heaven, but about leading them to the fulfillment of their human destiny as royal stewards of the new creation. The representative and corporate nature of Jesus's redemptive work is clearly stated in 2:10–13. Jesus became incarnate in order to come and help the descendants of Abraham (2:16), and the problem he came to help them with was not their embodiment but the problem of death (2:14–15).

In Hebrews 11:8–16 Abraham is held up as a paradigm of faith for the Hebrews in that "he looked forward to the city that has foundations, whose architect and builder is God" (11:10). Chapter 11:14 speaks of "a homeland," and verse 16 of "a better country, that is, a heavenly one." Verse 16 also states that God "has prepared a city for them." The urban imagery would speak powerfully to the Hebrews, threatened as they were by the power of Rome, a city which repeatedly showed itself not to be built by God! In 12:22 the author speaks of Mount Zion and the city of the living God, the heavenly Jerusalem. The image of a city fits well with the New Testament eschatology we have examined thus far, because the New Testament never indicates that

23. See Hurst, *Epistle to the Hebrews*, 110–13.
24. See ibid., 110–11.

God plans to lead his creation back to Eden, but rather forward to its destiny. But what of the adjective "heavenly"? Does it indicate that our destiny is not a new heavens and a new earth but "heaven"? The answer is, I think, no, not necessarily. "Heavenly," I suggest, qualifies "city" and "Jerusalem" not so as to imply that the city *is* heaven but so as to define a city and a place that is dominated by God, that is, the one who dwells in heaven.

In 12:25–29, "the main eschatological passage of the epistle,"[25] the author alerts his reader that God will shake the earth and the heaven. The NRSV translates verse 27: "This phrase, 'Yet once more,' indicates the removal of what is shaken—that is, created things—so that what cannot be shaken may remain." This translation appears to indicate that what is removed is "created things," that is, the whole creation. Adams argues strongly for this interpretation. He notes that 12:26 is referring to the promise in Haggai 2:6, although the author omits Haggai's "and the sea and the dry land" in order to keep the focus on earth and heaven. The reference to the time when "[God's] voice shook the earth" (v. 26) is a reference to Sinai, but now God is about to shake the entire cosmos. Adams rightly points out that *metathesin* can mean "change" or "alteration" but in Hebrews and here probably means "removal."[26] What is removed are the shakable things, and according to Adams these are defined as *pepoiēmenōn* ("created things"), so that "the author of Hebrews thus envisions in this passage a cosmic catastrophe that results in the dissolution of the cosmos. By declaring that heaven and earth, as created things, are destined for 'removal,' is he indicating that they are to be annihilated, that is, reduced to nothing? This seems unlikely since such a thought probably lay beyond his horizon. Most likely, he means that they will be reduced to their pre-created, *material* condition."[27] In a footnote Adams invokes 11:3, which he takes to indicate that the world was formed out of invisible matter.

Chapter 11:3 is a very weak foundation for this view, since the parallelism in 11:3 makes quite clear that the "invisible" in view is the "word of God" and not some invisible matter. Indeed, as W. L. Lane points out, the author's insistence in 11:3b that the cosmos was made from things that are not visible may directly critique the view of Plato and Philo that the world was made out of visible *material*.[28]

But what of the phrase *hās pepoiēmenōn*? An important clue as to how to interpret this verse lies in the metaphor of "shaking." The author gets this metaphor from Haggai, where it clearly refers to judgment. In 12:27–28 the shaking refers to the final eschatological judgment of God. The crucial question thus becomes how this judgment relates to the "removal" of verse 27. Adams's reading makes no sense of this passage, since in verse 28 the readers, "we,"

25. Adams, *Stars Will Fall from Heaven*, 185.
26. Cf. W. L. Lane, *Hebrews 9–13*, 482.
27. Adams, *Stars Will Fall from Heaven*, 190–91. Emphasis original.
28. W. L. Lane, *Hebrews 9–13*, 332.

who are very much part of the creation, are already receiving a kingdom that cannot be shaken! In biblical terms creation is hardly thinkable apart from humans, and the dissolution of the creation would imply the dissolution of the readers of Hebrews, but verse 28 clearly denies this. Thus G. Caird is right, in my view, that the difference between the shakable and the unshakable lies, contra Adams, not in their status as created, but in their relationship to God in terms of judgment.[29] Verse 27, in other words, does *not* teach the dissolution of the creation but its *purification*. In 12:25–29 it is thus God's final judgment which is in view, a judgment which will remove all that can be shaken, that is, all that is ripe for judgment; that which is righteous will remain, and the Hebrews are encouraged to persevere because they "are receiving a kingdom that cannot be shaken" (12:28).[30]

Hebrews clearly understands heaven as a place, indeed as the reference point of all other places. While Hebrews pays more attention to heaven than probably any other biblical book, this is only a problem for a theology of place if we read the duality of heaven and earth platonically. However, Hebrews maintains the duality within a typical New Testament eschatology which looks forward to the new creation, to the heavenly city, the new Jerusalem which will be ushered in when "the one who is coming will come" (10:37).

The central placial imagery of Hebrews, albeit negatively, is that of the sanctuary. As Hurst notes, "For Stephen [in Acts 7] *and Auctor* [the author of Hebrews], once the eschatological era has dawned, the days of the old center of worship are ended."[31] This is powerfully expressed in 13:7–19. Leviticus 16:27 stipulates that the carcasses of both animals may not be used as sacrificial food but must be burned outside the camp. The author relates this to Jesus's death outside the city gate of Jerusalem (13:12). But then comes an exhortation that must have hit the original readers right between the eyes: "Let us then go to him outside the camp and bear the abuse he endured." This exhortation is multilayered in its significance. Firstly it implies unequivocally that the old order centered on tabernacle and then temple is now obsolete. In Leviticus exclusion from the camp was a form of death, and the aim was always to be restored to the camp. But Jesus's death has changed all of this, and the readers must not seek to go back to the old cultus and practices. Secondly this exhortation implies that following Jesus will inevitably involve suffering. Thus it recalls Jesus's exhortation to his disciples to take up their crosses and follow him (Mark 8:34). With the dawning of the new age the LORD can be found only by going outside the camp to Jesus.

---

29. Caird, *Christian Hope*, 23.

30. Note that Adams ends up with a mass of contradictions by reading 12:25–29 as he does (*Stars Will Fall from Heaven*, 194–99). Despite his view of 12:27 he is compelled to acknowledge tantalizing indications that the author does indeed anticipate a new creation.

31. Hurst, *Epistle to the Hebrews*, 97. Emphasis original.

Positively, Hebrews does envision a new temple. In 12:22 the readers are reminded that they have already come to Mount Zion, a new-temple image. This is juxtaposed with the images of "the city of the living God," "the heavenly Jerusalem," and "the assembly of the firstborn." The description of Christians as "the firstborn" is related to the description of Christ in 1:6 as "the firstborn." Lane argues that 1:6 refers not to Jesus's incarnation but to his ascension.[32] If this is right, then "firstborn" would be associated with the resurrection of the dead, a major element in Jewish new-creation eschatology. Certainly the heavenly placial language must be read within the eschatological framework of Hebrews, so that, as in other parts of the New Testament, the vision of a new temple does not mean going to heaven, but refers to a creation in which God dwells, precisely the picture we find in Revelation 21. As Barrett points out, "The heavenly tabernacle in Hebrews is not the product of Platonic idealism, but the eschatological temple of apocalyptic Judaism, the temple which is in heaven primarily in order that it be manifested on earth."[33]

James

The letter of James was intended to circulate among the Jewish Christians of the Diaspora, the "nucleus of the Messianic renewal of the people of Israel."[34] James was written from Jerusalem, the geographical and religious center of the Dispersion. The letter's genre is that of "wisdom parenesis."[35] The wisdom character of James should not detract from the eschatological context in which it is set. Indeed, D. J. Moo argues that "what sets James's admonitions apart is the eschatological context in which they are placed."[36]

In terms of place several passages merit comment. "World" is used twice in a negative way: in 1:27 and 4:4. As is common in the New Testament, "the world" in these passages in James does not refer to the creation itself but to "the ungodly worldview and lifestyle that characterize human life in its estrangement from the creator."[37] Indeed it is easy to miss the very positive view of the creation and thus of place implied by James's appropriation of the wisdom tradition, with its presupposition of creation and its God-given order.

Although Christ's coming is "near," James sees it as imperative that the Jewish Christians live wisely in all areas of their life, as does Proverbs. The letter expresses this in its overarching theme, namely *wholeness*,[38] which is

32. W. L. Lane, *Hebrews 1–8*, 26–28.
33. Barrett, "Eschatology of the Epistle to the Hebrews," 389.
34. Bauckham, *James*, 16.
35. Ibid., 30.
36. Moo, *Letter of James*, 29.
37. Ibid., 97.
38. On the importance of this theme in James see Hoppe, *Der theologische Hintergrund des Jakobusbriefes*; Zmijewski, "Christliche 'Vollkommenheit'"; Martin, *James*; Tamez, *Scandalous*

introduced in 1:2–4: trials are to be embraced because they produce endurance, and the result is that the readers may be *teleioi kai holokleroi* (mature and complete). *Teleios*, with its cognate verb *teleioun*, is a favorite word group of James, and he uses it to articulate the theme of completeness or integrality (1:4, 17; 2:8, 22; 3:2). Significantly, the two words occur seven times—seven symbolizing completeness—just as God's wisdom is characterized in 3:17 by seven qualities.

Bauckham helpfully analyzes James's treatment of integrality in terms of five aspects. Firstly, integration concerns the wholeness of the individual and the community. James 1:18 extends the idea of wholeness to the whole creation! Secondly, wholeness entails the *exclusion* of that which militates against it. As 4:4 states, one cannot be friends with "the world" and with God. James's dualism is not one of earth versus heaven but one of life lived in obedience to God in opposition to life lived in disobedience to God.[39] Thirdly, in James wholeness is achieved by adding one thing to another (cf. 3:17). The law is a whole and must be fulfilled as such (2:8–13). Fourthly, wholeness involves consistency: "In other words, wholeness is about the consistent devotion of the whole person, the whole of life, the whole community, and ultimately the whole cosmos to God."[40] Fifthly, in James it is God who ultimately embodies wholeness. As Bauckham notes, "At stake is the belief that the wholeness of human life is possible only in relation to a specific centre outside of the self: God."[41]

James 5:1–6 is a warning against rich oppressors reminiscent of Jesus's warning against storing up riches while not being rich in relation to heaven. L. T. Johnson has shown that James works extensively with Leviticus 19:11–18,[42] and in 5:4 he refers to Leviticus 19:13: "Listen! The wages of the laborers who mowed your fields, which you have kept back by fraud, cry out, and the cries of the harvesters have reached the ears of the Lord of hosts." This is one of several passages in which we see how James understands the Torah. The "law" he refers to is the Torah, but understood now as the law of God's rule over his messianically renewed people.[43] As Bauckham notes, this has three consequences for James's understanding of Torah: internalization in terms of Jeremiah's understanding of the new covenant; ethical concentration in that the Torah is understood from the perspective of love of one's neighbor as a summary of the whole law; and, thirdly, intensification, since James's interpretation of the Torah is guided by Jesus's teaching.[44]

Message of James; Elliot, "Epistle of James in Rhetorical and Social Scientific Perspective"; and Tsuji, *Glaube zwischen Vollkommenheit und Verweltlichung.*

39. See Bauckham's helpful comments in this respect (*James*, 179–80).
40. Ibid., 181.
41. Ibid., 183.
42. L. T. Johnson, "Use of Leviticus in the Letter of James."
43. Bauckham, *James*, 147.
44. Ibid.

None of the placial specificity or comprehensiveness of the Torah is lost in James's reading of it. Agriculture continues to be practiced, but in a misdirected way; instead of justice for the laborers who mow the fields and harvest the crops, there is fraud and injustice. The problem is not the creation but its misdirection. Wholeness must extend to every aspect of human implacement.

1 Peter

First Peter is written by the apostle Peter to "the exiles of the Dispersion in Pontus, Galatia, Cappadocia, Asia, and Bithynia" (1:1). There is a virtual scholarly consensus that, unlike James, this apocalyptic, Diaspora letter was written to predominantly gentile Christians.[45] The places mentioned are ones to which Christianity spread at a very early stage. Indeed in 1:12 it appears that Peter refers directly to Pentecost: "the things that have now been announced to you through those who brought you good news by the Holy Spirit sent from heaven." Four of the places mentioned here, if we take the Phrygia of Acts 2 to refer to Galatic rather than Asian Phrygia, are represented among the pilgrims present on the day of Pentecost who heard Peter's interpretation of that event. Such pilgrims would have been the earliest to carry the gospel back to their homes:

> An excellent road ran from the Cilician Gates northwards through Cappadocia and Galatia to Amisus on the Euxine, probably the first city on that coast to receive the Gospel; and at Mazaca (Caesarea) it crossed another fine route which the enterprise of Ephesian traders had utilized so effectively as to direct the commerce of Cappadocia from Sinope to their own Levantine sea-board. Syrian Antioch occupied a key position in relation to both routes; and we can be sure that the Christian Church there would lose little time in following up with a more thorough evangelization the trail of the Gospel first blazed by the returning pilgrims. In the cities, and especially the coastal cities of these provinces, Jewish settlements abounded, and it was through the synagogues, no doubt, that Christianity first made headway.[46]

The recipients of 1 Peter are described as *eklektois parepidēmois diasporas*—"to the exiles of the Dispersion" (1:1). *Eklektois* describes their relationship to God; they are his chosen people. *Parepidēmois diasporas* describes their relationship to the places in which they found themselves. The theme of sojourning and exile is a major one in 1 Peter. J. Michaels is perceptive in noting that it is precisely their redemption in Christ that renders them sojourners and exiles: "Their divine election is a sociological as well as a theological fact,

45. Michaels, *1 Peter*, xlv–xlvi.
46. Selwyn, *First Epistle of St. Peter*, 46.

for it has sundered them from their social world and made them like strangers or temporary residents in their respective cities and provinces."[47] Ironically, whereas in the Old Testament it was non-Israelites who were sojourners, here it is Christians who find themselves in that position. Their redemption in Christ displaced them, but the whole point of 1 Peter is to re-implace them in the context of the larger Christian metanarrative.

And this Peter does through his eschatological explication of the Christ event. According to E. Selwyn, 1 Peter "is eschatology thoroughly appropriated and digested both in the mind of the author and in the life and thought of the Christians whom he addresses."[48] These Christians look forward to the revelation of an imperishable inheritance which is kept in heaven ready to be revealed in the last time (1:5). They look forward to the glory they will enjoy (4:13), but already they taste it: "the grace they enjoy is regarded as in a sense thrown backwards from the world to come (i. 13): it is a foretaste of the final revelation and the eternal glory."[49]

Selwyn, however, argues that there is nothing in 1 Peter about the geography or chronology of what follows the judgment. It seems to me that the eschatological language Peter uses and, as Selwyn so clearly points out, its background in Jewish thought indicate that Peter clearly has in mind a new creation; it is this that will be revealed in the last time. For example, 3:9 alludes to the Abrahamic covenant when it states, "It is for this that you were called—that you might inherit a blessing," so that what is in view is the blessing of the nations promised to Abraham. Similarly, the language of exile implies the hope of return from exile, which does not involve "going to heaven" but the restoration of the reign of God over his entire creation.

2 Peter

Adams asserts, "Of all the New Testament passages examined in the present study, 2 Peter 3:5–13 is the text that most ostensibly expresses the expectation of the catastrophic end of the cosmos."[50] He insists that attempts to read this passage otherwise are exegetically unsustainable. D. C. Allison says, similarly, "Here, it seems to me, is exactly the sort of expectation N. T. Wright wants to emphasize did not exist or at least was rare. But here it is in the New Testament."[51]

According to Adams, 2 Peter 3:7, with its statement that "the present heavens and earth have been reserved for fire," envisages the destruction

47. Michaels, *1 Peter*, 6.
48. Selwyn, "Eschatology in 1 Peter," 394.
49. Ibid., 396.
50. Adams, *Stars Will Fall from Heaven*, 200.
51. Allison, "Jesus and the Victory of Apocalyptic," 139–40. N. T. Wright discusses this passage in 2 Peter in *Resurrection of the Son of God*, 462–63.

of the cosmos. Adams reads verse 10 as describing the destruction of the heavens ("the heavens will pass away with a loud noise") *and* of the earth ("the elements will be dissolved with fire"). The loud noise associated with the passing of the heavens, which are "the created, material heavens,"[52] is best understood, not as the coming of God in judgment, but as the sound of the conflagration.

The meaning of "the elements" is disputed. Most commentators argue that the celestial bodies are being referred to. Adams argues that in verse 12 "the heavens" and "the elements" refer to the whole created universe and that the terms most likely have the same meaning in verse 10. When the letter was written, the common sense of "the elements" was the four elements: earth, water, air, and fire, and for the Stoics these elements constituted everything *on earth*. For Adams, the dissolving of the elements refers to the burning up and dissolution of the physical elements of which earthly things are made. He argues that the author of 2 Peter draws, albeit not uncritically, on Stoic cosmology, which manifests itself in three areas:

- the statement in verse 5 that the heavens and earth were formed out of water and through water. This reflects the Stoic account of the origins of the world.
- the depiction of the flood in Genesis as a cosmic deluge in verse 6, which reflects the Stoic belief that the cosmos is subject to destruction by water as well as fire.
- the assertion in verse 7 that the heavens and earth are destined for fire, which evokes the Stoic view of cosmic conflagration.

For Adams, "the author's adoption of these elements of Stoic cosmology is apologetically motivated. Faced with an objection to the parousia promise on the ground of the philosophical doctrine of cosmic indestructibility, he responds by invoking a traditional rival viewpoint. This enables him to offer a scientific defense of his eschatological convictions as well as a biblical one."[53]

How then to explain the phrase, "the earth and everything that is done on it will be disclosed" (v. 10)? There is widespread agreement that *heurethēsetai* means "will be found/disclosed" rather than "will be burned." Adams relates this being found to "discovery at the final judgment."[54] More problematic for Adams's view is that "*the earth* and everything that is done on it will be found." "Despite the wording, most think that human beings and their works are actually in view in this clause, and I share this opinion."[55] Thus for Adams

---

52. Adams, *Stars Will Fall from Heaven*, 222.
53. Ibid., 217.
54. Ibid., 228.
55. Ibid.

the "new heavens and a new earth" of verse 13 follow on from the destruction of the present cosmos.

For multiple reasons it seems to me that Adams and Allison are quite wrong in reading this section of 2 Peter as teaching the destruction of the creation. Second Peter 3 is about the coming "day of the Lord" (v. 10). Adams understands this expression as a synonym of *parousia*, but it has strong connotations of judgment, and this is central to chapter 3, as the life implications in verses 11–12 indicate.[56] Not only are the scoffers (v. 3) wrong, but when God comes it will be as *judge* of the earth. Verse 3, contra Adams,[57] does not indicate that the scoffers thought the creation was indestructible, merely that it continued as before with no sign of the promised day of the Lord.

Verse 5 does not, in my opinion, reflect a Stoic account of the origins of the world. The Stoics were ontological monists who considered "god" to be just as material as the cosmos. Stoic theology is thoroughly refuted by the statement that creation came about "by the word of the Lord." This refers to Genesis 1 and the Old Testament passages which speak of God creating by his word; "existed" fits with the Old Testament notion of initial creation and of creation as being sustained in existence. *Di' hydatos* is unusual but explicable from the Genesis 1 creation account: as P. Davids points out, in being gathered within its bounds the water was also the means of forming the earth or making it appear.[58] Thus the NLT accurately captures the meaning of this verse: "They deliberately forget that God made the heavens by the word of his command, and he brought the earth up from the water and surrounded it with water."

"Fire" in verse 7 is clearly a symbol for judgment[59] and destruction of the godless. Our author knows from Genesis that God has promised never again to "destroy" the earth by water, and thus this final judgment is envisioned as by fire. There is no reason why we should find here a reference to the Stoic doctrine of the cyclical conflagration of the world; indeed the very cyclical nature of the doctrine runs contrary to the linear eschatology articulated in this passage. "Whatever the source of his language, our author is moving within the world of Jewish ideas, not that of Platonic or Stoic ideas."[60] What the fire will destroy, according to this verse, is not the entire creation but *the godless*.[61] Davids also makes this observation:

---

56. Contra Adams (ibid., 215), who remarkably argues that "on linguistic content alone, cosmology is *self-evidently* the main interest of these verses."

57. Ibid., 206–9.

58. Davids, *Letters of 2 Peter and Jude*, 270. Note also that v. 6 begins "by these," so that it is likely that "the word" is part of the judgment in vv. 6–7.

59. Cf. Zech. 12:6; Mal. 4:1; Deut. 32:22; Isa. 33:11, 12; Zeph. 1:18.

60. Davids, *Letters of 2 Peter and Jude*, 273.

61. Cf. Jude 14–16 for a similar emphasis on judgment.

The judgment is not of creation but of human beings, just as the flood was not about the creation but about human evil. . . . Our author is not against the creation since that is something that God made. He does believe that it needs to be purified, but this purification is principally a purification of the human evil that has polluted it.[62] Presumably, as with the deluge, the extent of the destruction by fire will be limited by that needed to wipe out human evil.[63]

For Adams the author reaches for Stoic insights in order to show "scientifically" that the universe is destructible, but Stoicism teaches a doctrine of cyclical conflagration and understands the universe to be eternal, just the sort of doctrine Peter is arguing against.

Verse 10 does indeed speak of the heavens passing away and of the elements being dissolved, with the result that the earth and everything that is done on it will be disclosed. But the central motif here is judgment. Adams reads this verse as teaching the literal dissolution of the heavens, but when the verse refers to the earth being disclosed, he reverts to the earth as a metaphor for humans and their deeds. In my view something like the reverse is the case. Verse 10 evokes the day of the Lord in typical apocalyptic fashion, with the effect of God's coming being the passing away of the heavens and the dissolving of the elements with fire.[64] This is metaphorical, apocalyptic language evoking the reality of God's coming in judgment in history. It makes no sense to read "the elements" as the earth within this imagery, since "the earth" will then be disclosed.[65] What we have here is a powerful picture of the day of the Lord. It is as though the heavens are stripped away as God passes through them, so that nothing stands between the earth and God; life in this picture will truly be *coram deo*! As Davids notes, "And that is the goal: to expose all that has gone and is going on on the earth so that all those things that human beings thought they were getting away with or thought that God did not see are suddenly exposed to his unblinking eye. . . . The point is the uncovering and exposing and thus the purifying of the earth."[66]

62. See Wolters, "Worldview and Textual Criticism in 2 Peter 3:10," for the argument that the image in 3:10 is that of refining fire rather than destruction by fire.

63. Davids, *Letters of 2 Peter and Jude*, 274.

64. Thus it does not seem to me too important whether the "imagery" is that of destruction or purification. As with this sort of apocalyptic imagery in general, it is a mistake to take it too literally. However, it is worth noting that *kausoumena* need not imply burning up in the sense of destruction, but could refer to purification. Cf. Chrysostom as quoted in Harrisville, *The Concept of Newness in the New Testament*, 100. Harrisville's argument for purification rather than destruction anticipates Wolters's argument along similar lines in his "Worldview and Textual Criticism in 2 Peter 3:10." Wolters focuses on the word *heurethēsetai* and makes a good case for reading it as referring to the survival of purifying fire.

65. On the different interpretations of "the elements" see Davids, *Letters of 2 Peter and Jude*, 283–86.

66. Ibid., 286–87.

Central to how we understand this passage in 2 Peter is our diagnosis of what is wrong with the world. The problem is not whether the world is destructible or not, but sin and godlessness which have defiled God's good creation. Consequently the author speaks of the day of the Lord as "the day of judgment and destruction of the godless." And what will be the difference between the old heavens and earth and the new heavens and earth? Not the destruction of the creation but the fact that the new heavens and earth will be a place "where righteousness is at home" (v. 13).

Thus, far from teaching the dissolution of the creation, 2 Peter affirms the transformation of the creation at Christ's second coming. As Bauckham rightly notes of 2 Peter 3 and comparable passages in Jewish and Christian literature, "Such passages emphasize the radical discontinuity between the old and the new, but it is nevertheless clear that they intend to describe a renewal, not an abolition, of creation."[67]

The Johannine Epistles

First and Second John are important for our work on place because they oppose the (Hellenistic) attempt to deny the reality of the incarnation, a doctrine central to the theology of place.[68] As Inge rightly notes, "In defining the locus of God's relations with humanity to be focused in one particular individual the incarnation asserts the importance of place in a way different from, but no less important than, the Old Testament."[69] Thus 1 John begins with a wonderful declaration of the incarnation (1:1–3), and in 4:2–3 the mark of the Spirit is that one confesses that Jesus Christ has "come in the flesh." The spirit of the antichrist is to deny such a confession. Similarly 2 John warns against many deceivers who deny that Jesus came in the flesh (v. 7).

Revelation

This finally brings us to Revelation, a book in which place is central, ranging from John's implacement on "the island called Patmos" (1:9), to the seven churches *in Asia* (2; 3), to John's ascent *into heaven* through an open door (4:1), to his re-implacement *on earth* (19:11), to the destruction of Babylon (17:1–19:10) and the establishment of the new heaven and the new earth (21:1).

Revelation is thus full of placial data and also vitally important for any theology of place. Indeed appeal is regularly made to Revelation's vision of the new Jerusalem coming *down* to *earth* to support the New Testament

---

67. Bauckham, *Jude and 2 Peter*, 326.
68. See Inge, *Christian Theology of Place*, 51–54.
69. Ibid., 52.

teaching of a transformed creation rather than an eschatology of "going to heaven." Suffice it here to note that scholars are by no means agreed that in terms of its theology of place Revelation teaches a renewed creation. Thus, W. D. Davies, for example, asserts of the New Jerusalem, "It comes down. Yes. But it is *from heaven* that it comes and that to a new earth. Surely the earthly Jerusalem has here lent its name to a spiritual, transcendental reality."[70] Adams argues that Revelation 21:1 teaches the complete dissolution of the physical universe, which is followed by the act of re-creation. He focuses on 6:12–17, which, he argues, envisions a catastrophe which ends the cosmos or prefigures its dissolution.[71] There is, however, far more about place in Revelation than the references to the new Jerusalem and the new heaven and earth, and we will need to examine both the role of particular places in Revelation and its cumulative theology of place.

Although Revelation is more than a letter,[72] its epistolary character is an essential element.[73] In 1:11 John is told to write what he sees and to send it to the seven churches of Asia. And chapters 2 and 3 contain a specific message to each of the seven churches, and the imagery used indicates a detailed knowledge of their specific contexts. Indeed the messages are crafted out of the interface between the Old Testament, the gospel, and the historical conditions facing the individual churches, and as such are a good example of contextualization.

C. J. Hemer has alerted us to the connection of the letters not only into the biblical tradition but also into the historical contexts of the particular churches.[74] Placial analogues, he notes, appear in each letter. For example, the description of Pergamum as the locale of "Satan's throne" likely refers to its primacy in the imperial cult.[75] In each case, "the symbolism of the letters was forcibly applicable to the original readers."[76]

Seven is an important symbolic number in revelation, signifying completeness, and in Revelation it is no accident that there are seven letters to seven churches. Thus in their particularity the seven churches also symbolize the universal church. But this should not detract from their geographical and historical particularity; indeed the order in which the churches are addressed

70. W. D. Davies, *Gospel and the Land*, 162.

71. Adams argues for a position which, in my opinion, lacks coherence. He is adamant about the complete destruction of the creation and yet argues that "the new created order is both a restoration of the original and a transformation of it; it is the fulfillment of the creation's design" (*Stars Will Fall from Heaven*, 251).

72. On the genre of Revelation see Bauckham, *Theology of the Book of Revelation*, 1–22. Revelation falls into three categories of literature: letter, prophecy, apocalypse.

73. Chapters 3 and 4 appear distinct from the body of Revelation but are intimately linked into it. See Parez, "Seven Letters and the Rest of the Apocalypse"; Hemer, *Letters to the Seven Churches*, 16–17.

74. Hemer, *Letters to the Seven Churches*, 16–17.

75. Ibid., 82–87.

76. Ibid., 210.

is the order a messenger would follow in delivering the book to the churches in Western Asia Minor. Ephesus would have been a natural entry point to the mainland of the province of Asia for a messenger, and the remaining six cities lie in a circular route around its inner territories.[77] The letters to the churches embody the particularity and universality we noted at the conclusion to our discussion of place in the Gospels. As Bauckham notes of Revelation as a whole, "It combines a contextual specificity of relevance to its first readers with a kind of eschatological hyperbole that transcends their context."[78] As Caird perceptively notes,

> it is of the utmost importance for John's theology that the first statement he makes about the heavenly Christ is that he saw him *among the lamps*. He is no absentee, who has withdrawn from earth at his Ascension, to return only at his Parousia, meanwhile exercising his authority over the churches by remote control through their heavenly representatives, the angels. The first characteristic of Christ revealed to John in his vision is that he is present among the earthly congregations of his people, and whatever John has later to say about the coming of Christ must be interpreted in the light of this salient fact.[79]

Furthermore the symbolism of *seven* churches alerts us to the fact that this is true not just of the seven churches mentioned, but wherever a church may find itself located.

While we cannot explore 4–16 in any detail here, it is important to note the universality and comprehensiveness of God's judgment as depicted in Revelation. It is universal in that it relates to the whole creation and comprehensive in that no area of life is omitted from it. Particularly noticeable is the political and economic critique of Revelation. Thus, in his study of Revelation 4–5 Morton concludes that "the purpose of Rev. 4–5 is to affirm that Christ, not Caesar is Lord."[80] Of chapters 16–19 Bauckham notes that their judgments "are primarily aimed at destroying the *systems*—political, economic, religious—which oppose God and his righteousness and which are symbolized by the beast, the false prophet, Babylon, and the kings of the earth."[81] Bauckham's work is particularly insightful in showing that Revelation's critique is

77. The work of Ramsay, *Letters to the Seven Churches of Asia*, has been seminal in this respect. Hemer notes, "It may readily be supposed that a regular itinerary had been perfected since Pauline times and that the seven focal cities on the route had acquired a special importance as organizational and distributive centres for the church of the area" (*Letters to the Seven Churches*, 15).

78. Bauckham, *Theology of the Book of Revelation*, 155. Emphasis original.

79. Caird, *Commentary on the Revelation of St. John the Divine*, 25.

80. Morton, *One upon the Throne and the Lamb*, 196. On the ontological, cosmic unity depicted in chaps. 4–5 see R. D. Davis, *Heavenly Court Judgment of Revelation 4–5*, 148–57.

81. Bauckham, *Theology of the Book of Revelation*, 102.

not just of the idolatry of emperor worship but of the cultural implications that followed from this.[82]

Revelation climaxes in chapters 17–22. Chapters 17:1–19:10 deal with the destruction of Babylon, the city-symbol of Rome, and all that is in opposition to God. Chapters 19:11–21:8 parallel this section with the emergence of the new Jerusalem. Then, chapters 21:9–22:9 deal with the new Jerusalem itself. Note that 19:11 signals the end of the visions in heaven; after this all the action takes place on earth. The emergence of the new Jerusalem is of cardinal importance, tied as it is into the destiny of *this* creation. As Bauckham rightly notes, "Part of the strategy of Revelation, in creating a symbolic world for its readers to enter, was to redirect their imaginative response to the world. . . . John's readers need the vision of a centre in the eschatological future towards which they may live. . . . The New Jerusalem represents the true fulfillment of the ideal of the city, a city truly worth belonging to."[83]

Revelation is thus all about a counterrepresentation of reality,[84] and in terms of place it is crucial to discern what this counterrepresentation means for us today.

As Revelation comes to its climax in the vision of the new Jerusalem, it is important to note how creation and redemption are linked eschatologically. Throughout Revelation God is worshiped as Creator, and because he is creation's alpha he will also be its omega. "The scope of his new creation is as universal as the scope of creation. It is as Creator that he can renew his creation, taking it beyond the threat of evil and nothingness into the eternity of his own presence."[85] Revelation 21:1 might be thought to contradict the notion of re-creation: "Then I saw a new heaven and a new earth; *for the first heaven and the first earth had passed away*, and the sea was no more" (emphasis added). According to Aune, this verse, taken with 20:11b,[86] "makes it difficult

---

82. Bauckham notes that "it is a serious mistake to suppose that John opposes Rome only because of the imperial cult and the persecution of Christians. Rather this issue serves to bring to the surface evils which were deeply rooted in the whole system of Roman power" (*Climax of Prophecy*, 349–50).

83. Bauckham, *Theology of the Book of Revelation*, 129–30.

84. See in this respect Bauckham's very useful section on the relevance of Revelation today (ibid., 159–64). He notes that "one of the functions of Revelation was to purge and to refurbish the Christian imagination" (ibid., 159). On the literary nature of Revelation see Thompson, "Literary Unity of the Book of Revelation." He concludes that "the book of Revelation does not hold together oppositions and conflicts; rather it speaks from unbroken wholeness to unbroken wholeness" (ibid., 361). On the metaphoricity of the city image in Revelation see Räpple, *Metaphor of the City in the Apocalypse of John*. She rightly notes that, "as in artistic creations, the Apocalypse provokes its readers to uncover an 'unfinished world' as potential for change toward the possible" (ibid., 5).

85. Bauckham, *Theology of the Book of Revelation*, 163.

86. One is surprised at Aune's literalism in relation to 20:11. Carroll, "Creation and Apocalypse," 256, rightly notes, "The point therefore is that there is no escaping divine justice. . . . The first heaven and earth 'depart,' and the new heaven and earth come into view (21:1),

to avoid the conclusion that the author had in view the *complete destruction of the physical universe*."[87] However, with Harrisville,[88] Caird,[89] Bauckham,[90] Prigent,[91] and others,[92] it seems clear to me that Revelation envisions a renewal of the creation and not its destruction.[93]

When in verse 5 God declares, "See, I am making all things new," alluding to Isaiah 65:17, he then shows how significant this statement is by commanding John to write it down. "First" and "new" in 21:1, 5 carry the apocalyptic sense of the contrast between the present age and the age to come. In this way they refer to the renewal of the creation and not its dissolution. Verses 4 and 8 define this "newness": the complete absence of suffering, pain, and evil and of those who perpetrate such things. As Revelation makes clear, the creation comes from God and is thus fundamentally good; the problem is not with the creation per se, but with its perversion. Indeed God's faithfulness to his creation is a central theme of Revelation,[94] one that appears already in 11:15 in its declaration that "the kingdom of the world has become the kingdom of our Lord and of his Messiah," and again a few verses later (v. 18) in the announcement that the time has come, not to destroy the earth, but to destroy those who destroy the earth! This destroying of the destroyers is related intertextually to an equivalent wordplay in Genesis 6:11–13, 17, where the Hebrew verb *šāḥat* is employed with a similar double meaning. In the flood narrative in Genesis 6–9, the waters are the primeval waters which God had restrained but now allowed to "destroy" the earth. These same waters of chaos are the

---

but the meaning is that the present creation is renewed, not replaced." As Carroll notes, the implications for such a reading of Revelation are of great significance for how we approach our world.

87. Aune, *Revelation 17–22*, 1117. A similar view is held by Charles, *Critical and Exegetical Commentary on the Revelation of St. John*; Pohl, *Offenbarung des Johannes Erklärt*; Kraft, *Offenbarung des Johannes*; Müller, *Offenbarung des Johannes*; Wikenhauser, *Offenbarung des Johannes*; Ladd, *Commentary on the Revelation of St. John*; Kiddle, *Revelation of St. John*; Comblin, "Liturgie de la Nouvelle Jérusalem (Apoc 21:1–22:5)"; Vögtle, *Das Neue Testament und die Zukunft des Kosmos*; Günther, *Nah- und Enderwartungs-horizont*, 201–3; Fekkes, *Isaiah and Prophetic Traditions in the Book of Revelation*, 229–30.

88. Harrisville, *Concept of Newness in the New Testament*, 99–105.

89. Caird, *Commentary on the Revelation of St. John the Divine*, 260, 265–66.

90. Bauckham, *Theology of the Book of Revelation*, 49–50.

91. Prigent, "Trace de liturgie judéo-chrétienne dans le chapitre XXI de l'Apocalypse de Jean."

92. In terms of the reception history of 21:1, Irenaeus writes in his *Fragments* that it is not the substance or essence of the creation which disappears. In his *Apocalypse Commentary*, 221, published in 1329, Nicholas of Lyra says of 21:1 that "one should understand not that their substance is changed but that while this remains, they will be improved in their qualities and properties such that in clarity and transparency and similar things they will submit to the glory of the elect, who praise God by created things."

93. Aune (*Revelation 17–22*) and Adams (*Stars Will Fall from Heaven*) argue for the destruction of the "physical universe." This description of the "creation" seems to me anachronistic and reductive and alien to the holistic view of the creation we find in the Bible.

94. See Bauckham, *Theology of the Book of Revelation*, 51–53.

place in Revelation from which the destructive beast arises (13:1). Thus when the last clause in 21:1 says, "and the sea was no more," it signifies that "in the new creation God makes his creation eternally secure from any threat of destructive evil."[95]

It is eternally secure because of its source, and thus the city of the new Jerusalem comes *down* from heaven to earth (21:2). As a *place* the new Jerusalem is depicted as paradise, the holy city, and the temple. The motifs of the water of life and the tree of life characterize the city as paradise regained (21:6; 22:1, 2, 17; cf. 7:17).[96] The water and the fruit of the tree are the food of eternal life, life as God always intended it to be.

However, lest we think that the goal of history is a return to Eden, this paradise is a holy *city* (21:2, 9–27).[97] The connection of the city with paradise is evident from the precious stones and metals that constitute the city (cf. 21:15–21 with Ezek. 28:13–20). The city descends to a great high mountain (21:10), an image which has an extensive mythological ancestry as well as a more immediate background in Ezekiel 40:2. The mountain is the cosmic mountain where earth and heaven meet. The Old Testament looks forward to the day when Mount Zion will be elevated above all mountains and become the cosmic mountain it was intended to be. "All that the earthly Jerusalem could do no more than symbolize will be reality. Whereas the builders of ancient Babylon . . . sought to join earth to heaven with the self-defying pride John saw repeated in contemporary Rome, the New Jerusalem which comes from God will truly join heaven to earth."[98]

The trajectory in Scripture from the "garden" of Eden to a city reflects the role of the city as a symbol of God's intent and humankind's desire to develop the creation and to build places of culture and community. The holy city "points to that harmony of nature and human culture to which ancient cities once aspired but which modern cities have increasingly betrayed."[99] As 22:2 notes, the city will be the seat of God's kingdom; at its heart will be the throne of God, which is no longer in heaven but on earth. The city will be the light of the world; "the nations will walk by its light, and the kings of the earth will bring their glory into it" (21:24). "In offering their own glory to God's glory, of course the kings and the nations do not lose it, but acknowledge its source in God to whom all glory and honour belong."[100] The most unusual feature of

---

95. Ibid., 53.

96. For the Old Testament background to the water of life see Isa. 49:10; 55:1; Ezek. 47:1–12; Zech. 14:8, and for the background to the tree of life see Gen. 2:9; 3:24; Ezek. 47:12; Prov. 3:18.

97. Dumbrell argues the city imagery "indicates the completely political direction which the Kingdom of God assumed" (*End of the Beginning*, 1).

98. Bauckham, *Theology of the Book of Revelation*, 133.

99. Ibid., 135.

100. Ibid., 135–36.

the city is the absence of a temple (21:22).[101] This is because the whole city is filled with the glory of God—it has become a temple. This is confirmed by its cubic shape (21:16), the same as the Holy of Holies. As Dumbrell rightly notes,

> in Revelation 21 the concept of the sanctuary is enlarged to be co-extensive with the concept of "holy space" referred to in that chapter. Jerusalem is the sacred shrine of the new heavens and the new earth, the place from which the glory of God radiates throughout the new universe. . . . In brief, we may assume all aspects of the temple symbolism have come together in this pattern of expectation of the last two chapters of the Bible.[102]

People are integral to place, and not surprisingly the great covenant theme of God being "our God" and us being "his people" finds strong emphasis in this section (21:3, 7; 22:3–5). Intriguingly we find an emphasis on particularity both in the presence of God's covenant people and in the presence of the nations and the kings of the earth. In this way Revelation holds together the Old Testament promises to God's people and the hope that his blessing would come to *all the nations* of the earth.[103]

As we noted in our examination of Genesis 1–3, no philosophy of place is adequate without a theology of place. And in the climactic vision of Revelation we find the same emphasis; before chapter 21 God's presence is confined to heaven, but now his throne is on earth (22:3). This is not for a moment to suggest that before the parousia God is not present on earth—Christ's walking among the lampstands refutes any such view—but that his presence is to an extent hidden. He is present as the Lamb standing as if slaughtered (5:6), as the Spirit present in the faithful witness of the martyrs. While the beast holds sway over the earth, Christ's glory is fully apparent only in heaven, and hence John's need to walk through the door to see what is happening in heaven (4:1–2).

But with the emergence of the new Jerusalem, God's home is among mortals (21:3); God dwells with his people and is himself with them (21:3). The Greek words used in verse 3 for "home" and "dwell" are "virtual transliterations"[104] of the Hebrew *miškān* and *šākan*, used in the Old Testament of God's presence in both tabernacle and temple. In this way the whole of the new Jerusalem is depicted as the Holy of Holies, as we noted above—it is filled with God's

101. For the Old Testament temple background to Revelation see R. Briggs, *Jewish Temple Imagery in the Book of Revelation*. See ibid., 221–23, for the originality and radicality of Revelation's view that there will be no temple in the new Jerusalem.

102. Dumbrell, *End of the Beginning*, 38. Similarly Beale, *The Temple and the Church's Mission*, 25.

103. See in this respect Bauckham's excellent chapter "The Conversion of the Nations" (*Climax of Prophecy*, 238–337). Bauckham discerns an allusion to Genesis 12:3 in Revelation 1:7 and argues that 1:7 suggests that God's promise to Abraham will be fulfilled through the repentance of the nations (ibid., 318–22).

104. Bauckham, *Theology of the Book of Revelation*, 140.

unrestricted presence. "Like his presence in the temple (e.g. Ezek. 43), this eschatological presence of God entails holiness and glory. As his eschatological presence, it is also the source of the new life of the new creation. . . . God's presence . . . means life in the fullest sense: life beyond the reach of all that now threatens and contradicts life, life which is eternal because it is immediately joined to its eternal source in God."[105] In the Old Testament the only one allowed to enter the Holy of Holies was the high priest, and this only once a year during which he wore the name of God on his forehead. Now, however, God's servants will "see his face, and his name will be on their foreheads" (22:4). As in Eden, "life is now lived directly from its source."[106] And in stark contrast to the kingdom of the beast, God's servants will reign with him forever and ever (22:5). With God in place, humans and nations find their place, so that place itself is fulfilled. And in terms of how this representation of reality should affect our relationship to place now, W. Harrington is eloquent:

> The promise of a new world implies a radical questioning of our present relationship with the world. . . . It is a reminder that we human beings have sinned grievously against God's world, which was committed to our responsible care. . . . We are summoned to *metanoia*, called to work towards the new world held in prospect.[107]

105. Ibid., 140–41.
106. Harrisville, *Concept of Newness in the New Testament*, 103.
107. Harrington, *Revelation*, 210.

Place in the Western Philosophical and Christian Traditions

In the development of a Christian view of place for today a sense of the vicissitudes of place in history is essential. We will only be able to hear God's call to us in terms of placemaking if we understand how we have arrived where we are today. In this respect, the Western philosophical and theological traditions are foundational from a Christian perspective. As part 2 will demonstrate, place has been suppressed by philosophy in modernity and neglected by theology. Thus, our examination of the history of place in Western philosophy and theology will, in part, be an exercise in retrieval.[1] Both philosophy and theology contain rich resources but they need to be excavated and transfused into the present. The early church crafted its worldview in the context of Greco-Roman thought[2] and throughout the centuries the relationship between theology and philosophy has been complex but always interrelated. We will begin with the Western philosophical tradition and then attend to the theological tradition, taking note of their relationship. Wonderfully, we are witnessing a renewed interest in place by philosophers and theologians, but major work remains to be done.

1. Groundbreaking work in this respect has been done in philosophy by Casey, *Fate of Place*, and in theology by Santmire, *Travail of Nature*.
2. See Wilken, *Spirit of Early Christian Thought*.

9

Place in the Western
Philosophical Tradition

Christian thought never operates in a vacuum, and so we must note the various ways in which place has been construed in the Western philosophical tradition, since virtually from its inception the church has dialogued with this tradition as it has sought to contextualize the gospel. By the time the church fathers began relating the gospel to Greco-Roman culture, the thought of Plato and Aristotle—the high point of Greek philosophy—had existed for several centuries, and as we will see, Plato's and Aristotle's views of place cast a long shadow over the philosophical tradition.[1] In *The Fate of Place*, Casey demonstrates unequivocally the growing suppression of place in modernity by the philosophical tradition. He poses the question:

> Can we bring place out of hiding and expose it to renewed scrutiny? A good place to start is by a consideration of its complex history. To become familiar with this history is to be in a better position to attest to the pervasiveness of place in our lives: in our language and logic as in our ethics and politics, in our bodily bearing and in our personal relations. To uncover the hidden history of place is to find a way back into the place-world—a way to savor the renascence of place even on the most recalcitrant terrain.[2]

We will outline the contours of the Western philosophical tradition's handling of place as a background for exploring the idea's development in the Christian tradition.

1. Caygill, *A Kant Dictionary*, 368.
2. Casey, *Fate of Place*, xv.

Plato and Aristotle

Aristotle says of his master Plato, "I mention Plato because, while all hold place to be something, he alone tried to say *what* it is."[3] The major source for Plato's view of place is his *Timaeus*.[4] For Plato space preexists creation. The demiurge had the task of transforming this original space or receptacle into habitable places. This preexistent space is called Necessity (*anankē*) and Space (*chōra*). None of the basic elements of earth, air, fire, and water characterize this preexistent space.[5] It does not consist of matter, although it assumes material qualities; it is a nature "invisible and characterless."[6]

Contra the ancient atomists, the Receptacle is not a void, nor is it placeless. It may have no place of its own, but it offers place to things that come into existence. Its "winnowing" action generates regions, locatory matrices for things. The demiurge works with this preexistent space to configure things in particular places. Plato uses the images of a wet nurse[7] and a mother[8] for the Receptacle. He narrates a progressive implacement whereby space becomes primal regions and then particular places. K. Algra argues that Plato works with two conflicting views of space, one according to which it receives only qualities, the other according to which it receives actual phenomenal bodies.[9] There is thus validity in Aristotle's view that Plato's theory of space was incoherent and unable to account for the locomotion of physical bodies.

Unlike the Christian God, the demiurge does not create *ex nihilo* but from a primordial chaos and in accordance with the living archetype of the realm of Ideas. The demiurge creates the world soul, upon which the world is fastened. The world is visible, whereas the soul is invisible. But the soul is the most excellent of all the things produced by the demiurge, because it shares in reason and harmony. The gravitational pull in Plato's philosophy is always upward toward the realm of forms and Ideas, exemplified in the superiority of the world soul to the world itself. Because of the dualism in Plato's philosophy there is a profound tension in his view of the Receptacle as preexistent and yet also receiving actual material bodies. Plato's deprecation of the material makes a rich philosophy of place impossible.

Aristotle brought Plato "down to earth," and it is notable that his most substantial discussion of place—five chapters—occurs in his *Physics*.[10] Aristotle

---

3. Aristotle, *Physics* 209b17.
4. See Algra, *Concepts of Space*, 72–120. See ibid. for references to the debates about Plato's view of the Receptacle and the validity of Aristotle's critique of it.
5. Plato, *Timaeus* 51a.
6. Ibid., 51b.
7. Ibid., 49a.
8. Ibid., 50d.
9. Algra, *Concepts of Space*, 72–120.
10. Aristotle changed his view of place between his early composition of the *Categories*, in which place is construed as the equivalent to volume and extension, and the *Physics*, in which

focuses on the concrete world of the everyday, and in analyzing this he notes that "the potency of place must be a marvelous thing, and take precedence of all other things."[11] Indeed *where* a particular entity is, is one of the ten accidents characteristic of every entity.[12] Aristotle makes rare gestures toward myth, but in the *Physics* place is not (Plato's) space; rather he focuses on examining "in what way [place] is."[13]

Aristotle discerns two types of place: the common place (*topos koinos*) and the special place (*topos idios*). The former is that *in* which all bodies are, and the latter is the first *in* which a body is.[14] From the *in*-ness common to both, Aristotle proceeds to specify eight senses of being in something! The last is the most significant, containing the metaphor central to Aristotle's view of place: "as a thing is 'in' a vessel, and generally, 'in' place."[15]

Place is like a vessel in its containing and surrounding capacity. In its primary sense place is thus "what *primarily* contains each body."[16] However, place is unlike a vessel in that whereas a vessel can be carried around, place is unchangeable. "Hence we conclude that *the innermost motionless boundary of what contains is place*."[17] It is the "inner surface of the innermost unmoved container of a body."[18] As Casey notes, here Aristotle departs from Plato most clearly; for Plato the Receptacle is open to the limits of place, but for Aristotle delimitation is already present in place:[19] "the world is always already fully implaced."[20] For Plato place is imposed and geometrical; for Aristotle it is immanent and physical. Plato's and Aristotle's views continue to influence contemporary thinking about place. The geometric model, popular in early modern science, is still widely espoused today; phenomenological models which question the imposition of geometry and focus on the immanent order of the world have their ancient ancestry in Aristotle.[21]

Modern views of place have been influenced by Aristotle's understanding of *points*. For Aristotle four things lack place: the heavens, the Unmoved Mover, numbers, and points. Aristotle "resolves" his problem that points are indispensable, observable, but placeless by distinguishing between place and position. Points have no place, but they exhibit position. The one, as the

---

he rejects this earlier model. Cf. *Categories* 5a9–14 and *Physics* 211b14–28. On this change see Mendell, "*Topoi* on *Topos*," 206–31; Algra, *Concepts of Space*, 121–91.

11. Aristotle, *Physics* 208b35.

12. The fifth of Aristotle's categories.

13. Aristotle, *Physics* 208a28–29.

14. Ibid., 209a33–34.

15. Ibid., 210a23–24.

16. Ibid., 209b1; see also 210b34–35; 211a28. Emphasis added.

17. Ibid., 212a20–21. Emphasis added.

18. W. D. Ross's alternative translation of *Physics*, 212a20–21 (*Aristotle's Physics*, 56).

19. Casey, *Fate of Place*, 55.

20. Ibid., 56.

21. Ibid., 57.

basic unit of arithmetic, is "substance without position," whereas the point is "substance with position."[22] "That the point is a unit by which place, and still other regions of space, can be conceived and even experienced has been of perennial interest. If Plato regarded the point as a 'geometrical fiction' contra the Pythagoreans, Aristotle reinstated the abiding importance of the point, considering it to be as indispensable in geometry as it is problematic in physics."[23] Unlike Aristotle, Proclus absolutized the point in relation to place, regarding the point as generative of place: "We witness in Proclus the first appearance of a distinctive pointillism of place, where points, regarded as cosmically primary, give rise to places as if by natural extension."[24]

Aristotle's mature view of place is not without its problems:[25] firstly, by his emphasis on surface he views place as two-dimensional, whereas it is clearly three-dimensional; secondly, Casey discerns a tension between the localism of Aristotle's container model and the globalism implied by some of his descriptions of the physical universe; thirdly, the determination of the first unchangeable limit remains problematic; fourthly, it is not precisely clear what it means for place to *contain* something; and fifthly, it appears to be a theory of the location of static bodies and thus cannot help explain the movement of bodies. From a Christian perspective the "tension" between the local and global is not problematic. As we saw in part 1, Genesis envisions the whole earth as a home for humankind while also recognizing that humans will always be embodied in particular places. As Casey himself notes, "Problematic as we have just seen it to be, the very nesting of special *topoi* within an overarching *Topos* has the virtue of conceiving the cosmos not as an empty and endless Space but as an embracing Place, filled to the brim with snugly fitting proper places."[26] Aristotle's lasting contribution to studies of place is his recognition of it as an irreducible feature of the world with its own inherent power. Humans and entities are always dated *and* located.

The Middle Ages

During the Middle Ages and on into the modern era Western philosophy shifted its focus from place to space, and ultimately to the virtual obliteration of place by space. But this journey has its roots in Greek philosophy. Epicurus was the first philosopher to isolate space in its encompassing sense.[27] He posits a generic space (*chōra*) or the void (*to kenon*), which cannot be

---

22. Aristotle, *Posterior Analytics* 87a36–37.
23. Casey, *Fate of Place*, 65.
24. Ibid.
25. Ibid., 69–71. See also Algra, *Concepts of Space*, 192–260.
26. Casey, *Fate of Place*, 71.
27. Algra, *Concepts of Space*, 52–58.

recognized by the senses; it is an "untouchable substance."[28] The void provides the context for free atomic movement and is boundless, infinite in extent. Worlds are formed by atoms combining:[29] "The point seems to be that all void is potentially place and all place is potentially void."[30] Whereas for Aristotle it is all about being *in* place, space is about existing *through* the interval that space provides. Stoic thought, with its view that an infinite, empty void surrounds the finite placial cosmos, marks a further step toward the view that space is properly infinite.[31]

Neoplatonism introduced two novel ideas to the debate about place, namely that there are far more kinds of places than Aristotle recognizes, and that the less material place is, the more power it exerts. For Plotinus, "temporal and spatial priority are subordinates as wholes to other kinds of priority as coming at a later stage in the series of priority by nature, whereas, further up in the series, priority by order and difference are subordinate as wholes to the absolute priority by nature, power, and dignity of the One."[32] Philoponus (AD 490–570) approaches a spatial absolutism with his view that it is extension and not body that is the essence of place. As Philoponus states in his *De Opficio Mundi*, "If one abstracts the forms of all things, there obviously remains the three-dimensional extension only, in which respect there is no difference between any of the celestial and the terrestrial bodies."[33]

Medieval thought played a crucial role in the move from place to space.[34] The Middle Ages marks the transformation from a secular worldview "to a theological Weltanschauung in which the infinity of space becomes a primary preoccupation.[35] If God is limitless in power, then His presence in the universe at large must also be unlimited. Divine ubiquity thus entails spatial infinity."[36] While this is true, we need to be aware of the nature of that theological weltanschauung to which Casey refers. Scholastic theologians became deeply involved in natural philosophical reflections which were heavily logico-mathematical. As Grant notes, "Natural philosophy was never significantly

28. Rist, *Epicurus*, 56.

29. Ibid., 67–73.

30. Ibid., 57.

31. Cf. Algra, *Concepts of Space*, 261–339. Stoic thought identified four kinds of immaterial things which cannot be said to exist but can be thought of as subsistent: void, place, time, and lekta (things meant) (Rist, *Stoics*, 152). The Stoic doctrine of repetitive conflagration of the world necessitated the view that there must be empty space outside the world, since conflagration would cause expansion; Sandbach, *The Stoics*, 78.

32. O'Meara, "Hierarchical Ordering of Reality in Plotinus," 78.

33. Quoted by E. Grant, *Much Ado about Nothing*, 272.

34. Current recognition of the importance of medieval discussion for philosophy of science is largely the result of Pierre Duhem's groundbreaking work.

35. On the debate about God and the infinite in the Middle Ages see E. Grant, *God and Reason*, 228–52; idem, *Much Ado about Nothing*; Funkenstein, *Theology and the Scientific Imagination*, 23–116.

36. Casey, *Fate of Place*, 77.

infiltrated by theology, and natural philosophy was never really about God and his attributes. It was, of course, about God's creation, but it was about that creation as a rational construction that could only be understood by reason."[37] This alerts us to the *nature-grace* dichotomy at work in scholasticism, a dichotomy which would facilitate the secularization of science.[38] The scholastic theologians did, of course, endeavor to relate theology and science, and central to their reflections were God's omnipotence and God's omnipresence. The former relates to Aristotle's argument that a vacuum is impossible, which would mean that not even God could move the world and thus create a vacuum.[39] The condemnation of this view in 1277[40] inadvertently stimulated reflection on God and spatial infinity, a move which was central to the ultimate triumph of space over place.

Space features large in scholastic discussions, but this is not to say that place is entirely neglected. A notable medieval debate was over the different ways in which bodies and spirits occupy their places. Peter Lombard distinguished between *ubi circumscriptum*, the way in which a body is coextensive with the place it occupies, and *ubi definitivum*, the way in which an angel or spirit is delimited by its place but need not be coextensive with it.[41] Thomas Aquinas, similarly, devotes questions 50 to 64 of part I of his *Summa theologiae* to the nature of angels and poses the question, can an angel move from place to place?[42]

Two key figures of the Middle Ages who reflected on the infinity of space, both in the fourteenth century, were Jean de Ripa, a Franciscan theologian, and Thomas Bradwardine, a theologian as well as a mathematician. De Ripa assumed that God could or did create an infinite void space independent of himself, whereas Bradwardine argued that God did not need to create such an infinite space, since it already existed: it was the infinite omnipresence of God's immensity, which is without extension or magnitude.[43] God exists everywhere in an imaginary infinite void.[44] Casey acknowledges that the analysis of the world via mathematical quantification, a move which is at the heart of the absolutization of space, is a "resecularization of the world," but insists that it would not have been possible without the preceding theological reflections.[45] Grant agrees: "Except for extension, the divinization of space in scholastic

37. E. Grant, *God and Reason*, 197.

38. See Goheen and Bartholomew, *Living at the Crossroads*, 78–81.

39. See E. Grant, *God and Reason*, 223–28; Funkenstein, *Theology and the Scientific Imagination*, 117–20.

40. It was only in the latter half of the twentieth century that the significance of Étienne Tempier's condemnations was recognized. See Pieper, *Scholasticism*, 126–35.

41. E. Grant, *God and Reason*, 257.

42. Ibid., 255–264.

43. Ibid., 234–37.

44. Ibid., 236.

45. Casey, *Fate of Place*, 103–29.

thought produced virtually all the properties that would be conferred on space during the course of the Scientific Revolution."[46]

Central to medieval discussions was the question whether or not the whole world can move, and if so, into what does it move? If it cannot move, then a surrounding space is irrelevant. If it can move, then there must be a space beyond the world, through which and in which it can move. Theologically this question was framed in terms of whether or not God can create space which surpasses the space of the cosmos, that is, space unbounded by cosmic constraints and thus ultimately infinite.[47] Aquinas argued, in Aristotelian fashion, that the immobility required for a place to be more than a sheer container is not found immanently but in relation to the celestial sphere. The heavens provide the stable reference required by any particular place in the cosmos. Giles of Rome and Duns Scotus argued similarly for a cosmic relational model.

The year 1277, when the bishop of Paris, Étienne Tempier, issued 219 condemnations of doctrines that denied or limited God's power, marked an important turning point in the move toward an absolutization of space.[48] Two of Tempier's condemnations are particularly significant; first, he condemns the idea that God could not make several worlds.[49] Implied in Templer's view is that these worlds must share a space and that if an infinite number of such worlds is possible, then the shared space would have to be infinite. Second, Tempier condemns the view that God cannot move the world with rectilinear motion. In these medieval discussions absolute and infinite space must not be confused; the former implies something *self*-sufficient, which the latter does not. Significantly, no medieval thinker claims that God has created an infinite space distinct from himself; Orseme goes so far as to assert that the infinite space he is talking of is the immensity of God himself![50] Thomas Bradwardine (ca. 1290–1349) took the further step of divinizing the void in his *De causa Deit contra Pelagium*.[51] "But the move remains immensely significant, since it accustomed medieval minds to think in terms of a space without end, whatever they held to be in fact the case concerning the given material universe."[52]

Medieval theology and philosophy may have prepared the ground for the marginalization of place, but it took the resecularization of thought through the Renaissance and then on into the modern period to ultimately obliterate place. The two major views that influenced nonscholastic theory were those of Lucretian atomism and Stoicism. Bruno embodies the former, whereas

---

46. E. Grant, *God and Reason*, 237. See also idem, *Foundations of Modern Science*.

47. Casey, *Fate of Place*, 104.

48. On the significance of the condemnations for the development of science see E. Grant, *Foundations of Modern Science*, 70–85; idem, *Science and Religion*, 195–202.

49. See E. Grant, *Foundations of Modern Science*, 120.

50. Casey, *Fate of Place*, 111.

51. Ibid., 111–14.

52. Ibid., 111.

Telesio, Patrizi, Gassendi, More, Barrow, von Guericke, Locke, and Raphson represent the latter.[53] In his *De immenso et innumerabilibus*, Bruno lists fifteen characteristics of infinite space.[54] For Bruno space is "essentially an infinite, homogenous, immobile, physical, three-dimensional, continuous, and independent quantity that precedes, contains, and receives all things indifferently, despite the further assumption of its impenetrability."[55] Space is uncreated, eternal, and independent of God.[56]

The Renaissance and Modernity

The enthusiasm for Plato and neoplatonism, as well as a revival of interest in Epicurus, Lucretius, and the Stoics, influenced Renaissance reflections on place. "A sign of the times was the nearly universal rejection of space and place as categorical in status. No longer could 'where' (Aristotle's *pou*) be considered one of the ten basic metaphysical categories."[57] The secularizing direction is evident in Patrizi's view that not only is space unique, and the first element to be created, but God himself is subject to space! As Casey notes, this is the spatialization of the divine.[58] The relationship between space and place remains confused in Renaissance thought. The final ascendancy of space over place must await Newton's *Mathematical Principles of Natural Philosophy* in the latter seventeenth century; however, with Renaissance thought the critical turning point had arrived.

Casey discerns four stages in the ascendancy of space: modern space as absolute (Gassendi and Newton), modern space as extensive (Descartes), modern space as relative (Locke and Leibniz), and modern space as site and point. A cohering belief of these thinkers is in "simple location," a view which reduces place to position, to a "pinpointed spot in a massive matrix of relations."[59] A. Whitehead perceptively refers to this as the "fallacy of misplaced concreteness," which consists in "mistaking the abstract for the concrete."[60] The underlying shift, even in relation to Renaissance thinkers, is that infinite space is empty even of place itself, so that space is self-sufficient and independent of what is in it.

According to Gassendi (1592–1633),[61] who espoused a revived Epicurean atomism worked into a hybrid with Stoicism, "Place is nothing other than

53. See E. Grant, *Much Ado about Nothing*, 182–255.
54. Ibid., 186–87.
55. Ibid., 187.
56. Ibid., 190–92.
57. Casey, *Fate of Place*, 125.
58. Ibid., 126. See E. Grant, *Much Ado about Nothing*, 199–206.
59. Casey, *Fate of Place*, 138.
60. Whitehead, *Science and the Modern World*, 64.
61. For a useful analysis of Gassendi's view of space see E. Grant, *Much Ado about Nothing*, 206–21.

empty space."[62] For Gassendi, God created a single, finite world and placed it into an infinite three-dimensional void. The finite world surrounded by an infinite space indicates his Stoicism; however, his finite world was not the Stoic plenum (occupied space), but consisted of atoms and microvacula (minute places containing atoms). "Space is an absolutely immobile, homogeneous, inactive (resistanceless), and even indifferent, three-dimensional infinite void that exists by itself whether or not bodies occupy all or part of it and whether or not minds perceive it."[63] The purity of space is related to its measurability; it precedes creation and will exist after the universe disappears. Gassendi attempts to hold on to a notion of place, but now it is reduced to "some sort of extension," so that it is hard to distinguish it from space: "the leveling-down of place, its peculiar qualities and special tropisms, remains within the monolithic space with which it is now increasingly identified."[64] The dynamism of place yields to space as supine and passive. Gassendi's spatial framework formed the basic frame for Newton's scientific revolution.

Newton, in his *Mathematical Principles* (1687), incorporates Gassendi's theory of space and makes the concept of absolute space central to physics: "Prior to Newton, the doctrine of infinite void space played little role in science proper. As the chief architect of the Scientific Revolution, however, Newton would construct his new physics and cosmology within the frame of an infinite, absolute space."[65] Newton accepted the Stoic conception of the finite world of the universe surrounded by an infinite space. Space is neither substance nor accident but an emanant effect of God. Fundamentally, space for Newton is tridimensional—it has length, breadth, and depth—and into this space Newton set all possible geometrical shapes. These immaterial shapes enable material versions of them to move through and be contained in space. Space is the place in which God is omnipresent, and thus it is eternal and an attribute of God. "Newton appears to have held the position that God is literally an incorporeal, three-dimensional being actually possessed of length, breadth, and width and that His dimensionality is our absolute, three-dimensional, infinite space."[66] By the end of the eighteenth century the triumph of Newton's view of infinite space was established. "It was a triumph, however, only for the physical side of Newton's space. The God who filled it and whose property or attribute it was had vanished. . . . Space was now a pure, infinite, three-dimensional container for all things and activities. Its divinity was gone. . . . The properties remained with the space. Only God departed."[67]

62. Gassendi, *Opera Omnia* 3:216; Casey, *Fate of Place*, 390n113.
63. Grant, *Much Ado about Nothing*, 210.
64. Casey, *Fate of Place*, 141.
65. Grant, *Much Ado about Nothing*, 240.
66. Ibid., 245.
67. Ibid., 255.

In *The Discarded Image*, C. S. Lewis describes the radical shift in the experience of the cosmos that the modern, Newtonian view of space as infinite entailed. For medievals the universe may have been unimaginably large, but it was also finite and evoked wonder. Modern space may arouse terror or reverie, but unlike the medieval view, it is disorienting and provides no place within which the modern mind and spirit can dwell.[68]

Extension is the central concept of Descartes's view of space. It is the essence common to space and matter and determines the character of quality and dimension and consequently of all measurement of distance. "Anything that occupies space is extended and that extension *is* space."[69] Descartes, unlike More,[70] rejects any notion of spiritual extension; whatever is extended is a genuine body. Descartes aligns himself with Plato and Aristotle in their attempts somehow to make matter coextensive with space. Three consequences flow from the Cartesian equation of matter with space:[71] firstly, the world is indefinitely extended; secondly, no void can exist; and thirdly, place is subordinate to space and matter. "Its standing is either purely conceptual in character—that is, dependent on the merely reflective distinction between generic and individual unity—or else it is simply identified with empty space, that is to say, with something that is in itself an outright *contradictio in adiecto*."[72] Descartes does make an intriguing distinction between internal place (the volume occupied by an individual body) and external place (place as determined by the relationship between a body and other bodies). He does not, however, pursue the possibilities of this distinction, and "place, subordinated first to space . . . is subordinated a second time to vicinity—about whose exact meaning, however, we are given no determinate clue. The fate of place . . . is left dangling. . . . In the end there is no such thing as 'place,' while there *is* preeminently a single universal 'space.'"[73]

Descartes's mathematical approach to place is evident in his comments about architecture:

> It is observable that the buildings which a single architect has planned and executed are generally more elegant and commodious than those which several have attempted to improve. . . . Thus, also, those ancient cities . . . are usually but ill laid out compared with the regularly constructed towns which a professional architect has freely planned on an open plain; so that although the several buildings of the former may often equal or surpass in beauty those of the latter, yet when one observes their indiscriminate juxtaposition, there a large and here

68. Lewis, *Discarded Image*, 98–99; cf. Lundin, *Believing Again*, 126–29.
69. Angeles, *Dictionary of Philosophy*, 270.
70. For More on space see Grant, *Much Ado about Nothing*, 221–28.
71. Casey, *Fate of Place*, 154–56.
72. Ibid., 156. A *contradictio in adiecto* is a logical inconsistency between a noun and the adjective that modifies it.
73. Ibid., 161.

a small, and the consequent crookedness and irregularity of the streets, one is disposed to allege that chance, rather than any human will guided by reason, must have led to such an arrangement.[74]

Mumford notes that "there could be no sharper contrast between the two orders of thinking, the organic and the mechanical [Descartes], than here: the first springs out of the total situation, the other simplifies the facts of life for the sake of an artful system of concepts, more dear to the mind than life itself."[75]

Descartes hovers between the absoluteness of space and the relativism of external place. Locke, and then more fully Leibniz, follows the idea of space and place to the conclusion that both are altogether relative. Locke, in his *Essay Concerning Human Understanding* (1690), distances himself from Descartes in his insistence that space is not body. Open, empty space has three modes: capacity or volume, the relation between the extremities of a body, and distance, which is the space between two or more bodies.[76] Central to Locke's view of place is distance; indeed place is a "modification of distance,"[77] and modification is purely a matter of convention.

> Place is what human beings create when (for largely utilitarian purposes) they set about determining the distance between positions of things. The determination of distance is tantamount to its measurement. . . . The "mathematization of nature" . . . holds true for Locke as well. . . . With Locke's conception of place as distance-determined . . . the decisive steps have been taken toward that fateful reduction of place to "site" that will become the pervasive destiny of place in the eighteenth and nineteenth centuries. Place is no longer a genuine *measurant*, a measuring force, but something merely *measured.*[78]

For Leibniz, interval or situation rather than distance determines space and place. Space is relative and ideal: space "can only be an ideal thing, containing a certain order, wherein the mind conceives the application of relations."[79] What is extended for Leibniz is not a body but a quality of a body. "By assimilating space to quantity, Leibniz takes a crucial step towards the progressive objectification of space as a monolithic conception in relation to which place will perforce become increasingly insignificant, if never entirely irrelevant."[80] Leibniz reduces space to position, which is quite abstract, so that the density and particularity of place are subsumed into the abstractness of

74. Descartes, *Discourse on Method*, Part II, quoted in Mumford, *City in History*, 393–94.
75. Mumford, *City in History*, 394.
76. Locke, *Essay Concerning Human Understanding*, 167–69.
77. Ibid., 170.
78. Casey, *Fate of Place*, 165. Emphasis original.
79. Leibniz, *Philosophical Papers and Letters*, 1147.
80. Casey, *Fate of Place*, 171.

space.[81] Place is thereby lost in space: it is lost in the abstractness of space, it is lost in the infinity of space, and thirdly it is lost in the relativity of space.[82] Kant's legacy with respect to place is dual;[83] on the one hand he dealt the final blow to place, but paradoxically, he also suggested a way to recover the importance of place through the living human body. Kant's mature view is found, among other places, at the outset of his *Critique of Pure Reason*, in "Transcendental Aesthetic," section I. He defines space as "a necessary a priori presentation that underlies all outer intuitions."[84] We cannot know the world as it actually is, and space is a mental concept imposed on raw experience. In his mature work Kant reduces space to point. In his *Metaphysical Foundations of Natural Sciences* (1786) he declares straightforwardly that "the place of every body is a point."[85]

> Kant's focus on point represents the last step in the progression—or, more accurately, the regression—that manifests itself in the century and a half after the publication of Descartes' *Principles of Philosophy*. Reflecting the general dissolution of place in space, this stepwise series has consisted in two basic moves: first, the replacement of place by *position*, a move initiated by Descartes, continued and completed by Locke and Leibniz, and still tempting to Kant in his early writings; second, the shrinking of position itself into point. The last step, initiated by Leibniz and completed by Kant in the *Metaphysical Foundations of Natural Science*, is the most extreme. . . . A point brings with it no inherent nexus or scheme of relations; it is an isolated entity. . . . It is the ultimate form of simple location.[86]

From this time onward place is reduced to a bare point, depicted on geometrical axes that depict the dimensionality of space.

Casey argues that the best route to recover place is through a focus on the body,[87] because concrete phenomena, as epitomized in Kant's philosophy, have in modernity come to be thoroughly subordinated to mind. A shift of focus to the body opens up the phenomenon of embodiment and thus place.[88] It is by way of the body that place has begun to be recovered philosophically, and remarkably this can be traced back to Kant himself in an early essay of his

---

81. As Casey points out, although there are redemptive aspects in Leibniz's view of place, ultimately he identifies place with position and quantity (ibid., 172–73). For a positive appropriation of Leibniz in terms of place, see Harvey, *Justice, Nature and the Geography of Difference*, especially 248–55.

82. Casey, *Fate of Place*, 175.

83. For a useful summary of the development of Kant's view of space see Caygill, *A Kant Dictionary*, 367–73.

84. Kant, *Critique of Pure Reason*, 78.

85. Kant, *Metaphysical Foundations of Natural Science*, 21.

86. Casey, *Fate of Place*, 190. Emphasis original.

87. Ibid., 203.

88. From a Christian perspective, this retains the epistemological vs. ontological priority of modernity, and is by no means to be assumed as the best way into a philosophy of place.

published in 1768.[89] In his search for the ultimate grounds for the differentiation of regions in space, Kant argues that it is because our bodies are already divided into paired sides and parts that we can discern objects as placed and oriented. "In his tiny text of 1768 he demonstrates—for the first time ever in Western thought—that *the most intimate as well as the most consequential inroad to place is through the body.*"[90] Kant himself did not pursue the fecundity of the body with respect to place.

Whitehead was one of the first to contest the nineteenth-century denigration of space and place.[91] Whitehead focuses on human experience and asserts that no element among the main elements of nature is apprehended as simple location. The developments in reflection on space from the seventeenth to the nineteenth centuries have been guilty of "misplaced concreteness," in which abstractions are mistaken for the concrete.[92] Crucial elements of our experience are lost through this abstraction, and not least of these is place. Recovery of place requires a new view of the body:

> You are in a certain *place* perceiving things. Your perception takes place where you are, and is entirely dependent on how your body is functioning. But this functioning of the body in one *place*, exhibits for your cognizance an aspect of the distant environment, fading away into the general knowledge that there are things beyond. If this cognizance conveys knowledge of a transcendent world, it must be because the event which is the bodily life unifies in itself aspects of the universe.[93]

Central to the body's apprehension of places is its "withness." As we are always embodied, so we are also always implaced.

A renewed appreciation of place emerges in Husserl's phenomenology, and particularly, in terms of the body, in relation to Merleau-Ponty's work. Husserl's phenomenology is a last-ditch attempt to rescue the Enlightenment project, and in this respect he stresses, in reaction to Kant, that we need a foundation other than that of pure mind; the alternative foundation is to be found in the life-world. Central to this is the living body and the way in which it "holds sway." Husserl's journey toward place is complex and arduous, but in his late work, *The Crisis of European Sciences and Transcendental Phenomenology*, he rightly critiques the mathematical reductionism or abstraction of seventeenth-century science, and intriguingly traces this abstraction to the bodily activity of surveying land! Husserl singles out walking as the clue to

89. Kant, "Concerning the Ultimate Ground of the Differentiation of Directions in Space," in *Theoretical Philosophy 1755–1770*, 365–66.

90. Casey, *Fate of Place*, 210. Emphasis original.

91. See Whitehead, *Science and the Modern World* and *Process and Reality*.

92. Whitehead, *Process and Reality*, 51.

93. Whitehead, *Science and the Modern World*, 92. Emphasis added. See Temple, *Nature, Man and God*, 486, who agrees with Whitehead in his critique of idealism.

how the body holds sway in the lived world. Walking uncovers the mystery of how one builds up a coherent view of the world from the fragmentary appearances one receives.[94]

What is exploratory in Husserl becomes explicit in Merleau-Ponty, who asserted that we gain access to the "primary world" primarily through our lived body.[95] Bodily movement is "productive of space."[96] Bodily orientation and expressive movement result in inhabitation:

> We must therefore avoid saying that our body is in space, or in time. It inhabits space and time. . . . I am not in space and time; nor do I conceive space and time; I belong to them, my body combines with them and includes them. The scope of this inclusion is the measure of that of my existence.[97]

Aristotle's "in" of containment is here replaced by Merleau-Ponty's "in" of *in*habitation. Knowledge of place is a real thing and is characterized by familiarity. Implacement and embodiment go hand in hand; the tie between them is so "thick" that it can never be neatly divided.

With his emphasis on time, one might find it strange that Heidegger would be a key thinker in the recovery of place;[98] however, late in his life (1969) at a seminar in Le Thor he himself argued that his thinking had traversed three periods, each with a leading theme: meaning, truth, and place.[99] The potential for a robust philosophy of place is indeed present in *Being and Time*. *Dasein*, with its concomitant notions of gathering, nearness, and being ready-to-hand, would appear to lead naturally to a consideration of place; and indeed Heidegger does reintroduce the notion of "room" after a millennium of its neglect. Making room relates to the way *Dasein* arranges ready-to-hand things to create greater spaciousness. However, Heidegger's temporocentrism prevents place from emerging on its own terms until Heidegger's late work following his "turn."[100]

In his late work Heidegger focuses on the multiplicity of ways of *Dasein*, and this, combined with his preoccupation with "nearness," leads him eventually to place under the concept of "dwelling." Nearness results in neighborhood, and neighborhood means dwelling in nearness. In the last text he wrote, namely "Art and Space" (1969), Heidegger asks for the very first time, "Still, what is place?" He answers, "Place opens a region by every time gathering things into

94. See Casey, *Fate of Place*, 224–27.
95. Merleau-Ponty, *Phenomenology of Perception*, 130.
96. Ibid., 387.
97. Ibid., 139–40.
98. For a defense of Heidegger's early work in terms of its fecundity for a positive philosophy of the environment see Foltz, *Inhabiting the Earth*. On Heidegger and place, see also Sharr, *Heidegger's Hut*.
99. Casey, *Fate of Place*, 244.
100. See ibid., 243–84, for a detailed analysis of Heidegger's development.

their belonging together."[101] As Casey observes, "The circuitous and digressive character of Heidegger's path over more than four decades should not blind us to the fact that he ends by giving the most suggestive and sustained treatment of place in this century."[102]

Postmodernism

An encouraging development is the renewed interest in place in philosophically inclined authors. Much of this renewed interest is markedly postmodern. Bachelard worked for much of the twentieth century on the poetic imagination and in particular how this relates to psychology. Central to his work is the placiality of the psyche. Psychic place is nonphysical but is still fully place. For Bachelard, to resolve the tensions of the inner life one must do a topoanalysis of the different places one has experienced. In principle, the number of themes available for topoanalysis is limitless, but there is one that Bachelard privileges, namely that of *the house*.[103] Whereas Heidegger considered the world as the house in which mortals dwell, Bachelard argues that the house is a world. The house, he contends, is "one of the greatest powers of integration for the thoughts, memories, and dreams of mankind."[104] To inhabit a house is not only to be protected from the outside but also to experience the world in miniature, so that in Bachelard's theory space is now immanent in place rather than vice versa.

Attractive as Bachelard's approach is, it does not do justice to the realities of displacement in the world. Thus Foucault, for example, partially in response to Bachelard, focused much of his research on noncentral sites, so-called heterotopology. Foucault's work on the clinic, the mental asylum, and the prison is well known. He is also the first to assert the historicist thesis about place, namely that space and place are historical concepts and entities, subject to the flux of history. Casey considers this historicist approach Foucault's most important contribution to the analysis of place.[105]

Place comes to the foreground in Deleuze and Guattari's analysis of nomadism in their *A Thousand Plateaus*. They distinguish between smooth and striated space. The latter is subject to linear striation as seen from a fixed viewpoint. The former is heterogeneous and full of "qualitative multiplicities" which are particular and resist universalization. The great example of smooth space is nomad space; it is localized but not delimited. One becomes familiar

---

101. Heidegger, "Doch was ist der Ort," 207, quoted in Casey, *Fate of Place*, 283.
102. Casey, *Fate of Place*, 284.
103. Bachelard devotes the first two chapters of his *Poetics of Space* to the house.
104. Ibid., 6.
105. Casey, *Fate of Place*, 301. A useful entry point into Foucault's view of place is his interview with Rabinow. See Foucault, "Space, Knowledge, Power," in *The Foucault Reader*, 239–56.

with such space by experiencing it bodily. Deleuze and Guattari prefer smooth space but acknowledge that one cannot choose between it and sedentary space. However, as Casey rightly notes, "In their insistence on becoming and movement, . . . the authors of *A Thousand Plateaus* overlook the placial potential of *settled dwelling*—of what I have elsewhere called 'built places.' Instructive as is nomadic circulation in the smooth places of deserts and steppes, it represents only part of the full range of human habitation."[106]

Not surprisingly, Derrida, with his early interest in writing and "Archi-writing," later turned his attention to "Archi-tecture."[107] Derrida's discernment of the metaphysics of presence in institutional architecture led him to stress heterotopic places. However, as with so much of his philosophy, its practical outworking is not terribly helpful. This is evident in his role as a consultant to the Villette project, in which he was asked by the architect Bernard Tschumi to design a small park within the larger Parc. Derrida's exhortation was, "Here's my idea: design *chōra*, the impossible place: design it."[108] Casey perceptively and damningly notes that "indeed, one of the most fateful consequences of a deconstructive architecture is its critique of habitation in the usual Western and, more specifically, Heideggerian senses. . . . Derrida discerns in such values, even as thus uncomplicated, the shadow of an un-self-critical metaphysics of presence, an overestimation of the value of nearness and proximity."[109]

Casey's constructive phenomenology of place is found in his *Getting Back into Place*. Since we engage that work in detail in other parts of this book, we will not outline his approach here. Suffice it to note his historicist leanings as pointed out above. It is hard to reconcile these with his phenomenology of place, which would appear to lean toward a realist view of place.[110]

A phenomenology of place is attractive in its receptivity to the richness of creation as it presents itself to the mind, but the problem of abstraction as the key to true knowledge continues to overshadow such an approach. Indeed the great lesson from this history of the philosophy of place in the Western tradition is the skepticism about everyday, lived experience, and the trust in abstraction to lead us to true knowledge of the world. Abstraction is hereby separated from everyday experience and trumps it in terms of knowledge. A good example of how this approach continues to influence metaphysical reflection appears in Brian Greene's *The Fabric of the Cosmos: Space, Time,*

---

106. Casey, *Fate of Place*, 309. Emphasis original.

107. Derrida, "Point de folie."

108. Cited in Ulmer, "Electronic Monumentality."

109. Casey, *Fate of Place*, 318.

110. Casey criticizes Foucault for undercutting his historicist thesis by seeking to universalize heterotopology (ibid., 301). Consistent historicism seems to me impossible, and Casey himself undercuts his historicist aspirations with his outstanding phenomenological analysis of place in his *Getting Back into Place*.

and the Texture of Reality. Greene acknowledges the early influence of Camus upon him, alerting him to the priority of the question of the meaning of life over scientific analysis. However, when it comes to introducing us to current theories of space and time, he asserts, "For me, physical reality both sets the arena and provides the illumination for grappling with Camus' question." "*The* overarching lesson that has emerged from scientific inquiry over the last century is that human experience is often a misleading guide to the true nature of reality."[111] For Greene it is scientific analysis and not human experience that will get us to the truth about our world. Unsurprisingly, there is not one listing of "place" in Greene's index, despite his evocative subtitle about the "texture of reality."

A genuine recovery of place requires a reconfiguration of abstraction in terms of its relationship to everyday experience of the world around us. Fortunately a substantial body of philosophical work addresses precisely this issue. What we require is an understanding of ontology or metaphysics of the sort articulated by N. Wolterstorff in his *On Universals*:

> It is my conviction that all of us, apart from ontology, are aware of the structure of reality—always, of course, dimly, always somewhat askew, always overlooking things, never getting the whole picture. Yet the task of the ontologist is not to postulate new and astonishing entities, not to take us aback with his surmises, not to reveal secrets never suspected. His task is to describe that *rich reality* in the midst of which we live and act, believe and disbelieve, hope and despair. If he is successful, and if we are at all perceptive, we will not find him describing a terrain which, by his description, is astonishingly different from that in which we thought we lived. We will find him describing that terrain which has all the features of the familiar. The ontologist does not postulate unfamiliar things to account for the familiar. He calls our attention to the familiar. The danger that courts in his reader is not that of annoyed shock, but of dozing familiarity. He does not take us on long trails through dark woods into sunlit openings beyond. He points out to us the structure of the ground on which we have stood all along.[112]

Similarly Harvey, in his *Justice, Nature and the Geography of Difference*, addresses "the problem of theorizing"[113] in his introduction. Contra much postmodernism, Harvey seeks to rebuild a Marxist meta theory which does justice to the "permanences" that surround us.[114] The result is a penetrating analysis of the ideological realities of place and multiple insights into how humans construct place. Problematically, however, for Harvey we ourselves

111. Greene, *Fabric of the Cosmos*, 5. Emphasis original.
112. Wolterstorff, *On Universals*, xiii. Emphasis added. The number of placial metaphors in this paragraph is astonishing and significant.
113. Harvey, *Justice, Nature and the Geography of Difference*, 9–10.
114. Ibid., 8.

create the "permanences," and "it is formally true that everything can be reduced to flows."[115]

Astute philosophical analyses of the problem of abstraction are found, for example, in the works of Hamann,[116] Berdyaev, Marcel, Buber, Polanyi,[117] Whitehead, Wolterstorff, the Dutch philosophical tradition of Dooyeweerd, Vollenhoven, and Malpas.[118] All of these thinkers have in common a critique of post-Enlightenment epistemology insofar as it creates a bifurcation,[119] a cleavage[120] between lived experience and scientific analysis. "We have just now seen that theoreticians, because they habitually remain imprisoned by abstractions, are always liable to substitute what is often only a grotesque caricature for a reality which is living and, like everything which lives, is threatened."[121] Marcel rejects the "antiseptic objectivity"[122] of scientism and seeks a recovery of a science rooted in wisdom, communion, intersubjectivity, and wonder. "With the eclipse of mystery goes the atrophy of the sense of wonder."[123]

Marcel relates the intellectual and social alienation of modern humans to the spirit of abstraction that is so dominant in contemporary society. He seeks to elaborate a philosophy deeply in touch with concrete, everyday reality: "The spirit of abstraction results when we ignore the concrete reality from which the abstraction is taken."[124] Such an approach leads to reductionism, of having rather than being. Marcel does not by any means negate the value of abstraction, but carefully distinguishes between primary and secondary reflection. Abstraction is what Marcel calls primary reflection, but his goal is to recover secondary reflection, that reflection rooted in our participation in everyday life and the mystery of being.[125] Mystery breaks down the subject-object relation and alerts us to the truths that comprehend us, to types of truth inseparable from their appropriation: communion, testimony, witness.[126] Secondary reflec-

---

115. Ibid.

116. Haynes, "Introduction," x.

117. Polanyi, *Personal Knowledge*.

118. In terms of scientific abstraction, see the revealing series of interviews in Cayley, *Ideas*. I found the interviews with Wendell Berry, Sajay Samuel, and David Abram particularly helpful. Malpas notes, "While it is a widespread philosophical and scientific tendency to reduce complex structures to more primitive levels of analysis, such reductions typically involve a shift in that which is the focus of explanation—they do not explain, therefore, so much as change the subject" (*Place and Experience*, 196).

119. Whitehead's term. See his book, *Concept of Nature*, 26–48.

120. Berdyaev, *Destiny of Man*, 2: "A cleavage takes place in reality, and in knowledge it expresses itself as objectivization."

121. Marcel, *Tragic Wisdom and Beyond*, 101.

122. Keen, *Gabriel Marcel*, 1.

123. Ibid., 10.

124. Ibid., 13.

125. Ibid., 17.

126. Ibid., 21.

tion recovers the unity of experience, which is in fact fundamental to primary reflection. Marcel calls the central givenness of metaphysics *incarnation*: "We are not only inseparable from our bodies, but from the concrete situations in which we find ourselves. I *am* my habitual surroundings in the same way that I *am* my body."[127]

A vital insight in Marcel's work is that the concrete, everyday world of lived experience is *not* uninterpreted. As Keen notes of Marcel's thought,

> For the religious person the concrete situation in which he finds himself is experienced as the arena within which fidelity to God is to be exercised. Since God is understood as the creator of all, the empirical conditions of my life, my situation, my family, my vocation, are *places* not only of my participation in the mystery of being, but of my encounter with God. For the believer the grace and demand of God are mediated through the concrete situation.[128]

This is what I would call a person's or community's worldview, that pretheoretical orientation toward life which interprets the world and prescribes how to live in it.[129]

Neither I nor any of the authors mentioned above want for a moment to detract from the importance and insights of science. But what does cry out for critique is the overspecialization of science and the extrapolation from the limited, specialized focus of science to claiming to tell the truth about all of life. Wendell Berry has rightly referred to this faith in science as modern superstition and poor science.[130] Berry's critique of agricultural science is particularly interesting, because it alerts us that a major test for science is how it feeds back into and deepens everyday experience. Like too much modern science, agricultural science has taken on a life of its own, divorced from local, earthy realities, whereas, as Berry rightly insists, "to accept nature as a standard is to accept the local ecosystem and its health as the chief indicator of the health of the human economy in that place."[131]

It is easy to see how, once space is legitimately abstracted from our experience of place, the rich textured and local nature of place will be lost if it takes on a life of its own as the path to truth about place. This, as we have seen, is precisely what has happened, and with devastating consequences. For our purposes it will suffice to note that place is primary and that concepts of space are always an abstraction from our experience of place. Healthy science will

127. Ibid., 26.
128. Ibid., 28. Emphasis added.
129. See Goheen and Bartholomew, *Living at the Crossroads*. Probably the most important philosophical work in this area is that by Dilthey. See Goheen and Bartholomew, *Living at the Crossroads*, 12–14.
130. See W. Berry, *Life Is a Miracle*; and his interview, "What Needs to Be Subtracted," in Cayley, *Ideas*, 149–63.
131. W. Berry, "What Needs to Be Subtracted," 150.

deepen our experience of place rather than detract from it. A great parable of such an approach is the effect of the moon landing in 1968. This was hailed as a great example of the "frontier metaphor" at work in American society. As Ronald Reagan later said, "Space, like freedom, is a limitless, never-ending frontier on which our citizens can prove that they are indeed Americans."[132] All planning and attention was directed toward the moon, but, ironically, the greatest effect came from the unplanned photographs of the earth! Hence the title of Robert Poole's exploration of the effects of the moon landing in his aptly named *Earthrise*. The effect of the journey into space led, as should all good science, to a renewed appreciation of earthly life.

The problem of abstraction in relation to place has received detailed attention not only from philosophers but also geographers, and in particular *humanistic geography*.[133] Drawing on phenomenology and existentialism, humanist geographers sought to recover a rich, thick concept of place. Relph argues that "one of the first aims of a phenomenology of geography should be to retrieve these [everyday] experiences from the academic netherworld and to return them to everyone by reawakening a sense of wonder about the earth and its places."[134]

Humanistic geography has done important work in recovering place. However, some of its proponents are in danger of reducing place to human response.[135] Somewhat similarly, Marxists such as Harvey tend to reduce place to a social construct: "Place, in whatever guise, is like space and time, a social construct. This is the baseline proposition from which I start."[136] Sack[137] and Malpas have rightly argued that place is more fundamental to human existence than a human construct. Philosophically, Malpas's account of place is the most satisfying I have encountered.

Malpas draws on Heidegger, Proust, and the analytical tradition—Davidson, Kant, Strawson, and so on—to develop a coherent philosophy of place. He aims to understand place not in the narrow sense of space-time location but as "that wherein the sort of being that is characteristically human has its ground."[138] Malpas develops at length the intimate connections that human thought, knowledge, memory, and agency have with place. Knowledge, according to Malpas, is grounded in the concrete grasp of one's own located existence and in the spatio-temporal structure of the world.[139]

132. Quoted in Poole, *Earthrise*, 5. On the frontier metaphor and science see W. Berry, "What Needs to Be Subtracted," 156–57.

133. See Cresswell, *Place*, especially 18–26.

134. Relph, "Geographical Experiences and Being-in-the-World," 16.

135. Malpas, *Place and Experience*, 30–31.

136. Harvey, *Justice, Nature and the Geography of Difference*, 261. See Cresswell, *Place*, 26–33.

137. Sack, *Homo Geographicus*.

138. Malpas, *Place and Experience*, 33.

139. Ibid., 135.

Place is not merely physical extension or simple location, but neither can it be understood apart from objective space.[140] Malpas's philosophy of place is attractive for its attention to the complexity of place: place "must instead be understood as a structure comprising spatiality and temporality, subjectivity and objectivity, self and other. Indeed, these elements are themselves established only in relation to each other, and so only within the topographical structure of place."[141] Human subjectivity is embedded in the dense structure of place—without places beings would only be abstractions:[142]

> Our identities are thus bound up with particular places or localities through the very structuring of subjectivity and of mental life within the overarching structure of place. Particular places enter into our self-conception and self-identity inasmuch as it is only in, and through our grasp of, the places in which we are situated that we can encounter objects, other persons or, indeed, ourselves. . . . The claim is that we are the sort of thinking, remembering, experiencing creatures we are only in virtue of our active engagement in place; that the possibility of mental life is necessarily tied to such engagement, and so to the places in which we are so engaged; and that, when we come to give content to our concepts of ourselves and to the idea of our own self-identity, place and locality play a crucial role—our identities are, one can say, intricately and essentially place-bound.[143]

Place is thus to be understood as a complex of factors, subjective, intersubjective, and objective. Examinations of place will attend to dimensions such as the natural landscape, patterns of weather and sky, human ordering of space and resources, and the individual and communal narratives in which the place is imbued.[144]

> While the possibility of human involvement in the world is given only in and through such a place, the unity of the place is also evident in, and articulated by means of, the organised activity of the human beings who dwell within it. . . . The dependence of place upon subjectivity, and on objectivity and intersubjectivity, is a dependence (properly an interdependence) that results simply from the character of place as a structure that necessarily encompasses all of these elements and within which the elements are themselves constituted.[145]

We have explored some of the travails of place in the Western philosophical tradition. But how did place fare in the Christian tradition? Did the Christian tradition simply follow the Western in subordinating place to space, or does

140. Ibid., 157.
141. Ibid., 163; cf. 173–74.
142. Ibid., 175–76.
143. Ibid., 177.
144. Ibid., 185.
145. Ibid.

it have resources for recovering a robust theology of place? We have already demonstrated the fecundity of Scripture in terms of place, but as Christians articulated their faith at different times and places, did they plumb this resource, or capitulate to the growing espousal of space against place? It is to this question that we now turn.

10

Place in the Christian Tradition

Introduction

> All the colors of this most beautiful world grow pale once you ex-
> tinguish its light, the firstborn of creation. . . . Every creature will
> alternately become your sacrifice and your idol. . . . This analogy of
> man to the Creator endows all creatures with their substance and
> their stamp, on which depends fidelity and faith in all nature. The
> more vividly this idea of the image of the invisible GOD dwells in
> our heart, the more able we are to see and taste his loving-kindness
> in creatures, observe it and grasp it with our hands.[1]

> The universe is the first Bible. Each being manifests the creative
> word which gives it its identity and attracts it. Each being manifests
> a dynamic idea, something willed by God. Ultimately each thing is
> a created name of him who cannot be named.[2]

As we will see below, there is an abundance of literature nowadays on Christianity and nature and the environment. Christianity and *place*, however, has
received comparatively little attention. Not least of the reasons for this has
been the eclipse of creation in so much Christian thought and practice. Church
historians and theologians tend not to ask the questions I am after in this
book. Writing on place in the Christian tradition reminds one of the challenges

---

1. Hamann, *Writings on Philosophy and Language*, 78–79.
2. Clément, *Roots of Christian Mysticism*, 27.

scholars face who try to take women's experience seriously in historical writing; patriarchy meant that for centuries that experience was ignored, and one has to look hard to recover it. The more I have dug around in the Christian tradition, the more I have discovered both positively and negatively the ways in which Christians have indwelled and fashioned place. Of particular interest has been the discovery of a multitude of Christians who engaged place positively and creatively as an integral part of God's creation. My joyful discoveries reflected below are, however, only the tip of the iceberg; major research remains to be done on place in the Christian tradition.

In the light of the ecological crisis there has been no shortage of writers ready to lay the responsibility at theology's door. The most well known is Lynn White, in his famous article in 1967, "The Historical Roots of our Ecological Crisis." But others have been equally hard-hitting. In the nineteenth century L. Feuerbach asserted that "nature, the world, has no value, no interest for Christians. The Christian thinks of himself and the salvation of his soul."[3] The theologian G. Kaufman takes the biblical-classical theological tradition to have been thoroughly anthropocentric at the expense of nature. The great vocabulary of the Christian tradition—words such as salvation, hope, sin, redemption, righteousness—has to do primarily with humanity and excludes the rest of creation. For Kaufman this is no deviation: "An inner logic of consistency in Western religious traditions was being worked out here."[4] The very concept of God as it has developed in the West "has built into it a depreciation of the metaphysical, and certainly the religious, significance of nature."[5]

Christian scholars have responded to this critique in a variety of ways, all of which Santmire has described and evaluated in an accessible way.[6] Santmire discerns three categories of theological response: reconstructionists, apologists, and revisionists. *Reconstructionists* despair of traditional Christian thought and believe that a new "theology" must be constructed from the ground up. The most well-known reconstructionist is Matthew Fox. Many ecofeminists would also fall under this category. *Apologists*, by comparison, defend the ecological resources of the tradition. *Revisionists* work mainly within the classical Christian tradition but have recognized the problems in much Christian thought, and thus have sought to reexcavate the biblical and theological traditions in search of resources for a robust theology of nature. According to Santmire, the revisionist tradition surfaced in 1961 in Joseph Sittler's address to the World Council of Churches in New Delhi, reached its culmination in James A. Nash's *Loving Nature: Ecological Integrity and Christian Responsibility*, and has flowered more recently in works such as those of John

3. Feuerbach, *Essence of Christianity*, 287.
4. Kaufman, "A Problem of Theology," 351.
5. Ibid., 355.
6. See in particular Santmire, *Nature Reborn*.

Polkinghorne, Terence Fretheim, and Denis Edwards.[7] Note should also be taken of Santmire's series of excellent contributions to this debate.[8]

"Revisionist" is, in my opinion, a somewhat unfortunate name for what Santmire envisages, since it easily evokes the baggage of the reconstructionist position. It is important, therefore, to note what he means by it. The aim is not to abandon the classical theological tradition, but to reclaim it and reenvision it. Santmire is clear that the revisionist position presupposes the faith of the Christian story at the center, proclaimed and nurtured by the church in its worship. On the whole his corpus of work bears eloquent witness to these aims. However, because of the problems inherent in the word *revisionist*, and the ambivalence Santmire sometimes exhibits about the coherent witness of Scripture, I suggest we think of a fourth alternative, namely *Reformational*. *Reformational* evokes an approach which seeks to be re-formed through a renewal of our consciousness by the work of the Spirit through Scripture and the tradition. A Reformational approach seeks to honor the Protestant tradition's motto *semper reformanda* so that we keep reforming rather than get stuck in the past, especially as new challenges, such as place, present themselves to the church. However, a Reformational approach locates the problems in *us*, rather than in Scripture and the Christian tradition at its best.

In part 1 of this book we saw that both Old and New Testaments provide a solid, creative basis for a Christian view of place. However, too much of contemporary Christianity and much of the Christian tradition fails to build on this foundation. Our examination of the Christian tradition will attempt to discern how the rich scriptural witness has been blunted and also to attend to positive nodes in the tradition that we can transfuse into the present to forge a contemporary theology of place.[9]

My analysis below will focus on particular Christian thinkers, but also position them in their broader context. Like all humans, Christians are placed, and for better or for worse they will shape the contexts in which they live. As D. Bonhoeffer rightly notes of the mandate to labor, "It is a making of new things on the basis of the creation by God. No man can evade this mandate."[10] Much of that shaping is either lost to history or waiting to be excavated. As noted previously, placemaking has not drawn the attention of most church historians.

Two aspects of theology and culture in particular will affect the extent to which Christians engage actively and creatively in placemaking. The first is

7. Polkinghorne, *Faith of a Physicist*; Fretheim, *God and World in the Old Testament*; Edwards, *Jesus and the Wisdom of God*.

8. Santmire, *Brother Earth*; idem, *Travail of Nature*.

9. It goes without saying that this is a Herculean task. The equivalent of Casey's *Fate of Place* needs to be written for the Christian tradition. In this section I have aimed at an overarching sense of the tradition, noting the best scholarship and original sources, and attending in particular to constructive parts of the tradition.

10. Bonhoeffer, *Ethics*, 74.

their view of the relationship between Christ and culture. Historically five major models of the Christ-culture relationship can be discerned in the Christian tradition: Christ against culture, Christ of culture, Christ above culture, Christ in parallel to culture, and Christ the transformer of culture.[11] Clearly the first two models are unlikely to have a major effect on placemaking, although exponents of the Christ-against-culture model, embodied in some monasticism and nowadays in Amish culture, sometimes end up powerfully affecting our understanding of place by providing a prophetic, alternative model in times of crisis. Niebuhr rightly refers to churches espousing the latter three models as Churches of the Center, since they are less extreme and represent the views of most Christians. The final model, Christ the transformer of culture, which I regard as the most biblical, is likely to have the most conscious effect on placemaking.

The second aspect is the (political) room for placemaking. Placemaking, especially in the public domain, requires a degree of cultural freedom and power, and thus it is not surprising that it is mainly after Constantine's conversion, and the Edict of Milan in 392, that we witness Christians actively involved in building projects and in the building of churches in particular.[12] For the first three centuries Christians worshiped mainly in private houses. Some of these were renovated to accommodate Christian worship.[13] However, we know from Eusebius that even before the fourth century, Christians had begun to build their own churches.[14]

After Constantine's legalization of Christianity, church building exploded in the fourth century. Most church buildings would have been moderate in size, but they were fashioned according to the design of the great churches that now emerged. Vast amounts of imperial money were poured into the construction of churches, with the result that many were magnificent.[15] Intriguingly, the dominant style chosen for church buildings was that of the basilica, a large building originally designed for the conduct of public business. The building of churches in this style significantly affected the liturgy: "Much of the story attached to the development of the Eucharistic liturgy and the calendar is

11. See Niebuhr, *Christ and Culture.*

12. The vision for and practice of Christian influence on culture prior to 392 should not be underestimated. For example, Bardaisan (154–ca. 222), a Christian, was an influential and learned figure at the court of the kings of Orsene. He wrote *The Book of the Laws of Countries* to demonstrate that in whatever place Christians find themselves, they are free to live under the laws of the Messiah. On Bardaisan see P. Brown, *Rise of Western Christendom*, 3–7. On Christians in the third century see ibid., 18–33. He notes that this century was one of "surprising Christians" (ibid., 25).

13. See also ibid., 24.

14. Cf., for example, the Greek Chapel located in the second-century catacomb of Priscilla in Rome, shown in Wainwright and Westerfield-Tucker, *Oxford History of Christian Worship*, 59.

15. Eusebius devotes part of book 10 of his church history to the panegyric he delivered on the occasion of the dedication of a new basilica at Tyre.

associated with what was required by the sheer scale of the new buildings and by the fact that Christians could now make the public plazas and thoroughfares of the major cities their own."[16]

The legacy of Christendom is rightly controversial. But as Newbigin perceptively notes,

> What should the church of the fourth century have done? Should it have refused to baptize the Emperor on the ground that it is better for the spiritual health of the Church to be persecuted than to be in the seats of power? The discussion is unrealistic and futile. We have to accept as a matter of fact the first great attempt to translate the universal claim of Christ into political terms was the Constantinian settlement. Christ as Pantocrator took on the lineaments of the Roman Emperor.[17]

Positively, the Constantinian settlement provided the space for Christians to influence public building in a lasting fashion. In my opinion, perhaps the great example in this respect is the Hagia Sophia as rebuilt by Justinian in the sixth century.[18] Although it has been Islamized and is now a museum, it remains overwhelming both visually and aesthetically. Visiting it several years ago, I resonated with Paul the Silentiary's AD 562 description of it: "Thus, as you direct your gaze towards the eastern arches, you behold a never-ceasing wonder."[19]

When Augustine lay dying in the fifth century, so too did the Roman Empire. Brown notes the crucial role of many churches in Gaul amidst the consequent disarray:

> The intensely communal quality of the Christian churches, which we have seen developing in the cities of the fourth century, now stood out in pointed contrast to a divided and easily dispersed secular aristocracy. The local church became the "fixative" that held whole populations in place. The Church's charitable activities palliated the effects of famine and siege. . . . More important still, the building of the church spoke of the day-to-day determination of cities to survive and to be seen to survive.[20]

The emergence of monasticism during this time was vital for the reemergence of Europe, as we will see in part 3 in our examination of placemaking and the city. The monasteries were microcosms for the recovery of the macrocosm of

16. Baldovin, "The Empire Baptized," 78. See also Baldovin, *Urban Character of Christian Worship*.

17. Newbigin, *Sign of the Kingdom*, 47. For a similar view see O'Donovan, *Desire of the Nations*.

18. See Nelson, *Hagia Sophia, 1850–1950*.

19. See Paul Silentarius, "Descr. S. Sophiae" and "Descr. ambonis v. Soff," in Mango, *Art of the Byzantine Empire*.

20. P. Brown, *Rise of Western Christendom*, 62.

European cities. Though often neglected, the Byzantine Empire, which began in the early fourth century with the foundation of Constantinople and ended when the Ottoman Turks captured it in 1453, also contributed significantly to this recovery. The rebuilding of the Hagia Sophia is part of this rich legacy.[21]

This narrative takes us into the Middle Ages, and then on to the Renaissance and Reformation and the Enlightenment and post-Enlightenment eras, and then on to our late-modern day. In our examination of placemaking and the city we will explore the medieval city and subsequent developments. As we explore the views of central Christian thinkers, we will be looking for understandings of the Christ-culture relationship and practices that open up placemaking.

21. Among others, see Bullen, *Byzantium Rediscovered*; Wells, *Sailing from Byzantium*. Wells notes, "Measuring by cultural influence, however, more recent historical research has revealed a story of lasting achievement and vigorous expansion" (20). He explores the transmission of ancient Greek literature to the West, the contribution of Byzantine culture to Islamic science, and the empire's religious contribution to the Slavic world.

11

Early Church Fathers

For if the flesh were not in a position to be saved, the Word of God would in no wise have become flesh.[1]

Irenaeus

Irenaeus (130–200) was a bishop who wrote to defend the church against gnosticism and to interpret and celebrate the essentials of the gospel for the church of his day. Gnosticism is a complex phenomenon whose rise parallels that of Christianity. Central to gnosticism was the view that creation is evil: "The universe, the domain of the Archons, is like a vast prison whose innermost dungeon is the earth, the scene of man's life."[2] However, a spark of the divine is contained within the human soul, which sets humankind radically apart from the evil creation:

> Gnosticism . . . removes man, in virtue of his essential belonging to another realm, from all sameness with the world, which is now nothing but bare "world," and confronts him with its totality as the absolutely different. Apart from his accessory outer layers contributed by the world, man by his inner nature is acosmic; to such a one, the world is indifferently alien. While there is ultimate otherness of origin, there can be kinship, neither with the world nor with any part of the universe. The self is kindred only to other human selves in the world—and to

1. Irenaeus, *Against Heresies* 5.14.1.
2. Jonas, *The Gnostic Problem*, 43.

the transmundane God, with whom the non-mundane center of the self can enter into communion.[3]

Through a savior who descends from above, humans are provided with what they need for salvation, namely gnosis. After death, each soul, equipped with gnosis, travels upward until, stripped of all foreign accretions, it reaches its true home in God. According to some systems, the last act of the gnostic universal drama is the demolition of the cosmos. As Santmire notes, "Gnosticism is perhaps the most extreme example in Western history of a world view shaped by the metaphor of ascent—by that metaphor, indeed, and no other."[4]

Irenaeus rejected the gnostics' denial of the creator God and the Old Testament and their view of God as distant and removed from everyday life. He saw creation as humanity's God-given home, which was of great value to the God who became incarnate to redeem fallen humanity and to thereby renew the entire creation. In his struggle with Marcion and the gnostics over the unity of the Bible, Irenaeus articulates the unity of the Bible as a single story:

> Two histories converge in the biblical account, the history of Israel and the life of Christ, but because they are also the history of God's actions in and for the world, they are part of a larger narrative that begins at creation and ends in a vision of a new, more splendid city in which the "Lord God will be their light." The Bible begins, as it were, with the beginning and ends with an end that is no end, life with God, in Irenaeus's charming expression, a life in which one is "always conversing with God in new ways." Nothing falls outside of its scope.[5]

With Irenaeus's narrative approach to the Bible we have an incipient biblical theology articulated in terms of the story shape of the Bible as a whole. Furthermore, he explains the story in terms of the theme of renewal or re-creation. God's original intention for creation was dynamic; God intended to lead it from its original state to final fulfillment. Hence the incarnation is aimed not just at redeeming humanity but at leading the creation to its intended fulfillment. Christ recapitulates in himself what has preceded him in human history and thereby overcomes sin and leads the whole of human history to its consummation. "Creation, the incarnation of Christ, redemption, and resurrection, belong together as different parts of one all-embracing saving work of God."[6]

Irenaeus's eschatology of the final renewal of all things is a central part of his rejection of gnosticism. "Neither the substance nor the essence of the

---

3. Ibid., 17.
4. Santmire, *Travail of Nature*, 34.
5. Wilken, *Spirit of Early Christian Thought*, 63.
6. Grillmeier, *Christ in Christian Tradition*, 101.

creation will be annihilated . . . but the 'fashion' of the world passes away."[7]
After the resurrection and the judgment, the saints shall dwell in the terrestrial
kingdom of the new Jerusalem; for the earth will not be destroyed, but will
be accommodated to the new conditions.

Irenaeus does teach that the creation was made for humankind, but this is
an administrative anthropocentrism and decidedly not an ontological one.[8]
Creation is arranged for the well being of humans, but this is not its only
purpose—it has its own integrity in relation to God. Human dominion over
nature is muted in Irenaeus's theology: "The accent is not on teleological
activity, but on *communion*—eating in the midst of the overflowing blessings
that God gives in nature. For Irenaeus, this is true in this life; but it will be
all the more true of the times of the coming new heavens and new earth."[9]

Origen

There is no doubt that the Christian tradition is ambiguous as regards place.
Henri de Lubac notes a tendency in the Greek fathers especially, that "proceeds
unambiguously away from the material to the spiritual. . . . Spiritualization,
presented in a thousand different colorations, is the basic tendency of the
patristic epoch."[10] This becomes clear through a comparison of Irenaeus with
Origen (185–254).[11]

For Origen there was a time before creation when there was neither time nor
space. Creation occurs in two stages: primal or providential creation, and secondly the creation of the visible world. Before anything visible appeared, God
created the organizing principles for the visible world; these were the primal
object of creation.[12] The description in Genesis 1 of what God saw as good
refers to the first stage of creation, creation of divine wisdom and providence.

Similarly there are two stages in the creation of humankind. The first man
is created immaterial and superior to any corporeal nature. The *imago Dei*
of Genesis 1 applies to all humans and precedes what Adam became when
he assumed his earthly nature "because of sin."[13] Origen does not regard the
material world as evil, but it is subject in his thought to the very contradiction
Lovejoy identifies in the chain of being.[14] Matter is created by the goodness
of God, but merely in order to educate human beings so that they can return
to their higher spiritual destiny. For Origen, when it comes to creation, we

---

7. Irenaeus, *Against Heresies* 5.36.1.
8. Santmire, *Travail of Nature*, 42.
9. Ibid., 44. Emphasis original.
10. De Lubac, "*Un témoin dans l'Eglise*," 186.
11. Santmire, *Travail of Nature*, 44–45.
12. Tzamalikos, *Origen: Cosmology and Ontology*, 45.
13. Origen, *Homilies on Jeremiah*, 2, 1.
14. Lovejoy, *The Great Chain of Being*, 45–54.

need to think in terms of three realities: God, who precedes time and space; providential creation, coming into being out of nothingness; and the fall out of the body of Christ, which denotes actual creation coming into existence.

The materiality of the world is fundamental for Origen.[15] God is the original place (*hoinai topos*) of the Logos,[16] and the Logos created the world and is fundamentally related to it.[17] God is the primary place of the Logos but not the only place; the Logos is stretched out alongside with the world (*symparekteinomenos*). He is present with the world but not part of it. Time[18] and history are central to Origen's theology; they are the necessary means through which the world will be able to return to God. Thus there is no inherent antagonism between space and time. The incarnation is central to the historical process: "In his philosophy of history, the incarnation, passion, death, and resurrection of Jesus stands in the center and determines the core of his thought and exegesis of Scripture."[19]

Origen affirms the resurrection of the body and the soul,[20] but his eschatology leads not to a new heavens and new earth but ultimately to incorporeal existence in God. Origen has much to say about different places, and particularly the places that are *up* rather than down here.[21] With regard to the meek inheriting the earth, for example, Origen notes that there is another heaven which contains that earth which Jesus promises to the meek.[22] In his articulation of the final telos of living with God, Origen avoids any word that is explicitly placial.[23]

"The ultimate destination is a state *after* the eternal life: this state is the divine reality itself. To exist in space-time is *sojourning*, that is, a *temporary* status, which had a beginning and will come to an end. The absolute *end* is styled as 'entering into' the divine life."[24] The final end comes when the world "jumps" through Christ into the timeless being of God. God will then be seen as he is in himself, and those who are now rational hypostases will be in God, beyond time and corporeality. When this jump happens there will no longer be any reason for space and time and the corporeal world, and they will cease to exist.

> The notion of a certain "after the eternal life," which marks the final end of the world, points to the dissolution of corporeality into non-being. Going into the divine reality, "communion" with God and "deification" imply and entail sharing the divine nature. Although the ontology of creatures is not the divine

---

15. Tzamalikos, *Origen: Cosmology and Ontology*, 113–16.
16. Origen, *Commentary of Origen*, 20, 18.
17. Tzamalikos, *Origen*, 166.
18. See ibid. for Origen's philosophy of time.
19. Ibid., 424.
20. Ibid., 18.
21. Ibid., 102–4.
22. Ibid., 103.
23. Tzamalikos, *Origen: Philosophy of History*, 270.
24. Ibid., 272.

one . . . they are deified by divine grace. This entails that the essential elements of the make-up of the world, that is, space and time, will come to an end. Since corporeal nature is a demonstration of the reality of space, termination of existence of corporeal nature is due to the termination of existence of space proper.[25]

That Origen was a deeply philosophical theologian is clear. What is contested is the extent to which his theology is influenced by Greek philosophy.[26] In my view it is clear that in Origen's theology the biblical metanarrative has been reconfigured within a Neoplatonic schema, which denigrates the creation. We come from God and return to him.

Thus Origen denigrates the human body, and animals exist only in order to be agents of purgation in the education of humans. In his writings he compares the creation of humans to the birth of a child, and that of animals and inanimate entities to the afterbirth.[27] Origen's perspective is thoroughly anthropocentric[28] in that "the Creator, then, has constituted all things the servants of the rational being and of his natural understanding."[29] For Origen, unlike Irenaeus, God's goal with creation is a return to the beginning. The material world will collapse back into nothingness. Origen attempts to take seriously the church's affirmation of the resurrection of the body, but the resurrected body will perhaps be "like the ether, and of a celestial purity and clearness."[30] It will have lost its corporeality.[31]

As happens again and again in this strand of Christian thought, Scripture is interpreted to fit the paradigm. A good example of this is Origen's spiritualization of the Israelites' journey to the promised land:

> If you do not wish to fall in the wilderness, but to have attained the promised land of the fathers, you should have no portion in the land nor should you have anything in common with the earth. Let your portion be only with the Lord, and you will never fail. Therefore, the ascent from Egypt to the promised land is something by which, as I have said, we are taught in mysterious descriptions the ascent of the soul to heaven and the mystery of the Resurrection from the dead.[32]

As a Christian, Origen affirms the goodness of creation, but his embrace of the metaphor of ascent as articulated in the chain of being leads him inevitably

25. Ibid., 311.
26. For detailed discussions of the philosophical influences on Origen's theology, see Tzamalikos, *Origen: Philosophy of History*; idem, *Origen: Cosmology and Ontology*.
27. Origen, *Against Celsus* 4:74.
28. As Santmire notes, Origen's is an ontological anthropocentrism, compared with Irenaeus's administrative one (*Travail of Nature*, 50).
29. Origen, *Against Celsus* 4:78.
30. Origen, *First Principles* 1.6.4.
31. Ibid., 1.7.4.
32. Origen, "Homily 27 on Numbers," paragraph 4, in Greer, *Origen*.

to degrade creation and thus place. Although Origen's theology was eventually condemned by the church, he strongly influenced subsequent Christian thinkers, not least by his view of creation and thus of place.

Indeed, it is hard to overemphasize the negative effect of Neoplatonism on Christianity in terms of a positive theology of placemaking. As with Platonism, the gravitational pull of Neoplatonism is always upward and away from concrete, created reality, and as long as theology remained entrenched in such a framework, the framework would always detract from such issues as place.

Augustine

Augustine's legacy in terms of place is contested, not least because of the shifts in his theology, especially in his middle and later years. Like Origen, Augustine (345–430) was a philosophical theologian, and in his pilgrimage from one philosophical school to another he came to rest in Neoplatonism. "At the same time, in his middle and later years, Augustine was able to sense the textures and the resonances of biblical faith, above all the biblical concern for history, far more adequately than Origen was able to do. In this respect Augustine was much closer to Irenaeus than to Origen, and for this reason he may also be thought of as a confessional theologian."[33]

Alongside the decisive influence of Neoplatonism on Augustine came that of Genesis 1 and 2, which, engaging him on no less than five occasions, contributed to his mature thought about creation.[34] "Augustine's work with the Genesis creation narratives . . . helped him to reshape his thought so that it was no longer defined primarily by the spatial categories of Plotinus, but more and more by the temporal categories of biblical history."[35] Genesis 1 and 2 brought Augustine to a view of reality as creation history with a beginning, *creatio ex nihilo*; an end point; and a unique midpoint in the incarnation.

For Augustine, God is the unchanging One, but a God who is active and close at hand as well. He conceives of the primary material out of which the creation is made as good and receptive to the ordering of creation. However, it remains true that for Augustine, the spiritual dimension of creation is closer and more akin to God. Human utility is not, in Augustine's view, the sole function of the material world; the goal of the creation is beauty, and every part of the creation has its role in the hierarchy of being in glorifying God.

33. Santmire, *Travail of Nature*, 55.

34. His work on Genesis 1 and 2 was polemical, as in *Against the Manichees* (written in 388–89); exegetical and theological in his commentary (393–94; *De Genesi ad Litteram*); existential and personal in his *Confessions* (401); and synthetic in his *City of God* (417), Books 11 and 12. See Augustine, *On Genesis*, Books 11 and 12.

35. Santmire, *Travail of Nature*, 57. This is noted by Tillich in "The Struggle between Time and Space," chap. 3 of his *Theology of Culture*.

Certain parts of the human body, for example, appear to have no utilitarian value but are made solely for beauty's sake. "Therefore it is the nature of things considered in itself, without regard to our convenience or inconvenience, that gives glory to God."[36]

God is intimately involved in the world and governs all things by "concursus." Augustine invokes the metaphors of shepherding, the husbandman, and brooding as ways of depicting God's governance of the creation. The whole of the creation is charged with God's grandeur, and it is only the disordering of our senses and affections that prevents us from seeing this. Intriguingly, Augustine develops the concept of seminal ideas built into the creation. These contain within themselves the seeds of new development and allow for novelty in history:[37] "All these things indeed have originally and primarily already been created in a kind of web of the elements; but they make their appearance when they get the opportunity. For just as mothers are pregnant with their young, so the world itself is pregnant with things that are not created in it."[38] Augustine associates human domination with the fall rather than the true order for creation. Augustine appears to envision a communal and contemplative relationship between humankind and nature, what Santmire refers to as a contemplative dominion.[39] Interestingly, Augustine insists that the groaning of Romans 8 applies to humans and not the good creation as a whole; similarly, the curse of Genesis 3 applies to humans and does not disrupt the cosmos.

Crucially, Augustine's vision of creation history culminates not in a return to the beginning but in a new heavens and new earth:

> The form of this world will pass away in a blazing up of the fires of the world, just as the Deluge was caused by the overflowing of the waters of the world. . . . The qualities of the corruptible elements which were appropriate for our corruptible bodies will utterly perish in the burning, and our substance itself will acquire the qualities which will be suited, by a miraculous transformation, to our immortal bodies, with the obvious purpose of furnishing the world, now renewed for the better, with a fitting population of human beings, renewed for the better even in their flesh.[40]

Admittedly, this renewal follows a universal conflagration of all things, but nevertheless his view represents a considerable advance on Origen. The world itself will be renewed. In his mature thought Augustine evokes the metaphor of the "spouse" as an image for the body's relationship to the soul, in contrast

36. Augustine, *City of God* 12.4.
37. This is not unlike Dooyeweerd's idea of differentiation. See Chaplin, *Herman Dooyeweerd*, 71–85.
38. Augustine, *On the Trinity* 3.9, quoted in Santmire, *Travail of Nature*, 68.
39. Santmire, *Travail of Nature*, 69–70.
40. Augustine, *City of God* 20.16, quoted in Santmire, *Travail of Nature*, 68.

to his earlier images of the body as a "snare" or "cage."[41] As regards the resurrection body, he stresses its identity with the earthly body: "Take away death, the last enemy, and my own flesh shall be my dear friend throughout eternity."[42]

In view of the centrality of neoplatonism in Augustine's thought, it is not surprising that scholars remain divided over his legacy. Bonhoeffer rightly recognized that "it was a near catastrophe for Christianity when it became more closely related to neo-Platonic idealism than to Old Testament realism,"[43] and for all Augustine's progress, the neoplatonic pull toward that which is above is never finally eradicated from his theology.

Maximus the Confessor

Maximus the Confessor (ca. 580–662) was a Christian monk, theologian, and scholar. In his early life he was a civil servant and an aide to the Byzantine emperor Heraclius. However, he gave up his political life to enter a monastery. Brian Daley, in the preface of his translation of von Balthasar's *Cosmic Liturgy*, notes that in 1941 and even in 1961 "von Balthasar's concern was to find in the Catholic dogmatic tradition . . . an intelligent and convincing answer to the seductive call of German idealism to let *the concrete reality of creation* dissolve into being nothing more than the phenomena experienced by the thinking human subject."[44] Central to von Balthasar's theology is the quest for an approach which "affirms the world in all its finitude."[45] In Maximus the Confessor, von Balthasar finds the most world-affirming of all the Greek church fathers.[46] Maximus himself asserts that "whatever exists, has being according to a perfect law and cannot receive a better being."[47]

Maximus's theology is a synthesis of the mysticism and apophatic (negative) theology of Dionysius, the Aristotelian emphasis on the concrete universal, and an understanding of Jesus in terms of a Chalcedonian Christology.[48] Von Balthasar says of Maximus's theology, "In the sphere of a Christian philosophy of person and existence, the clarity of the Greek grasp of the world's being was to find its final fulfillment."[49] Maximus makes a clear ontological distinction between God and creation: God's immanent name is Being; his transcendent name is Not-being. No common concept of Being can span God and creature.

---

41. Miles, *Augustine on the Body*, 97.
42. Augustine, *Sermons* 155.5, quoted in Santmire, *Travail of Nature*, 68.
43. Dumas, *Dietrich Bonhoeffer*, 153.
44. Daley, translator's foreward to Balthasar, *Cosmic Liturgy*, 17. Emphasis added.
45. Löser, *Im Geiste des Origenes*, 211.
46. Balthasar, *Cosmic Liturgy*, 61.
47. Maximus, *Ambigua*, in Patrologia graeca (hereafter PG) 91:1189b. Translations from Maximus, *Ambigua*, are those of Balthasar, *Cosmic Liturgy*.
48. See Balthasar, *Cosmic Liturgy*.
49. Ibid., 65.

The creation has its *archē* in God as its sole cause; he brings it into "being" from nonbeing and sets it on its path that leads it via "well-being" to its goal in "eternal well-being," that is, union with God. Maximus thereby combines the neoplatonic cycle of procession and return with a more historical, developmental understanding of motion: "The whole intelligible-sensible universe presents itself as a real medium for the self-manifestation of God without being coextensive with his being."[50]

Maximus envisages the goal of creation as *deification* or union with God,[51] but he does not equate this with a loss of corporeality. He envisages a naturally lasting cosmos as the supporting ground for divinization. The preincarnate Logos is immanent, albeit in concealed fashion, in all the intelligible structures of the world. He sees the natural world contemplated in the light of wisdom as a source of revelation: "The wise person stands in the midst of the world's realities as in an inexhaustible treasury of knowledge. No being leaves him untouched; everything provides food for his intellectual nourishment."[52]

In the creation Maximus identifies three laws: the natural law, the written law, and the law of Christ. In line with the patristic tradition, he identifies the two books of Scripture and nature, but a unique development in his thought is the argument that the two are equally valuable.[53] The third law is spiritual law or the law of grace; it is a single law which converges in Christ, who is, after all, the author of natural law as creator and the giver of the written law as lawgiver. The three are thus one and the same; to break any of them is sin.[54] For the Logos's involvement in all three "economies" Maximus uses the metaphor of "thickening": in each economy the Word has thickened himself. "He indicates himself by analogy through each visible being, as through certain letters, wholly present in his utter fulness in the whole universe and at the same time wholly present in individual things."[55] The life of virtue is thus itself an incarnation of the Word.

The incarnation is central to Maximus's theology. It is not only the midpoint of world history but the foundational idea of the world itself. As A. Louth notes, "The body of Christ confers a redeemed significance on the cosmos and marks out a sacred space in which this redemption is celebrated and effected."[56] Maximus makes much of the transfiguration. It is an archetypal locus in which the human union with God by faith and the reciprocal universal theophany of divine glory is proleptically demonstrated.[57]

50. Cooper, *Body in St. Maximus the Confessor*, 18.
51. For a good explanation of this concept in Orthodox theology see Payton, *Light from the Christian East*, 132–54.
52. Ibid., 62.
53. Cooper, *Body in St. Maximus the Confessor*, 37.
54. Balthasar, *Cosmic Liturgy*, 66.
55. Maximus, *Ambigua*, PG 91:1285d.
56. Louth, "Body in Western Catholic Christianity," 121.
57. Cooper, *Body in St. Maximus the Confessor*, 36.

Through his death, resurrection, and ascension, Christ "reestablishes the continuity between heaven and earth 'and proves that heavenly and earthly beings join in a single festive dance, as they receive the gifts that come from God.'"[58] Maximus notes, "Because our earth was no longer, for him, a different reality from Paradise, he appeared to his disciples on it once again, after his Resurrection, and associated with them, so showing that from now on the earth was one, united with itself."[59] Christians are now the place and occasion of God's incarnation as it continues to be realized; we share with Christ in the transformation of the world.

As a body-soul unity, humans are a microcosm of the universe: "Man, as an intellectual and material microcosm, thus appears both as the midpoint of a universe arranged in a polar pattern and as its final synthesis."[60] While Maximus privileges mind over matter, we have seen already the positive role of matter and embodiment in his theology.[61] Von Balthasar notes that "dogmatic formulations, in fact, are often a step ahead of the full philosophical 'ownership' of a new way of thinking: with the assurance of a sleepwalker, the Church coins a formula that only later on reveals all the dimensions of its meaning."[62] As we saw in our overview of the history of the philosophy of place, one way in which place has been retrieved is through a recovery of embodiment. The church fathers are instructive in this respect, and not least Maximus, because of the way in which the Christian belief in the resurrection of body and soul forced them to engage critically with those tendencies in Greek thought which denigrated the body.[63] Maximus does not spell out in detail the shape of the deiform body, but he does note that it will be a perfected version of Adam's prefall body, truly corporeal, yet free from divisive, corrupting qualities.[64]

Maximus's high ecclesiology is integrally related to his cosmology: "It is not 'heavenly liturgy,' as it is for Pseudo-Dionysius, or 'cosmic gnosticism,' as it is for Erigena; theology, for Maximus, is Cosmic Liturgy."[65] For Maximus true cosmic being is fulfilled in the church.

Although Maximus's theology contains no developed theology of place, it clearly has great potential in this respect. He notes that "the whole universe, defined by the limits of its own intelligible principles (λογοι [logoi]), is called place (τοπος [topos]) and time (ἰων [iōn])."[66] All finite beings are located and

---

58. Balthasar, *Cosmic Liturgy*, 273, quoting Maximus, *Exposition of the Lord's Prayer*, PG 90:877a, b.

59. Maximus, *Ambigua*, PG 91:1309a, b.

60. Balthasar, *Cosmic Liturgy*, 175. Barth opposes this view (*Church Dogmatics*, vol. 3, pt. 2, pp. 15–16).

61. For an excellent treatment of this theme see Cooper, *Body in St. Maximus the Confessor*.

62. Balthasar, *Cosmic Liturgy*, 211.

63. Amongst many other sources, see the essays in Coakley, *Religion and the Body*.

64. Cooper, *Body in St. Maximus the Confessor*, 253.

65. Ibid., 85.

66. Maximus, *Ambigua*, PG 91:1292c.

dated.[67] Maximus also distinguishes between the right use as opposed to the abuse of creaturely things,[68] a distinction akin to the neo-Calvinist distinction between structure and direction (see p. 225). Right use is oriented toward the destiny of creation, namely transfiguration into God: "The image of the burning bush will then be completely realized: 'That ineffable, overwhelming fire, which burns away, hidden in the essence of things as in the bush,' will then burst out: not to consume the world, for it needs no fuel to burn. It will be a flame of love at the heart of things, and that flame is God himself."[69]

67. Balthasar, *Cosmic Liturgy*, 139.
68. Ibid., 304–5.
69. Ibid., 353.

12

The Middle Ages, the Reformers, and the Protestant Tradition

The Middle Ages

Remarkably, G. Chesterton, in his book on Thomas Aquinas,[1] discerns a common cause in Aquinas and Saint Francis: both were seeking to recover the incarnation. However, in terms of place Saint Francis is a more promising candidate than Thomas. Indeed with the possible exception of Saint Francis the potential flowering of place we witnessed in Augustine did not fully survive in the Renaissance and Middle Ages. There is a deep ambiguity in medieval thought; on the one hand Christians seek God through the world, but on the other they seek God through renunciation of the world.[2]

Alan of Lille (ca. 1128–1202) demonstrates this ambiguity. He assumes the great chain of being and describes the heavens as the citadel of a city where the everlasting Ruler dwells. The heavenly army of angels serves the Ruler, and further down God creates a beautiful material universe with a wonderful sensuous harmony about it. However, nature's goodness has no future: it will fade away, and while rational creatures are relevant to the end of history, irrational creatures are good only for the beginning. The material world has a subordinate, instrumental place in service of rational creatures.

1. Chesterton, *Saint Thomas Aquinas*, 1–28.
2. See in this respect Chenu, *Nature, Man, and Society*, 36; Santmire, *Travail of Nature*, 76.

There were countervailing tendencies, to be sure, as cities emerged in their own right and cathedral schools were established. Indeed L Mumford[3] and R. Dubos[4] find in Benedict a model for ecological responsibility.[5] Dubos argues that the Benedictine movement exercised a "creative stewardship of the earth." The Benedictine motto was *Ora et Labora*, and with their sense of mission, Benedictine communities played a major role in taming and developing Europe. However, the thought of the most influential theologian and philosopher of the medieval era, Thomas Aquinas, demonstrates the failure of medieval thought to escape from the inherent ambiguity we identified earlier.

Thomas Aquinas

E. Gilson rightly points out that Thomas's (1225–1274) view of the world was imbued with a "radical optimism,"[6] and this ties in with his appropriation of Aristotle. However, as Chesterton perceptively notes, the question is whether he brought Christ to Aristotle or Aristotle to Christ. Central to Thomas's scholasticism is a confidence in his ability to know the creation and a sense of its inherent goodness. In line with Aristotle, Thomas conceives of God as the first cause, and although this view is tempered by the Platonic notion of participation, his view of God's relationship to the creation tends to be slanted in this Aristotelian direction. Everything participates in Being, and thus God is in everything—"God is in all things, and innermostly"[7]—but he governs creation through the hierarchy he has created, and in particular through the spiritual beings, the angels.

Each creature has a life and telos of its own within the larger whole, and the world around us is the good world God created. The diversity of creation represents the goodness of God, but this approach is muted by Thomas's thorough subordination of nature to humankind. The plants and animals exist solely in order to serve humankind, what Santmire calls a kind of "*intramundane anthropocentrism*."[8] The tension in Thomas's thought between the good and the goodness is manifest in his concept of the eschaton. As a biblical scholar Thomas is constrained to take the resurrection of the body and the renewal of all things seriously, and so he does. However, as regards the animals and plants, mixed bodies and minerals, there will be no renewal at the end of time. In his articulation of the reasons for this, Thomas's anthropocentrism is foregrounded: "If the end ceases, those things which are directed to the end should cease. Now animals and plants were made for the upkeep of human life . . .

---

3. Mumford, *Myth of the Machine*, 263–67.
4. Dubos, *Reason Awake*, 126.
5. See White, *Machine Ex Deo*; Bosch, *Transforming Mission*, 230–36.
6. Gilson, *Christian Philosophy of St. Thomas Aquinas*, 189.
7. Thomas Aquinas, *Summa Theologica* 1.8.1.
8. Santmire, *Travail of Nature*, 91. Emphasis original.

therefore when man's animal life ceases, animals and plants should cease. But after this renewal animal life will cease in man. Therefore neither plants nor animals ought to remain." Again: "Dumb animals, plants, and minerals, and all mixed bodies, are corruptible both in their whole and in their parts, both on the part of the matter which loses its form, and on the part of their form which does not remain actually. . . . Hence they will not remain in this renewal."[9]

For all the deficiencies of Aquinas's eschatology, Chesterton is right about his concern to recover a robust doctrine of the incarnation, which facilitates a concern with the created order. Thus, in his political writings, for example, Aquinas demonstrates a real concern with city building:

> One who wishes to found a city or a kingdom must therefore first of all choose a place suitable to the preservation of the health of the inhabitants; fertile enough to provide them with sufficient food; pleasant enough to give them enjoyment; and well defended enough to ensure them protection against enemies. . . . Then, having chosen the site, it is necessary for the founder of a city or kingdom to divide it up in such a way as to supply all the needs which must be met if the kingdom is to be complete. . . . It will be necessary to provide locations suitable for the establishment of towns, farms and castles, and centres will need to be set up for the pursuit of learning, the training of soldiers, and the conduct of commerce . . . otherwise neither city nor kingdom could endure for long.[10]

Saint Francis

Francis's (1182–1226) attractiveness stems in particular from his care for God's creatures: he cared for fish and insects, he ordered honey and the best wine to be made available for the bees in the cold winters, and he referred to all animals as his brothers. The movement of ascent to God, so dominant in his time, was central to Francis's piety, but it resulted not in a movement away from the creation but in one of descent to the creation. Santmire discerns the source of this remarkable inversion of the piety of the day in Francis's relationship to Jesus:

> Francis's relationship with nature had a *cruciform* character. He became the Christ-like servant of nature. He impoverished himself in order that he might give himself to others, both to human and to natural creatures. So in his life and thought . . . he, in effect, united two grand theological themes: . . . the vision of the descending goodness of God, which makes all things good and worthy of respect in their own right, since they are indeed of God and for God; . . . the vision of the descending love of God in Christ, the self-giving Savior, who, in turn, mandated sacrificial love for the world.[11]

9. Thomas Aquinas, *Summa Theologica*, 5.91.5.
10. Thomas Aquinas, *Political Writings*, 38–39.
11. Santmire, *Travail of Nature*, 111. Emphasis original.

Similarly, Alan Paton notes that through a speech by Reinhold Niebuhr he learned from Saint Francis that "there is a wound in the Creation and that the greatest use we could make of our lives was to ask to be made the healer of it."[12] At a liturgical level a great gift of Francis was the introduction of the Christmas Christ mass, with living animals in a dark cave outdoors illuminated by candles and torches. In this "ritualization of nature" Francis bequeathed to the church a ritual that has been practiced by many churches ever since.[13]

Santmire finds evidence that Francis looked forward to the consummation of history in the renewal of the cosmos as a whole and concludes that Francis's life and death were shaped by the ecological motif of Western theology. It seems to me, however, that Dubos fingers an important issue in terms of a Christian theology of *place* rather than nature when he recommends Benedict over Francis as his patron saint of ecology. Dubos discerns, rightly in my view, a certain passivity in relation to nature in Francis, whereas in Benedict he finds a spirit of "creative intervention in the earth."[14] The key issue, which is at the heart of place as opposed to nature, is that of *cultivation*. Benedict certainly has a far more developed sense of this than does Francis.

> When practiced in the true spirit of the Benedictine rule, monastic life helped the monks to establish close contact with the natural world through daily and seasonal rituals and work which were coordinated with cosmic rhythms. . . . Benedictine architecture . . . achieved a functional beauty which made it a major artistic achievement of Western civilization. . . . The solution to the environmental crisis will not be found in a retreat from the Judeo-Christian tradition or from technological civilization. Rather it will require a new definition of progress, based on better knowledge of nature and on a willingness to change our ways of life accordingly.[15]

Francis's vision was deeply influential and appears clearly in the thought of both Bonaventure (1221–1274) and Dante (1265–1321).[16] However, in both thinkers the metaphor of ascent ultimately triumphs. As Santmire says of Dante, "His home is emphatically not on this earth, surrounded by the birds and snakes and trees and streams. His home is far above in the ethereal regions of absolute, pure, and imageless spiritual transcendence."[17] The proper end of humankind is the beatific vision, which involves leaving creation behind.

12. Paton, *Towards the Mountain*, 260.
13. See Santmire, *Ritualizing Nature*, 4–6.
14. Ibid., 118.
15. Dubos, "Franciscan Conservation versus Benedictine Stewardship," 58.
16. See Santmire, *Travail of Nature*, 98–106.
17. Ibid., 105.

The Reformers and the Protestant Tradition

There can be no doubt that the Reformers recovered the doctrine of creation in a major way,[18] but the question remains whether they went far enough theologically to provide a basis for a theology of place today. Santmire argues:

> One can say, as it were, that they inverted the metaphor of ascent: it was no longer a question of humanity ascending to God, whether by meritorious works or by indwelling gifts of grace or by any other way; now it was a question of God descending to humanity. But the legacy of the metaphor of ascent is still to be seen in their preoccupation with God and humanity, in general, and with the theme of human salvation in particular.[19]

Santmire contends that the Reformers' focus on *human* salvation—one thinks of Martin Luther's great struggle with how to be in a right relationship with a holy God—helped clear the ground for the Western secularization of nature that was to follow.[20] As we will see, there is far too much positive reflection on creation to suggest that the Reformers caused this secularization, and if guilt must be assigned, then the Thomistic tradition would have more to answer for than that of the Reformers.

At its core Luther's and John Calvin's theology was, according to Santmire, "theanthropocentric." It is true that for Luther justification was central, and it clearly deals, in his theology, with God and humanity. However, it must be noted that Luther broke with the medieval dualism of matter and spirit, insisting that the fundamental dichotomy is between faith and works and not between matter and spirit. Central to Luther's diagnosis of the human condition is that sinners exchange the glory of God for the worship of the creation, as Paul notes.[21] Luther's break with the medieval dichotomy of spirit and matter opens up a far more positive view of the creation. For Luther all created things are really masks of God (*larvae Dei*); on Galatians 2:6 Luther comments, "Now the whole creation is a face or mask of God. . . . There must be masks or social positions, for God has given them and they are his creatures."[22] This implies the contingency of all things, but also the fact that these masks—which include created objects *as well as* stations in life such as magistrate, schoolteacher, parent, and so on—should be honored as means through which God may be revered. The God revealed in Jesus is for Luther also the Creator who is constantly active

---

18. A good example of this is the way in which Luther broke the back of Jerome's interpretation of Ecclesiastes, which had dominated scholarship for some one thousand years. See Bartholomew, *Ecclesiastes*.

19. Santmire, *Travail of Nature*, 121.

20. Ibid., 122.

21. Luther, *Lectures on Romans*, 23–24.

22. *Luther's Works* 26:95; Dyrness, *Reformed Theology and Visual Culture*, 52.

in all his creatures.[23] Luther asserts that Christ's presence is everywhere in the world even as he sits at the right hand of God.

The Lutheran Tradition: Dietrich Bonhoeffer

Luther made much of vocation or callings but continued to think of society as it was as God-ordained, as Troeltsch notes:

> The vocational system was not consciously designed and developed for the purposes of the holy community and of Christian Society, but it was accepted as a Divine arrangement. The individual, moreover, regarded his work, not as a suitable way of contributing to the uplift of Society as a whole, but as his appointed destiny, which he received from the hands of God. That is why it was possible for the Lutheran to regard the work of his vocation in an entirely traditional and reactionary way. . . . This point of view coincides with the traditional Catholic view.[24]

For the development of a Christian view of place, one of the most fertile theologies from within the Lutheran tradition is that of Bonhoeffer, the twentieth-century martyr. Bonhoeffer's life was cut short in its prime, and one can only imagine what he might have produced if he had lived a long life. What he did write has been very influential, and the development of his thought and his relationship to philosophy have been explored in a vast body of literature.[25] In terms of place his last work, *Ethics*, is particularly fecund, and I will focus my attention on this work while cross-referring to his other writings.[26]

Dualism of one sort or another has bedeviled the Christian tradition, not least the Lutheran one with its doctrine of two kingdoms, but Bonhoeffer rejects any concept of a two-spheres approach to the world:[27] "There are not two realities, but only one reality, and that reality is the reality of God, which has become manifest in Christ in the reality of the world. . . . The reality of Christ comprises the reality of the world within itself."[28] In continuity with his earlier work *Act and Being*, Bonhoeffer stresses the congruity of the ontological presence of the Word *in* the world and the transcendent coming of the Word *to* the world, a coming which that presence makes the world receptive to.

Bonhoeffer's theology is profoundly ecclesial: "Church history is the hidden center of world history."[29] Bonhoeffer rightly notes that the church does

23. Dyrness, *Reformed Theology and Visual Culture*, 52.

24. Troeltsch, *Social Teaching of the Christian Churches* 2:610.

25. See, e.g., Bethge, *Dietrich Bonhoeffer*; Bonhoeffer, *Dietrich Bonhoeffer Works*; Gregor and Zimmermann, *Bonhoeffer and Continental Thought*.

26. Naturally Bonhoeffer's *Ethics* needs to be seen in the context of his work as a whole. For a useful overview see Dumas, *Dietrich Bonhoeffer*.

27. Bonhoeffer, *Ethics*, 62–72.

28. Ibid., 63–64.

29. Bonhoeffer, *Dietrich Bonhoeffer Werke* 1:142–43.

indeed occupy a definite space in the world, a space marked out by her public worship, institutional structures, and parish life. His ecclesiology is insepara-bly related to his Christology. In Christ God has claimed space in the world, and even though it be only an inn, "then in this narrow space He comprises together the whole reality of the world at once and reveals the ultimate basis of reality."[30] As the community of Christ, the church always reaches beyond itself; it is the place where witness is borne to the foundation of all reality in Christ. "If one wishes to speak, then, of the space or sphere of the church, one must bear in mind that the confines of this space are at every moment being overrun and broken down by the testimony of the church to Jesus Christ."[31] The church has a place not in order to deprive the world of territory, "but precisely in order to prove to the world that it is still the world, the world which is loved by God and reconciled with Him. . . . The only way in which the Church can defend her own territory is by fighting not for it but for the salvation of the world."[32]

Withdrawal from the world is not an option for Bonhoeffer. Darkness and evil—and Bonhoeffer is under no illusion about the extent of these—must not be abandoned; every area of life must be claimed for Christ because "Christ gives up nothing of what He has won. He holds it fast in His hands."[33] The incarnation is the ultimate affirmation of finite reality: "Christ died for the world, and it is only in the midst of the world that Christ is Christ."[34] In terms of the form that human life takes in the world, Bonhoeffer identifies four divine mandates: labor, marriage, government, and church. For our interest in placemaking, labor is the most significant: "From the labour which man performs here in fulfillment of the divinely imposed task there arises that like-ness of the celestial world by which the man who recognizes Jesus Christ is reminded of the lost Paradise."[35] God's will is that the reality of Christ with us and in our world becomes efficacious. Bonhoeffer's theology is strongly eschatological, and he describes the time between the coming of Christ and the consummation of the kingdom as the "penultimate." This does not downplay the importance of life today; indeed the penultimate receives its profound meaning from the ultimate.

Bonhoeffer recognizes that the penultimate is characterized by an antithesis, but insists that Christians should not abandon the "secular"; they should op-pose the secular only in the quest for a "better secularity."[36] "It is only in this sense, as a polemical unity, that Luther's doctrine of the two kingdoms is to

30. Bonhoeffer, *Ethics*, 68.
31. Ibid., 69.
32. Ibid., 68.
33. Ibid., 70.
34. Ibid., 71.
35. Ibid., 74–75.
36. Ibid., 65.

be accepted, and it was no doubt in this sense that it was originally intended."[37] The penultimate is characterized by a preparing of the way for the return of Christ, and this preparation is not only inward, but "a formative activity on the very greatest visible scale."[38] Bonhoeffer deplores the loss of "the natural" in Protestant theology and seeks to recover it.[39] The natural is that which is, after the fall, directed toward the coming of Christ, whereas the unnatural is that which closes its doors to Christ.

In the context of his discussion of the natural, Bonhoeffer offers a profound reflection on bodily life. "Man is a bodily being, and remains so in eternity as well."[40] "It is my body that separates me in space from other men and that presents me as a man to other men."[41] He rightly recognizes in the carpe diem passages of Ecclesiastes the affirmation and joy of bodily life. He notes that homes are not just for protection and rearing of the young, as are animals' shelters; "they are places in which a man may relish the joys of his personal life in the intimacy and security of his family and of his property."[42]

For Bonhoeffer the world is the place of concrete responsibility which is given to us in Christ. He articulates a keen sense of the particularity of implacement: our task is not to transform the world but "to do what is necessary at the given place and with a due consideration of reality."[43] This sense of particularity is especially clear in Bonhoeffer's reflections on vocation.[44] Grace comes to the human in his or her place, and it is in this place that we are called to hear and respond to Christ's call. "The calling is the call of Jesus Christ to belong wholly to Him; it is the laying claim to me by Christ at the place at which this call has found me; it embraces work with things and relations with persons; it demands a 'limited field of accomplishments,' yet never as a value in itself, but in responsibility towards Jesus Christ."[45]

Calvin

Calvin's understanding of the creation as fallen meant that he developed a significantly different view of vocation from that of Luther. The structures

---

37. Ibid., 66.
38. Ibid., 93.
39. Ibid., 101–41. Bonhoeffer grew in his appreciation of the importance of the Old Testament for a biblical theology. He concludes his *Creation and Fall* with a reference to the second tree of life, now planted in the garden of the Mount of Olives and Golgotha. The fall involves a rejection of what I call implacement in the world, whereas redemption (the second tree) opens up the possibility of re-implacement within God's good but fallen world.
40. Bonhoeffer, *Ethics*, 113.
41. Ibid., 115.
42. Ibid., 114.
43. Ibid., 203.
44. Ibid., 222–30.
45. Ibid., 225.

of society as well as individual human beings are fallen and require transformation, said Calvin. God's written Word provides the glasses by which we
can read his word in the creation, and in this light Christians are, in obedient
gratitude, to work to renew all of human life so that it achieves God's purpose for it. Indeed Calvin's *Institutes* are intended to shape all of life. "For
Calvin," notes W. Dyrness, "the impact of the performance of worship and
of Christian discipleship was to extend to the reforming of the structures of
everyday life. The theological plan of the *Institutes* was to be reflected in the
structures that became visible in the communities and cultures that lived by
this plan."[46] And N. Wolterstorff points out, similarly, "Original Calvinism
represented, then, a passionate desire to reshape the social world so that it
would no longer be alienated from God. Thereby it would also no longer be
alienated from mankind, for the will of God is that society be an ordered
'brotherhood' serving the common good."[47]

Wolterstorff characterizes Calvinism helpfully as "world-formative,"[48] and
this formative dimension of early Calvinism is more fecund for a theology of
place than Santmire recognizes. The radicality of Calvinism in this respect
should not be underestimated; Wolterstorff distinguishes between avertive
and formative religion and notes that whereas the dominant character of
medieval Christianity was avertive,[49] that of Calvinism was formative. Calvin
does indeed stress God's sovereignty and his consequent role as lawgiver, but
"fundamental in the structure of Calvin's thought about God is the idea that
he dispenses good gifts to his children. . . . Obedient action in society enters
the picture as one of the manifestations of gratitude; as such, it is to God's
glory. Thus deeper in Calvin's thought than the image of God as lawgiver is
the image of God as the 'Author of all blessings.'"[50]

Max Weber falsely sees in Calvinist activism a desire to ensure that one is
part of God's elect.[51] Santmire sets up a false antithesis when he claims that
Calvin's affirmations of the majesty of creation are designed to reassure believers that their God is the sovereign Lord, "not that the Creator is carrying
out some purpose with the whole creation, with nature in particular, which is
somehow independent of his will for human salvation."[52] By contrast, Troeltsch
movingly captures the motivation for Calvinist activism when he writes:

> The Calvinist knows his calling and election are sure, and that therefore he is
> free to give all his attention to the effort to mould the world and society to the

46. Dyrness, *Reformed Theology and Visual Culture*, 109.
47. Wolterstorff, *Until Justice and Peace Embrace*, 21–22.
48. Ibid., 3.
49. Ibid., 6. Wolterstorff relates this to the great chain of being underlying medieval thought.
50. Ibid., 14.
51. See M. Weber, *Protestant Ethic*, 51–79.
52. Santmire, *Travail of Nature*, 126.

Will of God. He does not need to cling to God lest he should lose Him. . . . His duty, therefore, is not to preserve the "new creation" and its intimacy with God, but to reveal it. . . . The individual was drawn irresistibly into a wholehearted absorption in the tasks of service to the world and to society, to a life of unceasing, penetrating, and formative labor.[53]

Undoubtedly early Calvinism and its successors manifested serious problems.[54] However, it is clear that in terms of *place* early Calvinism is a rich resource. Calvin, in his commentary on Genesis 1:26, asserts,

And hence we infer what was the end for which all things were created; namely, that none of the conveniences and the necessities of life might be wanting to man. In the very order of creation the paternal solicitude of God for man is conspicuous, because he furnished the world with all things needful, and even with an immense profusion of wealth, before he formed man. Thus man was rich before he was born.[55]

Santmire finds such an assertion in tension with certain other statements by Calvin, such as, "For it is true that this world is like a theatre in which the Lord shows to us a striking spectacle of His glory."[56] However, Calvin's theology is more coherent than Santmire allows. Genesis does indeed depict the world as a wonderful home for humankind, as we saw in part 1. And in his commentary on Genesis 2:15, Calvin is quite clear that this "anthropocentrism" does not allow for abuse:

The custody of the garden was given in charge to Adam, to show that we possess the things which God has committed to our hands, on the condition, that being content with a frugal and moderate use of them, we should take care of what shall remain. Let him who possesses a field, so partake of its yearly fruits, that he may not suffer the ground to be injured by his negligence; but let him endeavour to hand it down to posterity as he received it, or even better cultivated. Let him so feed on its fruits, that he neither dissipates it by luxury, nor permits it to be marred or ruined by neglect. Moreover, that this economy, and this diligence, with respect to those good things which God has given us to enjoy, may flourish among us; let every one regard himself as the steward of God in all things which he possesses. Then he will neither conduct himself dissolutely, nor corrupt by abuse those things which God requires to be preserved.[57]

53. Troeltsch, *Social Teachings of the Christian Churches* 2:589.
54. Although these are often overstated. For a judicious exploration of the early Calvinists see Little, *Religion, Order, and Law*. See also Graham, *The Constructive Revolutionary*; Lindberg, *Beyond Charity*.
55. Calvin, *Genesis*, 96.
56. Calvin, *First Epistle of Paul to the Corinthians*, 40.
57. Calvin, *Genesis*, 125.

The beauty and splendor of creation play a major role in Calvin's theology.[58] Food and clothes are not just for necessity, but for delight and good cheer and decency.[59] Calvin intended that the splendor of the church should spill out into the world. Outside of regular worship hours Calvin insisted that churches in Geneva should be locked, not only in order to avoid "superstitious" practices, but because "all of life has become an arena of faith and spirituality. No particular space is sacred; but all spaces are potentially sacred."[60]

This is not to suggest that we find in Calvin a full-blown contemporary theology of place, but it is to insist that the potential is there. Because of its opposition to images and Catholic styles of church architecture—for much of which it is justly criticized—the broader contribution of Calvinism to place and architecture is regularly ignored.[61] Calvinist Bernard Palissy (1510–90) planned the Tuileries Palace and Gardens for Catherine de Medici. In 1536 he published his views of architecture and agriculture in his *La Recept veritable*. Palissy advocates working with nature and respecting the dignity of creation; he has harsh words for those who destroy the forests and thereby their own future in their ignorance.[62] His approach to architecture develops out of a meditation on Psalm 104. "The object then of his work in planning, planting and building, is to make his work an image of his 'delectable garden,' that is an image of redemption. . . . His imaginary garden . . . is an 'entextured structure' that reflects the transformation that Christ has made possible."[63]

The French Calvinist Salomon de Caus came to England in 1611 to redesign the gardens of Richmond Palace; he laid out his views in his work on perspective published in London in 1612.[64] Thus, in the late sixteenth and seventeenth centuries some of the most important architects were Calvinists, but the religious aspect of their work has been largely ignored. Partially this is because that dimension of their work is indirect. "Art here serves religion, but not at all in the medieval sense. It now serves what is to these architects the higher calling of religion, that program of making right a distorted created order."[65]

Two streams flowing from Calvinism, namely Puritanism and Dutch neo-Calvinism, also require comment in terms of a theology of place because they are either misrepresented or neglected. Santmire castigates the former:

58. Dyrness, *Reformed Theology and Visual Culture*, 72–76.

59. Ibid., 73.

60. Ibid., 82.

61. The best, most comprehensive recent book on this subject is Dyrness, *Reformed Theology and Visual Culture*.

62. Ibid., 110.

63. Ibid., 111.

64. De Caus, *La Perspective avec La Raison des ombres et miroirs*.

65. Dyrness, *Reformed Theology and Visual Culture*, 112. Cf. Randall, "Structuring Protestant Scriptural Space," 346.

The way for the ethic of exploitation was also prepared by the earlier Puritan doctrine of the dominion of man over nature. . . . From its earliest days, this Puritan doctrine tended to coalesce with what Weber called the spirit of Capitalism. . . . We can conveniently refer to this coalescing of the Puritan doctrine with the apology of capitalism as the utilitarian view of nature. This view depicts nature essentially as a realm defined by its openness to manipulation and exploitation.[66]

With his focus on nature, it would appear that Santmire confuses exploitation with formation; intriguingly both Wolterstorff and Taylor appeal to the Puritans to support their view of the Reformers as life affirming.

J. I. Packer notes that the name "Puritan" was mud from the very start.[67] Puritanism undoubtedly had its problems;[68] however, in terms of place—and many other areas—Puritanism does not deserve to be the whipping boy its critics have made it. In the sixteenth century Puritan Phillip Stubbes forbade bearbaiting and cockfighting and hunting; God is abused when his creatures are![69]

In New England the Puritans sought to restore creation to its original splendor.[70] Edward Johnson declared, "This is the place where the Lord will create a new Heaven and a new Earth, in new Churches, and a new commonwealth together."[71] There is some hubris in this comment, but the Puritans worked deliberately to ensure that their townscapes reflected their understanding of redemption.[72] Within a short time they established an unprecedented number of townships, centered on the meetinghouse, and, intriguingly for our purposes, once settled they stayed put: "What New Englanders lacked in outward expression and understanding they seemed to make up for in inward intensity about the spatial relationship they knew."[73] Eschatologically the Puritans "lived and died in keen expectation of God's greater work in the new creation."[74]

In his marvelous chapter, "God Loveth Adverbs," C. Taylor articulates the contribution of the Reformers as follows:

As a result, certain of the original potentialities of Christian faith, which tended to be neutralized in the amalgam with ancient metaphysics and morals, were allowed to develop. The crucial potentiality here was that of conceiving the

66. Santmire, *Brother Earth*, 30–31.
67. Packer, "Foreword: Why We Need the Puritans," ix.
68. Ryken, *Worldly Saints*, 187–202. On the alleged connection between Puritanism and capitalism see Robinson, *Death of Adam*, 23–24.
69. Dyrness, *Reformed Theology and Visual Culture*, 127.
70. Ibid., 213.
71. Quoted in ibid.
72. Ibid.
73. D. Allen, quoted in ibid., 213–14. See ibid., 212–39, on Puritan towns, houses, and meetinghouses.
74. Ibid., 215.

hallowing of life not as something which takes place only at its limits, as it were, but as a change which can penetrate the full extent of mundane life.[75]

This vision is crucial for a Christian theology of place. In some later Calvinism this transformative vision often virtually disappears, with its emphasis on praxis being replaced by an exclusive focus on ecclesiology, soteriology, and theology. However, the holistic, transformative vision of early Calvinism was revived and developed particularly in the neo-Calvinism that developed through the labors of G. van Prinsterer, H. Bavinck, A. Kuyper, and their successors, which we will come to below.

---

75. Taylor, *Sources of the Self*, 221. See ibid., the whole of chap. 13.

13

The Modern Period

Modern Secularization of Nature

In our examination of the history of the philosophy of place we have already noted the effect of secularization upon place. The Reformed tradition was not immune to the powerful forces at play: the influence of the natural sciences, of Kant's philosophy, and of industrialization was such that "we may legitimately speak of the secularization of nature in the Reformation tradition in the nineteenth and twentieth centuries. . . . Nature came to be viewed by many modern Protestant thinkers as a mere thing, a world of objects, closed in upon itself, moved only by its own laws, not open to any other dimensions of reality, and therefore a world which humans must constantly transcend if they are to be rightly related to God."[1]

The effect of the natural sciences was that nature came to be thought of mechanically and abstractly.[2] Kant affirmed the mechanical view of nature, and related to this is his separation of the ideas of nature and God. In Kant's system belief in God is allowed "no immanent use whatever, that is, no use admissible for objects of experience."[3] As Dooyeweerd has noted, the nature-freedom ground motive is dominant in modern thought, and this is certainly true of Kant: humanity is distinct from nature, and man's greatness is precisely his freedom from deterministic nature.[4] Intriguingly, Kant retains the biblical

1. Santmire, *Travail of Nature*, 133.
2. Berman, *Reenchantment of the World*.
3. Kant, *Critique of Pure Reason*, 732.
4. For Dooyeweerd a ground motive is a fundamental motivation or driving force in culture.

notion of the kingdom of God, but he spiritualizes it as an ethical common-wealth or a people of God under ethical laws.[5]

> We can instructively think of Kant's philosophy as an ecological sieve. As the flow of the Reformation tradition passed through his thought—which has been profoundly influential ever since within the Reformation tradition—the theocentric-ecological circumference of Reformation thought was largely filtered out. Most major Protestant theological systems after Kant would be radically theanthropocentric. God would be viewed essentially in isolation from nature, and humanity would be viewed essentially in isolation from nature.[6]

However, it was not just the world of ideas that affected Reformed views of the world; industrialization further consolidated the mechanical view of the world. As Mumford observes, "The power that was science and the power that was money were, in the final analysis, the same kind of power: the power of abstraction, measurement, quantification."[7] Tremendous progress resulted, but, as has become increasingly apparent, at a tremendous cost, and not least to place. The secularized view of the world driving modernity became, as Nietzsche articulated, a will-to-power, especially in regard to place and nature. The result was a profound loss of Calvin's vision of the creation as the theater of God's glory.

Kant and post-Kantian thought affected theology profoundly, especially as theologians assumed the insights of that tradition and sought to corre-late Christian thought with it. The resultant anthropocentrism appears, for example, in Schleiermacher, "the Kant of modern Protestantism."[8] "Schlei-ermacher led a revolution by shifting the metaphysical doctrine of the con-tingency of all things to the epistemological doctrine of the human feeling of unqualified dependence. . . . The Human is the basis for the affirmation of the divine."[9]

As we saw in part 1, the spiritualization of the kingdom of God continues to affect biblical interpretation. Santmire tracks the influence of Kant through Ritschl (1822–89), J. Herrmann (1846–1922), A. von Harnack (1851–1930), R. Bultmann (1884–1976), and E. Brunner (1889–1966).[10] Ritschl focuses on the question of how humans as part of nature can transcend its limitations. He finds Christianity's answer in the kingdom of God, through which people are enabled to rise above nature. From this perspective the world exists solely

---

5. Santmire, *Travail of Nature*, 135; Kant, *Religion within the Limits of Reason Alone*, bk. 3, 85–138.
6. Santmire, *Travail of Nature*, 135.
7. Mumford, *Technics and Civilization*, 25.
8. Buckley, *At the Origins of Modern Atheism*, 330.
9. Ibid., 331–32.
10. Santmire, *Travail of Nature*, 138–40.

for humans. Herrmann further reveals the growing anthropocentrism of the age, arguing that Christianity has to do with communion between Christians and God. For von Harnack, Christianity is concerned with "God the Father and the human soul so ennobled that it can and does unite with him."[11] Bultmann, in developing the existentialism for which he is well known, argues that faith can have to do only with self-understanding and not with an abstract worldview. Thus God cannot be understood as active throughout the creation! "Only statements about God are legitimate as expressing the existential relation between God and man. Statements which speak of God's actions as cosmic events are illegitimate."[12] Bultmann clearly reveals Kant's influence on him in his view of nature as self-enclosed, a realm in which the cause-effect nexus dominates.[13]

Santmire finds Kierkegaard, a complex thinker, unhelpful for developing a theology of place, but I think his work may offer significant potential. In *Fear and Trembling* this potential emerges in the quest for a knight of faith. The "author"[14] notes that "the movements of faith must constantly be made by virtue of the absurd, yet in such a way, be it observed, *that one does not lose the finite but gains it every inch.*"[15] In other words, the decentering of the ego that is involved in faith leads, not to a loss of the finite, but to its true recovery! The imagined knight of faith is a fully embodied human being:[16]

- He is solid through and through.
- His walk is vigorous.
- He takes delight in everything, thus manifesting the mark of the earthly man.
- He takes walks into the forest, in which he delights.
- He engages imaginatively with a building site.
- He lounges at the window of his home, taking an interest in everything that goes on outside.
- He smokes his pipe!

Indeed, "the whole earthly form he exhibits is a new creation by virtue of the absurd. He resigned everything infinitely, and then he grasped everything again by virtue of the absurd."[17]

---

11. Harnack, *What Is Christianity?*, 63.
12. Bultmann, *Jesus Christ and Mythology*, 69.
13. Ibid., 15, 61.
14. Kierkegaard commonly wrote under a pseudonym and his *Fear and Trembling* is no exception. The author is identified as Johannes de Silentia.
15. Kierkegaard, *Fear and Trembling*, 29. Emphasis added.
16. Ibid., 30–31.
17. Ibid., 32.

Anglican Sacramentalism

"Whereas classical Protestantism never developed a theory of the sacramental universe or a sacramental principle, Anglicanism did."[18] This sacramental worldview is rooted in the writings of Calvin's great English contemporary, Richard Hooker: "It is largely because of Hooker that there has been greater attention paid to the doctrine of creation in the theology of the Church of England than in any other Church in the West."[19] Aiming to develop a comprehensive theory of law, Hooker focused on the relationship between salvation and creation. Thus he came to link the sacraments to God's providential activity throughout the universe:

> All other things that are of God have God in them and he them in himself likewise. . . . God hath his influence into the very essence of all things, without which influence of Deity supporting them their utter annihilation could not choose but follow. Of him all things have both received their first being and their continuance to be that which they are. All things therefore are partakers of God, they are his offspring, his influence is in them, and the personal wisdom of God is for that very cause said to excel in nimbleness or agility, to pierce into all intellectual pure, and subtile spirits, to go through all, and to reach unto everything that is. Otherwise, how should the same wisdom be that which supporteth, beareth up, and sustaineth all?[20]

C. S. Lewis notes of Hooker that "few models of the universe are more filled— one might say drenched—with Deity than his."[21] Hooker's sacramental approach to the creation did not disappear, but is found in the writings of Lancelot Andrewes and George Herbert, contemporaries of Hooker's; in the works of seventeenth-century poet, writer, and theologian Thomas Traherne; and in Pearson's seventeenth-century *Exposition of the Creed.*[22]

Interest in Traherne's works has recently revived. Theologically the notion of transfiguration is at the heart of his trinitarian theology, which mitigates the effect of Platonism on his work. Transfiguration operates in three ways in Traherne's thought: (1) as the process wrought in the individual by God's Spirit whereby one is transformed increasingly to be like Christ; (2) as a momentary revelation of the fullness of life to come in eternity; and (3) as an action of the transfigured individual whereby one's transformed perceptions in turn transform all that one encounters.[23] The effect of Traherne's

---

18. Horne, "Sacramental Use of Material Things," 9.
19. Ibid., 10.
20. Hooker, *Works* vol. 2, book 5, chap. lvi, 247.
21. Lewis, *English Literature in the Sixteenth Century*, 459.
22. See Horne, "Sacramental Use of Material Things."
23. On this theme see C. D. Macfarlane, "Transfiguration as the Heart of Christian Life."

centering of his theology in transfiguration comes wonderfully to the fore in his extended poem, "A Wise Man Will Apply His Mind":

2

A Righteous Man will duly Prize
  The Sun, the Stars, the Skies
The earth, the Seas, the Clouds, the Rain
  The Mountains, and the Hills,
And evry Spring that back again
  From all those Hills distills,
The Thunders, Lightenings, Meteors Hail and Snow
With evry thing in Heaven or earth below.

3

A Man that hath a Tender Sence
  Feels all the Excellence
Of evry Creature, and doth See
  In evry Kind of thing
Vast Treasures of felicitie
  Giv'n him by the King.
A Pious Man adores the Lord of Glory:
A Learned Man with Joy doth read his Story.[24]

The most comprehensive explication of this Anglican sacramental vision appears at the conclusion of W. Temple's Gifford Lectures, published in 1934 as *Nature, Man and God*. In lecture 29, entitled "The Sacramental Universe," he defines a sacrament as "a spiritualization of a material object whereby a spiritual result is effected."[25] Conceptually, Temple works with the relationship of matter to spirit; spirit is the highest principle of unity in the creation, and because "the whole cosmic system exists by the will of a Creative Spirit, then in all things that Creative Spirit exercises control, and all other entities are truly intelligible and explicable only by reference to Him. He is παντοκρατωρ [*pantokratōr*]. The whole universe is the expression of His Will."[26] Temple insists that the creation is historical and carefully avoids the dangers of pantheism; God is transcendent over the universe but also immanent within it. Temple's privileging of spirit over matter leads him to the view that the lower (material) orders of reality find their fullness only when utilized by the higher as a means of self-actualization. Spirit expresses its actuality not by ignoring matter but by controlling it.[27] Temple aims to explicate the unity of matter

24. Extract taken from ibid., 219. It is a poem of fifteen stanzas, each of eight lines.
25. Temple, *Nature, Man and God*, 491.
26. Ibid., 479.
27. Ibid., 477.

and spirit in the creation and affirms that "one ground for the hope of Christianity that it may make good its claim to be the true faith lies in the fact that it is the most avowedly materialist of all the great religions. . . . Its own most central saying is: 'The Word was made flesh.'"[28] The result is a sacramental view of the universe:

> This conception does not only mean that a mind of sufficient insight can detect the activity of God in all that happens if it can be seen in its true context and perspective, so that the sublimity of nature is an expression of the divine majesty, and its beauty of the divine artistry, and love's sacrifice . . . of the divine heroism. . . . More than this is involved. The world, which is the self-expressive utterance of the Divine Word, becomes itself a true revelation, in which . . . what comes is not truth concerning God, but God Himself. This . . . does not exclude the possibility of special revelations; rather it is the condition of that possibility.[29]

Temple further insists that not only is the creation sacramental of God to God's creatures, but it becomes "sacramental of Him to Himself."[30]

Temple's sacramental theology contains remnants of the chain of being, as is evident in his statement that "we pass from God through the world of process and history to God."[31] He further notes that "*as the spiritual elements in the organism become predominant, the concomitant physical relations become relatively less important and may finally drop away.*"[32] Nevertheless his approach is a fecund source for a contemporary theology of place and has been appropriated as such by Inge, as we will see below.

Sacrament also plays a major role in Orthodox and Catholic views of the creation. In the view of the Eastern Orthodox theologian A. Schmemann,[33] humans should relate to the world as priests who bless God in thanksgiving and worship and who, by filling the world with this Eucharist, transform life into communion with God. The fall involved the loss of this sacramental, priestly perspective on life; redemption involves its recovery. In Christ, "the true life that was lost by man was restored, for redemption as new creation means 'that in Christ, life—life in all its totality—was returned to man, given again as sacrament and communion, made Eucharist.' . . . In redemption, the world is restored as God's creation and human beings resume their priestly vocation."[34]

---

28. Ibid., 478.
29. Ibid., 493.
30. Ibid., 495.
31. Ibid., 493.
32. Ibid., 487. Emphasis original.
33. Schmemann, *For the Life of the World*.
34. Naugle, *Worldview*, 52. In this passage Naugle quotes Schmemann, *For the Life of the World*, 20–21.

Thus Schmemann exhorts Christians to witness to the reality of the world as God's good creation, and to be busy with transforming every aspect of life. Similarly, in his recent work on the Eucharist, the Catholic theologian R. Kereszty asserts,

> To the extent that we enter into the heavenly liturgy of the glorified Christ, we begin to see the universe in a new light. We anticipate the vision of the end times when the glory of the Lord will radiate through all of God's creation. . . . The Eucharist thus foreshadows the role which to some extent all of the cosmos will fulfill at the end of times: we will see and love God in and through Christ directly but we will also see his glory shining through all of nature. Thus, in some way, all of nature will be our "eschatological food" in the heavenly kingdom.[35]

Neo-Calvinism

Among Christian traditions that provide resources for a recovery of place, the Dutch neo-Calvinism that developed from van Prinsterer, Kuyper, Bavinck, and their successors has contributed significantly. Philosophically, neo-Calvinism has developed in two directions in the last century: the Reformational philosophical tradition of H. Dooyeweerd and D. Vollenhoven and their colleagues and students, including H. Runner; and the more analytical tradition of A. Plantinga and N. Wolterstorff, which has led to a remarkable widespread renaissance of Christian philosophy in North America.

For neo-Calvinists, Christianity is truly world-formative; it provides a worldview, a way of understanding all of reality, with radical consequences for every part of our lives. Its distinctive emphases are as follows.

1. Neo-Calvinism insists on a comprehensive and integrated understanding of creation, fall, and redemption.

The whole world belongs to God. At the same time, all of reality is under the curse of sin—and all of reality lies within range of redemption in and through Jesus Christ. In Kuyper's justly celebrated words: "There is not a square inch of the entire world of which Christ does not rightly say, 'That is mine.'" Or as B. Zylstra says, "The covenant is as wide as creation."[36] There is a good creational structure for everything, but after the fall, the serious possibility of misdirection is opened up. Neo-Calvinism does not recognize any conflict between gospel and creation. Neo-Calvinists understand the gospel to be the healing power which restores creation, in line with God's original

35. Kereszty, *Wedding Feast of the Lamb*, 200–201.
36. Zylstra, "Preface," 30.

design and toward its originally intended consummation. Bavinck articulates this beautifully when he asserts that

> the essence of the Christian religion consists in the reality that the creation of the Father, ruined by sin, is restored in the death of the Son of God and re-created by the grace of the Holy Spirit into a kingdom of God. Dogmatics shows us how God, who is all-sufficient in himself, nevertheless glorifies himself in his creation, which, even when it is torn apart by sin, is gathered up again in Christ (Eph. 1:10). It describes for us God, always God, from beginning to end—God in his being, God in his creation, God against sin, God in Christ, God breaking down all resistance through the Holy Spirit and guiding the whole of creation back to the objective he decreed for it: the glory of his name.[37]

2. Neo-Calvinism emphasizes God's good and dynamic order for creation.

If the resurrection is, as O. O'Donovan rightly asserts, the reaffirmation of creation and its order, then the order for kinds of things and the means by which things can be distinguished from other kinds of things comes from this wise order embedded in creation. God establishes the possible structure and distinctive identity of created things: linden trees, cigars, human beings, states—everything. The order of creation is constant, grounded in the covenantal faithfulness of God. There is a close connection for neo-Calvinists between creation and the rich diversity of things in this world. God not only brought reality into existence, but brought it into existence as an extraordinarily rich, complex, and diverse order of distinct kinds of things. As Bavinck notes: "The world is a unity, but that unity manifests itself in the most magnificent and beautiful diversity. Heaven and earth were distinct from the very beginning; sun and moon and stars each received their own task; plant and animal and man each have their own nature. Everything is created by God with a nature of its own, and exists and lives according to a law of its own."[38]

Kuyper developed this sense of ordered diversity in relation to society in his doctrine of sphere sovereignty and argues that, for instance, the family has sovereignty in its own sphere in the face of both the state and the church, and should not be internally made subject to these other relationships. All human authority, every human relationship, is subject to the sovereign rule of God. This view does not deny historical changes in society but rather emphasizes the possibilities given in creation which provide room and set limits for the emergence of a wide range of different relationships in society.

---

37. Bavinck, *Reformed Dogmatics*, 1:112. See also Bavinck's profound "The Catholicity of Christianity and the Church."

38. Bavinck, *Schepping of Ontwikkeling*, 41–42.

3. Neo-Calvinism affirms the historical development or differentiation of creation.

Neo-Calvinism has a deep appreciation for the historical development of human cultures and societies. The development of technology, the advances of the sciences, the building of cities, and the disentanglement of various distinct relationships in society (often referred to as "differentiation")—these are all fundamentally appropriate human responses to God's command to realize the possibilities of creation, the cultural mandate (see Gen. 1:28; 2:15). Christians are responsible for affirming and advocating such advances in the context of the coming of the kingdom of God[39]—while opposing their misdirection away from the glory of God.[40]

4. Neo-Calvinism recognizes an ultimate religious conflict—the antithesis—in all of life.

A battle is being fought at the deepest level in every society and within every human person—a struggle between the inclination to submit to God and the inclination to rebel against God. This personal and public conflict between the kingdoms of light and darkness is called by neo-Calvinists *the antithesis*. This struggle is not, they insist, to be relegated to some spiritual realm above or alongside everyday life: it is a spiritual struggle for everyday life itself. The antithesis issues forth a clarion call for Christian cultural activity in opposition to every manner of idolatry.

Clearly neo-Calvinism has major resources for a contemporary view of place, though these remain largely undeveloped.

Paul Tillich

Paul Tillich (1886–1965), who did his doctorate on Schelling and drew consciously on the Romantic movement, retained an interest in the theology of nature throughout his academic career and was critical of the post-Kantian Protestant surrender to the natural sciences and industrialization. Tillich argued for an understanding of God as the ground of being in an attempt to transcend the post-Kantian view of God as quintessentially a moral being with little interest in the creation. He excavated resources in Augustine and Luther as he sought to develop a theology which did justice both to God's transcendence and the participation of nature in the life of God. The crucial

39. H. Ridderbos notes that in Reformed theology the church has occupied a more prominent place than the kingdom of God, but that in the neo-Calvinist revival of Reformed theology the kingdom moves center stage ("Church and the Kingdom of God," 9).
40. See C. Seerveld, "Dooyeweerd's Idea of 'Historical Development.'"

question to which Tillich addressed himself was, "How is the reality manifested by revelation related to the reality which we know and experience? How is faith related to thought, prayer to work, religion to culture, in short, how is God related to the world?"[41]

Tillich worked in the context of the two world wars. For him the first war indicated the collapse of the lifestyle of the nineteenth century and, with it, idealist philosophy and liberal theology. His worldview is thoroughly historical, but with a stress on all of historical reality. Tillich interprets the fall existentially, as a move from essence to existence, that is, as a move to estrangement from that to which man belongs.

Christology is rightly central for Tillich, and he interprets it in terms of new being:

> If I were asked to sum up the Christian message for our time in two words, I would say with Paul: It is the message of a "New Creation" . . . the New Being, the New Reality which has appeared with the appearance of Jesus. . . . The New Creation—this is our ultimate concern; this should be our infinite passion—the infinite passion of every human being. . . . The message of Christianity is not Christianity, but a New Reality.[42]

Tillich articulates the relationship between God and our world in terms of his doctrine of "belief-ful realism." Realism means that religion is concerned with our world. "Belief-ful" does not equate God with our world but indicates how God appears as its transcendental ground and meaning:

> It is as in a thunderstorm at night, when the lightning throws a blinding clarity over all things, leaving them in complete darkness the next moment. When reality is seen in this way with the eye of a self-transcending realism, it has become something new. Its ground has become visible in an "ecstatic" experience, called "faith." It is no longer merely self-subsistent as it seemed to be before; it has become transparent or, as we would say, "theonomous." . . . We are grasped, in the experience of faith, by the unapproachably holy which is the ground of our being and breaks into our existence and which judges us and heals us. This is "crisis" and "grace" at the same time.[43]

Thus Tillich's belief-ful realism manifests a kinship with the sacramental view of the universe discussed above.

Central to Tillich's theology is a concern to recover the whole of reality as the province of faith. Faith takes hold of the whole person, and no sphere of life can be withdrawn from its domain. Protestantism is, according to Tillich, "radial laicism":

41. Zahrnt, *Question of God*, 295.
42. Tillich, *The New Being*, 15–19.
43. Tillich, "Realism and Faith," quoted in Zahrnt, *Question of God*, 326.

Every person, every place and every action is qualified by this association with the unconditional; it penetrates every moment of daily life and sanctifies it: "The Universe is God's sanctuary. Every work day is a day of the Lord, every supper a Lord's supper, every work a fulfilment of the divine task, every joy a joy in God. In all preliminary concerns, ultimate concern is present, consecrating them."[44]

Tillich's theology has been heavily criticized for obscuring the boundary between God and the world. Positively, he represents a major pastoral attempt to help his contemporaries find God in the daily reality of the world and their lives amidst catastrophic times. Certainly his thought can contribute much to a theology of place.

Karl Barth

One would hope that the mature Barth would offer a fertile theology for place. With his christocentric focus, he asserts, "This man is the secret of heaven and earth, of the cosmos created by God."[45] However, the adequacy of Barth's doctrine of creation and his view of human culture are still disputed.

In his discussion of God's omnipresence, Barth explores God's own spatiality and his relationship to created space. For Barth, God's presence "necessarily means that He possesses a place, His own place, or we may say safely, His own space. The absolute non-spatiality of God, deduced from the false presupposition of an abstract infinity, is a more than dangerous idea. If God does not possess space, He can certainly be conceived as that which is one in itself and in all. But He certainly cannot be conceived as the One who is triune."[46] God is spatial in a unique way that befits him as God; he is the Creator of space and is completely present in the space that rightly belongs to him. "There is no place where He is not present in His essence, which includes, of course, His knowledge and power. . . . This is the general nature of His omnipresence."[47] God is free and superior in relation to created space, but this does not imply that he has a negative relationship to space: "There is nowhere where God is not, but He is not nowhere."[48]

> The truth is rather this, that God is present to other things, and is able to create and give them space, because He Himself possesses space apart from everything else. The space everything else possesses is the space which is given it out of the fulness of God. The fact is that first of all God has space for Himself and that

44. Zahrnt, *Question of God*, 331.
45. Barth, *Church Dogmatics* (hereafter *CD*), vol. 3, pt. 1, p. 21.
46. Barth, *CD*, vol. 2, pt. 1, p. 468. T. Gorringe notes here Barth's originality (*Theology of the Built Environment*, 42).
47. Barth, *CD*, vol. 2, pt. 1, p. 470.
48. Ibid., 471.

subsequently, because He is God and is able to create, He has it for everything else as well; just as He is life and love ad extra because He is first in Himself with primal power and fulness.[49]

God's omnipresence does not mean that he cannot be present in different and special ways; this is clear from Scripture. God is present, and this for Barth implies both distinction and relationship: "there are certainly different forms, very different forms, of God's presence in His creation, but there is no absence of God in His creation."[50] Barth distinguishes three ways in which God is present in his creation: firstly his general presence; secondly his special presence in revelation and reconciliation; and thirdly his presence in Jesus, "the basis and constituent centre of His special presence."[51] Jesus is "the place to which every examination of the Old and New Testament witness to God's special presence must necessarily and unequivocally point in the last instance."[52]

Barth emphasizes the Word as God's address to humankind, found preeminently in Jesus Christ, and he articulates a doctrine of God's eternal election of Jesus and his people.[53] This twin focus of God in Jesus and humanity in Jesus alerts us to the possibility of a marginalization of nature. For Barth redemption is actualized through the history of salvation; redemption requires a theater outside of God, and thus God brings creation into existence. However, "the covenant is not only quite as old as creation; it is older."[54] In the *Church Dogmatics* Barth makes much of creation as the theater of God's glory, but according to H. Zahrnt, "The whole creation—nature, the world, man and history—is now forced into the Christological pattern and so deprived of its own meaning and status."[55] Creation is the external ground for the establishment of the covenant, but as such, its being is instrumental and made subservient to election. Similarly Santmire argues, "Barth presents us by default with a view of nature that is radically interpreted in terms of personal being. It therefore allows little room, if any, for a sense of human solidarity with and cooperation with, not to speak of wonderment before, nature as a realm of fellow creatures worthy of respect in their own right."[56]

While there are, in my view, problems with Barth's theology of creation, his theology is far more nuanced than the rather blunt criticisms of Zahrnt and Santmire give it credit for. In *Church Dogmatics*, Barth is in fact highly

49. Ibid., 474.
50. Ibid., 476.
51. Ibid., 483.
52. Ibid., 483–84.
53. As Zahrnt notes, "This is the apex of his theology, if one can name as apex what in fact is the root of everything" (*Question of God*, 107).
54. Quoted in ibid., 96.
55. Ibid., 113.
56. Santmire, *Travail of Nature*, 155.

critical of the anthropocentrism of theology from the Middle Ages and Renaissance onward[57] and its failure to develop a coherent theology of creation, though he finds exceptions in Polanus in the seventeenth century and the neo-Calvinists Kuyper and Bavinck in the nineteenth century. Barth himself is quite clear that

> man is certainly not His [God's] only creation. Man is only *a* creature and not *the* creature. The creature of God is the totality, the whole cosmos of the reality posited by Him and distinct from Him, in the plenitude of which man is only a component part, very inconsiderable in some important ways and deeply dependent on creaturely elements and factors which are greatly superior to him. . . . Besides man there are other creatures posited by God and distinct from God, with their own dignity and right, and enveloped in the secret of their own relation to their Creator. Man is a creature in the midst of others which were directly created by God and exist independently of man.[58]

In a lengthy exegesis of Genesis 1–2 Barth[59] prophetically anticipates the animal rights concerns of our day by noting how animals suffer at the hands of humans. He proposes that every slaughter house should have written over it in fiery letters Paul's reference in Romans 8 to the groaning creation! He even picks up on the significance of Mark 1:13 for a doctrine of the animal creation, a point we discussed in part 1.[60]

It is thus false to simply accuse Barth of anthropocentrism and a marginalizing of the creation. Nevertheless, there remains a tension in Barth's thought in this respect. The Word of God comes to humankind, and as such it can only "glance" at the surrounding world.[61] Barth resists any notion of theology becoming a worldview or developing a cosmology. He defends the neutrality of "genuine science": "Exact science dedicated to its object and its method, working positively and not dreaming and romancing, is in fact pure knowledge."[62] However, in the same volume Barth asserts unequivocally that "it is impossible to maintain at one and the same time the concept of man as constituted by the Word of God and the idea of a neutral capacity in man."[63]

At the start of the twenty-first century we are far more aware of the problems with the alleged neutrality of science and of the view that it yields pure knowledge. Barth, in my view, manifests here something of a nature/grace dichotomy whereby theology is a response to God's grace but genuine science does indeed operate according to a neutral capacity in humankind. As

---

57. Barth, *CD*, vol. 3, pt. 2, pp. 4–6.
58. Ibid., 3–4. Emphasis original.
59. Barth, *CD*, vol. 3, pt. 1, pp. 98–228.
60. Ibid., vol. 3, pt. 2, p. 5.
61. Ibid., 11.
62. Ibid., 12.
63. Ibid., 131.

we saw in our overview of the history of place in Western philosophy, such a view of science leads to the suppression of place. Barth rules out of court the possibility that a worldview, and disciplines apart from theology, may also take as their starting point an encounter with the Word, whereas, as I have argued above, a coherent Christian view of place requires just such insights.

14

Contemporary Theologies of Place

Al Gore, in his *Earth in the Balance*, insightfully notes that

> the old story of God's covenant with both the earth and humankind and its assignment to human beings of the role of good stewards and faithful servants, was—before it was interpreted and twisted in the service of the Cartesian worldview—a powerful, noble, and just explanation of who we are in relationship to God's earth. What we need today is a *fresh telling of our story with the distortions removed.*[1]

The crucial question is just what will constitute such a retelling.

As we noted at the outset of our discussion of place in the Christian tradition, Christian scholars have responded to the ecological critique in three main ways: as reconstructionists, as apologists, and as revisionists. *Reconstructionists* despair of traditional Christian thought and believe that a new "theology" must be constructed from the ground up. Indeed, Gore himself believes that such a retelling will involve "a renewed investigation of the wisdom distilled by all faiths."[2] Many ecofeminists, such as Mary Daly and Rosemary Radford Ruether, the latter with her appropriation of *gaia*, would also fall under this category.

The most well-known reconstructionist is Matthew Fox. Fox locates the problem with Christian theology in its understanding of fall-redemption. "The

1. Gore, *Earth in the Balance*, 218. Emphasis added.
2. Ibid., 258.

original sin, as Fox sees the matter, is for all intents and purposes the traditional Christian doctrine of original sin itself, as that doctrine has allegedly shaped the history of Western culture."[3] Fox replaces this pernicious theology of fall-redemption with a theology of original blessing and the coming Cosmic Christ: "What is needed . . . is a spiritual vision that prays, celebrates, and lives out the reality of the Cosmic Christ who lives and breathes in Jesus and in all God's children, in all the prophets of religion everywhere, in all the creatures of the universe."[4] Fox understands Christ's salvation in terms of example: the historical Christ reveals the universality of the Cosmic Christ and calls us to awareness of his workings everywhere. He also discloses to us that we too are divine! Fox's is a realized eschatology, and on the basis of his theology he anticipates a global renaissance in our time.

Fox's creation theology is admirable in its attempt to recover the doctrine of creation, but deeply deficient in other ways. His theology is akin to the antiurban romanticism of Thoreau. Its most serious deficiency is his passing over of the problem of radical evil, to which the doctrine of original sin bears witness. As Santmire notes, "But a cosmic Christology must be predicated, as Sittler knew so well, and Jürgen Moltmann has forcefully reminded us, on a theology of *the blood of the cross*, according to the witness of Colossians."[5] The Bible begins with a park and ends with a city, and contra Fox, a theology of place requires a sense of the cosmic history of the Bible.

Apologists, by comparison, defend the ecological resources of the tradition. *Revisionists* work mainly within the classical Christian tradition but have recognized the problems in much Christian thought and thus have sought to reexcavate the biblical and theological traditions in search of resources for a robust theology of nature. The issue at stake between apologists, revisionists, and reconstructionists is the extent to which the biblical and Christian tradition contains the resources for a fresh telling of the story adequate to the challenges of placemaking today. Lynn White rightly notes that "since the roots of our trouble are so largely religious, the remedy must also be essentially religious, whether we call it that or not."[6] But is the Christian tradition up to the challenge?

As we saw in part 1, the Bible is more than up to the challenge. From our discussions above, however, it is clear that much work remains in reforming the tradition of its distortions, an ongoing challenge. A central example in this respect is the spiritualizing of the New Testament concept of the kingdom of

---

3. Santmire, *Nature Reborn*, 18.

4. Fox, *Coming of the Cosmic Christ*, 7.

5. Santmire, *Nature Reborn*, 23. Emphasis original. Although we will not discuss Moltmann's theology in detail, it is clearly important for a recovery of the creational dimensions of faith. Later in his career Moltmann did recognize the importance of theology of place; see Moltmann, *A Broad Place*, 361–63.

6. White, "Historical Roots of Our Ecological Crisis," 1207.

God, a distortion that can be traced back at least as far as Kant, but which continues to bedevil biblical theology today. The extent to which this distortion remains dominant appears poignantly in Al Gore's question: "Why do our children believe that the Kingdom of God is *up*, somewhere in the ethereal reaches of space, far removed from this planet?"[7] Our explorations in the Christian tradition have revealed that there are countless points in the tradition from which a vibrant view of place can be developed for today.

Santmire

Santmire's theology of nature is expounded in his *Travail of Nature*[8] and *Nature Reborn*, but the most extensive and systematic discussion is in his earlier work, *Brother Earth*,[9] in which he notes that "the 'biblical world-view' is by no means a self-evident unity."[10] Santmire is conscious of the challenge historical criticism presents to the unity of Scripture but proposes that we attend to the biblical witness of a God who plays out a history with man and nature: "Together these two histories, inseparable yet distinct, comprise the Universal Divine Story of creation, redemption, and consummation."[11]

In his explication of the biblical story Santmire focuses on creation, history, and the kingdom of God. He rightly stresses that in the Bible creation is not an isolated event but the beginning which anticipates its telos, the consummation of all things under the rule of God. Every created entity has integrity, "a life of its own with God. Every natural entity, first of all, has its own *place*."[12] God delights in all of creation, so that the created realm has intrinsic value to God: "He wills to have the galaxies and the icthyosaurs and the alligators and the lilies and the infinite seas of electrons, mesons, photons, and all other particles and forces for their own sakes quite apart from what they all may or may not mean for our being and well-being, as well as for the sake of our being and well-being."[13] Nature, for Santmire, has *spontaneity*: it is open to new possibilities. It has *continuity*: it is channeled in a well-marked course. And it has *congruity*: God is pleased with it.[14] Creation is like a building structured by the wisdom of an architect; each part has its own role and sphere. Santmire understands sin as "a discordant note

7. Gore, *Earth in the Balance*, 264. Emphasis original.
8. Santmire, *Travail of Nature*, 189–218.
9. Santmire, *Brother Earth*, 80–200.
10. Ibid., 80.
11. Ibid., 81. Note the similarities in this respect between L. Newbigin and Santmire. In *Nature Reborn*, Santmire uses the language of "the biblical Story" and structures the entire book around that theme.
12. Santmire, *Brother Earth*, 85. Emphasis original.
13. Ibid., 130.
14. Ibid., 133–39.

against the rule of God."[15] He is emphatic that there has been no cosmic fall; humankind has fallen, but nature has not.[16] Sin transforms the beautiful into the ugly and taints God's good creation.

As the Psalms make clear, nature's worshipful response to God is as pleasing to him as the appropriate sacrifice. Humankind's dominion involves a positive responsibility to care for the creation, with a care which embraces wonder and delight. Humankind is crowned with glory (Ps. 8), but God's glory is also manifest throughout the creation: "This theme of God's glory manifest throughout the whole creation is congruent with all the other themes suggesting that nature in itself has its own value and integrity in his eyes, quite apart from its other function as a vehicle of blessing for man."[17] Humankind is essentially united with nature, so that a human can say of it "Brother earth": "Trees, rivers, flowers, stars, desks, tables, buildings, bombs, rust tin cans, and similar natural entities are constituents of man's homeland, however it may be distorted."[18] A person cannot say "I" without implicitly referring to nature. Noah would have denied himself if he had not taken the animals with him!

As image-bearer, humankind also transcends nature as overlord and caretaker. Nature is spontaneous, but humans are free; nature is continuous, but humans can order their lives; nature is congruous, but humans can worship God. As caretaker, "one should so order one's life that the whole of nature, including *wild* nature, can flourish. This means not only to respect nature's rights but to *act to preserve and to defend* those rights."[19] Humankind also images God by relating to nature as a wondering onlooker. Wonder involves attention, and as Luther commented, "If you really examine a kernel of grain thoroughly, you would die of wonder."[20] This can be as true of the city as of the wilds.

Jesus, in the prophetic tradition, conceived of the kingdom of God coming in his life as well as in a final consummation which involves a renewed creation.[21] In its worship the church celebrates both the restoration of its relationship to creation and the coming new creation. "All of the Church's worship, when it is right, is sacramental."[22] Indeed, "the Eucharistic meal functions as the

---

15. Ibid., 124. Emphasis original.
16. See ibid., 163–70, 192–200.
17. Ibid., 88.
18. Ibid., 143.
19. Ibid., 150. Emphasis original.
20. Luther, *Weimarer Ausgabe*, 19:496, quoted by Santmire, *Brother Earth*, 256.
21. On the centrality of Christ see Santmire, *Brother Earth*, 163. In his *Travail of Nature*, 196–218, Santmire finds a conflict in New Testament writings between those dominated by the metaphor of ascent (John, Hebrews) and those which, under the motif of the universal lordship of Christ, are guided by the metaphor of migration to a good land.
22. Santmire, *Brother Earth*, 177. See Santmire, *Nature Reborn*, 85–92, on the cosmic meanings of baptism and Eucharist.

supreme anticipation of the end, at which time the life-giver, the Spirit—who now dwells in and enlivens the Church—will create all things new."[23] With humankind, nature too is renewed and transformed. For Santmire this renewal of the whole creation is vital; if nature is to fall away, then it is of no ultimate value. However, he nuances this by noting both the continuity of the new creation with the old and the discontinuity between them: the first creation will not be destroyed, but renewed, all the "chaotic elements" of nature will be removed.[24]

For Santmire, history is a key component of a biblical view of nature. "[God's] wise shaping of the universe is temporally as well as spatially oriented."[25] The goal of creation is the divine Sabbath rest, and this determines all God's other works. Creation is totally dependent on God, and he rules it immediately;[26] however, his speaking of it into existence does give it a certain structure: "In a certain sense, then, nature does have a law, but this law is not a permanently fixed, self-sufficient, immanent force, it is the faithful and powerful presence of God working within his domain, directing it toward his Final Future."[27] In an attempt to protect the real participation of creatures in God's history with creation, Santmire argues that even God does not know all the details of the future, which remains open.[28] God's plan for the creation is not an abstract map, but concrete and dynamic, and involves God's pervasive governance now so as, one day, to usher in the new creation.

Biblically, Santmire finds that the notion of the kingdom of God as both creative rule and created realm provides the most helpful scaffolding for a theology of nature.[29] He rightly notes that *kingdom* refers not only to reign but to the geographical territory of that reign as well:

> It refers to a Divine *rule* and to a Divine *realm*. The first idea points primarily to activity by the Sovereign; the second primarily to the sphere governed by the sovereign. This double connotation expresses the fundamental biblical conviction that God both *rules majestically* throughout his creation and rules majestically throughout his *creation*. The biblical writers take seriously both the government of God and the world in which his rule holds sway.[30]

For Santmire the idea of the kingdom of God also validates both nature and civilization: "*nature and civilization are fellow citizens of the Kingdom of God.*"[31]

---

23. Santmire, *Brother Earth*, 91.
24. Ibid., 109.
25. Ibid., 107.
26. See ibid., 114–20, on this theme.
27. Ibid., 97.
28. Ibid., 111–13.
29. Ibid., 101.
30. Ibid., 104. Emphasis original.
31. Ibid., 133. Emphasis original.

Inge

As we have seen, sacrament plays a prominent part in Santmire's theology of place. For Inge, however, working consciously in the Anglican tradition, it is center stage. "I would not," he says after examining the biblical material, "want to argue with Davies' conclusions about the land question, and would agree with him about the Christocentricity of the New Testament."[32] Inge finds in the incarnation,[33] however, the means of reconciling the New Testament with the centrality of place in the Old Testament. He[34] quotes T. Torrance with approval: "Unless the external breaks into the temporal and the boundless being of God breaks into the *spatial* existence of man and takes up dwelling within it, the vertical dimension vanishes out of man's life and becomes quite strange to him—and man loses his place under the sun."[35] Inge asserts, *"Places are the seat of relations or the place of meeting and activity in the interaction between God and the world. . . .* Place is therefore a fundamental category of human and spiritual experience."[36]

The danger of a sacramental approach to the world is that if everything is a sacrament, then nothing is. Inge avoids this danger by arguing that a sacramental approach means that the world can become the place of God's revelation to us. Sacraments are "those rents in the opacity of history, where God's concrete engagement to change the world becomes visible. It is therefore to speak of the Holy Spirit, which is today the awareness of events which are wholly worldly, opaque and ordinary on the one hand and wholly divine, radiant and mysterious on the other, for such a duality is the mark of the Spirit."[37] For Inge we must start with events in our understanding of sacramentality. The Old Testament is full of events at particular places where God manifests himself to particular people. Furthermore, many central events in church history have been sacramental, such as Constantine's vision and the vision of Saint Francis. Inge provides contemporary evidence that such particular experiences of the divine are far more common than is often acknowledged. This does not mean that we should work via a phenomenology of such experiences, but the possibility of sacramental encounters fits within a biblical worldview: "The biblical narrative leads us to expect God's self-revelation and, therefore, that the world is a possible place of sacramentality."[38]

A sacramental approach to place follows from New Testament eschatology: "Christ himself is the reintegration of God's original creation, and in Christ

32. Inge, *Christian Theology of Place*, 51.
33. Lilburne, *Sense of Place*, also makes the incarnation central.
34. Inge, *Christian Theology of Place*, 51.
35. Torrance, *Space, Time, and Incarnation*, 75.
36. Inge, *Christian Theology of Place*, 52. Emphasis original.
37. Gorringe, "Sacraments," 165.
38. Inge, *Christian Theology of Place*, 74.

God has restored the sacramental nature of the universe."[39] Everything will be in place in God's time! However, Inge rejects the notion that some places, such as Iona, for example, are intrinsically holy. We need a relational view of place, in which the relationships between God, place, and humans provide the possibility for sacramental events. "The world in itself is not sacramental, because sacramentality is an event that involves action by God and a response by unique human beings."[40] Such disclosures take place in and outside the church. Ritual has a crucial role to play in this respect, and the church sacraments should prepare Christians for the possibility of sacramental encounter in God's world.

This relational view of place and sacramentality does mean that once God discloses himself in a particular place, it is possible for his disclosure to continue to be associated with that place. Time and history are central components of place, and just as places can be desecrated, so they can be redeemed. A place was redeemed, for example, when the Anglican Cathedral of Zanzibar was built over the site of the slave market with the high altar placed precisely where the whipping post had been. A relational view also means that associations with God can diminish and wither over time if not sustained by ritual and tradition. Indeed a holy place is "set aside not in order to deny the holiness of other places, but for human perception to intensify the sanctification of all places. . . . Because a priest is set apart for holy things, it does not mean that the laity are licensed for profanity."[41]

39. Ibid., 76.
40. Ibid., 81.
41. Sykes, "The Holy Place," quoted in Inge, *Christian Theology of Place*, 87.

PART 3

A Christian View
of Place for Today

The biblical and theological dynamic motivating Christians to take place seriously is the incarnation and redemptive work of Christ. Athanasius's exploration of the incarnation is profoundly moving as he explains to his readers that the renewal of creation has been achieved by the same Word who made it in the beginning. The effect of the incarnation is

> like as when a great king has entered into some large city and taken up his abode in one of the houses there, such city is at all events held worthy of high honour, nor does any enemy or bandit any longer descend upon it and subject it; but, on the contrary, it is thought entitled to all care, because of the king's having taken up his residence in a single house there: so, too, has it been with the Monarch of all.[1]

Place is a constituent part of God's good creation that he is already renewing and will finally renew at the end of the ages. Thus, it is "entitled to all care" because God's glory and our well being are at stake in our placemaking. As we saw in part 2, place has been neglected in far too much of the Western tradition. Retrieval and renewal of placemaking is a challenge, albeit an exhilarating

1. Athanasius, *On the Incarnation of Our Lord*, ix.

one! A recovery of place and placemaking cannot afford to be simplistic and superficial—too much is at stake.

In part 3 I will map out a theology of place for today and then explore its implications for some of the myriad different types of places. A Christian view of place requires the biblical and historical work of parts 1 and 2, but it is also wonderfully practical. As will become apparent, all of us can start to make a difference today.

15

Contours of a Christian View of Place

Theologically, there are multiple entrances into a Christian view of place for today. Inge uses the concepts of the incarnation and sacrament; P. Scott develops a trinitarian, eucharistic theology of place.[1] Both develop rich and insightful theologies of place. If we imagine theology as a grand cathedral with multiple entrances, then the question becomes which of the many possible entrances provides the most comprehensive and insightful perspective. In my opinion it is a *trinitarian* theology of place that is the most fruitful way into a Christian view of place for today.

Any theology of place worth its salt must be *christocentric*. As Newbigin asserts, Christ is the clue to all that is.[2] Thus Inge is right to make the incarnation central to a theology of place. However, precisely because such a theology is christocentric, it will be *trinitarian*. The remarkable flowering of trinitarian theology in the latter half of the twentieth century is important because "prime reality" for the Christian is the God who has come to us in Jesus, and epistemologically it is essential that a theology of place take this prime reality as its starting point.

Thus a Christian view of place should be trinitarian. But how we proceed from here is less clear. C. Gunton and others have sought to develop conceptual frameworks from the doctrine of the Trinity for theological work in science, art, and other disciplines.[3] As I have argued elsewhere, these frameworks are simply not up to the task of rigorous analysis.[4]

---

1. P. Scott, *Political Theology of Nature*.
2. Newbigin, *Light Has Come*.
3. Gunton, *The One, the Three, and the Many*, 3. Gorringe, *Theology of the Built Environment*, develops a trinitarian approach, but without resort to Gunton's transcendentals.
4. Bartholomew, "The Healing of Modernity: A Trinitarian Remedy?"

Marshall's trinitarian theology is more helpful, in my view, because it fore-grounds the relationship between the Trinity and Scripture: "The action whereby the Spirit induces us to love God by sharing in the mutual love of the Father and the Son is epistemically decisive: from it ultimately stems our willingness *to hold true the narratives which identify Jesus and the triune God, and to order the rest of our beliefs accordingly.*"[5] Hence the importance of part 1 of this book; a healthy trinitarian theology of place will attend closely to the ways in which place is rendered in Scripture. A doctrine such as that of the Trinity is an abstraction from Scripture. However, as Calvin notes of his *Institutes* that their aim is to equip the reader to attend to Scripture more rigorously, the same should be true of all Christian doctrine, and not least that of the Trinity; it emerges from, among other things, Scripture, and in turn illuminates our reading of Scripture. It will not do to settle, like Inge, with Davies's claim that the New Testament spiritualizes place, and then appeal to the doctrine of the incarnation to circumvent the implications of that spiritualization. Rather, the doctrines of the Trinity and the incarnation will lead us to reexamine the New Testament to see if Davies's influential reading is correct. As we have seen, it is not; on the contrary, while the New Testament's theology of place is refocused, it is just as materialist as that of the Old Testament.

The doctrine of creation is fundamental to a theology of place. Indeed the failure of Christians to attend to place is largely owing to the eclipse of the doctrine of creation.[6] A theology of place is rooted in the sort of theology of creation we discussed in relation to Genesis 1–2, which is itself fundamental to the entire biblical narrative. The doctrine of creation resists all dualisms which undermine the good materiality of our world and any attempt to privi-lege the soul or the "spiritual" over the material. A theology of place requires in addition a sense of the *dynamism* of the creation order:

> By his Word God established a well-ordered creation. By that same Word he continually calls it to order. His Word is our life. For by it he put in place the permanently normative environment for our life together in his world. This network of structures and functions, governed by creational law, manifests his loving care for all creatures. Every creature, in its own unique way, is subject to this constant yet dynamic ecosystem of creational laws. . . . The creation order is evidence of the caring hand of the Creator reaching out to secure the well-being of his creatures, of a Father extending a universe full of blessings to his children. . . . It enables us to become all we are meant to be.[7]

A major challenge to contemporary theologies and philosophies of place is historicism. A dynamic understanding of the creation order offers the requisite

---

5. Marshall, *Trinity and Truth*, 209. Emphasis added.
6. See Spykman, *Reformational Theology*, 176–78.
7. Ibid., 178. On creation order see ibid., 178–91.

resistance to such historicism; God's order holds for the whole creation, yet it is not static but provides for the normative development of history and culture. The fall opens up the possibility of the misdirection of God's good structures of the creation, such as place, but amidst sin and rebellion his order for creation continues to hold.

God has ordered creation such that the whole earth is designed as a home for humankind; hence a theology of place will always have a cosmic concern, including the well being of outer space and other planets. But, as we saw in terms of the relationship between Genesis 1 and 2, the embodied nature of human beings means that our placedness is always local and particular; so too will be our primary responsibility for placemaking. Just as the first couple is called to tend to Eden, so we are called to tend to the respective places in which we have been put.

As becomes apparent in Genesis, a biblical view of creation resists a nature-culture dichotomy which privileges wilderness over placemaking. Cultural development, including placemaking, is normative and fundamentally good. The fall opens up the possibility for the disastrous misdirection of cultural development and placemaking, the evidence of which is all around us. However, the temptation to collapse structure into direction must be resisted, lest we set "unblemished" nature in opposition to culture and placemaking. The challenge of the fall and sin is rather to work hard at practicing placemaking in such a way that it takes place along the grain of God's order for creation, and thereby enhances the shalom of all the creation. In the diverse places we explore below, that will be our major concern.

The incarnation, life, death, and resurrection of Jesus are the center of the biblical narrative and must also be so for a theology of place. In opposition to a Lutheran doctrine of two spheres, Bonhoeffer rightly notes that

> there are not two realities, but only one reality, and that is the reality of God, which has become manifest in Christ in the reality of the world. Sharing in Christ we stand at once in both the reality of God and the reality of the world. The reality of Christ comprises the reality of the world within itself. . . . It is now essential to the real concept of the secular that it shall always be seen in the movement of being accepted and becoming accepted by God in Christ.[8]

Central to a theology of place is the way in which we construe the relationship between the Christ event/redemption and creation. As O'Donovan has insisted, we must resist distinguishing between a kingdom ethics and the ethics of creation. The incarnation and the resurrection are the ultimate affirmation of creation.[9] O. Tjørhom rightly notes, "Actually, without creation there is

---

8. Bonhoeffer, *Ethics*, 64–65.
9. See O'Donovan, *Resurrection and Moral Order*. In *Christ and Creation*, C. Gunton makes use of the theology of Irenaeus to articulate the creation-redemption relationship.

nothing to save—creation is the 'stuff' of salvation."[10] Christ's redemption is aimed at the recovery of God's purposes for the whole creation, not in the sense of leading it back to Eden, but in the sense of leading it forward to the destiny God always intended for it. Correctly understood, the Eucharist embodies such a theology; hence the fecundity of P. Scott's eucharistic theology of place.[11]

But what is the destiny God intends for his creation? One's eschatology is crucial for a theology of place. Christian eschatologies have often made Christianity vulnerable to the charge that it is opium for the masses, designed to detract from earthly, material realities through its focus on the spiritual realm.[12] However, as we saw in part 1, biblical eschatology is not about the destruction of the world but about its renewal to become the new heavens and the new earth. As N. T. Wright notes,

> Take away the goodness of creation, and you have a judgment in which the world is thrown away as garbage, leaving us sitting on a disembodied cloud playing disembodied harps. Take away judgment, and you have this world rumbling forward with no hope. Put creation and judgment together, and you get new heavens and new earth, created not *ex nihilo*, but *ex vetere*, not out of nothing, but out of the old one, the existing one.[13]

Hence the provocative title of Wright's contribution to *The Green Bible*: "Jesus Is Coming—Plant a Tree!" Or, in our terms, Jesus is coming, get on with placemaking!

Few things would help the church in its engagement with culture as much as the recovery of a rich theology and practice of the Eucharist, as we will see below. Scott resists extending the notion of sacrament to place, whereas, as we saw in part 2, Inge has argued for a sacramental theology of place. Inge develops his theology of place in terms of sacramental encounters with God,[14] whereas Bess argues that "spaces and material objects may be deemed sacred when they are offered up by human beings to the sacred in the hope of their sanctification—when they are made as a *sacrifice* (literally, a gesture of 'making holy')."[15] In terms of placemaking, Bess's sacramental approach offers greater possibility than Inge's. As Bess notes, we humans lack the power to make places sacred or to initiate placial encounter with God, but we are able to offer the "sacrifice represented in the lavishness and care bestowed by human beings upon the works of our minds and hands that we offer to the sacred."[16]

---

10. Tjørhom, *Embodied Faith*, 36.
11. P. Scott, *Political Theology of Nature*.
12. See Ingraffia, *Postmodern Theory and Biblical Theology*, for these critiques and his right critique of them.
13. N. T. Wright, "Jesus Is Coming—Plant a Tree!," I-72–I-85.
14. Inge, *Christian Theology of Place*, 59–90.
15. Bess, *Till We Have Built Jerusalem*, 69. Emphasis original.
16. Ibid., 69–70.

To actually engage in placemaking in the myriad types of places in our modern world, a Christian view of place will need to provide conceptual resources for place-specific-making. What makes Bess's work so helpful, for example, is his overtly Thomistic framework and his intimate knowledge of architecture at a theoretical and practical level. As soon as one discusses places in depth, issues like philosophy of society, anthropology, and a host of others surface, and nuanced engagement with these issues requires philosophical insight as well as discipline-specific knowledge. We live amidst a renaissance of Christian philosophy and therefore have ample resources to draw on for developing an integrally Christian view of place. Disciplinary knowledge requires foundational Christian insights, but there is no shortcut to the knowledge gained from immersion in a discipline and its practices, what we might call "professional knowledge." Christian placemaking requires an ecology constituted by the biblical narrative, a theology of place, a philosophy of place, and the professional knowledge acquired from immersion in specific types of placemaking.

As we have seen, it is hard to specify with precision just what constitutes place. Place is real but complex and difficult to conceptualize. An attractive feature of Malpas's philosophy of place, as we saw, is his attention to its complexity. Place is a creational structure involving space and time, subjectivity and objectivity, self and other. God has made the world such that these components are established in relation to each other only within the structure of place.[17] Human subjectivity is embedded in the dense structure of place—without places, beings would only be abstractions.[18]

Place is thus to be understood as a complex of factors, subjective, intersubjective, and objective. Examinations of place will attend to dimensions such as the natural landscape, patterns of weather and sky, human ordering of space and resources, and the individual and communal narratives in which the place is imbued.[19]

> While the possibility of human involvement in the world is given only in and through such a place, the unity of the place is also evident in, and articulated by means of, the organised activity of the human beings who dwell within it. . . . The dependence of place upon subjectivity, and on objectivity and intersubjectivity, is a dependence (properly an interdependence) that results simply from the character of place as a structure that necessarily encompasses all of these elements and within which the elements are themselves constituted.[20]

A vital dimension in a philosophy of place is the relationship between lived experience and the abstraction that constitutes theory. Lived experience is

17. Malpas, *Place and Experience*, 163; cf. 173–74.
18. Ibid., 175–76.
19. Ibid., 185.
20. Ibid.

primary, and a philosophy of place will be serviceable only insofar as it feeds back into, is tested by, and deepens lived experience. Concepts of place and placemaking are indispensable, provided they do not take on a life of their own and become *the* route to truth because lived experience cannot be trusted. This is not—precisely not!—to lapse back into a naïve realism. All experience is interpreted, and in my opinion this is where the concept of a worldview is invaluable.[21] Not everyone is a philosopher, scientist, or theologian, but everyone has a worldview, conscious or not. A worldview is rooted in the religious orientation of a person and community and interprets the world for them and orients their life in the world. Hence the importance for placemaking of the development of a Christian worldview and its embodiment in practice.

Previously, we noted the element of temporality in a philosophy of place. A Christian view of placemaking ignores this at its peril. Date and place are fundamental elements in human existence. It is a not-quite-accurate truism that knowledge of the past alone will enable us to understand the present, but I have been struck time and again with how indispensable a historical perspective is to even begin to tackle issues like a Christian perspective on gardening or the city today. There is a timed, historical dimension to place, awareness of which is vital if we are to engage in placemaking today. In this respect I have found Dooyeweerd's notion of "cultural differentiation" of great heuristic value. In Dooyeweerd's philosophy the historical aspect of reality is about culturally formative power. For Dooyeweerd it is normative for culture to become more differentiated through history, although, as he himself asserts, we need to carefully distinguish healthy from unhealthy differentiation. Such an approach will prevent us from lapsing back into a nostalgic romanticism while simultaneously refusing to accept the way things are, as inevitably so. Such an approach believes in progress but never uncritically espouses modern progress or globalization as normative. Instead it does the hard work of imagining what normative cultural differentiation might look like so as to identify the genuinely progressive elements of modernity and globalization as well as its shadow side. Only thus will we be able to begin to practice placemaking in a genuinely missional way.

---

21. Goheen and Bartholomew, *Living at the Crossroads.*

16

Placemaking and the City

The city is understood best as a community of communities, the foremost purpose of which is to enable its citizens to live the best life possible.[1]

For the first time in history the world is now predominantly urban.[2] In the second half of the twentieth century the world's urban population increased nearly fourfold, from 732 million in 1950, to 2.8 billion in 2000, and to more than 3.2 billion in 2006. Growth has been rapid in Africa, Asia, and Latin America but significantly slower in Europe and North America. This urban growth is unprecedented and expected to continue as a result of both immigration to cities and natural growth. "The world is on the threshold of change as consequential as any in the history of civilization."[3] By 2010 the percentage of the urban population living in low- and middle-income nations will have grown from 40 percent in 1950 to 75 percent. Urbanites in these contexts face acute problems of clean water, sanitation, housing, transport, energy, and adequate health care. The symbol of this explosive growth is the emergence of the megacity, a large urban grouping with more than ten million inhabitants.

As we noted in part 1, Scripture affirms the development of cities, which should be seen as the normative opening up of the cultural potentials built into the creation. However, the Bible is acutely aware of the power of demonic forces and the possibility for radical misdirection of city life, Babel being

1. Bess, *Till We Have Built Jerusalem*, 52.
2. Precisely what constitutes "urban" is disputed. See Lee, "An Urbanizing World," 6.
3. De Blij, *Power of Place*, 186.

the most poignant symbol of this. As T. Gorringe notes, "The city is both Babylon, the place of alienation, exile, estrangement and violence, and Jerusalem, the place where God dwells, sets God's sign, and invites humankind to peace."[4] A Christian view of the city for today must also take account of its historical development. Reader[5] and Mumford[6] note the continuity in cities throughout the millennia. As true as this may be, in order to avoid anachronistic applications of the Bible to urban life today, it is vital that we have a sense of the historical development of cities and the important differences that industrialization and globalization have introduced. "The prime need of the city today is for an intensification of collective self-knowledge, a deeper insight into the processes of history, as a first step toward discipline and control."[7]

The Origin of the City

The origin of the city is shrouded in mystery. The common narrative sequence for explaining the origin of the city is that of hunting and gathering, agriculture, villages, cities, states. Permanent settlement requires a reliable food supply, and archaeologists discern traces of such development in the Mesolithic period, some fifteen thousand years ago. Some twelve thousand years ago, in the Neolithic period, they identify a second stage, which involved settlement, dietary continuity, and domestication, thus providing for permanence and continuity in residence and control over natural processes. The emergence of the Neolithic village marked a new kind of settlement: "Village life is embedded in the primary association of birth and place, blood and soil."[8] Out of the village emerged the granary, the bank, the arsenal, the library, the store, and thus the embryonic structure of the city.[9]

The city emerged some five thousand years ago as the result of the union between Neolithic and more archaic Paleolithic culture. The city brought together the earlier cultural elements, a gathering that was facilitated by the introduction of the plow and large-scale irrigation. The first evidence for urban life is found in Mesopotamia, although these cities were small. Even by the third millennium BC Ur probably occupied no more than 150 acres with a population of about twenty-four thousand people.[10]

4. Gorringe, *Theology of the Built Environment*, 140.
5. Reader, *Cities*, 32.
6. Mumford, *City in History*, 74.
7. Ibid., 526.
8. Ibid., 14.
9. Ibid., 19. D. Miller notes that "the cities Mumford has always favored are those that retain these village values, well-proportioned cities with compact civic centers and a vivid neighborhood life. The village in the city is his ideal community" (*Lewis Mumford*, 464).
10. Kotkin, *The City*, 4.

By 1900 BC Mesopotamian power shifted to Babylon, which would rank as one of the world's greatest cities for the next 1,500 years. Here Hammurabi (1728–1686 BC) would enact his famous laws, covering a range of civil and ceremonial cases that form an important context for the interpretation of Old Testament law.[11] His achievement was to attain supremacy in the eastern world of his time; his empire stretched from the Persian Gulf in the south to Kurdistan in the north and included virtually the whole of Mesopotamia and its neighboring countries. The control that empires exerted over vast areas facilitated trade, but trade never dominated imperial life as it does in cities today.

The development of the city was multifaceted, but two vital components were religion and politics:

> To interpret what happened in the city, one must deal equally with Technics, politics, and religion, above all with the religious side of the transformation.[12] If at the beginning all these aspects of life were inseparably mingled, it was religion that took precedence and claimed primacy, probably because unconscious imagery and subjective projections dominated every aspect of reality, allowing nature to become visible only in so far as it could be worked into the tissue of desire and dream.[13]

Politically the most important agent of this development was the king: "He is the polar magnet that draws to the heart of the city and brings under the control of the palace and temple all the new forces of civilization."[14]

E. Soja suggests that another geohistorical narrative may better explain the evidence, namely that the city precedes the development of agriculture and villages. He discerns three major urban revolutions: the first in the upland regions of southwestern Asia more than ten thousand years ago, which led to the urban-based invention of agriculture; the second five thousand years later in the lowlands of the Fertile Crescent, and the third some five thousand to six thousand years later with the start of the Industrial Revolution in western Europe.[15] Needless to say, this is a minority view, but intriguing in terms of our analysis of Eden as urban and of Mesopotamian creation stories which start with the city.

Between the eighth and sixth centuries BC the Greek polis emerged as a result of the devolution of power from the citadel to the village community. Greece was a conglomerate of small city-states clustered around an urban core. By the end of the sixth century BC the Hellenic city had begun to take form, characterized by the acropolis. The city-states were fiercely independent,

11. See Boecker, *Law*, 67–133.
12. Cf. Kotkin, *The City*, 4–5.
13. Ibid., 33.
14. Ibid., 35.
15. See Soja, *Postmetropolis*, 19–94.

but the Greeks nevertheless developed a remarkable culture that continues to influence urban life today. Athens was at the center of this civilization, presided over by gifted amateurs.

Alexander the Great's urban legacy lay in the cities he and his successors founded: Antioch, Seleucia, and especially Alexandria "employed rational planning principles on a scale rarely seen in older Greek cities. Starting from scratch, each city was designed with a proper agora, temple, and government buildings. Here we see the systematic planned development of large-scale public works."[16] Alexandria was "the first and greatest universal city, the supreme Hellenistic melting pot."[17]

The Romans were an extraordinary city-building people, and by the Augustinian period (63 BC–14 AD) they had built hundreds of new towns, laid out simply and in human proportion, so that *Romanization* became a synonym for *urbanization*. The cities of the Roman Empire were characterized by the wall, the forum (public spaces), human scale, and the bath: "the one supreme god they really worshipped was the body."[18] With a population of greater than one million, Rome was two to three times as large as cities such as Babylon. The Romans developed the legal, economic, and engineering infrastructure that allowed their empire to flourish for some five hundred years. The result of Rome's size was that "urban retail on a modern scale here makes its first sustained appearance. . . . At its most sophisticated, Rome presaged the contemporary shopping center; the Mercatus Traini offered a vast array of products in its five stories of shops."[19]

Rome's size resulted in what Mumford calls "megalopitan elephantiasis."[20] Over time the empire came to be centered more and more on rites of extermination: "Even before Rome had changed from Republic to Empire, that city had become a vast collective torture chamber."[21] Rome's decadence and overextension led to its demise.

The Medieval City

Amidst the urban decay of Rome, slow, fresh life was, however, already sprouting in the form of the medieval city. "The new religious vision that made this life possible gave a positive value to all the negations and defeats that the Romanized people had experienced: it converted physical illness into spiritual health, the pressure of starvation into the voluntary act of fasting, the

16. Kotkin, *The City*, 24.
17. Grant, *From Alexander to Cleopatra*, 37–40, 194–96, 198–203.
18. Mumford, *City in History*, 226.
19. Kotkin, *The City*, 32.
20. Mumford, *City in History*, 237.
21. Ibid., 230.

loss of worldly goods into increased prospects for heavenly salvation."[22] The monastery was central to the emergence of the medieval city: "It was in the monastery that the ideal purposes of the city were sorted out, kept alive, and eventually renewed."[23] Indeed, "the medieval city in Europe may be described as a collective structure whose main purpose was the living of a Christian life."[24] Within this Christian ethos hospitals and almshouses sprang up throughout cities. The Christian ethos dignified work, as is apparent in the guilds, which were religious associations based on the Benedictine principle of *ora et labora*. "A city that could boast that the majority of its members were free citizens, working side by side on a parity, without an underlayer of slaves was, I repeat, a new fact in urban history."[25]

The university was invented during this period, beginning with Bologna in 1100, Paris in 1150, Cambridge in 1229, and Salamanca in 1243. The university laid down a cooperative organization of knowledge on an interregional basis, and scholars flocked to these centers from all over Europe; in turn, the masters taught at distant centers. The combination of sacred, scientific, and political knowledge which the university offered had no exact parallel in any other culture.[26]

The medieval city was profoundly communal. Artisans and dealers had, for the most part, their shops in their houses.[27] By the thirteenth century the main form of the medieval city was fixed; in most towns a central quarter or core was surrounded by a series of irregular rings which enclosed and protected the core. The economic quarters were located around the town gate. At the heart of the medieval city was the cathedral. Christianity shaped all of life in the medieval city. As A. Frugoni notes,

> The peal of a bell rings through the air and other bells respond to it, muffled by distance. It is the start of another day, a day that still takes its rhythm from the bells that set the pace of monastic life. . . . The sun has not yet risen when people leave the house to go to church. Everyone who is physically able and can find the time attends mass. . . . The supernatural and the earthly interpenetrated one another.[28]

Apart from cathedrals and perhaps town halls, builders kept to human dimensions. At its widest, no medieval town normally extended more than half a mile from its center, so that every necessary institution, every friend, relative,

22. Ibid., 243.
23. Ibid., 247.
24. Ibid., 267.
25. Ibid., 271.
26. Ibid., 276.
27. See C. Frugoni, *Day in a Medieval City*, 45–116.
28. A. Frugoni, introduction to ibid., 8–9.

and associate, was in effect a close neighbor, within easy walking distance.[29] All in all, the medieval city was an extraordinary achievement:

> What was involved in a realization of the Christian city? Nothing less, I submit, than a thoroughgoing rejection of the original basis on which the city had been founded: the renunciation of the long-maintained monopoly of power and knowledge; the reorganization of laws and property rights in the interests of justice, free from coercion, the abolition of slavery and of compulsory labor for the benefits of a ruling minority, and the elimination of gross economic inequalities between class and class.[30]

However, the medieval city flourished best in adversity, and its very success proved its undoing. Ultimately religion conceded to commerce; success embroiled the church in the affairs of the world until, ironically, sin became the church's principal source of revenue.

The Baroque City

Between the fifteenth and eighteenth centuries the form and content of urban life were radically altered in Europe, a change which emerged from mercantilist capitalism.[31] This climaxed in the seventeenth century, when the old order began to break up and then religion, trade, and politics went separate ways. Under the rule of the prince, the modern state began to appear in the fourteenth century, with its capital city and the concomitant rise of bureaucracy and the office, the royal court, gunpowder, fortifications, and the garrison. The dominant symbol of the Baroque city was the avenue, which facilitated military traffic and, by comparison with pilgrimage, was a place for spectators, not participants. "We have seen what became of the medieval cathedral. But what became of its God? Here the transformation can be recorded only in terms of blasphemy. The absolute ruler by divine right usurped the place of the Deity and claimed his honors."[32] This was manifest in the city in the form of the palace, the hotel, the theater, the pleasure garden, the museum, the art gallery. The home became separated from the workplace, and furniture was invented. The city was sacrificed to traffic, and, à la Descartes, geometric order was prized. "The palace: the exchequer: the prison: the mad-house—what four

---

29. Mumford, *City in History*, 313.

30. Ibid., 317. It is important not to overromanticize the medieval city. See Girouard, *Cities and People*, 159, for a critique of the medieval city in terms of its oppressiveness and hierarchical nature.

31. Cf. Kotkin, *The City*, 65–82.

32. Mumford, *City in History*, 372.

buildings could more completely sum up the new order or better symbolize the main features of its political life."[33]

The Transition to a Market Economy

From the seventeenth century onward urban stimulus came from the market. London's commercial ascendancy prepared the way for this next major shift in the evolution of cities, one driven by developments in manufacturing technology. The Industrial Revolution transformed the city, and often in decidedly negative ways.

> But liquid capital proved to be a chemical solvent: it cut through the cracked varnish that had long protected the medieval town and ate down to the raw wood, showing itself even more ruthless in its clearance of historic institutions and their buildings than the most reckless of absolute rulers. One might characterize this whole change as the replacement of the concrete market place of the medieval town by the abstract transnational market, which flourished wherever a profitable deal could be made.[34]

The urban growth stimulated by the market flourished amidst religious schism and was characterized by individualism and utilitarianism. Land became a commodity, with the result that slums appeared. As P. Geddes noted: "Slum, semi-slum and super-slum, to this has come the Evolution of Cities."[35]

The poor in particular suffered. F. Engels noted of Manchester that "everywhere one sees heaps of refuse, garbage and filth. . . . One walks along a very rough path on the river bank, in between clothes-posts and washing lines to reach a chaotic group of little, one storied, one room cabins. Most of them have earth floors and working, living and sleeping all take place in one room."[36] In the latter half of the nineteenth century the focus of industrial growth was North America, where the factory town developed on a scale beyond that of Britain. In 1850 the United States had only some six large cities; by 1900 it had thirty-eight cities with a population of over one hundred thousand. As industrialism spread across the globe, it ushered in an unprecedented era of urbanization, but as Mumford notes,

> At the very moment that cities were multiplying in numbers and increasing in size all through Western civilization, the nature and purpose of the city had been completely forgotten: forms for social life that the most intelligent no longer

33. Ibid., 395.
34. Ibid., 413.
35. Geddes, *City Development*, quoted in ibid., 433.
36. Engels is quoted in Koditschek, *Class Formation and Urban Industrial Society*, 107.

understood, the most ignorant were prepared to build. Or rather, the ignorant were completely unprepared, but that did not prevent their building.[37]

The gridiron planner became the dominant model of city planning, with traffic its great priority. The mine, the factory, the railroad are the great symbols of this era.

Suburbia: "Crisis in Jerusalem"[38]

> There are people, products of modern times, with little or no sense of place. These are the rootless ones. There are the people of the suburbs, those places of interchangeable parts strung like beads on a commuter line. One such place is much like another, and sometimes the only way you can tell your home from your neighbor's is by the color of the front door. Such people move from place to place as their careers or their wishes dictate. . . . They are places for the nomad heart. . . . Deep within, they suffer the malaise of the fugitive heart.[39]

Suburbs were evident as early as the city itself, but mass movement to the city produced the suburb as refuge. "Beginning as a mechanism of escape, the suburb has turned into its very opposite. All that is left of the original impulse toward autonomy and initiative is the driving of the private motor car."[40] The suburban superblock appeared in the mid-nineteenth century but was transformed with the appearance of the car: "Under the present dispensation we have sold our urban birthright for a sorry mess of motor cars. . . . Our cities are being destroyed for the same superstitious religious ritual: the worship of speed and empty spaces."[41] Industrialism was damaging in multiple ways to urban life and created the impetus toward the suburbs. Los Angeles was designed with suburban living in mind.[42] D. Bartlett, in his book *The Better City* (1907) set out a vision for a "City Beautiful" that would provide residents with easy access to nature. Factories would be situated outside of the city center, and housing for workers would be spread out to prevent overcrowding. Bartlett was a Protestant minister, and he had been appalled by the urbanism he experienced in St. Louis. He moved to Los Angeles, which he hoped could become "a place of inspiration for noble living."[43] What began so hopefully has become a symbol of the problem of suburbia: "Now the results of this

37. Ibid., 419.
38. I have adapted this phrase from Norris Kelly Smith, "Crisis in Jerusalem." For a history of suburban sprawl see Bruegmann, *Sprawl*.
39. Paige, "Leave If You Can," 13.
40. Mumford, *City in History*, 492.
41. Ibid., 509. See Kunstler, *Geography of Nowhere*, 85–112. On the history of suburbanism in Canada see Harris, *Creeping Conformity*.
42. See Kotkin, *The City*, 112–13.
43. Bartlett, *The Better City*, 37, 211.

grand experiment are in, and the news is not good: the metropolis is stran-
gling on its own patented brand of 'growth.' . . . [The city] is stuck with its
sprawling low-density single-family house monoculture communities, with
its long commutes, and its addiction to gas."[44] Los Angeles is crime ridden,
and M. Davis describes it as the "carceral city,"[45] because of its omnipresent
security cameras, police officers, and private security guards, as well as gated
communities, the fastest-growing type of community in the United States.[46]

Megalopolis

The twentieth century has witnessed the emergence of the megacity, characterized by the ever taller skyline as well as the clustering of tall office buildings,
hotels, and apartments in new forms of central business districts.[47] In postco-
lonial contexts this has had its worst effects, with huge growth in population
but no accompanying growth in and distribution of wealth. The result is that
in the early twenty-first century some six hundred million urbanites live in
squatter settlements. Calcutta, Lagos,[48] Mumbai, and many Middle Eastern
cities show this trend. Mother Teresa's work has acquainted many of us with
the challenges of life in Calcutta, and the rise of Islamic fundamentalism is
connected to the impoverished megacities of the Middle East.[49] Some megacities
have been far more successful than others: Seoul, Hong Kong, and Singapore
stand out as success stories in many respects. But megacity development often
comes at great cost. China's development of Beijing for the 2008 Olympics,
plus its creation of the world's largest dam, swept away entire historic neighborhoods. The environmental costs are also staggering.[50] If the sort of patterns
of consumption that characterize America were to become global, it would
require four more Earths to sustain the world.[51]

   Little-known Curitiba[52] forms an astonishing example of positive city development in stark contrast to fellow Brazilian cities such as São Paulo.[53] In
the 1960s, attempts were made to reconstruct Curitiba along the model of

---

44. Kunstler, *Geography of Nowhere*, 212–13.
45. M. Davis, *City of Quartz*, 316.
46. Twenty-eight million Americans now live in gated communities. See Smith, Whiteleg, and
Williams, *Greening the Built Environment*, 146.
47. De Blij, *Power of Place*, 203.
48. On Lagos see ibid., 192–96.
49. Kotkin, *The City*, 135.
50. Baichwal, *Manufactured Landscapes*, DVD.
51. De Blij, *Power of Place*, 204.
52. See McKibben, *Hope, Human and Wild*, 57–113. His chapter on Curitiba is a must read!
Register, *Ecocities*, 315–21, also uses Curitiba as an example of an ecocity, but he is not uncritical
of recent developments.
53. See De Blij, *Power of Place*, 187–89, on the magnitude of the urban problems facing Brazil,
chiefly in terms of social inequality and corruption.

American cities. At this critical stage Jaime Lerner, who had grown up in Curitiba, became mayor of the city. He recognized the danger—"They were trying to throw away the story of the city"[54]—and acted quickly, courageously, and successfully to take Curitiba in a very different direction. Today the bus system is the best on earth; it is not subsidized, and yet it is profitable. A municipal shepherd and his flock of thirty sheep trim the grass in Curitiba's vast parks. There are few cars in the city center, which is safely walkable. Curitiba is a relatively poor city; the per capita income of its population of 1.8 million is approximately $25 a year. It has no beaches to boast of, and yet 99 percent of the population declare themselves fully happy with their city. It has slums, but they are clean; practices are in place such that a slum dweller who collects a sack of garbage gets a sack of food in return. "The downtown, though a shopping district, is not a money-making machine. It is a habitat, a place for *living*—the exact and exciting opposite of a mall."[55]

On the whole, however, the megacity is facing a crisis. The communications revolution has undermined the importance of urban centers, the emergence of the "ephemeral city"[56] based on consumerism and tourism is hardly promising, and the challenges of crime and international terrorism are potentially catastrophic. "The metropolitan world, then, is a world where flesh and blood are less real than paper and ink and celluloid."[57]

With the megacity has come the "world city," the city that forms part of a global urban network that links it more closely internationally than locally. The top three world cities are New York, London, and Tokyo. Contemporary urbanism is integrally related to globalization, and a characteristic of our times is the development of a global core which contains only 15 percent of the world's population but records approximately 75 percent of the world's annual income.[58] "Even supporters of economic globalization concede that the concentration of corporate power and decision making in major cities has created a global urban hierarchy in which the top-ranked centers in the global core dominate the worldwide network of which they are part."[59] The core attracts millions of what De Blij calls "mobals," risk-taking migrants mainly seeking employment. However, the norm is that "in the global core, piecemeal control takes precedence over comprehensive negotiation. . . . This control takes various forms, but in combination it has the effect of walling off core from periphery."[60] De Blij likens this to South African apartheid: "There is more than a hint of apartheid in the regional geography of the world today.

54. McKibben, *Hope, Human and Wild*, 64.
55. Ibid., 101. Emphasis original.
56. Kotkin, *The City*, 151.
57. Ibid., 547.
58. De Blij, *Power of Place*, 13.
59. Ibid., 201.
60. Ibid., 16.

Keeping locals in their place and restricting mobals to the greatest degree possible perpetuate the global dichotomy."[61]

Twentieth-Century Visions for the City

As suburbia mushroomed, attempts were made to rejuvenate the city. Hall notes that twentieth-century city planning was fundamentally a reaction to the evils of the nineteenth-century city, exemplified in the Victorian slums and accompanied by the threat of crime and violence.[62] Secondly he notes that "there are just a few key ideas in twentieth-century planning, which re-echo and recycle and reconnect. Each in turn stems from one key individual, or at most a small handful of such: the true founding fathers of modern city planning."[63] Hall identifies multiple models for the city that developed in the twentieth century. We have already taken note of his first model, namely mass suburbanization facilitated by the market.

The second is that of the garden-city, articulated by Ebenezer Howard. Following World War II, planners in the United Kingdom consciously sought to relocate industry and people to the peripheries of London. The Abercrombie Plan (1943) emphasized the development of new towns enveloped by green space, the so-called "garden-city." Mumford, though disappointed by the UK garden-cities, never let go of the garden-city as the ideal: "a constellation of medium-sized communities set in publicly protected open spaces given over to agriculture and recreation."[64] J. Jacobs and W. Whyte strongly disagreed.[65] Ironically, Jacobs's famous book was published in the same year as Mumford's *The City in History*. Contra Mumford, for Jacobs and Whyte, cities need lots of streets full of people and activity.[66]

The third model is that of the regional city, developed soon after 1900 by the Scottish biologist Patrick Geddes. This envisions regional planning according to which each subregion would be carefully developed on the basis of its natural resources.[67] The fourth model is that of a revived vision of the monumental city, expressing civic pride and prosperity. Most well known is the fifth model, Le Corbusier's vision of the vertical city.[68] Corbusier's *Toward an Architecture* was hugely influential, and a refrain of the book is that "*a great era has just*

61. Ibid., 18.

62. Hall, *Cities of Tomorrow*, 7. On the problems of the nineteenth-century city, see ibid., 13–46.

63. Ibid.

64. D. L. Miller, *Lewis Mumford*, 471.

65. See Whyte, *The Last Landscape*, and Jacobs, *Death and Life of Great American Cities*.

66. See D. L. Miller, *Lewis Mumford*, 473–77.

67. Hall, *Cities of Tomorrow*, 8, locates Mumford in this group.

68. Published in his *La Ville radieuse*. A spate of recent books have been published on Le Corbusier. See Filler, "Maman's Boy," 33–36.

begun. There exists a new spirit.[69] He despised the city's collection of small cottages and apartments and envisioned high-rise blocks with massive towers set aside for commerce as a way of solving the city's density with increased density. Corbusier tells us that "a cathedral is not beautiful"[70] and welcomes American grain elevators as the "magnificent first-fruits of the new age."[71] As Trigg notes, Corbusier "is governed in everything he says by an almost missionary zeal to spread the message that a new age demands a new architecture for a new kind of man."[72] For Corbusier the metaphor for the new age and thus the new man was that of the machine, and he says that "economic law inevitably governs our acts and thoughts."[73] The imprint of this vision is clearly apparent in major cities throughout the world today. The sixth model rejects large-scale planning and argues for a bottom-up approach whereby the people build for themselves, known as the community-design movement.

New Urbanism Recontextualized

Recently movements such as New Urbanism (NU) have sought to develop models for recovering human scale and community-based urban development.[74] NU developed in North America in the 1980s with the aim of reforming all aspects of real estate development and urban planning.[75] It is also known as "traditional neighborhood design." NU argues that in the first quarter of the twentieth century in North America, cities were characterized by compact, mixed-use neighborhoods, but that this changed with the car and resultant urban sprawl. The heart of NU is the design of neighborhoods, which should be self-governing and have

1. a discernible center;
2. most dwellings within five minutes' walk of the center;
3. a variety of dwelling types;
4. shops and offices on the edge of the neighborhood;
5. small garages, but not at the front of houses;
6. an elementary school close enough for walking;
7. small, accessible playgrounds;
8. streets which form a connected network and are narrow and shaded by trees;

69. Le Corbusier, *Toward an Architecture*, 146. Emphasis original.

70. Ibid., 32.

71. Ibid., 33.

72. Trigg, *Shaping of Man*, 4. For an insight into what drove Le Corbusier's work, see Weber, *Le Corbusier: A Life*.

73. Le Corbusier, *Toward an Architecture*, 12.

74. See www.cnu.org/charter for the charter of NU.

75. See Hall, *Cities of Tomorrow*, 412–15, for concurrent developments in Australia, California, and Florida, where the well-known New Urbanist development "Seaside" was central.

9. buildings close to the streets;
10. prominent sites reserved for civic buildings.

Hall notes of these developments,

> The odd fact was that the resulting prescription sounded and looked uncannily like Ebenezer Howard's Social City of 1898; or, for that matter, Sven Markelius's and Göran Sidenbladh's Stockholm General Plan of 1952. Planners, it seemed, had reinvented the wheel.
> One could say that it was a good wheel, worth reinventing.[76]

Philip Bess, a Catholic professor of architecture, engages positively but not uncritically with NU in his *Till We Have Built Jerusalem*. His conceptual framework is Thomistic: "There is a sacred order to which we are all accountable and relative to which we discover our own good, but also a rightful 'autonomy of earthly affairs.'"[77] With Aristotle he affirms that the city is the ultimate human community. Bess argues that architecture is best understood as a craft; as A. MacIntyre notes, "To share in the rationality of a craft requires sharing in the contingencies of its history, understanding its story as one's own, and finding a place for oneself as a character in the enacted dramatic narrative which is that story thus far."[78] For Bess,

> the Congress for the New Urbanism . . . is shooting straight for the heart of the contemporary building culture by first challenging and then engaging and converting the public officials, legislators, planners, traffic engineers, bankers, developers and homebuilding executives who are collectively responsible for the vast majority of new building being done in the United States—almost all of which is in the form of sprawl development, and almost all of which is done with minimal or no assistance from architects.[79]

In Bess's view NU is the only movement around with a coherent alternative to suburban sprawl.[80]

Bess's major critique of NU is its potential reductionism,[81] its implication that if we get the built environment right, healthy community will inevitably result.[82] Bess rightly notes the dangers with this; the built environment is an

---

76. Ibid., 413.
77. Bess, *Till We Have Built Jerusalem*, xv.
78. MacIntyre, *Three Rival Versions of Moral Enquiry*, 65.
79. Bess, *Till We Have Built Jerusalem*, xxiii–xxiv.
80. Ibid.
81. As W. Berry rightly notes, "Biblical religion . . . is also explicitly against reductionism" (*Life Is a Miracle*, 101).
82. Gorringe notes that "it is not possible to build people into virtue" (*Theology of the Built Environment*, 175).

indispensable part of an urban community, but it is insufficient by itself. The healthy neighborhood requires a virtuous community;[83] Bess stresses the importance of moral virtues, such as civility. Such communities are not "built" overnight; they require slow, careful nurture. North America, Bess notes, has few resources in this respect.[84]

Bess notes four orders that constitute the city: the ecological,[85] the economic, the moral, and the formal (architectural). He also notes the importance of the sacred for the city,[86] and uses the concept of "sacrament" to evoke the potential for the city to "be offered up by human beings to the sacred in the hope of their sanctification."[87] Kotkin similarly notes the historical importance of religion for cities; New Urbanists, however, "rarely refer to the need for a powerful moral vision to hold cities together."[88] For Kotkin, "Cities can thrive only by occupying a sacred place that both orders and inspires the complex natures of gathered masses of people. . . . It is in this city, this ancient confluence of the sacred, safe, and busy, where humanity's future will be shaped for centuries to come."[89]

What might a sacramental approach mean for city building? Bess suggests six characteristics:[90]

1. A sense of verticality, in which height and depth are allowed sacred significance
2. Concern for light as symbolic of the immateriality of the sacred
3. Care for and delight in craftsmanship redolent of the goodness of material things and their sacramental potential
4. The use of geometric ordering systems as emblematic of the order in creation
5. Compositional and artistic unity
6. A sense of hierarchy

Bess's antireductionistic approach to the city is very helpful in my opinion. Reformational philosophy offers a similarly antireductionistic approach. From its perspective every concrete entity, including the city, functions in fifteen

83. Intriguingly, McKibben says, "I've come to think that the solution to our environmental problems has more to do with rebuilding working communities even than with reworking our engines and appliances" (*Pieces from an Active Life*, 5).

84. Bess, *Till We Have Built Jerusalem*, 54. W. Berry lists seventeen things a local community should do if the residents want their community to flourish ("Conserving Communities," in *Another Turn of the Crank*, 19–21).

85. See in this respect Register, *Ecocities*.

86. Bess, *Till We Have Built Jerusalem*, 65–77.

87. Ibid., 69.

88. Kotkin, *The City*, 158.

89. Ibid., 160.

90. Bess, *Till We Have Built Jerusalem*, 73–74.

modal aspects: the arithmetic, placial, kinematic, physical, biotic, sensitive, logical, historical, lingual, social, economic, aesthetic, juridical, ethical, and pistic. The city is founded in the historical mode because it does not come "with" creation but is developed in history as the urban potential of creation is activated. It is qualified by the social modality,[91] which gives it its distinctive character as a "community of communities." The development of cities is part of normative cultural differentiation, but this differentiation can be skewed and misdirected. As a social entity, a city is composed of manifold complex interrelationships. There are natural communities, such as the family, and there are organized communities, such as city government, schools and universities, parks, shops and commercial institutions, churches, synagogues, and mosques. A city is a hub of intercommunal and interindividual relationships, all of which compose the hustle and bustle of city life.

The qualifying social mode alerts us that a city is about facilitating healthy, life-giving social life.[92] From this perspective a city is distorted when it becomes above all a commercial entity. The economic dimension is indispensable, but it must be subservient to the qualifying social dimension. Consumerism is written so deeply into the fabric of contemporary North American culture that it is genuinely hard to imagine what this relationship between the social and the economic might look like. And in such a culture, as Z. Bauman notes, those who resist the seduction of the market become the dirt of contemporary society. For the "seduced," consumerism becomes the source of liberty, but for the growing number of those who cannot afford this liberty, it becomes oppressive.[93]

> And as to the "glocalizing" impact, the cultural landscape of globalization, from the *maquiladora* cities of Mexico to the conurbations of Pacific Rim China, presents vistas of low-rise factories the size of football fields, enormous parking lots, drab basic, and usually over-crowded apartment buildings, polluted waterways, and sun-obscuring smog. Tens of millions of locals and mobals prove their willingness to take the job opportunities globalization creates, but let us not misinterpret motivations. Not many walk to work celebrating their absorption of foreign ideas and global best practices.[94]

As has often been noted, the result is that the mall has become the cathedral of our day, except that it has now been superseded by the "power centre."[95]

---

91. This is recognized by Mumford, "What Is a City?"; Wolterstorff likewise notes that "fundamentally a city is a shared environment for human activity" (*Until Justice and Peace Embrace*, 127).
92. Aristotle says that "friendship would seem to hold cities together" (*Nicomachean Ethics*, bk. viii, chap. 2, 115a, 208).
93. Z. Bauman, *Freedom*.
94. De Blij, *Power of Place*, 198.
95. Bunting and Filion, *Canadian Cities in Transition*.

To make the economic dimension genuinely subservient to the social in the city will mean that the autonomous market will have to be recontextualized in the context of a more human, more holistic story, and for us that is of course the biblical story. In response to this postcare economy, Goudzwaard and de Lange offer a wonderful and realistic vision for an "economy of care."[96] McKibben similarly calls for a "deep economy."[97] As McKibben rightly notes, the key question for any economy is whether it simply produces a larger pile of stuff or whether it builds community.[98]

The Reformational, antireductionist approach is illuminating in many, many ways. Take the aesthetic dimension of the city for example.[99] The city is not an artwork[100] and should not be turned into one. But the opening up of its aesthetic mode has major implications for city dwellers. Wolterstorff appropriately asks in this respect, why can we no longer build cities of delight? He finds the causes in Western individualism and private capitalism.[101] High art is venerated in cities but is locked away in museums.[102] And of the effect of the car, Wolterstorff rightly notes,

> Huge bleak parking areas are introduced. And, perhaps worst of all, wide expressways are sent crashing like destructive tornadoes through our cities. . . . Thus our commitment to the car as our principal means of transportation reinforces our tendency to think of the city not as an integrated public environment for our life together, but as a collection of individual buildings.[103]

As Wolterstorff points out, God ushers in the new Jerusalem, "yet in the eschatological image of the city we have the assurance that our efforts to

96. Goudzwaard and de Lange, Beyond Poverty and Affluence.
97. McKibben notes, "In choosing the phrase 'deep economy,' I have sought to echo the insistence, a generation ago, of some environmentalists that instead of simply one more set of smokestack filters or one more set of smokestack laws, we need a 'deep ecology' that asked more profound questions about the choices people make in their daily lives. . . . We need a similar shift in our thinking about economics—we need it to take human satisfaction and societal durability seriously; we need economics to mature as a discipline" (Deep Economy, 2–3).
98. Ibid., 2.
99. In this respect see also Gorringe, Theology of the Built Environment, 193–221. He identifies five "constituents of the image of the city" which will make a city beautiful: respect for the natural environment, an exuding of life, respect for the past and corporate memory, community buildings and public space, and genuine concern for the poor.
100. Jacobs rightly notes that "a City cannot be a work of art" (Death and Life of Great American Cities, 372; emphasis original). In terms of enhancing the visual order of the city, Jacobs focuses on streets, landmarks, and eye-catchers (ibid., 372–91).
101. Wolterstorff, Until Justice and Peace Embrace, 135. See also Wolterstorff, Art in Action, 178–83.
102. Wolterstorff, Art in Action, 138.
103. Ibid., 136. McKibben notes that "a car is the ultimate symbol of individualism; a crosswalk is about community" (Deep Economy, 152). Cf. Gorringe, Theology of the Built Environment, 220.

make these present cities of ours humane places in which to live—efforts which so often are frustrated, efforts which so often yield despair—will, by way of the mysterious patterns of history, eventually provide the tiles and timber for a city of delight."[104] Both Wolterstorff and C. Seerveld highlight the invaluable role of creative, appropriate public art in the city.[105] The integration of the built environment with the natural landscape is another important element in this respect, as are the creative development of public spaces which enhance community and buildings which facilitate and embody community.

The communal nature of the city raises tough questions about how big a city can become and still be a context for human flourishing. Certainly, the larger the city, the more important the sort of neighborhood envisioned by NU becomes. The multifunctional, human-scale neighborhoods aimed at by NU are urgently needed to create the multiple centers that would interact in order to constitute a vibrant, life-giving city. The scale of the problems of urbanism is so large that one is easily overwhelmed by the challenge. But again, attention to neighborhoods reduces the challenge to something doable, as long as city government provides the freedom and support for such initiatives. At a very practical level, Bess suggests that a Christian community with ten acres on hand might, instead of building a church and a large parking lot, consider building the core elements of a potential neighborhood: a church building of a reasonable size, a public square, a school, and the beginnings of a mixed-use neighborhood.[106] Bess asks poignantly,

> Why couldn't churches use this strategy to begin to integrate housing and commercial buildings into suburbia as part of mixed-use neighborhoods? And who's to say that an initially random proliferation of such developments across suburbia—once the exemplary pattern was established—over time might not become, as it did in London, the very physical and spiritual centers so pointedly lacking in contemporary suburbia?[107]

The prospect is exhilarating! A vibrant church could work to help its members grasp the vision involved and thereby work to cultivate the communal virtues required. The ecology of the land could be taken seriously in its development; for example, old trees need not just be bulldozed down, but, where appropriate, could be retained. Planting of indigenous species of plants would encourage vibrant bird and insect life.

104. Wolterstorff, *Until Justice and Peace Embrace*, 140.
105. Seerveld, "Cities as a Place for Public Artwork."
106. On the relevance of the church community to the city see also Gorringe, *Theology of the Built Environment*, 183–92.
107. Bess, *Till We Have Built Jerusalem*, 132–33. Bess also has a diagram illustrating what such a ten-acre development might look like (ibid., 132).

Such a neighborhood could provide space for one or two *third places*, so missing nowadays from the North American urban context. Oldenburg describes third places as "the core settings of informal public life."[108] According to Oldenburg, third places provide

- neutral ground for friendships and informal association;
- a leveling context in which all are welcome;
- context in which conversation is the main activity;
- a group of people who make up "the regulars";
- a plain, homely context whose aesthetics and sociality is low-profile;
- a mood of playfulness; and
- a home away from home.

Oldenburg's *The Great Good Place* and his edited volume *Celebrating the Third Place: Inspiring Ideas about the "Great Good Places" at the Heart of Our Communities* are must reading to get a sense of the potential for community of healthy third places.[109]

Such a neighborhood could also encourage and enable the presence of the small-mart,[110] which could make local produce and food and other products available to the neighborhood. Community gardening could flourish in such a context,[111] and the community could connect into healthy farms in the locality.

Quo Vadis?

Depth engagement with the city requires a (Christian) conceptual framework of a philosophical nature for the city and the expertise of builders, architects, engineers, planners, and so on in the service of such a framework. The task is as big as the city! Take the juridical dimension of the city for example. Zoning laws have inhibited healthy city development all over the Western world, and even healthy neighborhood developments such as we discussed above will require lawyers and city managers to get involved in reforming the legal apparatus of cities in order to facilitate healthy development. Thus, redemption of the city will inevitably involve a multiprong strategy drawing on a variety of expertise. Change will not be easily achieved, and yet, as we have indicated,

108. Oldenburg, *Great Good Place*, 16.

109. I am indebted to Larry Bourgeois for introducing me to this literature. See www .espressoguild.org for an initiative by Larry to promote coffeehouse culture.

110. See Shuman, *The Small-Mart Revolution*. He pleads for "'place-based' businesses," which he calls LOIS: economic development rooted in local ownership and import substitution (ibid., 7–8).

111. See Lawson, *City Bountiful*; Ableman, *On Good Land*.

there are a myriad of practical initiatives that Christians could take today in order to start the process of transforming their cities into places for human flourishing. It is critically important to remember that communities and not individuals by themselves will be the mechanism of change; hence the potential of the local church or Christian community.

17

Placemaking in Garden and Home

Placemaking and Gardens

As we noted in our discussion of Genesis 1–3, we must not construe the biblical story as the move from wilderness to urbanism. The depiction of the city coming down from heaven in Revelation 22 depicts cultural development—the kings of the earth bring their glory into the city (21:24)—the goal is not a return to Eden. Nevertheless the city retains its links with Eden; one might say it is depicted as a garden city. The vision of the new Jerusalem is a powerful, metaphorical depiction of the renewal of the entire creation. In line with the Old Testament passages Revelation draws on, "the unusual combination of water metaphors with urban road portrayals"[1] is intriguing in terms of place.

A river flows from the throne "not on some urban back street but 'in the middle of' the city's main 'street' because the imparting of eternal fellowship with God is an essential characteristic of the city."[2] Whereas Eden had one tree of life, now trees of life line both sides of the river, bearing twelve kinds of fruit, and producing fruit each month (22:2)![3] "Both Ezekiel and Revelation thus envision an *escalated reestablishment* of the garden of the first creation in which God's presence openly dwelled."[4] If Eden is more "garden" than urban, then it is important to note that the "garden" is not lost in the new Jerusalem but is part of creation's renewal.

1. Beale, *Book of Revelation*, 1105.
2. Ibid., 1104.
3. Ibid., 1106.
4. Ibid., 1106. Emphasis added. Cf. in particular Ezek. 36:35.

Figure 17.1 The Risen Christ Portrayed as a Gardener (cf. John 20:15) and Appearing to Mary Magdalene; Painting by Rembrandt (Erich Lessing/Art Resource, NY)

In the Old Testament, apart from Genesis 1–3, gardens are regularly mentioned in connection with the palaces of kings (cf. 2 Kings 21:18): as a Solomon-like figure, Qohelet built extensive gardens (Eccles. 2:4–6); garden and rural imagery is prominent in Song of Songs, although, intriguingly, the woman personifies the built environment, and in particular that of Jerusalem.[5] Jesus refers to gardens in his teaching, retreats to a garden before his trial and crucifixion (John 18:1), and is buried in and rises from a garden tomb (John 19:41). Mary mistakes Jesus for the gardener (John 20:15). C. de Witt suggests she made this "mistake" because Jesus appeared as—he in fact was—*the* gardener,[6] an interpretation depicted by Rembrandt (see figure 17.1)! Scripture thus provides us with ample precedent for taking gardening seriously.

Gardening has a long and diverse history. In Europe, gardening revived in the French cities of Languedoc and the Ile-de-France in the thirteenth century, and in the Italian villa gardens of the early Renaissance. French *parterres* developed at the end of the sixteenth century and reached high development

5. See E. Davis, *Scripture, Culture, and Agriculture*, 168–75.
6. Public lecture at Redeemer University College on January 10, 2009.

under André Lenôtre. English landscape gardens opened a new perspective in the eighteenth century. The nineteenth century saw a smorgasbord of historical revivals and Romantic cottage-inspired gardening. In England, William Robinson and Gertrude Jekyll championed the wild garden and the perennial garden, respectively. Andrew Jackson Downing and Frederick Law Olmsted adapted European styles for North America, especially influencing public parks, campuses, and suburban landscapes. Olmsted's influence extended well into the twentieth century. The twentieth century also saw the influence of modernism in the garden, from Thomas Church's kidney-shaped swimming pool to the bold colors and forms of Roberto Burle-Marx. A strong environmental consciousness is driving new considerations in gardening today.

The variety and traditions of gardens are vast. In our own day we are familiar with public and home gardens, inside and outside gardens, vegetable and flower gardens. Public gardens and the specialist horticulturalist clearly have an important part to play in making towns and cities pleasant places in which to live, work, and relax.[7] But in our predominantly suburban homes, how seriously should we take gardening? In my opinion, very!

We really have no choice. Suburban homes come, in most cases, with gardens, which are part of the cultivated landscape. One would love to see developers not just bulldoze all trees and plants before building, as they tend to do in North America, but we have to work from where we are, and most homeowners can make an immediate difference to the creation by starting with what is at hand: their garden. As D. Browning perceptively notes in her *Paths of Desire: The Passions of a Suburban Gardener*,

> Because the suburban garden begins as a blank slate, the effort of creation is more apparent than in those beds long ago carved out of a rolling, generous, seductive—and instructive—countryside. . . . The suburban garden is all about ushering nature back into the very plot of land from which it has been recently banished, then controlling and ordering it, the better to appreciate it and live with it.[8]

The neglected suburban garden may be as much a scandal as the misdirected pride and domination embodied in the gardens of Versailles.[9] Not all of us will be like Čapek's "real gardener":

> I will now tell you how to recognize a real gardener. "You must come to see me," he says: "I will show you my garden." Then, when you go just to please him,

---

7. For the wonderful story of a farm garden in Ontario see Chambers, *Stonyground*. He notes that "a true garden is never apart from its landscape. It arises from it like Eve from Adam's rib; it makes love to the fields in the language of botany. What I am doing in the gardens of Stonyground speaks back to the landscape what I have learned from it" (ibid., xiii).

8. Browning, *Paths of Desire*, 4.

9. See Harrison, *Gardens*, 109–13.

you will find him with his rump sticking up somewhere among the perennials. "I will come in a moment," he shouts to you over his shoulder. "Just wait till I have planted this rose." . . . After a while he must have planted it; for he gets up, makes your hand dirty, and beaming with hospitality, he says: "Come and have a look; it's a small garden, but—Wait a moment," and he bends over to weed some tiny grass. "Come along. I will show you Dianthus musalae; it will open your eyes. Great Scott, I forgot to loosen it here!" he says, and begins to poke in the soil. A quarter of an hour later he straightens up again. "Ah," he says, "I wanted to show you the bell flower, Campanula Wilsonae. That is the best campanula which—Wait a moment, I must tie up this delphinium." . . . After that you must go away, leaving his behind sticking up among the perennials.[10]

Once you start gardening, it has a habit of getting under your skin, so don't be surprised if this image becomes one your friends have of you!

Suburban life has become boringly predictable across the globe. But this is one thing that developing a suburban garden can and should undermine. I simply cannot develop my small Canadian garden along the same lines as our half-acre family plot in South Africa. The climate is very different, but so are the soil and the neighborhood. Gardening leads us into a relationship with the place where we live. You soon discover that your soil is of a particular type: full of clay and tough work here in Hamilton, Ontario; rich and much easier to work in Hillcrest, in KwaZulu-Natal, South Africa. Here in Canada gardening brings you into a close relationship with the seasons, especially as you wait for the spring bulbs to start appearing. Pollan rightly notes that "it is gardening that gives most of us our most direct and intimate experience of nature—of its satisfaction, fragility, and power."[11] As Pollan says,

> Gardening, I had by now come to appreciate, is a painstaking exploration of place; everything that happens in my garden—the thriving and dying of particular plants, the maraudings of various insects and other pests—teaches me to know this patch of land more intimately, its geology and microclimate, the particular ecology of its local weeds and animals and insects. My garden prospers to the extent I grasp these particularities and adapt to them.[12]

Suburbanites urgently need to reconnect with their place, and gardening is a wonderful, slow way to do this. "Indeed, the gardener is an Adam who

---

10. Čapek, *The Gardener's Year*, 7–8, quoted in Harrison, *Gardens*, 26. See also Page, *Education of a Gardener*, a delightful book. R. Page notes that "'book learning' gave me information, but only physical contact can give any real knowledge and understanding of a live organism. To have 'green fingers' or a 'green thumb' is an old expression which describes the art of communicating the subtle energies of love to prosper a living plant. Gradually I came to recognise through idiosyncrasies of colour, texture, shape and habit the origin of a plant and its cultural needs" (16).

11. Pollan, *Second Nature*, 3–4.

12. Ibid., 62–63.

has reengaged with the element of which he is made (for 'out of [the ground] wast thou taken' [Gen. 3:19])."[13] But gardening is far from exempt from the larger, cultural dynamics, and one needs to be aware of these.

In North America gardening has become an industry. In South Africa, where my family lives, many permanent nurseries are within easy reach, where one can go and browse in landscaped surroundings, attend lectures, consult with staff, and generally enjoy a cappuccino and a meal or snack in a relaxing context. Here in Ontario it is quite different. Once spring approaches, a multitude of temporary nurseries spring up, normally in the barren parking lots of malls and supermarkets. Of course there are permanent nurseries, but it is rare to find one that hosts a coffee shop and places to sit and relax. Gardening has been industrialized here in North America to an extent unknown in South Africa. Partially, of course, this is a seasonal issue, but there is more to it than that—the ubiquitous dollar has come to dominate the gardening and flower "industries."[14]

How do we resist the unhealthy industrialization of gardening? We can do many things. Growing your own seedlings is one way—one soon has enough to give away to friends and bypass the often inflated plant market. And gardening should enhance community. Gardens should have boundaries, but these need to be porous: "An essential tension is lost when gardens do not have porous, even promiscuous openings onto the world beyond their boundaries. . . . They open their enclosures in the midst of history, offering a measure of seclusion that is not occlusion."[15] Boundaries should "keep the garden intrinsically related to the world that they keep at a certain remove."[16] Indeed, as I have discovered, it is hard to attend to your garden without making contact with your neighbors and thus starting to build that community which is so essential but so elusive in our day. Before you know it you are discussing particular weeds, sharing plants, and entering into local community.

Here in Hamilton, as is common in suburbia, we are obsessed with developing immaculate, green *lawns*. Again, this is big business: "Nowhere in the world are lawns as prized as in America. In little more than a century, we've rolled a green mantle of it across the continent, with scant thought to the local conditions or expense. America has some 50,000 square miles of lawn under cultivation, on which we spend an estimated $30 billion a year."[17] Neglecting your lawn can make you a pariah in your neighborhood![18] Intriguingly, this can be traced back to, among others, F. Scott's *The Art of Beautifying Suburban Home Grounds*, published in 1870. In England lawns were generally found

13. Harrison, *Gardens*, 29.
14. For an eye-opening examination of the flower industry see Stewart, *Flower Confidential*.
15. Harrison, *Gardens*, 57.
16. Ibid., 56–57.
17. Pollan, *Second Nature*, 55.
18. Ibid., 55–56.

on estates, but America democratized them. In England the lawn was not an end in itself but the backdrop for games, and for flower beds and trees. Scott subordinates all other elements to the lawn: "Let your lawn be your home's velvet robe, and your flowers its not too promiscuous decoration."[19] The result is the macro lawn business, with its chemicals and pesticides. "Lately we have begun to recognize that we are poisoning ourselves with our lawns, which receive, on average, more pesticide and herbicide per acre than any other crop grown in this country."[20] What is the solution? Subordinate lawn care to gardening![21] "Gardening, as compared to lawn care, tutors us in nature's ways, fostering an ethic of give-and-take with respect to the land. Gardens instruct us in the particularities of place."[22]

The use of chemicals and pesticides is an important example of how the smallest cultivated garden brings the suburbanite in touch with the larger issues facing us on the planet nowadays.[23] Rachel Carson's classic *Silent Spring* is justifiably famous for her exposé of the effect of large-scale and indiscriminate use of pesticides and chemicals on the environment. "Through her mother, Maria Carson, and her Presbyterian forebears she imbibed a reverence for nature, an antimaterialist ethic, and a reformist impulse."[24] Amidst corporate and scientific opposition and debilitating health problems, Carson fought to bring the effect of these chemicals to public attention and in the process made a huge contribution to the environmental movement.[25]

So, relaxing about the immaculate lawn and canceling the contract with the lawn maintenance company frees up money and more space for cultivation! And here is where the creativity and the importance of local knowledge come to the fore. As I learned in South Africa, it is good to keep an eye out for indigenous plants and flowers, for not only will these grow well and flower abundantly, but they will attract and nurture the bird life. Indeed, it is astonishing to see how a garden comes alive in unexpected ways once the soil is cultivated and the garden developed to be a place for birds and other creatures to find a home. One finds oneself waking up to bushes full of small birds and long-neglected plants start coming into bloom, and even in suburbia you find surprising visitors in your

19. Quoted in ibid., 59.

20. Ibid., 63.

21. For examples of what this might mean in practice in North America see Rubin, *How to Get Your Lawn off Grass*. Joan Gussow, in her *This Organic Life*, proposes that suburbanites could raise much of their own food on what are currently grass lawns. She does this because of the "irrepressible joy in tending to and eating from that part of the natural world to which I have bound myself" (120). Her other best reason is "deliciousness" (ibid., 215).

22. Lytle, *The Gentle Subversive*, 63–64.

23. See Pollan, *Second Nature*, 190–201, for what gardening might offer us in terms of an environmental ethic.

24. Lytle, *The Gentle Subversive*, 11.

25. See ibid. The literature on the effect of pesticides is extensive. On pesticides and grassland birds of the prairies in Canada see Herriot, *Grass, Sky, Song*, 133–219.

garden. For two years in a row in suburban Hamilton, I have had the experience of a wild rabbit or two regularly occupying my small garden. Earthworms start to appear in abundance, as of course do weeds![26]

Gardens, mercifully, "have a way of slowing time down—allowing its flow to gather in placid ponds, as it were—but that is part of their power of enchantment, not their power of endurance."[27] Even the homeless carefully create gardens out of whatever is available, as a means of finding their place in a displaced world. In their 1993 book *Transitory Gardens, Uprooted Lives*, D. Balmori and M. Morton provide a visual and written documentation of gardens made by the homeless in the slums of New York.[28] The terrible displacement of the homeless is an image of the displacement so many of us experience in our dromocratic societies. Gardening provides an important way of recentering. "Gardens are not memorials. . . . If anything they exist to reenchant the present."[29]

One important way to recover a rhythm of grace is to reappropriate the church calendar, and in his fascinating book *Inheriting Paradise: Meditations on Gardening*, theologian V. Guroian connects his love of gardening to living the church year. As M. Silf notes in her foreword, "If our desire is for the presence of God, this book offers us 'the tomatoes and squash, the wild geese and the chickadees'—the very places where the presence of God is vibrantly incarnate, palpable, alive, and accessible to our own hands and feet."[30] Thus the practice of cultivation needs to be attended to slowly, as legitimate in itself.

Homemaking

> "He doesn't care about houses," is in my lexicon a statement as serious and final as . . . an essential lack of ethical sense would be, if discovered in a colleague. . . . Occasionally I have paled at seeing some friend I have known for years in his home for the first time. . . . The man who has no sense of the house and who is not moved by the harmony of handsome furnishings is for me, as for Shakespeare, the man who "hath no music in himself, a man fit for treasons, stratagems and spoils. The motions of his spirit are dull as night, and his affections dark as Erebus. Let no such man be trusted!"[31]

The home is central to the Old Testament covenant. Deuteronomy 6, in the *shema* (vv. 4–9), tells the Israelites to repeat God's words "at home" and to

---

26. On weeds see Pollan, *Second Nature*, 98–116.
27. Harrison, *Gardens*, 39.
28. See ibid., 39–48.
29. Ibid., 39.
30. Silf, foreword to Guroian, *Inheriting Paradise*, ix.
31. Praz, *Illustrated History of Interior Decoration*, 19.

write them on the doorposts of their houses and gates. While this "writing" is metaphorical, it could well also be literal; there is evidence from Egypt of sacred inscriptions on doors.[32] As P. Craigie notes, "The commandments were to be the subject of conversation both inside and outside the home, from the beginning of the day to the end of the day. In summary, the commandments were to permeate every sphere of the life of man."[33] This comprehensive vision is rooted firmly in the home. Not surprisingly, parental obedience and not coveting one's neighbor's *house* or field figure prominently in the Decalogue (Deut. 5:16, 21).

In the New Testament the house and the household are central to the life of Jesus and the mission of the early church. Domestic life plays a key role in the teaching of Jesus, and homes provide the setting for many events in his ministry. In Luke-Acts the home and household is the basic social unit through which the gospel spread from Palestine to Rome.[34] "Here among the households of the holy and the unholy, the wealthy and the poor, Jews and Gentiles of high and low degree, the good news of a holiness and wholeness available to all made its initial and sustained advance."[35] Not surprisingly, therefore, Paul repeatedly addresses the ethics of the household in his so-called *Haustafel*, household codes, such as in Colossians 3:18–4:1.

Paul's household codes reveal that the New Testament shares its culture's view that concord is vital in the household. The ancient household is not, of course, the equivalent of the modern home. "It is rather the equivalent of a modern family business, an economic unit at whose core is a family."[36] Yet Paul embraces the social structure of the household, while also transforming it:

The effect . . . is to bring even mundane duties under the lordship of Christ. Ordinary tasks are placed in a different interpretative framework. They are now performed to and for the Lord, whatever mundane purposes they may also serve. Each act gains a new meaning. Whereas the daily tasks might appear to serve only human needs and demands, the Christians can think of themselves as obeying their heavenly master. Life thus becomes an unseen transaction between believers and Jesus.[37]

Thus, in both Old Testament and New Testament the home is of fundamental importance as a social, educational, and ecclesial institution. However, the modern home must not quickly be equated with the New Testament household, any more than with the ancient Roman household. There is an overlap,

32. Walton et al., *Bible Background Commentary*, 178.
33. Craigie, *Book of Deuteronomy*, 170.
34. See Elliott, "Temple versus Household."
35. Ibid., 229.
36. Talbert, *Ephesians and Colossians*, 234.
37. Ibid., 234–35.

but there are also important differences. The historical development of the home is tracked by W. Rybczynski in his *Home: A Short History of an Idea*.[38] Rybczynski traces the origin of our idea of the home back to the Middle Ages. The poor lived in poverty, but town dwellers had homes. These were, however, very different from the contemporary Western home. They combined living and working, generally consisting of two floors over a basement for storage.[39] Until the seventeenth century, change in the home was slow.[40] M. Praz discerns *Stimmung*—the sense of intimacy in a room—as developing first in northern Europe.[41] The development of the stove meant better heating and easier subdivision of houses into different rooms. This made possible the discovery of privacy and intimacy: "before the idea of the home as the seat of family life could enter the human consciousness, it required the experience of both privacy and intimacy, neither of which had been possible in the medieval hall."[42] Rybczynski traces the discovery of domesticity to the Netherlands in the seventeenth century. Dutch religion, with its simplicity and thrift, manifested itself in the home. By midcentury, Dutch houses were divided into public and private rooms. As one still notices today, Dutch houses began to be constructed to allow light to stream through them. The Dutch prized their children, their homes, and their gardens. The Dutch garden was an indication of the transition from the communal large house to the individual family home. "To speak of domesticity is to describe a set of felt emotions, not a single attribute. Domesticity has to do with a family, intimacy, and a devotion to the home, as well as with a sense of the house as embodying—not only harboring—these sentiments. It was the atmosphere of domesticity that permeated de Witte's and Vermeer's paintings."[43]

By the eighteenth century privacy and domesticity had spread to the rest of northern Europe. Houses were now smaller and less public; they had become a place for personal, intimate behavior. Comfortable furniture developed in this period,[44] a challenge solved by rococo cabinetmakers.[45] Rococo was also the first style developed exclusively for the interior of the house, thereby introducing the distinction between architecture and interior décor, a distinction we take for granted today. The stage was set for the discovery of the idea of comfort: "It developed over a long period of time, and although it made great progress in Rococo France its evolution did not end there. From about the middle of the eighteenth century, or slightly earlier, it came increasingly

38. See also T. Putnam, "Beyond the Modern Home."
39. Rybczynski, *Home*, 32.
40. On the domestic interior from 1620–1920, see Thornton, *Authentic Decor*.
41. See Praz, *Illustrated History of Interior Decoration*, 49–55.
42. Rybczynski, *Home*, 48.
43. Ibid., 75.
44. Ibid., 77–84.
45. Ibid., 96.

under the influence of Georgian England. Here, thanks to a happy confluence of economic and social conditions and national character, it flowered."[46]
The Georgian influence has been embodied in the novels of Jane Austen, who
perfected the domestic genre of novel-writing, "the literary equivalent to the
seventeenth-century Dutch school of interior painting."[47]

In terms of physical amenities, the history of the home can be divided into
two phases: pre-1890 and post-1890. All the modern devices with which we
are familiar—central heating, plumbing, hot and cold running water, electricity—became available only after 1890. These devices allowed for greater
domestic comfort but, intriguingly, did not much change the style of houses. It
was the *Exposition Internationale des Arts Décoratifs et Industriels Modernes*
in Paris in 1925 that produced a major change in how we view home style.
Style was to be new and modern and not simply a recovery of period styles.
Significantly, Le Corbusier designed a pavilion called *Esprit Nouveau*, which
in its minimalism embodied his view that "A house is a machine for living
in. . . . An armchair is a machine for sitting in, etc."[48]

The resulting austerity of minimalism that has dominated much twentieth-
century décor is described by Rybczynski as a rupture in the development of
comfort.

> And what does the twentieth-century chair offer us? It shows an optimistic
> belief in technology and the efficient use of materials. It shows a concern for
> fabrication, not craftsmanship in the traditional sense, but in precise and exact
> assembly. It is a purposeful object, without frivolity or frills. It offers status; you
> can buy a used car for less than many modern chairs. It exhibits lightness and
> movability, and it invites admiration for these qualities—just as a well-made
> camp cot does. But it does not ask to be sat in, or at least not for long. . . . It is
> about many things, this chair, but it is no longer about ease, leisure, or, if truth
> be told, about comfort.[49]

For Rybczynski, the home is above all about comfort, and at the end of his
Home he develops his nonreductionistic, multilayered Onion Theory of Comfort, though

> hardly a definition at all . . . It may be enough to realize that domestic comfort
> involves a range of attributes—convenience, efficiency, leisure, ease, pleasure,
> domesticity, intimacy, and privacy—all of which contribute to the experience;
> common sense will do the rest. . . . We should resist the inadequate definitions
> that engineers and architects have offered us. Domestic well-being is too impor-
> tant to be left to experts; it is, and it has always been, the business of the family

46. Ibid., 104. See ibid., 104–21.
47. Ibid., 112.
48. Le Corbusier, *Toward an Architecture*, 151.
49. Rybczynski, *Home*, 212.

and the individual. We must rediscover for ourselves the mystery of comfort, for without it, our dwellings will indeed be machines instead of homes.[50]

The danger with dealing with the home as a separate place is that we reinforce the contemporary fragmentation of modern life. For too many the big suburban box with the double garage doors as the main feature has become our refuge from work and daily life. But, of course, the house is inevitably intricately connected with the rest of life, even if we refuse to take note. Not only do we need to become conscious of these connections; we need to redirect them along healthy lines. W. Berry is scathing in his critique of the modern home:

> With its array of gadgets and machineries, all powered by energies that are destructive . . . the modern home is a veritable factory of waste and destruction. It is the mainstay of the economy of money. But within the economies of energy and nature, it is a catastrophe. It takes in the world's goods and converts them into garbage, sewage, and noxious fumes—for none of which we have found a use. . . . The modern home is so destructive, I think, because it is a generalization, a product of factory and fashion, an everyplace or a noplace. Modern houses, like airports, are extensions of each other; they do not vary much from one place to another. . . . The modern house is not a response to its place, but rather to the affluence and social status of its owner.[51]

Homes and housing have many dimensions, and healthy development will need to attend to them all. Most houses are parts of neighborhoods, towns, and cities, and our discussions above will bear integrally on the home. Like the city, the house has become a consumer product, so that it is often thought of, above all else, in terms of its monetary value. The commercialization of the home reveals the destructiveness of consumerism, and as Berry notes,

> if it is to cohere, a community must remember its history and obligations; it is therefore irreconcilably opposed to "mobility" as a social norm. Persons, places, and things have a practical value, but they are not reducible to such value; they are not interchangeable. That is why we outlawed slavery. That is why a house for sale is not a home.[52]

We urgently need property developers to work with architects to design good neighborhoods and healthy houses,[53] and there is now a considerable literature and practice available of "Building Green."[54] However, most of us will have

50. Ibid., 231–32.
51. W. Berry, *Unsettling of America*, 52.
52. W. Berry, *Way of Ignorance*, 79.
53. On the challenges and possibilities of property development see Rybczynski, *Last Harvest*.
54. See, e.g., Snell and Callahan, *Building Green*; Roy, *Earth-Sheltered Houses*.

to work, for now, with what we have.[55] What might a Christian view of place deliver in terms of the home?

From a Christian perspective the home is of fundamental importance because it is the place in which the family is implaced and flourishes or destructs. The home thus needs to be a place for human flourishing and the nurture of children. Homemaking skills are an essential component of parenting, but as Berry notes, in our culture, "housewifery . . . was reduced to the exercise of purchasing power."[56] Thus parents must make it a priority to recover and practice homemaking skills. How might we do this?

We might begin by realizing that *less is more* and *slower is faster*. Even as the family continues to disintegrate in the West, houses get bigger. Here in Hamilton, where I live, the middle class cityscape is dotted with huge, virtually identical box houses a few meters apart from each other. Family life and homemaking will never be recovered with the big house, several cars, and the essential two jobs to maintain this standard of consumerism. Homemaking takes time and is slow work; far better for a couple to opt for a smaller house so as to free up the time for homemaking. When it comes to homemaking in the West, less is invariably more.

We will also need to recover a sense of the home as a permanent place. This is so alien to mobile North American culture that Berry's statement above about a house for sale not being a genuine home sounds absurd. Of course moving has its place, but the absurdity we feel when we read what Berry says may merely reflect the profound extent to which we have become displaced and lack any strong sense of connection to our locale. A comparison with other cultures is revealing. In his discussion of the French café as a third place, Oldenburg notes,

> Conservatism grows with the investment in a locality. . . . Once the French worker finds a tolerable work situation, a suitable dwelling for his family, and a bistro at which to enjoy the companionship of his pals, he becomes an immovable object. Why should he move? . . . Having established his first, second, and third place, the Frenchman wisely proceeds to enjoy them. They are satisfied individuals, neither lonely nor dependent upon tomorrow to bring life's rewards.[57]

The home needs to become *our* home. Amidst the uniformity of boringly repetitive housing units, we can work to make the "unit" our distinctive home. The use of color, additions to the house, development of the garden, and many other strategies can move us in this direction. And why not recover the

---

55. For a wonderful perspective on the value of building one's own place see Pollan, *Place of My Own*; Kidder, *House*.

56. W. Berry, *Unsettling of America*, 114–15.

57. Oldenburg, *Great Good Place*, 154.

practice of giving our house a name, which humbly evokes the ethos of this permanent place in our lives?

An important part of homemaking will be to connect into local culture and recover community. We should not underestimate what this may require. For Berry it meant returning to his home in Kentucky and changing his profession from English professor to farmer and writer.[58] Reflecting on his return, Berry notes,

> That return made me finally an exile from the ornamental Europeanism that still passes for culture with most Americans. What I had done caused my mind to be thrown back forcibly upon its sources: my home countryside, my own people and history. . . . It occurred to me that there was another measure for my life than the amount or even the quality of the writing I did; a man, I thought must be judged by how willingly and meaningfully he can be present where he is, by how fully he can make himself at home in his part of the world. I began to want desperately to learn to belong to my place.[59]

For K. Norris it took a move back to Dakota.[60] For B. Hooks, as for Berry, it involved returning to Kentucky.[61]

A recovery of the suburban or inner-city home as a place for dwelling will thus involve a radical change in mind-set. Community, the very thing that suburbia undermines, will be essential. Those of us who remain in suburbia must be willing "to trade their problems for their possibilities."[62] "What makes community building so complex is that it occurs in an infinite number of small steps, sometimes in quiet moments that we notice out of the corner of our eye."[63] Fortunately the desire for slow food, neighborhood community, connection with the land, and so on is gaining momentum in the West, so that there is invariably a community, however small, waiting to connect with. Where I live in Hamilton there are regular farmers' markets, farms that function as community supported agriculture within easy reach, and so on.

Homemaking will involve becoming connected deeply into these local networks; not only will this deepen the roots of the home, but it will also allow the home to become again a unit of production rather than mere consumption. Where time permits, homeowners can grow some of their own produce

---

58. See W. Berry, *The Long-Legged House*, part 3.

59. Quoted in Hooks, *Belonging*, 175.

60. Norris, *Dakota*. Norris notes, "I live in an American desert, without much company, without television, because I am trying to know where on earth I am" (ibid., 23).

61. Hooks, *Belonging*.

62. P. Block, *Community*, 4.

63. Ibid., 9. W. Berry rightly notes that "the only real, practical, hope-giving way to remedy the fragmentation that is the disease of the modern spirit is a small and humble way. . . . One must begin in one's own life the private solutions that can only in turn become public solutions" (*Unsettling of America*, 23).

at home. It is astonishing how much produce can emerge from small patches of cultivated land.[64]

The home is above all else about the inner community of the family, and the home will need to be developed to facilitate deep relationship. The kitchen will need to be recovered as the place where meals are prepared:

> The modern kitchen, in which everything is hidden in artfully designed cabinets, looks well organized, like a bank office. But a kitchen does not function like an office; if anything, it is more like a workshop. Tools should be out in the open where they are accessible, near those places where the work is done, not secreted below counters or in deep, difficult-to-reach cupboards.[65]

Mealtimes will have to be recovered as slow times of reflection and enjoyment.[66] The TV and Internet will have to be carefully controlled or retired. Comfortable, relaxing living spaces conducive to rest and conversation will have to be developed. The bathroom, often an important place for privacy and relaxation, will need to be spacious and conducive to relaxation.

Seerveld expresses his concern that we "find out how we Christians can live in the rush without becoming part of the rush, because heading into the Canadian Northern wilds for good or moving to Montana is not a sanctifying solution: it treats one's neighbor like the pell-mell Gadarene swine."[67] How do we restore "ludic sanity"[68] to our homes in a culture of efficiency, technological mastery, and mass-produced (plastic) goods, now mainly coming from China? This is not how God wants us to live, and we need to break with this approach starting right where we do have some control, namely in our homes. As Rybczynski notes, postmodern collage is not the answer; we will need to look into the history of homemaking and find models that we can transfuse into the present. Has the TV den replaced rocking chairs on front porches? Then perhaps it is time to recover the front porch, or, as we call it in South Africa, the veranda. Are our kitchens full of plastic? Then perhaps it is time to slowly hunt out durable "old stuff."[69] Like Berry, Seerveld encourages us to start *now* in small ways:

- Put homemade bread on the table instead of "the carbohydrated, synthetic pulp supermarkets sell in vain under that name."[70]
- Purchase one well-crafted thing for your home.

---

64. For a delightful story of the recovery of production see Woginrich, *Made from Scratch*.

65. Rybczynski, *Home*, 222.

66. See Postman, *Disappearance of Childhood*, for a critique of what is happening to children in America today. Central to this is the home.

67. Seerveld, *Rainbows for the Fallen World*, 62.

68. Ibid., 68. Ludic here means "playful."

69. See Woginrich, *Made from Scratch*, 77–88.

70. Seerveld, *Rainbows for the Fallen World*, 69.

- One good linen tablecloth will add nuance to eating in a way that multiple vinyl place mats will never achieve.[71]
- Don't make the mistake of thinking that aesthetic depth necessarily means great expense. Simplicity is a great virtue in contemporary culture, and one can work slowly to develop the home into a vibrant, playful environment conducive to rest and relationship. I have a book on my shelves called *Shack Chic*, a photographic documentation of poverty-stricken shack homes in South Africa. The richness of exteriors and interiors is astonishing and ample evidence that nuance and wealth do not necessarily go together.
- Find artwork for your house that evokes the spirit of the home. The sort of art we need in our homes is that described by Lewis Hyde in *The Gift*: "I went to see a landscape painter's works, and that evening, walking among pine trees near my home, I could see the shapes and colors I had not seen the day before. The spirit of an artist's gift can wake our own."[72]
- While *home*, in the best sense of the word, should refer to a place whose entirety embodies a Christian spirit in today's world, it is vital that the home also contain the resources for spiritual renewal. This can take many forms: a comfy chair which the family understands one withdraws to if one needs silence and is not to be unnecessarily disturbed. A young architect friend of mine has designed and built two delightful chapels in the grounds of relatively small Cotswold properties in Gloucestershire in southwest England. Between these extremes you might do as I and so many others do, and reserve a niche of your home as a prayer area. Christian art should never be reduced to "religious" art, but there remains a place for creative religious artifacts and icons to remind us that our life is hidden in Christ.[73]

As Seerveld notes, there is no one Christian style; rather, "Whatever is in your power to firm up allusively—heightening ordinary things and everyday activities in gentle, surprising, celebrating ways—do it with all your might."[74]

The inner community of the home always reaches out into the local community, and the home is *the* place of hospitality in the Christian tradition. In her delightful book on the home, Edith Schaeffer notes that the home should be an open door with hinges.[75] There will be times to close the door for the sake of the family, but there will also be times to have the door wide open to

71. See Schaeffer, *Hidden Art*, for delightful attention to these issues.
72. Hyde, *The Gift*, xvii.
73. See Vitale and Saralegui, *The Divine Home*, regarding a tendency nowadays for religious artifacts to become collectors' items.
74. Seerveld, *Rainbows for the Fallen World*, 69.
75. Schaeffer, *What Is a Family?*, 211–34.

entertain friends and relatives, and strangers! The design of the home may need attention in this respect. The double garage at the center of the front of the home does nothing to encourage openness to the community. Hospitality has many dimensions to it, but one could do worse than start with the front door. And fortunately North Americans are starting to recover the front door! "Now, in the twenty-first century, front entrances are being rediscovered and appreciated. Seldom-used front doors are being unstuck, doorways widened, and whole façades reimagined to reclaim that entrance as the true portal into the house."[76] According to Vicente and Connor doorways are most successful when they[77]

- satisfy owner's tastes and needs;
- enhance the existing style of the house;
- are in proportion and scale to the rest of the house;
- draw the eye to the door without overpowering the façade;
- subordinate details and ornaments to the entrance;
- invite guests waiting for the door to be answered to admire the detail and workmanship.

The connection of the home with the rest of the world is symbolized nowadays by the mailbox (see figure 17.2). In parts of Canada a "flag" attached to the mailbox is raised to indicate the mail has arrived. In Kriger's painting a bird delivers the letter, evoking the wonderfully human dimension of postal communication. Although letter writing has been undermined by email and the Internet, letters and stamps have great potential for enhancing *glocality*, that is, being rooted in a place while connected globally. Stamps are like ministories[78] and invariably evoke the places from which they originate. Ironically, even as electronic mail franking and email facilitate a bland delocalized form of communication, stamps are increasingly being produced, which evoke particular places. For example, in Malaysia there are some four hundred species of palm trees. In May 2009 Malaysia released a set of four stamps depicting their palm trees: the Fan Palm, the Fish Tail Palm, the Serdang Palm, and the Joey Palm, an endangered species.

Stamps thus have great potential to raise our consciousness of place. We could work to recover the letter sent by the postal service. An example of this is Calvin Seerveld's letter writing. He recycles envelopes, and his letters invariably arrive with the address written in his black fountain pen and adorned with a colorful variety of local stamps. Collecting stamps and being aware of those our country is producing are also useful ways of recovering a sense

76. Vicente and Connor, *Language of Doors*, 11.
77. Ibid., 13.
78. On stamps and the Old Testament see Matek, *Bible through Stamps*.

Figure 17.2 Evocative Painting of a Mailbox with a Bird Personally Delivering a Letter; Painting by Henk Krijger, "Somebody Loves Me, I Wonder Who . . ." (Patmos Workshop and Gallery, Toronto)

of place. Having grown up in Pinetown in KwaZulu-Natal in South Africa, I still recall the stamp shop I used to visit in search of stamps. Nowadays it is hard to find a stamp shop in KwaZulu-Natal, and, as I discovered recently, none of the major stationery shops even sell stamp albums. The home is the obvious place for the recovery of such practices.

The *shema*, as we saw above, recognizes that faith will live or die in terms of what happens in the home. It is *the* place in which deep faith and the emerging generation are to be nurtured. Bachelard argues that "all really inhabited space bears the essence of the notion of home."[79] An essential ingredient in the redemption of our towns, cities, and countryside is a proliferation of houses that are in fact homes.

79. Bachelard, *Poetics of Space*, 5.

18

Placemaking in Various Facets of Life

To be healed we must come with all the other creatures to the feast of Creation.[1]

Placemaking and Farming

In his classic work on culture and agriculture, *The Unsettling of America*, W. Berry begins by distinguishing between exploiters and nurturers: "Whereas the exploiter asks of a piece of land only how much and how quickly it can be made to produce, the nurturer asks a question that is much more complex and difficult: What is its carrying capacity?"[2] For decades Berry has argued persuasively that modern agribusiness, developed in North America after World War II, is exploiting the land with devastating consequences to the land, food, and community.[3] The reductive metaphor of the "machine" has been brought to bear on agriculture with the result that "farming . . . is an industry known as 'agribusiness,' which looks upon the farm as a 'factory,' and upon farmers, plants, animals, and the land itself as interchangeable parts of 'units of production.'"[4] Character and community are the first casualties of exploitation, and significantly, they "constitute, just as much as

---

1. W. Berry, *Unsettling of America*, 103–4.
2. Ibid., 7.
3. According to one survey, farmers in the United States are five times as likely to commit suicide as to die from farm accidents. Halweil, *Eat Here*, 70.
4. W. Berry, *Standing on Earth*, 77.

nature, the source of food."[5] Subsequent decades have more than confirmed Berry's analysis.[6]

Ever attentive to the interconnectedness of creation, Berry argues that the crisis of farming in North America is a crisis of character, a crisis of agriculture, and a crisis of culture. In terms of character Berry notes that modern specialization has become a disease, with the result that relations and interconnectedness, and thus character, are lost. Agribusiness, which treats land and animals as units of production, is normed by merely economic and quantitative standards, with devastating consequences. "We are eating—drawing our lives out of the land—thoughtlessly. . . . It is a crisis of culture."[7] Berry continually emphasizes that we need to think of land and people *together*,[8] but this does not let us off the hook in terms of preserving wilderness areas. Wilderness is vital because[9]

1. our biological and cultural roots are in nature;
2. humility demands places that we do not use at all;
3. since wilderness is a standard of civilization and a cultural model, it is essential as a barometer of the effect of our civilization upon nature.[10]

Industrial agriculture has worked on the bigger-is-better principle, with devastating consequences for rural communities and farmers in particular, but also for food production and food consumers. As Pollan observes:

All of our uncertainties about nutrition should not obscure the plain fact that the chronic diseases that now kill most of us can be traced back directly to the industrialization of our food. . . . Wherever in the world people gave up their traditional way of eating and adopted the Western diet, there soon followed a predictable series of Western diseases, including obesity, diabetes, cardiovascular diseases, and cancer.[11]

W. Berry argues that we need to recover "kindly use" of the land. "Kindly use depends upon intimate knowledge, the most sensitive responsiveness and responsibility."[12] Berry's thought is deeply Christian, and his vision of such recovery revolves around the idea of creation order: "Fidelity to human order,

---

5. W. Berry, *Unsettling of America*, 9.
6. The evidence is overwhelming, but for a reality check see Baur, *Farm Sanctuary*, on slaughterhouses, and Pollan, *The Omnivore's Dilemma*, on food production.
7. W. Berry, *Unsettling of America*, 38.
8. Pollan, *Second Nature*, 4, notes that "Americans have a deeply ingrained habit of seeing nature and culture as irreconcilably opposed."
9. W. Berry, *Unsettling of America*, 29–30.
10. On the challenge of recovering wilderness see McKibben, *Hope, Human and Wild*.
11. Pollan, *In Defense of Food*, 10, 11.
12. W. Berry, *Unsettling of America*, 31.

then, if it is fully responsible, implies fidelity also to natural order. Fidelity to human order makes devotion possible."[13] Berry is never merely a prophet of doom; like the messages of the biblical prophets his diagnosis of the crisis in agriculture is unflinching, but he always attends to positive ways forward. His books are filled with practical reflections on farming and on examples of good practice, such as that of the Amish: "It is possible, I think, to say that this is a Christian agriculture, formed upon the understanding that it is sinful for people to misuse or destroy what they did not make. The Creation is a unique, irreplaceable gift, therefore to be used with humility, respect, and skill."[14] W. Berry is acutely sensitive to the historical development of farming, and in his startling reflections on mechanization he rightly notes, "The coming of a tool, then, is not just a cultural event; it is also an historical crossroad—a point at which people must choose between two possibilities: to become more intensive or more extensive; to use the tool for quality or for quantity, for care or for speed."[15] Berry thus rightly rejects the modern faith in progress and subjects "progress" to searching critique. In the process he comes up with surprising solutions: he continues to farm with horses and has also refused to acquire a computer for his writing.[16]

Recovery of kindly use in farming requires, according to Berry, that we do the following:[17]

1. Attend to the issue of the appropriate scale of farms. In any region there is a size limit beyond which the farmer cannot provide the affection and care farming requires.
2. Attend to the problem of balance. The proper proportions between people and land, and between plants and animals, must be discerned and respected.
3. Attend to diversity. Farms should aim at a diversity of species, and farming should encourage as many different kinds of good farming as possible.[18]

13. Ibid., 130.
14. Ibid., 213.
15. W. Berry, *Standing on Earth*, 72.
16. See W. Berry, "Why I Am Not Going to Buy a Computer;" "Feminism, the Body, and the Machine." In the former article, Berry, 171–72, lists nine criteria for technological innovation. One does not have to agree with Berry on these issues but the questions he asks are crucial.
17. W. Berry, "Agricultural Solutions," 82–85. At the conclusion to *Unsettling of America* Berry, 218–22, lists twelve public remedies. Remedy six is the promotion of local food markets. Remedy seven is that every town and city should operate an organic waste depot for sewage, garbage, etc., which is composted and sold at cost to farmers.
18. Midkiff, *The Meat You Eat*, 3, notes how agribusiness has reduced farmers to specializing in one crop and asserts that "monoculture is what has led to the decline, even the demise, of the American farmer."

4. Attend to quality: "A good farmer is a craftsman of the highest order, a
   kind of artist. It is the good work of good farmers—nothing else—that
   assures a sufficiency of food over the long term."[19]

Berry strongly emphasizes the need for us to reconnect with our sources of
food. Contra agribusiness, he argues that as many as possible should share
in the ownership of the land and be connected to it. This could and should
involve producing what we can of our food even in small city gardens, but it
will also involve taking an active interest in local food production and supporting local, good practice.[20]

The plausibility of Berry's trenchant critique requires better, much better,
models of farming that can be pointed to as viable alternatives. Berry has
attended to this on his own farm in Kentucky and also documents countless
examples of good practice, as do McKibben, Pollan, and many others.[21] Berry
has also evoked his vision powerfully in his novels and poetry. As McKibben
writes, "Wherever we live, however we do so, we desperately need a prophet
of responsibility; and although the days of the prophets seem past to many
of us, Berry may be the closest to one we have. But, fortunately, he is also a
poet of responsibility. He makes one believe that the good life may be not only
harder than what we're used to but sweeter as well."[22]

Since Berry published *The Unsettling of America* in 1977, many of his night-
mares have become reality.[23] But there are signs of change and of wonderfully
plausible alternatives, and they are sometimes encountered in the most unexpected places. When the Soviet Union withdrew its support from Cuba, American
analysts predicted that the country would soon collapse. The US embargo ensured that Cuba became an island hermetically protected from globalization.
The result is fascinating: "Cubans have created what may be the world's largest
working model of a semisustainable agriculture, one that relies far less than the
rest of the world does on oil, on chemicals, on shipping vast quantities of food
back and forth. . . . Mostly they grow their own."[24] Another example is the global
trend toward starting to farm the cities once again. In Shanghai 60 percent of
the vegetables and 90 percent of the milk and eggs come from urban farms.[25]

One may imagine Detroit as a failed city; in recent decades some one million
people have moved away as the motor industry has declined, so that much of the

19. Berry, "Agricultural Solutions," 85.
20. See, for example, Estill, *Small Is Possible*.
21. See in particular Pollan, *The Omnivore's Dilemma*; McKibben, *Deep Economy*; Vitek
and Jackson, *Rooted in the Land*.
22. McKibben, *Pieces from an Active Life*, 277.
23. For a good introduction to the horrors of contemporary meat production, see Midkiff,
The Meat You Eat.
24. McKibben, *Deep Economy*, 73. For the story see ibid., 71–77.
25. Ibid., 82.

139 square miles of Detroit consists of vacated lots and dilapidated buildings. But gradually some of Detroit is being cultivated; forty community gardens and microfarms have developed in recent years. After some one hundred years, vacant-lot farming is back in Detroit.[26] As Lawson notes in her inspiring book, *The City Bountiful: A Century of Community Gardening in America,*

> the notion of a City Bountiful suggests a city abounding with vegetables, fruits, and flowers that people grow for themselves and their community. Such a city provides opportunities for people to engage with their environment through the process of gardening and with their community through the social interaction of organizing and maintaining the gardens. Like the garden itself, the City Bountiful is a vision that needs to be nurtured.[27]

Placemaking and the University

As we noted in our discussion of the history of the city, the university was largely a Christian invention, an invention to which the rich architecture of universities like Oxford and Cambridge bear ample witness. The founding of the University of Halle in Germany in 1694 marks the start of the modern, secular university.[28] Universities became allied with the needs of government, and their goal became universal public education.

The third phase of the university, according to M. Ford, comes after World War II; the unifying mission of this development Ford calls "economism," or what we might call a mission to produce the consumer university. Out of this has emerged the higher education *industry*; the university has expanded to become "an economic actor in its own right."[29] With this expansion has developed a profound dependence of governments upon universities to help them solve the complex problems they face: "In the knowledge economy, it [the university] is literally the mother of all industries!"[30] According to Soley, "The story about the university . . . is that they will turn a trick for anybody with money to invest; and the only ones with money are corporations, millionaires and foundations. These investments in universities have dramatically changed the mission of higher education; they have led universities to attend to the interests of their well-heeled patrons, rather than those of students."[31]

26. See ibid., 82, 83; E. F. Davis, *Scripture, Culture, and Agriculture*, 176–78; Solnit, "Detroit Arcadia"; Lawson, *City Bountiful.*
27. Lawson, *City Bountiful*, 302. On the comparable allotment in the UK, see Crouch and Ward, *The Allotment.*
28. Ford, *Beyond the Modern University*, 27.
29. Ibid., 35. See ibid., 35–36, for the evidence.
30. Ibid., 36.
31. Soley, *Leasing the Ivory Tower*, 9.

We should not, therefore, underestimate the influence of the university in contemporary culture. In 1967 D. Bell wrote, "The university will become the central institution of the next one hundred years because of its role as the new source of innovation and knowledge."[32] P. Berger has recently reneged on his secularization hypothesis—he now speaks of "desecularization"—with a few exceptions. For our purposes an important exception is the

> international subculture composed of people with Western-type higher educa-
> tion, especially in the humanities and social sciences, that is indeed secularized.
> This subculture is the principle "carrier" of progressive, Enlightened beliefs
> and values. While its members are relatively thin in the ground, they are very
> influential. . . . They are remarkably similar all over the world today, as they
> have been for a long time.[33]

The university is thus a major player in globalization. Universities are also cultivated places which occupy large amounts of land and generally bear all the marks of suburbia: huge parking lots, a plethora of fast-food chains, and often unattractive, modern, functional buildings. Adopting Kunstler's meta-phor expressed in the title of his book *Home from Nowhere*, M. M'Gonigle and J. Starke assert that "at the university, *nowhere* is evident in the sprawl-ing acres of parking lots filled with mass-produced cars, the cafeteria food delivered via an exclusive servicing contract with a nameless multinational, and the standard-issue buildings heated and lit by energy from the void."[34]

There are, however, signs of change. *Planet U* emerged out of the suc-cessful struggle at the University of Victoria in British Columbia, Canada, to preserve woodland. And the authors document many similar cases. An encouraging example is the new campus of Kyushu University in suburban Fukuoka, Japan.[35] The site designated for the new campus was a rolling landscape of rice paddies, orchards, and forests. The plan was to level the landscape with bulldozers so as to facilitate construction. But the initiative of a biologist at the university, Tetsukazu Yahara, changed all that. The plan was revised to "maintain existing contours, concentrate the buildings along a curving central spine, and leave the flanks of the campus for preservation."[36] Upon completion, oaks and pines, turtles and salamanders, and ponds will have been protected. The university has also adopted a "no species loss" policy, with 270 species of plants and animals on the site, some of which are endangered. New courses and research related to this innovative approach have been introduced.

32. D. Bell, quoted in M'Gonigle and Starke, *Planet U*, 17.
33. Berger, "Desecularization of the World," 10.
34. M'Gonigle and Starke, *Planet U*, 65. Emphasis original.
35. Ibid., 115–16.
36. Normile, "Conservation Takes a Front Seat," 330.

When one contemplates the number of universities around today and their sprawling campuses, it is easy to be overwhelmed by the challenge they present in terms of placemaking. M'Gonigle and Starke helpfully suggest that "the university, every university, begin in a place where it can truly act, which is to say, in a place where the university actually *is*—the place where the sod's been turned."[37] Whether in a Christian or public university, we should have a vested interest and active participation in the growing commitment to developing "green" universities. A growing number of universities are intentionally building sustainable structures, the sort of development that needs public support.[38]

Universities need to be places that offer courses which facilitate reflection on place, and by professors who embody a commitment to place: "What is needed is a class of cosmopolitan educators willing to live where they work and to work where they live, a class of educators willing to take root, willing to cultivate a sense of place."[39] W. Jackson has appropriated the metaphor of "becoming native" for implacement. He notes that

> our task is to build cultural fortresses to protect our emerging nativeness. They must be strong enough to hold at bay the powers of consumerism, the powers of greed and envy and pride. One of the most effective ways for this to come about would be for our universities to assume the awesome responsibility for both validating and educating those who want to be homecomers—not that they necessarily want to go home, but rather to go someplace and dig in and begin the long search and experiment to become native.[40]

In this respect the plethora of Christian colleges, universities, seminaries, and Bible colleges that are spread across North America have a crucial role to play. It is one thing to offer courses on environment and place; however, as M'Gonigle and Starke note, "Without a coherent world-view to shape these disciplines, many instead reflect the economism in which the university is situated."[41] In today's consumer, postmodern culture it is well-nigh impossible for public universities to recover anything approaching a coherent worldview. But this is precisely what Christian colleges are supposed to specialize in! Thus a place to begin for Christians is the Christian colleges and universities. We need to

1. ensure that our colleges and universities are genuinely providing a coherent, integrated curriculum;
2. ensure that we have a variety of courses in different disciplines teaching about place; and

37. Ibid., 41.
38. See Ferrera and Visser, *Canada Innovates*, 110–35.
39. Zencey, "The Rootless Professors," 19.
40. Jackson, "Matfield Green," in Vitek and Jackson, *Rooted in the Land*, 101.
41. *Planet U*, 65.

3. most importantly, work to ensure that what we teach is backed up by a *plausible* development of the faculty and the college or university as a place. This would involve many components.

Among other things, it would mean becoming aware of the history of the place, since, as B. Penn notes, "What is lacking these days is historical imagination. People don't ask questions about place or historically what has gone before it."[42] The built environment would need to be taken seriously, with sustainable buildings which encourage learning and evoke the Christian worldview in the best sense of the word. In my opinion a chapel should be at the heart of the Christian university, and there should be ample places for reflection and contemplation, such as the prayer garden at Fuller Seminary. Buildings should have a multitude of public spaces designed for conversation and the development of intellectual community. There should be a third place or two, where faculty and students can meet in relaxed fashion for fun and conversation. Classrooms should be designed to evoke dialogue and exploration.

The role of food also requires scrutiny. "Colleges and universities are an obvious market, since they offer a captive population, and one likely to be receptive to the environmental and community impulses behind local food."[43] Sodexho, a massive food-service group, lost its contract with the University of California at Santa Cruz as a result of a student campaign in favor of local foods, a campaign that has spread to all the UC campuses. Some years ago, Fanny Singer graduated from Yale. While visiting her there, her mother, Alice Waters, a founder of the local food movement,[44] decided she did not want her daughter eating cafeteria food. Yale gave her Berkeley College dining hall to experiment with, and she raised the funds to convert it to a seasonal and local menu. It was not easy, but once the program was launched, students started lining up from other Yale colleges to get in!

The Christian colleges and universities across North America already occupy large tracts of land. The challenge for them is to repent of the functionalism so characteristic of contemporary evangelicalism and to take the task of placemaking seriously if they wish to be plausible embodiments of a Christian worldview at this time. A Christian view of the university also needs to attend to the extraordinary placemaking achievements of the past which remain, even while the ethos of the university may have become thoroughly secular. In his provocative novel *I Am Charlotte Simmons*, Tom Wolfe evokes the disconnect between the cultured place of Du Pont University and the lifestyle of students and faculty. This alerts us that healthy place, akin to the speech of the creation in Psalm 19:1–6, itself issues a call to recover healthy academic communities.

---

42. Penn, interview in M'Gonigle and Starke, *Planet U*, 116.
43. McKibben, *Deep Economy*, 84.
44. See McNamee, *Alice Waters and Chez Panisse*. Waters has been influenced by and acquainted with Christopher Alexander, Michael Pollan, and Wendell Berry.

With their spires and chapels and extraordinary architecture, universities like Oxford and Cambridge witness to the possibility of scholarship done *coram Deo*, before the face of God.

Placemaking and the Church

> The space for worship is the space for the enacting of a particular story, the story of Jesus as the story in which the worshipers may find their destiny. On this stage it is always the same play that is performed. . . . As we live in a church building, the story of Jesus of Nazareth should surround us, in sculpture, fresco, stained glass, mosaic, and other forms.[45]

The life of the people of God far exceeds that of the institutional church, and Christians are called to give expression to their faith in all aspects of life. In our modern differentiated societies Christians belong to several different places at the same time, and we should be concerned with placemaking in all these areas. This should not, however, detract from the unique role of the local congregation, the *ekklēsia*, which Newbigin rightly describes as the hermeneutic of the gospel.[46] As Newbigin notes: "I do not think that the geographical parish can ever become irrelevant or marginal. There is a sense in which the primary sense of neighbourhood must remain primary, because it is here that men and women relate to each other simply as human beings and not in respect of their functions in society."[47]

Christians are not agreed as to whether a worshiping community needs its own building or not. Clearly a church is far more than a building, but as I have argued elsewhere, it is to be expected that as a worshiping community takes root in a place, it will need a building of its own set apart for worship and institutional church activities. Worship of God clearly does not demand a place set aside for the gathered church, but then neither is a house essential to a family or an auditorium to an orchestra. However, normal cultural development as we experience it would require that a church would sooner or later require a building of its own.[48]

However we resolve this issue theologically, most Christian communities do end up building churches; indeed in the West the amount of land occupied by churches and religious orders is huge. The critical issue, then, is how churches are doing at placemaking. In cultures where Christianity has been part of the fabric for centuries, the landscape is littered with generally attractive buildings; the problem is finding Christians to occupy the buildings and maintain

45. Jenson, "God, Space, and Architecture," 15.
46. See Newbigin, *The Gospel in a Pluralistic Society*, 222–33.
47. Newbigin, *Sign of the Kingdom*, 64.
48. Bartholomew, "The Church and the World."

Figure 18.1 Example of an Ornate Orthodox Church

them. In "younger" cultures like North America, churches are also scattered throughout the landscape, but they bear the mark of modern trends in architecture, and many of them leave a lot to be desired.

Most contemporary churches, like malls, focus on the experience inside the building, and clearly this is of utmost importance. The church gathers to meet with Christ through Word and sacraments and for fellowship, and the interior needs to be designed to facilitate that. Different traditions will, of course, move in very different directions at this point, ranging from the simple Puritan-style meetinghouse to the ornate Orthodox church (see figure 18.1). R. Jenson, as quoted above, is right in my view that the church is the place where, in a variety of forms, the biblical story with its center in Jesus is enacted and reenacted so that amidst the challenges of life it increasingly becomes for us, in practice and not just theory, the true story of the world which we indwell.

It is crucial that our liturgies embody the creation-wide vision of placemaking.[49] S. Langer has appealed for public symbols that will orient us in material and social realities and thereby provide a cosmology which will orient our lives.[50] She despairs of the churches providing such symbols, but this is precisely what good liturgy, with its dramatic embodiment of the comprehensive vision of the gospel, should achieve. "*Ritualizing nature*, then, means standing within the cultural world of Christian worship and seeing what one can see as one

49. See in this respect Lathrop, *Holy Ground*, and Santmire, *Ritualizing Nature*.
50. Langer, *Philosophy in a New Key*, 288–89.

contemplates the world of nature from that standpoint."[51] As G. Lathrop notes, "The Word and Sacraments of Jesus Christ are surprisingly resilient. Allowed some presence in our assemblies, they will call us to the surprise of a reoriented cosmos. If we lay down our heads on them, even a little, they will be Bethel-stones for us, full of the presence of the triune God and enabling a new view of the world."[52] Healthy liturgy is "full of lines that run out to the world, full of communal orientation that is also a personal ethical formation."[53]

This means that our worship continues or begins when we leave the church door (cf. Rom. 12:1–2), *and* that the public witness borne by the architecture and grounds of the church are of vital importance. Pope Benedict XVI has remarked that "the only really effective apologia for Christianity comes down to two arguments, the saints that the Church has produced and the art which has grown in her womb."[54] Vavarek reminds us that the church building "is to be an image of the Church as a whole, the communion of God and human beings across time wrought through Christ's death, resurrection, and ascension. The entire building is therefore 'sacramental' in that it visibly represents the Church, the Kingdom of God present now in mystery."[55] Several years ago in Durban, South Africa, I was powerfully struck by the contrast between a new Orthodox church and a charismatic church just down the road from it (see figures 18.2 and 18.3). I would not have believed that in the "new" South Africa it was possible to build such a stunning church as this Orthodox one. It stands out like a beacon of light in the residential neighborhood in which it is situated. By contrast, the charismatic church has a factory- or warehouse-like appearance. It is remarkable and scandalous that the public witness borne by so many church buildings simply reinforces modern, functional, boring architecture. Bess similarly notes of modernist Catholic architecture that "most modernist Catholic churches have been a spiritual, aesthetic, and evangelical disaster."[56] We need to find much better models for contemporary churches so that our built environment witnesses to the God we worship in the building.

Different Christian denominations will have to ransack their own traditions and those of others to find contemporary models for church buildings that will publicly embody our faith in Christ. There is, of course, no one legitimate, Christian architectural style for churches. Bess discerns eight styles in his taxonomy that he considers still applicable for Catholic churches today:

1. The centralized plan based on the circle
2. The basilican plan

51. Santmire, *Ritualizing Nature*, 4. Emphasis original.
52. Lathrop, *Holy Ground*, 49.
53. Ibid., 59.
54. Ratzinger and Messori, *The Ratzinger Report*, 129–30.
55. Vavarek, "Church Building," quoted in Bess, *Till We Have Built Jerusalem*, 139.
56. Bess, *Till We Have Built Jerusalem*, 144.

Figure 18.2 Orthodox Church in Durban, South Africa (Peter Koch)

Figure 18.3 Charismatic Church in Durban, South Africa (Peter Koch)

3. The cruciform plan
4. The elliptical plan
5. The classical tradition
6. The Gothic tradition
7. Localized vernacular
8. Monastic simplicity and austerity

In today's context Bess urges restraint and argues that the cruciform plan might best function as the model for parishes and cathedrals. In our discussion of the city above, we also noted Bess's creative suggestion that, where a church is building and has multiple acres of land available, it should consider developing the plot into the seed of an urban neighborhood. When one thinks of all the church buildings in existence, the potential for a powerful public witness is staggering!

Bess notes the significance of the cemetery for the local church and suggests that where there is a cemetery there ought to be a visual and or processional link between the living community and the cemetery as a sign of the one, holy, catholic church.[57] Cemeteries have their own intrinsic importance and ought to be places for reflection and peaceful contemplation. They also have a public face, and both public and "private" faces ought to be developed imaginatively to reflect and embody the Christian understanding of death.

The modern funeral industry—for that is what it is—has, however, a vested interest in complicating what would appear to be a straightforward process of dissolution in the ground. The modern American funeral industry[58] developed at the end of the nineteenth century, and nowadays the average American funeral costs $10,000 and invariably includes embalming and other procedures to ensure that the deceased looks at peace and at rest.[59] Among other things, embalming involves the draining of the blood and toxic liquids from the visceral organs and the injecting of chemicals, mainly formaldehyde, in their place. Coffins, or what Americans now prefer to call caskets, are another industry, and, like embalming, are not generally environmentally friendly:

> The major casket manufacturers make the EPA's biennial list of each state's top fifty hazardous waste generators, and they are required to post to the agency's toxic release inventory the quantities of chemicals they release into the atmosphere: methyls, xylene, and other regulated emissions generated in the spraying of coatings onto casket exteriors.[60]

57. Ibid., 148.
58. See in particular Mitford, *American Way of Death Revisited*.
59. See M. Harris, *Grave Matters*, 14–29, for what is involved in embalming.
60. Ibid., 34.

When it comes to death, nowadays appearance would seem to be everything, and cemeteries are deliberately designed to appear like peaceful parks and lawns: the quintessential natural environment. However, as Harris notes,

> For all their landscaping aboveground, our cemeteries function less as verdant resting grounds of the dead than as landfills for the materials that infuse and encase them. Over time the typical ten-acre swatch of cemetery ground, for example, contains enough coffin wood to construct more than forty houses, nine hundred-plus tons of casket steel, and another twenty thousand tons of vault concrete. To that add a volume of formalin sufficient to fill a small backyard swimming pool and untold gallons of pesticide and weed killer to keep the graveyard preternaturally green.[61]

Little wonder that many Americans are rediscovering more traditional ways of handling death. A movement is afoot to help people rediscover the practices of the home funeral, and some are starting to opt for simple, crafted wooden caskets rather than the industrial ones. There is also a growing movement in different parts of America to establish natural burial grounds which avoid the concrete vault and whose graves are marked with simplicity. In the influential book *Pattern Language*, C. Alexander advises: "Never build massive cemeteries. . . . Instead, allocate pieces of land throughout the community as grave sites—corners of parks, sections of paths, gardens, beside gateways—where memorials to people who have died can be ritually placed with inscriptions and mementos which celebrate their life."[62]

In the light of Genesis 3:19 one would hope that Christians would be at the forefront of such developments. We need to find ways to cut through the misdirected commercialization of death and to lay our loved ones to rest so that they may indeed return to and revitalize the ground from which they have come.

Public Memorials and Battlefields

Joshua 3–4 tells the story of the Israelites crossing the Jordan River to the plains of Jericho in preparation for receiving the gift of the land. While the Israelites cross on dry land, the priests bearing the ark stand in the middle of the Jordan. The LORD commands Joshua to have twelve stones taken from the Jordan where the priests stood, carried to their camp, and then re-placed in the middle of the Jordan as a memorial "in the place where the feet of the priests bearing the Ark of the Covenant had stood; and they are there to this day" (4:9).

61. Ibid., 38.
62. Alexander, Ishikawa, and Silverstein, *Pattern Language*, 354–56.

The stones are to be a "sign," "a memorial forever," among the Israelites, a public memorial of the Lord's enabling them to enter the land. The number twelve is deliberate; each stone symbolizes one of the twelve tribes of Israel, and together they symbolize the whole people of God. The stones are taken from the place in the Jordan where the priests stood with the ark and returned to that place, a reminder once again that the land is all gift. The anticipated question of future generations (4:6) implies that Israelites will bring their children to see the stones, so that pilgrimage and ritual are bound up in this memorial.

Especially in Protestantism, reaction to what have been seen as the excesses of Catholic ritual has led to a loss of a theology of memorial and ritual. However we conceive of ritual in the institutional church—and in one way or another it is unavoidable—memorial and associated ritual are vital ingredients in human culture. Through memorials and associated rituals we embody and relive the stories and values that shape or should shape our societies.

Take battlefields, for example. They are public memorials to wars won and lost. McKibben notes just how important such places are in our consumer culture:

> Most Civil War battlefields haven't been handed over to the themepark developers, thank heaven. Many of them, in the custody of the Park Service, lie in that fast-suburbanizing corner of Maryland and Virginia and Pennsylvania, curious eddies of open space in a tide of pavement that has swept by on all sides. They have very little to do with that culture—the battlefields speak not to convenience or comfort, but to honor, obedience, glory, to that whole compound of older martial virtues now mostly mysterious to us. . . . Glory and honor and obedience have caused their share of pain over the years. But the mere existence of these spots helps keep these alternate conceptions of human life alive and real. . . . The encounter with history at a battlefield or a shrine might be like the encounter with real wildness in a forest or a mountain or a seacoast; each might hold the power to break us out of the enchantment under which we now labor, the enchantment of things, an enchantment that is quite literally wrecking the world.[63]

Christians should therefore have a vested interest in the creation of public memorials and public art that redemptively evokes our history and enables us to imagine what we might, with God's help, become. The Christian community should do this for itself but also for the world. The twelve stones of Joshua 4 are put in place "so that *all the peoples of the earth* may know that the hand of the Lord is mighty, *and* so that you may fear the Lord your God forever" (4:24; emphasis added).

The South African sculptor Gert Swart has produced a significant body of public art, and two of his projects bear powerfully on this issue. Swart,

63. McKibben, *Pieces from an Active Life*, 38–39.

Figure 18.4 "Peace Tree" by Gert Swart
and Fellow Artists, Pietermaritzburg, Natal,
South Africa (Zak Benjamin)

born of an English mother and an Afrikaans father, embodies in his life and work the struggle to be integrated and the struggle of service in the traumatic history of South Africa. Swart's adult conversion to Christianity focused his desire to serve Christ redemptively in art in South Africa.

In 1991, amidst some of the worst days of apartheid, Swart came up with a community project to build a peace tree in the grounds of Pietermaritzburg's main square, which is dominated by colonial buildings. At the time the use of car tires in so-called necklace murders was receiving much publicity as a horrible weapon of some of the liberation movements. Gert assembled used tires and colorful paint and, amidst resistance from the city, assembled a team of locals—black and white—to paint the tires and then assemble them as a tree (see figure 18.4). The resulting peace tree was a Christmas gift to the people of Pietermaritzburg. Seerveld says of the tree:

> The Peace Tree (1991) is great artistry with breath-taking relevance. Its workshop, people-friendly feel, quietly shared—without pointing fingers—humbled the memorials to conquest and victory which otherwise fill Pietermaritzburg's main square. Gert Swart and fellow artists gaily painted tyres and hung them up to convert necklaces of death into festive decorations, which herald the coming South Africa where all things can become new. The Peace Tree shows startling

Figure 18.5 Isandlwana Monument by South African Sculptor Gert Swart (Associated Magazines, Cape Town, South Africa)

metaphoric ingenuity within an idiom known to ordinary people, and its luster breathes the love of Christ which forgives, beckoning neighbors to joy in their belonging together.[64]

In the post-1994 South Africa, Swart was commissioned to design and produce a memorial for the 1879 battle of Isandlwana, a famous battle at which the Zulus wrought havoc among the British.[65] Understandably, an appropriate memorial at the battlefield was high on the agenda of Zulus in the new South Africa. But how could this be done without glorifying war in a mirror image of the colonial mentality that sparked the battle in the first place? The commissioning body initially requested a frieze of fearsome warriors brandishing spears.

As is evident in figure 18.5, Swart chose the "isiqu," or necklace of valor, as an appropriate symbol to honor the fallen Zulu warriors. Zulu warriors deemed worthy were allowed to wear a special necklace, which they generally carved themselves. The powerful, bronze necklace evokes a brave warrior laying down his weapons in order to engage reflectively in the intricate carving of his necklace. The ornate beads and lion's claws were normally reserved for

64. Calvin Seerveld, "Peace Tree (1991) Gert Stuart," *Many-to-Many* 25 (Dec. 1998).

65. The British had a vested interest in covering up their incompetence and the extent of their defeat at Isandlwana. For a recent narration of the events, see Lock and Quantrill, *Zulu Victory*.

high-ranking Zulus; here they honor all the warriors. In the perimeter wall of the base of the monument are four bronze headrests. These represent the four Zulu regiments employed in the battle, as well as evoking rest and cessation of violence. There are steps so that the visitor can mount the platform and stand amidst the "regiments" and contemplate the battlefield of Isandlwana.

Placemaking and Pilgrimage

The Importance of "Pilgrimage" for the Church Today

Mainline church attendance is in serious decline in the secular UK and Europe, but Christian pilgrimage and religious tourism are booming. The experiential, visual, communal nature of pilgrimage is attracting Christians and others in a way that the mainline churches are not. "Pilgrimage sites offer stories of saints and of God interacting with ordinary people; they provide an intensely visual environment; they draw the pilgrim into an atmosphere of corporate spirituality which yet allows infinite scope for individual response."[66] It is to phenomena like pilgrimage that Christians will have to attend as they seek afresh to make the gospel incarnate in secular Western culture.

In the Old Testament God is particularly present in Jerusalem, and pilgrimage there is mandatory. The New Testament contains a lot about pilgrimage. Consider:

- Jesus and his disciples are pictured as pilgrims to Jerusalem.
- The gospels are structured around the pilgrim festivals, especially the Passover.
- The Ethiopian eunuch went on pilgrimage to Jerusalem (Acts 8:26–40).
- The converts at Pentecost were pilgrims.
- Saint Paul hurried to Jerusalem to be there for the feast of Pentecost (Acts 20:16).
- Presumably many of the trips to Jerusalem reported in the Acts and Epistles were in connection with the festivals.

However, the particularity of Jerusalem is radically altered by its fulfillment in Jesus. How then does one read the relationship between Old and New Testaments in this respect, and what are its theological implications? Are the pilgrimages of the disciples holdovers from preresurrection practices, or are they models for postresurrection Christians? How does one construe Scripture as a unity such that one can make the theological connections with pilgrimage?

66. Dyas, "Pilgrimage," 94.

On the one hand it is clear that in Scripture Christians can no longer regard Jerusalem as God's "address" now that Christ is risen. God is now universally available in and through the risen Christ. O'Donovan relates this aspect of the New Testament fulfillment of the Old Testament to "an apophatic tradition in Christian thought with regard to all the concrete structures of Old Testament society."[67] O'Donovan is quite clear about the difference between the Old Testament and the New Testament as regards holy place. He argues that in the New Testament we have a "theological desacralisation" of special places: "The revelation to Israel had been a situated revelation, in a land which Yahweh had hallowed, and in a city where he had chosen to dwell. But the revelation in Christ broke down the elective particularity, not only of race but also of place."[68]

But does such fulfillment mean that the Old Testament now has nothing to teach us about land, politics, ritual, and so on? Surely not. O'Donovan argues that an apophatic approach to the Old Testament is complemented by a cataphatic or positive one, which continues to find instruction in the concrete structures of Israel: "We can at least try to learn about place from the Old Testament theology of the land without flying in the face of all that the New Testament has done with it."[69] Such a cataphatic approach is vital if we are to construe Scripture rightly in relation to pilgrimage.

For the church the concept of the people of God as a nation has been superseded by an understanding of the people of God scattered throughout the nations of the world. Nevertheless, the paradigm of Israel has much to teach us about ritual, and place. Humans embody their most important values in solemn rituals, such as the opening of parliament or the marriage ceremony, and Israel is no exception to this. At a positive level the Old Testament alerts us to the place of ritual in human society and God's concern with the values and perspectives embodied in such ritual. Thus Christians would do well to shape up rituals and public art that embody appropriate values and perspectives for our societies.

In ancient Israel pilgrimage is akin to ritual. Pilgrimage to Israel is ritualized in that it is mandatory and formalized: it is decreed that the tribes go up to Jerusalem regularly (Psalm 122:4), and the place of pilgrimage is formally fixed, as are the times of pilgrimage and the activities involved. The songs, like the journeys, are designed to center the life of God's people in the great realities on which its life is built. Commenting on the instruction in Psalm 122 for the pilgrim to pray for the peace of Jerusalem, McCann perceptively notes that such prayers

> amount to the [pilgrim's] recognition of God's reign and his or her commitment to live under God's reign. . . . For the psalmist, to enter Jerusalem *really does*

67. O'Donovan, "Loss," 49.
68. Ibid., 44.
69. Ibid., 50.

mean to enter a new world. The joy is real. . . . To live for God's sake . . . and for the sake of others . . . is to experience, embody, and extend the justice God intends for the world. This life-style, this commitment *is* reality.[70]

In this way pilgrimage functioned as ritualized practice designed to embed in the consciousness of the Israelites their identity as God's people.

God has made humans such that they need rituals in which they embody their highest values. These rituals help keep our lives centered on these values and on the associated narratives. In a fallen world such rituals become more, not less, important. Pilgrimage is one such practice. As E. Peterson notes, "We necessarily live much of our lives in exile, so to be able to spot the people and places that re-establish our true identity is *so* important."[71] Thus, while in the light of the New Testament, pilgrimage to Jerusalem or to anywhere else cannot and should not be mandatory, this does not preempt the role of Christian pilgrimage. The need for ritual and pilgrimage will remain, and I see no reason why Christians should not take seriously the task of shaping up pilgrimages as *a* means of recentering our lives on the Christian narrative.

Thus Peterson seems to me quite right to distinguish between the basic, nonnegotiable practice of daily praying with the Psalms, Lord's Day worship with one's community, and recollected prayer through the day on the one hand, and, on the other, the various spiritual disciplines that are not compulsory but on hand when we need them.[72] Peterson describes the disciplines, of which he lists fourteen, as a toolshed, well stocked for use when required, but otherwise left alone. The tools include spiritual direction, journaling, retreats, confession, and pilgrimage! This, I suggest, is the right place to position pilgrimage theologically: a useful discipline, but not compulsory.

The Development of Christian Doctrine and Pilgrimage

There is much pilgrimage in the New Testament, but it is unclear whether it was a holdover from the past or a legitimate expression of Christian life. Christian pilgrimage really got going when Constantine became emperor. In the course of this historical development, theologies of pilgrimage emerged.[73] This means that any assessment of a Christian theology of pilgrimage will have to wrestle seriously with the way in which Christian doctrine develops. This is the topic that Newman discusses in his *Essay on the Development of Christian Doctrine*. Under the theme of the sacramental principle, Newman defends the fourth-century appropriation by the church of many outward rites

70. McCann, *Theological Introduction*, 154.

71. E. Peterson, *Wisdom of Each Other*, 85. Emphasis original.

72. E. Peterson, *Under the Unpredictable Plant*, 104–9.

73. A useful text on the development of Palestine into the Holy Land is Wilken, *Land Called Holy*.

that were taken over from their culture and became a means of grace.[74] "In like manner the Sign of the Cross was one of the earliest means of grace; then holy seasons, *and holy places, and pilgrimages to them*; holy water; prescribed prayers, or other observances; garments, as the scapular, or coronation robes; the rosary; the crucifix."[75] Pilgrimage to holy places has often been connected with the relics of saints, and intriguingly, Newman relates this development theologically to the *materiality* of Christianity; it is anti-gnostic and takes the body seriously.

It is fascinating to note how N. T. Wright changed his mind about pilgrimage:

> A lot has to do with the slow turning away from various forms of dualism, to which evangelicalism is particularly prone, and towards a recognition of the *sacramental* quality of God's whole created world. . . . With the incarnation itself being the obvious and supreme example, and the gospel sacraments of baptism and eucharist not far behind, one can learn to discover the presence of God not only in the world . . . but through the world.[76]

Wright goes on to note that the cult of relics can itself be explained in relation to the grace of God at work in the embodied person. Wright is not persuaded by this argument, but it is interesting to see how he connects pilgrimage with the same doctrines as Newman: creation, incarnation, and sacrament.

Many Protestants would, of course, find Newman's apologia for high-church practices altogether unconvincing. Yet doctrines do arise and develop historically,[77] and Christian pilgrimage presents us with a classic case of early church development of a particular branch of practice and theology. It is too easy to simply dismiss this as the spin-off of a perverse Christendom. Contemporary pilgrimage thus presents the church with a challenge as to how to relate Christian doctrine to life today. Doubtless Catholics and Protestants will do this differently, but any fresh engagement with the issue of pilgrimage will have to think through the doctrines of creation, incarnation, and sacrament. Indeed a major issue underlying all pilgrimage is the theology of place. In *The Wisdom of Each Other*, written as letters to a friend and recent convert, E. Peterson, a leading evangelical authority on spirituality, writes,

> Your delight in coming across that monastery isolated out there on those austere plains, "miles from nowhere," and finding a community of praying brothers there is contagious. I am more and more convinced that holiness does indeed infiltrate *place*. In such places, I have always a sense of homecoming—*heaven*-coming.[78]

74. Newman, *An Essay*, 365–66.
75. Ibid., 374. Emphasis added.
76. N. T. Wright, *Way of the Lord*, 4. Emphasis added.
77. For an Anglican perspective on doctrinal development see McGrath, *The Genesis of Doctrine*.
78. E. Peterson, *Wisdom of Each Other*, 85. Emphasis original.

Wright affirms Peterson's theology of place in his experience of visiting a school building in Canada that had been a church:

> I walked in and sensed the presence of God, gentle but very strong. I sat through the loud concert wondering if I was the only person who felt it, and reflecting on the fact that I had no theology by which to explain why a redundant United church should feel that way. The only answer I have to this day is that when God is known, sought and wrestled within a place, a memory of that remains, which those who know and love God can pick up.[79]

What are we to make of Peterson's and Wright's experientially shaped reconsiderations of place? Doesn't the New Testament rule this out of court? Possibly, but even the biblical narrative is more complex than sometimes meets the eye as regards place. Thus the temple is above all else where Yahweh dwells and is thus quintessentially a holy place. But even within the temple there are degrees of holiness. And even while the temple occupies a special status within Israel, the Old Testament depicts the land of Israel as a whole as holy. And at other places in the Old Testament the whole of the earth is said to be "mine," according to Yahweh, thus making it holy too. These clues may indicate that we need not assume that to call one place holy is to imply that other places are irrelevant and "secular."

For God's people in the Old Testament the story of Jerusalem was unique; God lived there, and this made Jerusalem special or holy in a distinct way. For Christians Palestine is also special, but for different reasons—it was there that God established his Old Testament people, from whom came Jesus, who lived, died, and rose again in Palestine. As an inscription found in Amaseia, in Pontus, western Asia Minor, delightfully puts it, Palestine is a "'God-trodden' land."[80] The difference between these approaches is important and will shape pilgrimage to Jerusalem in a significantly different way.[81] The effect of this is that while Christians ought no longer to regard Jerusalem as "the place of the name," this does not dispense with the need or responsibility to take place seriously as part of God's good creation. Healthy pilgrimage, not least to Palestine and Jerusalem, is one way to do so.

Pilgrimage and Politics

A pilgrimage can be thought of as a microjourney by means of which one explores the macrojourney of one's life. Thus, Christian pilgrimage to Israel would be aimed at helping one to live out the gospel more comprehensively

79. N. T. Wright, *Way of the Lord*, 5.
80. See Wilken, *Land Called Holy*, 192.
81. See, for example, N. T. Wright's explanation of how he sees Christian pilgrimage to Israel (*Way of the Lord*, 9–11).

when one returns to one's daily life. It is vital that this connection with the whole of life be present in pilgrimage—the *journey in*, as it were, becomes the foundation for the *journey out*, and the aim of the journey out in pilgrimage is to deepen the journey in.

It is a scandal, and pilgrimage of a very distorted sort, when so many Christians visit Jerusalem without a second thought about the church in Israel and the suffering in the Middle East. In *From the Holy Mountain*, W. Dalrymple exemplifies a healthier type of pilgrimage in the Holy Land. In the context of his arrival in Jerusalem, he is attentive to the change in the fortunes of Christians in the old city. In 1992, 52 percent were Christian; now Christians make up fewer than 2.5 percent of the population. In the context of his pilgrimage in Jerusalem, Dalrymple connects the ancient Christian sites to contemporary oppression of Christians in Israel by the Israeli government. "All this is part of the most dramatic decline in a Christian population to have taken place anywhere in the modern Middle East, with the single exception of Turkish Anatolia."[82] And Dalrymple insightfully asserts that this makes a significant difference to the pilgrimage sites in the Holy Land: "All this matters very much. Without the local Christian population, the most important shrines in the Christian world will be left as museum pieces, preserved only for the curiosity of tourists. Christianity will no longer exist in the Holy Land as a living faith; a vast vacuum will exist in the very heart of Christendom."[83]

If Christians are genuinely concerned to follow the Jesus who was born and died in Israel, then, like him, they will need to take the whole of life, including politics, seriously. The Old Testament prophets were deeply concerned for justice in Israel—and while human bombs are immoral and unacceptable, so too is Israeli oppression of the Palestinians. Part of all Christian pilgrimage to Israel ought as a matter of principle to connect with these issues.

On the Journey

In my opinion Christian involvement in pilgrimage is legitimate and important in our (post)modern context. The real challenge, however, is *how* to shape the practice of pilgrimage such that Christians' identity as God's people is deepened in their day-to-day lives, and such that those unfamiliar with the narratives associated with sites of pilgrimage will have ample opportunity to connect with them. At a conference on pilgrimage I organized several years ago in Cheltenham, there were two fine discussions of such creative shaping of pilgrimage.

Robert Trimble, then of McCabe Pilgrimages, addressed the important topic of tourism and pilgrimage at a conference on pilgrimage. Trimble made

82. Dalrymple, *From the Holy Mountain*, 316.
83. Ibid., 317.

the point that pilgrimage has always had its facilitators, its tour operators, as it were. Many, of course, were unscrupulous![84] But the point is well taken—someone has to plan the journey and make it happen. The important thing is that the plans facilitate *healthy* pilgrimage rather than just tourism of a consumerist sort. The Muslim thinker Ziauddin Sardar describes tourism as "consumerism writ large, naked and unashamed, and to feed the insatiable need of tourists whole nations are converting themselves into vast emporia, havens of everything under the sun that can be bought."[85] It is too easy for Christian pilgrimage to become an extension of Western consumerism, so that we bring back souvenirs rather than blessings.[86]

Pilgrimage does need to be distinguished from travel in general. Dispenza rightly notes that "all our travel is sacred,"[87] but I think that his concern to make every trip a journey of self-discovery is to blur the boundaries between pilgrimage and travel. Nevertheless pilgrimage does illumine travel in interesting ways, since travel, too, often exemplifies consumerism. R. Steves addresses this issue in his delightful *Travel as a Political Act*. He suggests the following strategies for traveling more intentionally:[88]

- Travel like a medieval jester so that you can bring back home valuable insights.
- Choose to travel on purpose so that your travel can become life enhancing.
- Connect with locals.
- Take history seriously.
- Overcome fear.
- Celebrate diversity.
- Expand your view of Christianity.
- Choose to be challenged.
- Experience the rich/poor gap for yourself.

McCabe Pilgrimages exemplified how pilgrimage can be shaped along healthy lines with the plans they made in the year 2000 for links between churches in the UK and church projects in Israel. This ensured that Christian pilgrims from the UK made contact with the living stones[89] in the Holy Land.

84. See Sumption, *Pilgrimage*, for the realities of medieval pilgrimage.

85. Sardar, *Postmodernism*, 136. For a fascinating discussion of tourism from a Christian perspective see Aay, "Tourism."

86. Northcott, *Moral Climate*, 223, notes that "this slow pace of movement is the strongest point of contrast between traditional pilgrimage and modern mass tourism."

87. Dispenza, *Way of the Traveler*, 1.

88. Steves, *Travel as a Political Act*, 3–24.

89. "Living stones" is a metaphor for the Christians in the Holy Land. See, for example, Hilliard and Bailey, *Living Stones Pilgrimage*.

As Trimble noted, "The connections between a church in Durham and an orphanage in Bethany help to ground the experience of pilgrimage."[90]

Tewkesbury Abbey affords another example. A visit to the abbey highlights the serious attempts made there to connect visitors with the Christian faith. Among other things, in a small room near the entrance a short video runs continually, welcoming visitors and introducing them to the abbey; in the process, people make clear connections with the living faith the abbey stands for. In our secular societies thousands continue to visit cathedrals and abbeys—it is a creative challenge to find ways of making such visits a means to connect with the Christian story as embodied in such places. At the very least it means that these places need to continue to be steeped in prayer and worship; otherwise they will simply become museum pieces to be seen by curious tourists.

Placemaking and the Planet

A great deal has been and is being written about climate change and potential major damage to the planet. Many scientists are working on this issue, and almost daily the scientific body of data grows exponentially. The United Nations Intergovernmental Panel on Climate Change (IPCC) maintains that while the surface temperature of the earth has risen by 0.8 °C in the last century, most of the warming has taken place in the last three decades, with a rise of 0.2 °C per decade.[91] At this rate global temperatures will rise by a further 2 °C by the end of the century. Such a rate is unprecedented. In the IPCC's view this rise is caused by the increase in emission of the so-called greenhouse gases—carbon dioxide, methane, nitrous oxide—which have increased exponentially since the Industrial Revolution, so that they now far exceed preindustrial concentrations. The most important of these gases is carbon dioxide, resulting mainly from the use of fossil fuels; when too much carbon is present in the atmosphere, it traps more of the heat that is emitted from the earth's surface and leads to the heating of the surface of the planet. Scientists have now documented serious changes in climate patterns at global, regional, and continental levels. The danger is not only unexpected climatic events, but a tipping point will be reached so that in terms of positive feedback, a mechanism whereby the heating is amplified, the effect of the rise will be irreversible and very dangerous indeed.

A small minority of scientists, including some vociferous evangelicals,[92] continue to argue that global warming can be accounted for in terms of natural

90. From Trimble's notes.

91. As Flannery, *Weather Makers*, 246, notes, the IPCC estimates represent "lowest common denominator" science and are thus conservative. The problem may well be much more serious.

92. E. Calvin Beisner is a well-known example. See his *Where Garden Meets Wilderness*; and Spencer, Driessen, and Beisner, "An Examination of the Scientific, Ethical and Theological Implications of Climate Change Policy."

variations in climate, but most scientists agree that it is related, especially since 1970, to the increase in greenhouse gas emissions driven by global economic growth and trade. M. Northcott thus argues that "global warming . . . is the global market empire hitting its biopolitical limits."[93] The "ecological and social costs of a deregulated and growing market empire are now implicated in a potential global collapse in the earth system."[94] As is so often the case, it is the South and the poor who suffer the effects of global warming to a greater degree than the wealthy North.[95] "As a result of a combination of historic and amnesic conditions, more than two billion people live in areas of high environmental danger, millions of them by choice. Accelerating climate change is now worsening the odds for many of them."[96]

China is a good example of present industrialization if one wants to get a feel for its scale, its impact on the environment, and the global connections of such large-scale industrialization. For five years Edward Burtynsky documented industrial development in Shanghai; his documentation was turned into the award-winning film *Manufactured Landscapes* by Jennifer Baichwal. About half of cast-off American computers are sent back to China for dismantling in order to recover the metals. Among other things, Burtynsky documents poor villages whose houses are surrounded by mounds of computer parts as the poor dismantle the computers by hand; toxins from this process can be smelled kilometers away from the villages.

In December 2006 it was reported that the Chinese river dolphin, the *baiji*, was now extinct as a result of pollution and heavy traffic in the Yangtze River. Since the 1950s the baiji was the first large aquatic animal to become extinct, but news of this event barely caused a ripple in the People's Republic of China. Most of the worst-polluted cities are in China, and air and water resources are becoming toxic. A new coal-fired power plant is opened every ten days in China. The nation is consuming natural resources at an extraordinary rate and scouring the planet for raw materials; such action has included entering into agreements with unsavory regimes such as Zimbabwe and Sudan. "From South America to Central Asia, China is literally consuming the world."[97] In 2001 China's greenhouse gas emissions were 42 percent of that of the United States but by 2006 they were 97 percent. As Campanella notes, "The nation's current course of fast growth and expanding resource use is utterly unsustainable."[98]

China's growth is dependent on Western consumerism and our voracious appetite for cheap Chinese goods. Global markets are flooded with Chinese

93. Northcott, *Moral Climate*, 7.
94. Ibid., 5. See McKibben, *Eaarth*.
95. See S. Anderson, *Views from the South*.
96. De Blij, *Power of Place*, 109.
97. Campanella, *Concrete Dragon*, 295.
98. Ibid., 296.

goods, and, as is so typical of globalization, all we see and desire is the cheap price. It takes something like Burtynsky's *Manufactured Landscapes* to bring home to us the cost of such cheap goods, but of course China is far away and his film will never make the mainstream theaters.

There are some positive signs amidst China's industrialization: China is constructing more kilometers of subway and rail public transportation than any other nation; China is home to some 60 percent of the world's solar water heaters, and some 30 million households use solar power in some form; an ambitious sustainable urban development is under way for Chongming Island.[99] Architect William McDonough suggests that China is the only nation which may be able to make photovoltaic arrays cheap enough so that solar electricity becomes a viable option around the globe.[100]

If the warnings about the dangers of climate change are even close to the truth, then it has potential implications for every aspect of place discussed above. As McFague rightly notes, "Climate is our planet's largest, most important, and most vulnerable interlocking system: it allows for and sustains life."[101] In his analysis of why societies fail, Jared Diamond notes that a society's response to environmental problems is always significant.[102] The good news is that we now have the technology to begin to tackle this problem, and the cost globally would be about 3 percent of the global GNP.[103] Action needs to be taken at the personal, national, and international levels, but the problem is that economic globalization, central to the problem, is unlikely to easily face up to the challenge; global warming is indeed an inconvenient truth, as Al Gore has pointed out.

Saul argues persuasively in *The Collapse of Globalism* that a reaction to American-style globalization is already well under way. He notes that "none of this means that the global economy is coming to an end. What it does mean is that the Globalization model of the 1970s and '80s has faded away. It is now, at best, a regional project—that region being the West."[104] If there is any hope for solving the challenge of global warming, it will require a very different model of globalization; the danger is that the reaction will create a new vacuum.[105]

In Genesis 1 we saw that the whole universe is created as a home for humankind. Climate change threatens that home, but as we wake each day, it is hard for us to take this threat seriously, especially in the comfortable North. It is difficult to make the link between driving our SUVs, consuming endless

---

99. Ibid., 300–301.
100. Ibid., 300.
101. McFague, *New Climate for Theology*, 14.
102. Diamond, *Collapse*, 11.
103. Ibid., 23.
104. Saul, *Collapse of Globalism*, 204.
105. Ibid., 217–31.

cheap Chinese goods, purchasing cheap goods at Walmart, flying around the world to consume other cultures on our quick vacations, and the threat to the planet. But the link is there and we need to face up to it.

How ought Christians to respond to global warming? At present "conservative" Christians are often vociferous on issues like abortion and homosexuality while embodying a Western consumer lifestyle and laughing off global warming. Liberal Christians tend to take environmental issues more seriously but are cautious on "sin" and tend to be pro-choice and in favor of blessing same-sex unions. A recovery of the biblical notion of creation order and its allied motif of the antithesis that runs through the *whole* of creation would go a long way toward challenging this polarity. God's order applies as much to marriage and sexuality as it does to how we care for the earth. So, just as it is important that Christians hold on to God's order for marriage and sexuality and thus refuse to affirm same-sex relationships as normative, and just as they uphold the sanctity of human life and refuse to condone most practice of abortion, so too Christians must be clear that environmental destruction and Western-style consumerism is downright sin.

As McKibben notes, some welcome signs of such a stance have appeared among evangelicals.[106] He refers to the laudable work of C. DeWitt[107] and the courage it took for many evangelicals to distance themselves from George W. Bush on environmental issues. "It's far from clear, however, that faith communities will take this fight as far as it needs to go."[108]

To take the fight as far as it needs to go we would need:

1. To face up to the challenge of global warming and to stay abreast of the best science in this respect. Among other things, this will involve, as discussed above, a recovery of the creation-wide dimension in our liturgies. Rasmussen notes that a "significant work for Christian communities for the foreseeable future is adapting their major teachings and practices—the 'deep traditions' of Christianity, together with its reading of Scripture—to the task of revaluing nature/culture together so as to prevent their destruction and contribute to their sustainability."[109]

2. To recognize our complicity in the problem. This is far easier said than done! In an extremely important article, "Christianity and the Survival of Creation," W. Berry asserts that "Christian organizations, to this day, remain largely indifferent to the rape and plunder of the world and of its traditional cultures. It is hardly too much to say that most Christian organizations are as happily indifferent to the ecological, cultural, and religious implications of industrial economics as are most industrial

106. McKibben, "Will Evangelicals Help Save the Earth?"
107. DeWitt, *Earth-Wise.*
108. Ibid., 231.
109. Rasmussen, "Eco-Justice: Church and Community Together," 7.

organizations. The certified Christian seems just as likely as anyone else to join the military-industrial conspiracy to murder Creation."[110] Berry thinks that such approaches are contrary to Scripture and the Christian tradition, but if he is right about our complicity in the ecological problem, then change will not come easy, and we should anticipate considerable resistance.

3. To repent and to call our brothers and sisters to repent of this complicity. Our destruction of nature must not just be reduced to poor stewardship; "it is the most horrid blasphemy. It is flinging God's gifts into His face, as if they were of no worth beyond that assigned to them by our destruction of them."[111]

4. To own the radical change in perspective that such repentance will involve. Again this is no quick task: "Our predicament now, I believe, requires us to learn to read and understand the Bible in the light of the present fact of Creation. This would seem to be a requirement both for Christians and for everyone concerned, but it entails a long work of true criticism—that is, of careful and judicious study, not dismissal."[112]

5. To find the myriad small and big ways of making changes in our daily lives. Yet again this is hard: "It is understandably difficult for modern Americans to think of their dwellings and workplaces as holy, because most of these are, in fact, places of desecration, deeply involved in the ruin of Creation."[113] Chapter 5 of DeWitt's *Earth-Wise*, "Putting Creation Care into Practice," is jam-packed with practical suggestions for finding ways forward.[114]

6. To work together with Christians and other cobelligerents locally, nationally, and internationally to bring about change.

As Berry notes, the better possibility for Christianity is that "this, our native religion, should survive and renew itself so that it may become as largely and truly instructive as we need it to be. On such a survival and renewal of the Christian religion may depend the survival of the Creation that is its subject."[115]

Place and . . .

One could explore myriad areas in relation to place. On the website for this book readers will find resources and information about other aspects of

110. W. Berry, *Sex, Economy, Freedom & Community*, 94.
111. Ibid., 98.
112. Ibid., 94, 95.
113. Ibid., 100.
114. DeWitt, *Earth-Wise*, 65–76.
115. W. Berry, *Sex, Economy, Freedom & Community*, 96.

placemaking. In this section I attend briefly to areas that strike me as too important to omit.

The Arts and Place

Literature, art, and poetry are indispensable resources in excavating *and* developing a thick notion/practice of place. It is thus no coincidence that in his efforts to articulate a philosophy of place, J. Malpas finds in M. Proust's *Time Regained* a major resource.[116] In geography it was only some thirty years ago, in reaction to the abstraction of spatial science, that humanistic geography turned to literature as a source for recovering a thick view of place, a trend that continues to thrive.[117] Literature has a unique capacity to evoke the multidimensional nature of place.[118] Indeed, every theme that we have examined in part 2 would be illumined by a study of relevant literature. In literary studies it is now commonplace to find courses taught on the environment and literature.[119] The great thing about place is that it is always particular, and so considerations of *place* and literature inevitably draws attention to particular, placed bodies of literature, a concern that postcolonialism has rightly highlighted.

Pulitzer Prize–winning author A. Dillard has rightly been described by E. Peterson as an exegete of the creation, just as Calvin is an exegete of Scripture. The opposite of attention is distraction, and in today's busyness attentiveness suffers. Dillard has made it her task as a writer to attend to the creation. The doctrine of creation calls us to attention, because "matter is real. Flesh is good. Without a firm rooting in creation, religion is always drifting off into some kind of pious sentimentalism or sophisticated intellectualism. . . . The physical is holy."[120] Dillard spent a year attending to a creek and its surroundings and published her experiences in *Pilgrim at Tinker Creek*. Her explorations are rigorous and, at times, puzzling and mysterious. But she "ends up on her feet applauding."[121]

Emerson saw it. "I dreamed that I floated at will in the great Ether, and I saw this world floating also not far off, but diminished to the size of an apple. Then an angel took it in his hand and brought it to me and said, 'This must thou eat.' And I ate the world." All of it. All of it intricate, speckled, gnawed, fringed,

---

116. Malpas, *Place and Experience*.

117. Gregory et al., "Literature," *Dictionary of Human Geography*, 419–22.

118. Buell, *Writing for an Endangered World*, 2, identifies four types of engagement with the world that acts of environmental imagination have the potential to energize: they may connect readers with the experience of others, human and nonhuman; they may reconnect readers with places they have known and send them to new places they would otherwise never visit; they may open up alternative visions of the future; and they may evoke care for the physical world.

119. See, for example, Buell, *Environmental Imagination*; *Writing for an Endangered World*; *Future of Environmental Criticism*.

120. E. Peterson, *Contemplative Pastor*, 68.

121. Ibid., 69.

and free. Israel's priests offered the wave breast and the heave shoulder together, freely, in full knowledge, for thanksgiving. They waved, they heaved, and neither gesture was whole without the other, and both meant a wide-eyed and keen-eyed thanks. Go your way, eat the fat, and drink the sweet, said the bell. A sixteenth-century alchemist wrote of the philosopher's stone, "One finds it in the open country, in the village and in the town. It is in everything which God created. Maids throw it on the street. Children play with it." The giant water bug ate the world. And like Billy Bray I go my way, and my left foot says, "Glory," and my right foot says, "Amen": in and out of Shadow Creek, upstream and down, exultant, in a daze, dancing, to the twin silver trumpets of praise.[122]

Another Christian novelist who has also won the Pulitzer Prize is Marilynne Robinson. Her novels *Gilead*, *Housekeeping*, and *Home* profoundly evoke the complex experience of home in a fallen world. Berry, though probably best known for his collections of essays, has also published a series of novels and multiple books of poetry. His series of novels set in Port William, Kentucky, are wonderfully rich in place. The title of one of them, *A Place on Earth*, captures the thick, complex, richly human sense of place summoned up by Berry in this series. In one scene of the novel Old Jack falls asleep in a field; on waking, he is startled and hurries toward the barns.

But before he has gone much further, his mind has completely changed its subject. He has left the wheel tracks and begun to wander, though he keeps the same general direction. He goes out through the grove of oaks, down across the small wet-weather stream at the bottom of the swag, and up the opposite slope to the high point of the ridge. Now and again he stops and stands a long time, looking. He is studying his land, the shape of it, the condition of the growth on it, with the interest in it that he has had all his life.[123]

Poetry is a great resource for evoking the experience of place.[124] One of the most popular poems in the UK today is Davies's "Leisure,"[125] alerting us to the indispensable requirement of stopping, like Old Jack, if we are to attend to place.

Leisure

by William Henry Davies

> What is this life if, full of care,
> We have no time to stand and stare.

---

122. Dillard, *Annie Dillard Reader*, 424.
123. W. Berry, *A Place on Earth*, 212.
124. The literature is, of course, immense. Bate's *Song of the Earth* is a recent reflection on the capacity of poetry to help us become re-implaced in our technological age.
125. On the life of Davies see Hooper, *Time to Stand and Stare*.

No time to stand beneath the boughs
And stare as long as sheep or cows.

No time to see, when woods we pass,
Where squirrels hide their nuts in grass.

No time to see, in broad daylight,
Streams full of stars like skies at night.

No time to turn at Beauty's glance,
And watch her feet, how they can dance.

No time to wait till her mouth can
Enrich that smile her eyes began.

A poor life this if, full of care,
We have no time to stand and stare.

In our discussion of the city we drew attention to art in public places.[126] There is a real need for attention to public art that enhances city life outside of museums and the temples of high art, valuable as they are.[127] Recently there has been a flourish of publications on graffiti as a form of street art.[128] Some graffiti is indeed *art* and powerfully shapes its context, but much of it seems to be more of a bland expression of the brokenness of urban life. Seerveld rightly draws attention to murals and sculpture that genuinely enhance the urbanscape.[129]

Art plays an indispensable role in fashioning our places into human environments, and not least through its depiction of place. Simon Schama's *Landscape and Memory* is a tour de force of critical reflection on this subject. Among other things, in a section on the "verdant cross" he discusses the provocative painting of the Romantic artist Caspar David Friedrich, who dared to position the cross in the mountains and amidst winter landscape.[130] Friedrich's contemporaries were outraged; surely the cross belonged in churches and not amidst the creation! But Friedrich's point is powerfully made; the cross belongs amidst the entire creation.

The Politics of Place

Having grown up in apartheid South Africa, I find it simply impossible to ignore the politics of place. The control of place and its unjust distribution were key planks in the edifice of apartheid, in which 15 percent of the population

126. See Seerveld, "Cities as a Place for Public Artwork."
127. See Wolterstorff, *Art in Action*, and his chapter on "A City of Delight" in *Until Justice and Peace Embrace*.
128. For a good introduction see Stahl, *Street Art*.
129. Ibid.
130. Schama, *Landscape and Memory*, 207, 238–39.

owned 70 percent of the land. The Group Areas Act ensured that "white" towns remained just that, although "nonwhites" were allowed to enter such areas as servants and laborers. Whole "nonwhite" districts were forcibly removed to enact apartheid, perhaps the most famous being District 6 in Cape Town.

Apartheid as a metaphor has been rightly invoked for placial injustice way beyond South Africa. De Blij notes that the forces that drove apartheid can be seen today, albeit in different constellations, from Myanmar to Sudan and from North Korea to Zimbabwe. Jimmy Carter has invoked the metaphor of apartheid for the Israeli treatment of the Palestinians, particularly in relation to the "security" wall they are building; a very literal, placial apartheid.[131] De Blij suggests that a form of apartheid also operates globally; the global core contains some 15 percent of the world's population but records 75 percent of the world's annual income.[132]

In our global culture my neighbor may be thousands of miles away and yet be one of the displaced poor working in sweatshops to provide us with cheap consumer goods. Thus a politics of place alerts us unequivocally to the fact that a politics of place must be local *and* global, or, to use a recently invented word, glocal. The right to a place is surely an inalienable right of an embodied person. But it is not one that sits easily with Western consumerism. The house has become a consumer product par excellence in the fat, bloated, individualistic West, often far beyond the size required and eating up huge amounts of energy. Juxtaposed with this, but often far removed, are the really poor of the world, homeless and displaced. The apartheid of globalism means that in the West we are rarely confronted with the genuinely poor. Polish journalist R. Kapuściński describes his experiences of living in different parts of Africa. He describes the homeless who lived in the street outside his apartment and who often owned one possession that enabled them to survive. He relates the harrowing story of a homeless woman whose only possession was a bowl with which she could cook and sell some food to enable her to live literally from day to day. One day he heard a terrible scream from below in the street; this woman's one possession had been stolen.[133]

The politics of place is complex and multifaceted. The lack of place can have major political and psychological consequences. Jared Diamond points out that an unnoticed element in the cauldron of the Rwandan genocide was the inability of the land to provide adequate place for all its inhabitants.[134] A constitutive element of place is memory and history, and there must be few places on earth that do not contain memories of political injustice and oppression. Indeed the challenge of the politics of place threatens to be overwhelming. As with place in general, we have to start where we are, in our

---

131. Carter, *Palestine*; see also Backmann, *Wall in Palestine*.
132. De Blij, *Power of Place*, 7–17.
133. Kapuściński, *Shadow of the Sun*, 111–12.
134. Diamond, *Collapse*, 311–28.

place. Through taking the local politics of place seriously we will inevitably be drawn into global politics. The giant corporations are in our backyard, and many of their CEOs will be in our churches on Sundays. In North America we are part of the global core, part of that 15 percent of the world's population which records 75 percent of the world's income. Our places are formed by such global apartheid, and it should be impossible to attend to placemaking locally without taking account of the global context.

Epilogue

Spirituality and/of Place

Only when it is possible to gear regular *practices* to specifics of place
can re-embedding occur in a significant way: but in conditions of
high modernity this is difficult to achieve.[1]

We end where we began, but now to know our place more fully. As we saw
in Genesis, the tree of life indicates that God is the co-inhabitant of Eden.
No view of place, from this perspective, is complete without taking into account God's presence. We will not attain the practice of place without a deep
spirituality; sensitivity to place requires restful attentiveness, and it is only as
we are deeply and existentially centered in Christ that we become alive and
attentive to a world "charged with the grandeur of God."[2] After his tragic
death, what would be published as Dag Hammarskjöld's remarkable *Markings* was discovered in his briefcase. He notes that

> to have humility is to experience reality, not in relation to ourselves, but in its
> sacred independence. It is to see, judge, and act from the point of rest in ourselves.
> Then, how much disappears, and all that remains falls into place.
>
> In the point of rest at the center of our being, we encounter a world where
> all things are at rest in the same way. Then a tree becomes a mystery, a cloud,
> a revelation, each man a cosmos of whose riches we can only catch glimpses.
> The life of simplicity is simple, but it opens to us a book in which we never get
> beyond the first syllable.[3]

1. Giddens, *Modernity and Self-Identity*, 147. Emphasis added.
2. Hopkins, "God's Grandeur," in *Poems*.
3. Hammarsköld, *Markings*, 148.

319

The Jesuit poet Gerard Manley Hopkins wrote of a world alive with God amidst the rolling hills and valleys of Wales. In another poem he speaks of Christ as the one who "plays in ten thousand places."[4] The world is indeed charged with the grandeur of God but it is in our place, *one* of those ten thousand places, that we are called to find and join Christ at play.

Christ taught his disciples that *where* two or three are gathered in his name, *there* he is in the midst of them. The primary place in which we encounter Christ is in the local congregation, as we gather around him to hear his address and to eat and drink of his life. The Christ we encounter is the one who *stands with his face turned toward his world*; having borne in his body the wound of the world, he sends us out from his table to work alongside the Spirit (*missio Dei*) in bringing hope and healing to his world. Having partaken of his body and his blood at this table, we go out to incarnate his presence in all the places we inhabit of his creation.

Merton poses the question:

> Have we ever yet become Christians?
>
> The duty of the Christian is to see Christ being born into the whole world and to bring Him to life in all mankind.
>
> But we have sought to bring to birth in the world the image of ourselves and of our own society and we have killed the Innocents in doing so, and Christ flees from us into Egypt.
>
> Have we ever yet become Christians?[5]

In the language of Paul, justification is always followed by *sanctification*, that process of becoming who we now are in Christ. It has been illuminating to me to think of holiness, of sanctification, as *wholeness*,[6] as personal integrity as the image of God is being restored in my whole being. Central to this wholeness is deep relationship with God. In his Gospel, John uses a placial metaphor to evoke this reality: "Those who love me will keep my word, and my Father will love them, and we will come to them and make our *home* with them" (14:23). Implacement ultimately means that by the Spirit we have the Father and the Son as our co-inhabitants. Such at-homeness is the key to being at home in our particular places in God's good but fallen world, and is the place from which we derive the vision and resources for birthing Christ again and again in his world.

The best writers on place speak of the need for attentiveness, familiarity, silence, slowness, stability, repetition, particularity, hope, respect, love. These are all characteristics and the fruit of Christian spirituality, but rare in our speed-driven, consumerist Western culture. If placemaking is part of

4. Hopkins, "As Kingfishers Catch Fire," in *Poems*.
5. Merton, *Search for Solitude*, 197.
6. Cf. our discussion of James in part 1.

our journey out into the world, then it needs to be funded by a *deep journey in*—engagement with God, engagement with ourselves, and engagement with one another.

In the Western church in which so many pastors have exchanged their calling for that of shopkeepers,[7] ecclesial life often fails to nurture the inner journey fundamental to placemaking, and even where it does, congregational life *must* be complemented by personal spirituality. And place plays an important part in personal spirituality as well as spirituality providing the attentiveness requisite for placemaking.

Jesus models such a spirituality in his ministry, regularly withdrawing to solitary places for time in secret with the Father, and on occasion to very particular places (cf. Mark 1:35; *eis erēmon topon*). In John 10, Jesus's ministry repeatedly encounters strong opposition; he is accused of being possessed; they want to stone him to death; they want to arrest him. In response he returns to the place of his baptism and he remained there (10:40). The verb "remain" (*menein*) is an important word in John's Gospel; it is the same verb used in John 15 to "abide" in Christ. Why, in the face of such opposition, did Jesus return to the place of his baptism and remain there? Presumably because the strong opposition raised the question as to whether or not he was on the right track, whether or not he was being faithful to God's call in his life. He returns to the place of his baptism, his call, to hear again the word of the Father that he is indeed the Son, the beloved, with all the overtones those words carry of a journey to Calvary.

The place of prayer is not insignificant; because prayer and place affect each other, privacy and solitude are essential. In both the Old Testament and the Gospels the wilderness is regularly identified as a place where one encounters God. It is as though an empty place with no distractions allows our own empty inner places to be opened up to God and filled by him. Historically, withdrawal into the desert has been acted upon literally by some monks and, perhaps most well known, by the desert fathers and mothers of the fourth century. Merton explains the motivation behind this withdrawal from society into the desert:

> The simple men who lived their lives out to a good old age among the rocks and sands only did so because they had come into the desert to be themselves, their ordinary selves, and to forget a world that divided them from themselves. . . . And thus to leave the world, is, in fact, to help save it in saving oneself. . . . They knew that they were helpless to do any good for others as long as they floundered about in the wreckage. But once they got a foothold on solid ground, things were different. Then they had not only the power but even the obligation to pull the whole world to safety after them. . . . We cannot do exactly what they did. But we must be as thorough and as ruthless in our determination to break all spiritual chains, and cast off the domination of alien compulsions, to find our

7. E. Peterson, *Working the Angles*, 1.

true selves, to discover and develop our inalienable spiritual liberty and use it to build, on earth, the Kingdom of God.[8]

Historically the Christian church has not always understood the relationship between the active and the contemplative lives in a healthy way. At its best the two have been taken to be thoroughly interrelated and each indispensable for the other. Certainly some are called to be full-time contemplatives and others to the active life, but both need each other and both should contain elements of each other. The great challenge today is how to live the active life—in our terms, how to engage in placemaking—from a deep center in Christ.

Recovery of the true self and a sense of place—the two are inseparable— may indeed require something akin to the desert fathers' jumping off the shipwreck of society and swimming for their lives.[9] When one is amazed by the productivity of someone like Wendell Berry, it is vital to remember that his productivity stems from his becoming implaced by returning with his wife to Kentucky and staying put *there*.

For those of us who are called to be placemakers amid the desert of con- temporary urban life, we will have to be ruthless in finding ways to nurture a deep spirituality that will hold us as we seek to incarnate Christ in our contexts. For Western urbanization has produced its own kind of desert: "In our age we have also known another kind of desert—one that is constructed either by human malevolence (the gulags and the camps which dot our sorry history) or by human indifference and neglect (the slums and inner cities of our urban landscape)."[10] Alessandro Pronzato encourages us to find *our* desert in this urban desert:

> The crowded bus, the long queue, the railway platform, the traffic jam, the neigh- bours' television sets, the heavy-footed people on the floor above you, the person who still keeps getting the wrong number on your phone. These are the real conditions of your desert. Do not allow yourself to be irritated. Do not try to escape. Do not postpone your prayer. Kneel down. Enter that disturbed solitude. Let your silence be spoilt by those sounds. It is the beginning of your desert.[11]

True as this is, if we are to flourish in the modern, urban environment, we will need oases, places of solitude, deserts within the desert into which we can withdraw and find ourselves and Christ once again. Intriguingly, the Little Brothers and Sisters, founded in the 1930s, have set about doing just this, seeking to make available a desert spirituality of silent adoration adapted to our societies of sprawl, slums, and abandoned neighborhoods. Such oases

8. Merton, *Wisdom of the Desert*, 23–24.
9. The metaphor is from ibid., 3.
10. Cunningham, "Foreword," vii.
11. Pronzato, *Meditations on the Sand*, 98–99.

can take many forms: a side chapel in an urban church open to the public, a labyrinth for meditation, a prayer garden, a chapel in a busy college or business, a comfortable chair in our house demarcated for silence, no interruption. As we fashion such places they will fashion us; Christ will be born in us and we will be free to give birth to him in his world, fashioning places amidst the city and town that are alive, nurturing, and human.

In his eucharistic theology of place, Peter Scott rightly connects such a theology with Golgotha and suffering. Attempts at placemaking will not always be welcome in the modern West, to put it mildly. Who are we to resist the power center, the acres and acres of concrete parking lots, the millions of miles of tarred roads where each of us can drive our cars, bumper to bumper? Placemaking, like all mission worth its name, will be accompanied by resistance and suffering. Looking back on his own journey through the desert of his mother's slow death from cancer, Belden Lane found an unusual sense of recognition in Laura Gilpin's searing poem "The Two-Headed Calf." So too, I suggest, will we. Gilpin describes the birth of a two-headed calf. Tomorrow farm boys will carry its corpse off to the museum as an example of a freak of nature. But tonight the calf is alive and with his mother in the north field. The evening is perfect, and as the calf gazes into the sky, "there are twice as many stars as usual."[12]

12. Gilpin, *Hocus-Pocus of the Universe*, 59; http://writersalmanac.publicradio.org/index .php?date=2004/04/30.

Bibliography

Aay, H., and S. Griffioen, eds. *Geography and Worldview: A Christian Reconnaissance*. New York: University Press of America, 1998.

Ableman, M. *On Good Land: The Autobiography of an Urban Farm*. San Francisco: Chronicle Books, 1998.

Adams, E. *The Stars Will Fall from Heaven: Cosmic Catastrophe in the New Testament and Its World*. London: T&T Clark, 2007.

Agnew, J. A. *Place and Politics: The Geographical Mediation of State and Society*. Boston: Allen & Unwin, 1987.

Aharoni, Y. *The Land of the Bible: A Historical Geography*. Philadelphia: Westminster Press, 1979.

Aitken, S. C. *Place, Power, Situation, and Spectacle: A Geography of Film*. Lanham, MD: Rowman & Littlefield, 1994.

Alexander, C. *The Timeless Way of Building*. Oxford: Oxford University Press, 1979.

Alexander, C., S. Ishikawa, and M. Silverstein. *A Pattern Language: Towns, Buildings, Construction*. New York: Oxford University Press, 1977.

Alexander, C. *The Production of Houses*. New York: Oxford University Press, 1985.

Alexander, L. C. A. *Acts in Its Ancient Literary Context: A Classicist Looks at the Acts of the Apostles*. London: T&T Clark, 2005.

Alexander, P. H. et al. *The SBL Handbook of Style: For Ancient Near Eastern, Biblical, and Early Christian Studies*. Peabody, MA: Hendrickson, 1999.

Alexander, T. D. *From Paradise to the Promised Land: An Introduction to the Pentateuch*. Grand Rapids: Baker Academic, 2002.

Algra, K. *Concepts of Space in Greek Thought*. Leiden: Brill, 1995.

Allen, D. E. *The Naturalist in Britain: A Social History*. Princeton: Princeton University Press, 1994.

Allen, L. C. *Ezekiel 1–19*. Word Biblical Commentary 28. Dallas: Word Books, 1994.

Allison, D. C. "Jesus and the Victory of Apocalyptic." In *Jesus and the Restoration of Israel: A Critical Assessment of N. T. Wright's Jesus and the Victory of God*, edited by C. Newman, 126–41. Downers Grove, IL: InterVarsity, 1999.

Alston, W. P. *Beyond "Justification": Dimensions of Epistemic Evaluation*. Ithaca, NY: Cornell University Press, 2005.

Alter, R. *Imagined Cities: Urban Experience and the Language of the Novel*. New Haven: Yale University Press, 2005.

Anderson, A. A. *2 Samuel*. Word Biblical Commentary 11. Nashville: Nelson, 1989.

Anderson, F., and D. N. Freedman. *Amos*. Anchor Bible 24A. New York: Doubleday, 1989.

Anderson, H., and E. Foley. *Mighty Stories, Dangerous Rituals*. San Francisco: Jossey-Bass, 1998.

Anderson, S., ed. *Views from the South: The Effects of Globalization and the WTO on Third World Countries*. Oakland; Chicago: Food First Books and the International Forum on Globalization, 2000.

Andrews, C. *Slow Is Beautiful*. Gabriola Island, BC: New Society Publishers, 2006.

Angel, A. *Chaos and the Son of Man: The Hebrew Chaoskampf Tradition in the Period 515 BCE to 200 CE*. New York: T&T Clark, 2006.

Angeles, P. A. *Dictionary of Philosophy*. New York: Barnes & Noble, 1981.

Arendt, H. *The Human Condition*. Chicago: University of Chicago Press, 1958.

Aristotle. *The Physics*. Translated by P. H. Wicksteed and F. M. Cornford. 2 vols. Loeb Classical Library. London: William Heinemann; New York: Putnam, 1929.

———. *Posterior Analytics*. Translated by H. Treddenick and E. S. Forster. Cambridge, MA: Harvard University Press, 1960.

———. *Nicomachean Ethics*. Translated by T. Irwin. Indianapolis; Cambridge: Hackett, 1985.

———. *The Basic Works of Aristotle*. Edited by R. McKeon. New York: The Modern Library, 2001.

Athanasius. *On the Incarnation of Our Lord*. Willits, CA: Eastern Orthodox Books, n.d.

Auerbach, E. *Mimesis: The Representation of Reality in Western Literature*. Translated by W. R. Trask. Princeton: Princeton University Press, 1953.

Augustine. *Confessions*. Translated by R. S. Pine-Coffin. New York: Penguin, 1961.

———. *Concerning the City of God Against the Pagans*. Translated by H. Bettenson. Middlesex, UK: Penguin, 1972.

———. *On Genesis*. New York: New City Press, 2002.

Aune, D. E. *Revelation 1–5*. Word Biblical Commentary 52A. Nashville: Nelson, 1997.

———. *Revelation 17–22*. Word Biblical Commentary 52C. Nashville: Nelson, 1998.

Bachelard, G. *The Poetics of Space: The Classic Look at How We Experience Intimate Places*. Boston: Beacon Press, 1994.

Backmann, R. *A Wall in Palestine*. New York: Picador, 2010.

Baichwal, J, director. *Manufactured Landscapes*. DVD. Mercury Films Inc, National Film Board of Canada, Foundry Films Inc, 2006.

Baird, G. B. *A Commentary on the Revelation of St. John the Divine*. London: A&C Black, 1966.

Baldovin, J. F. *The Urban Character of Christian Worship: The Origins, Development, and Meaning of Stational Liturgy*. Rome: Pontifical Institutum Studiorum Orientalium, 1987.

———. "The Empire Baptized." In Wainwright and Westerfield-Tucker, *The History of Christian Worship*, 77–130.

Balthasar, H. U. von. *Cosmic Liturgy: The Universe according to Maximus the Confessor*. Translated by B. Daley. San Francisco: Ignatius, 2003.

Barnard, R. *Apartheid and Beyond: South African Writers and the Politics of Place*. Oxford: Oxford University Press, 2007.

Barrett, C. K. "The Eschatology of the Epistle to the Hebrews." In *The Background of the New Testament and Its Eschatology: Studies in Honor of C. H. Dodd*, edited by D. Daube and W. D. Davies, 363–93. Cambridge: Cambridge University Press, 1956.

———. *The Gospel according to St. John*. 2nd ed. London: SPCK, 1978.

———. *A Commentary on the First Epistle to the Corinthians*. 7th ed. London: Adam & Charles Black, 1983.

Barth, K. *Church Dogmatics*. Translated by G. W. Bromiley et al. Edited by G. W. Bromiley and T. F. Torrance. 4 vols. Edinburgh: T&T Clark, 1958.

Bartholomew, C. G. "Covenant and Creation: Covenant Overload or Covenantal Deconstruction." *Calvin Theological Journal* 30, no.1 (April 1995):11–33.

——— "The Healing of Modernity: A Trinitarian Remedy? A Critical Dialogue with Colin Gunton's '*The One, the Three and* the Many.'" *European Journal of Theology* 6, no. 2 (1997): 11–130.

———. "The Church and the World: The Power of Identity." In *Signposts of God's Liberating Kingdom: Perspectives for the 21st Century*, 1:21–30. Potchefstroom, SA: Institute for Reformational Studies, Potchefstroom University for CHE, 1998.

———. "The Theology of Place in Genesis 1–3." In *Reading the Law: Essays in Honour of Gordon J. Wenham*, edited by J. G. McConville and K. Möller, 173–95. Edinburgh: T&T Clark, 2007.

———. *Ecclesiastes*. Grand Rapids: Baker Academic, 2009.

———. "Journeying On: A Concluding Reflection." In Bartholomew and Hughes, *Explorations in a Christian Theology of Pilgrimage*, 201–15.

Bartholomew, C. G., and F. Hughes, eds. *Explorations in a Christian Theology of Pilgrimage*. Aldershot, England: Ashgate, 2004.

Bartlett, D. W. *The Better City: A Sociological Study of a Modern City*. Los Angeles: Neuner Company Press, 1907.

Bartoszewski, W. *The Convent at Auschwitz*. New York: G. Braziller Inc., 1991.

Bassler, J. M., ed. *Pauline Theology: Thessalonians, Philippians, Galatians, Philemon*. Minneapolis: Fortress, 1991.

———, ed. *Pauline Theology: 1 and 2 Corinthians*. Minneapolis: Fortress, 1993.

———, ed. *Pauline Theology: Romans*. Minneapolis: Fortress, 1995.

Bate, J. *The Song of the Earth*. Cambridge, MA: Harvard University Press, 2000.

Bauckham, R. J. "The Delay of Parousia." *Tyndale Bulletin* 31 (1980): 3–36.

———. *Jude and 2 Peter*. Word Biblical Commentary 50. Waco: Word Books, 1983.

———. *The Climax of Prophecy: Studies on the Book of Revelation*. Edinburgh: T&T Clark, 1993.

———. "Jesus and the Wild Animals (Mark 1:13): A Christological Image for an Ecological Age." In *Jesus of Nazareth: Lord and Christ; Essays on the Historical Jesus and New Testament Christology*, edited

by J. B. Green and M. Turner, 3–21. Grand Rapids: Eerdmans, 1994.

———. *James*. New York: Routledge, 1999.

———. *Bible and Mission: Christian Witness in a Postmodern World*. Grand Rapids: Baker Academic, 2003.

———. *The Theology of the Book of Revelation*. Cambridge: Cambridge University Press, 2003.

Bauman, Z. *Freedom*. Minneapolis: University of Minnesota Press, 1988.

Baur, G. *Farm Sanctuary: Changing Hearts and Minds about Animals and Food*. New York: Simon & Schuster, 2008.

Bavinck, H. *Schepping of Ontwikkeling*. Kampen: Kok, 1901.

———. "The Catholicity of Christianity and the Church." Translated by John Bolt. *Calvin Theological Journal* 27, no. 2 (1992): 220–51.

———. *Reformed Dogmatics*. Vol. 1, *Prolegomena*. Grand Rapids: Baker Academic, 2003.

Beale, G. K. *The Book of Revelation*. Grand Rapids: Eerdmans, 1999.

———. *The Temple and the Church's Mission: A Biblical Theology of the Dwelling Place of God*. Downers Grove, IL: InterVarsity, 2004.

Beale, G. K., and D. A. Carson, eds. *Commentary on the New Testament Use of the Old Testament*. Grand Rapids: Baker Academic, 2007.

Beisner, E. C. *Where Garden Meets Wilderness: Evangelical Entry into the Environmental Debate*. Grand Rapids: Eerdmans, 1997.

Beker, C. *Paul's Apocalyptic Gospel: The Coming Triumph of God*. Philadelphia: Fortress, 1982.

Benjamin, D. C. *Deuteronomy and City Life*. Lanham, MD: University Press of America, 1983.

———. "Stories of Adam and Eve." In *Problems in Biblical Theology: Essays in Honor of Rolf Knierim*, edited by H. T. C. Sun and K. L. Eades, 38–58. Grand Rapids: Eerdmans, 1997.

Berdyaev, N. *The Destiny of Man*. New York: Harper & Row, 1960.

Berger, P. L. "The Desecularization of the World." In *The Desecularization of the World: Resurgent Religion and World Politics*, edited by P. L. Berger, 1–18. Grand Rapids: Eerdmans, 1999.

Bergmann, S. *Creation Set Free: The Spirit as Liberator of Nature.* Grand Rapids: Eerdmans, 2005.

Berman, M. *The Reenchantment of the World.* Ithaca, NY: Cornell University Press, 1981.

Berry, R. J., ed. *Environmental Stewardship.* London: T&T Clark International, 2006.

Berry, W. *The Long-Legged House.* New York: Audubon/Ballantine, 1969.

———. "Agricultural Solutions for Agricultural Problems." In *The Gift of Good Land: Further Essays Cultural and Agricultural*, 113–24. New York: North Point Press, 1982.

———. *A Place on Earth.* Washington, DC: Counterpoint, 1983.

———. *What Are People For?* New York: North Point Press, 1990.

———. "Why I Am Not Going to Buy a Computer." In Berry, *What Are People For?* 170–77.

———. "Feminism, the Body, and the Machine." In Berry, *What Are People For?* 178–96.

———. *Standing on Earth: Selected Essays.* Suffolk, UK: Golgonooza Press, 1991.

———. *Sex, Economy, Freedom & Community.* New York: Pantheon, 1993.

———. *Another Turn of the Crank.* Washington, DC: Counterpoint, 1995.

———. *The Unsettling of America: Culture & Agriculture.* San Francisco: Sierra Club Books, 1997.

———. *The Gift of Good Land.* New York: North Point Press, 2000.

———. *Life Is a Miracle: An Essay against Modern Superstition.* Washington, DC: Counterpoint, 2000.

———. *The Way of Ignorance.* Shoemaker & Hoard, 2005.

———. "What Needs to Be Subtracted." In Cayley, *Ideas: On the Nature of Science*, 149–63.

———. *Imagination in Place: Essays.* Berkeley: Counterpoint, 2010.

Bess, P. *Till We Have Built Jerusalem: Architecture, Urbanism, and the Sacred.* Wilmington, DE: ISI Books, 2006.

Bethge, E. *Dietrich Bonhoeffer: Theologian, Christian, Contemporary.* London: Fountain Books, 1970.

Bietenhard, H. *Die himmlische Welt im Urchristentum und Spätjudentum.* Tübingen, Germany: Mohr, 1951.

Bird, J. et al., eds. *Mapping the Futures: Local Cultures, Global Change.* New York: Routledge, 1993.

Birkhead, T. *The Wisdom of Birds: An Illustrated History of Ornithology.* Toronto: D&M, 2008.

Blanchette, O. *The Perfection of the Universe according to Aquinas: A Teleological Cosmology.* University Park, PA: Penn State University Press, 1992.

Blenkinsopp, J. "The Structure of P." *Catholic Biblical Quarterly* 38 (1976): 278–83.

Blocher, H. *In the Beginning: The Opening Chapters of Genesis.* Downers Grove, IL: InterVarsity, 1984.

Block, D. I. *The Book of Ezekiel, Chapters 25–48.* Grand Rapids: Eerdmans, 1998.

Block, P. *Community: The Structure of Belonging.* San Francisco: Berrett-Koehler, 2008.

Boake, T. M., I. Chodikoff, and P. Busby. *Canada Innovates: Sustainable Building.* Edited by L. Ferrara and E. Visser. Toronto: Key Porter, 2008.

Bock, D. L. *Luke.* Vol. 2, 9:51–24:53. Grand Rapids: Baker Academic, 1996.

Bockmuehl, M. *Jewish Law in Gentile Churches: Halakah and the Beginning of Christian Public Ethics.* Grand Rapids: Baker Academic, 2000.

Boecker, H. J. *Law and the Administration of Justice in the Old Testament and Ancient East.* Minneapolis: Augsburg, 1980.

Bonhoeffer, D. *Dietrich Bonhoeffer Werke.* 17 vols. München: Kaiser, 1986–99.

———. *Ethics.* Edited by E. Bethge. Translated by N. H. Smith. Library of Philosophy and Theology. London: SCM, 1995.

———. *Dietrich Bonhoeffer Works.* Edited by W. W. Floyd Jr. Minneapolis: Fortress, 1996–.

———. *Creation and Fall: A Theological Exposition of Genesis 1–3*. Minneapolis: Fortress, 1997.

Borgman, P. *Genesis*. Downers Grove, IL: InterVarsity, 2001.

Boring, M. E. "The Gospel of Matthew." In vol. 8 of *The New Interpreter's Bible*, 87–505. Nashville: Abingdon, 1995.

Bornkamm, G. *Jesus of Nazareth*. Translated by I. McLuskey, F. McLuskey, and J. M. Robinson. New York: Harper & Row, 1960.

Borowski, O. *Daily Life in Biblical Times*. Atlanta: Society of Biblical Literature, 2003.

Bosch, D. J. *Transforming Mission: Paradigm Shifts in Theology of Mission*. New York: Orbis, 2003.

Bouma-Prediger, S., and B. J. Walsh. *Beyond Homelessness: Christian Faith in a Culture of Displacement*. Grand Rapids: Eerdmans, 2008.

Bradshaw, P., and J. Melloh, eds. *Foundations in Ritual Studies*. Grand Rapids: Baker Academic, 2007.

Braude, W. G. *Pesikta Rabbati: Homiletical Discourses for Festal Days and Special Sabbaths 1&2*. New Haven: Yale University Press, 1968.

Braudel, F. *The Mediterranean in the Ancient World*. Edited by R. De Ayala and P. Braudel. New York: Penguin, 2001.

Brenk, B. *Die Christianisierung der Spätrömischen Welt: Stadt, Land, Haus, Kirche und Kloster in Frühchristlicher Zeit*. Wiesbaden, Germany: Reichert Verlag, 2003.

Briggs, M. S. *Puritan Architecture and Its Future*. London: Lutterworth, 1946.

Briggs, R. A. *Jewish Temple Imagery in the Book of Revelation*. New York: Peter Lang, 1999.

Broad, W. J. *The Universe Below: Discovering the Secrets of the Deep Sea*. New York: Touchstone, 1997.

Bromiley, G. W., ed. *The International Standard Bible Encyclopedia*. Vol. 1. Grand Rapids: Eerdmans, 1978.

Brown, P. *The Rise of Western Christendom: Triumph and Diversity, AD 200–1000*. London: Blackwell, 1997.

Brown, R. "Translating the Whole Concept of the Kingdom." *Notes on Translation* 14, no 2 (2000): 1–48.

———. "A Brief History of Interpretation of 'The Kingdom of God' and Some Consequences for Translation." *Notes on Translation* 15, no 1 (2001): 3–23.

Brown, W. P., and S. Dean McBride Jr., eds. *The God Who Creates: Essays in Honor of W. Sibley Towner*. Grand Rapids: Eerdmans, 2000.

Browning, D. *Paths of Desire: The Passions of a Suburban Gardener*. Toronto: Scribner, 2004.

Bruce, F. F. *The Acts of the Apostles. The Greek Text with Introduction and Commentary*. Grand Rapids: Eerdmans, 1979.

———. *The Epistle to the Galatians*. Exeter, UK: Paternoster, 1982.

Brueggemann, W. *Genesis*. Interpretation. Atlanta: John Knox, 1982.

———. *Using God's Resources Wisely: Isaiah and Urban Possibility*. Louisville: Westminster John Knox, 1993.

———. *Deuteronomy*. Abingdon Old Testament Commentaries. Nashville: Abingdon, 2001.

———. *The Land: Place as Gift, Promise and Challenge in Biblical Faith*. Philadelphia: Fortress, 1977.

Bruegmann, R. *Sprawl: A Compact History*. Chicago: University of Chicago Press, 2005.

Bruggink, D. J., and C. H. Droppers. *When Faith Takes Form: Contemporary Churches of Architectural Integrity in America*. Grand Rapids: Eerdmans, 1971.

Bruner, F. D. *Matthew: A Commentary*. Vol. 1, *The Christbook: Matthew 1–12*. Rev. and exp. ed. Grand Rapids: Eerdmans, 2004.

———. *Matthew: A Commentary*. Vol. 2, *The Churchbook: Matthew 13–28*. Rev. and exp. ed. Grand Rapids: Eerdmans, 2004.

Buber, M. *The Writings of Martin Buber*. Edited by W. Herberg. New York: Meridian Books, 1956.

———. *Kingship of God*. New York: Harper & Row, 1967.

———. *I and Thou*. Translation by W. Kaufmann. Edinburgh: T&T Clark, 1970.

———. "Abraham the Seer." In *On the Bible: Eighteen Studies*, 22–43. Syracuse: Syracuse University Press, 2000.

Buckley, M. J. *At the Origins of Modern Atheism*. New Haven: Yale University Press, 1987.

Budd, P. J. *Numbers*. Word Biblical Commentary 5. Nashville: Nelson, 1984.

Buell, L. *The Environmental Imagination: Thoreau, Nature Writing, and the Formation of American Culture*. Cambridge, MA: Belknap Press, 1995.

———. *Writing for an Endangered World: Literature, Culture, and Environment in the U.S. and Beyond*. Cambridge, MA: Belknap Press, 2001.

———. *The Future of Environmental Criticism: Environmental Crisis and Literary Imagination*. Oxford: Blackwell, 2005.

Bullen, J. B. *Byzantium Rediscovered*. London: Phaidon, 2009.

Bultmann, R. *Jesus Christ and Mythology*. New York: Charles Scribner's Sons, 1958.

———. *This World and the Beyond: Marburg Sermons*. New York: Charles Scribner's Sons, 1960.

Bunting, T., and P. Filion, eds. *Canadian Cities in Transition: Local through Global Perspectives*. 3rd ed. Oxford: Oxford University Press, 2006.

Burgess, J. *Geography, the Media, and Popular Culture*. London: Croom Helm, 2010.

Burnett, F. W. "Philo on Immortality: A Thematic Study of Philo's Concept of παλιγγενεσία [palingenesia]." *Catholic Biblical Quarterly* 46 (1984): 447–70.

Buttimer, A., and D. Seamon. *The Human Experience of Space and Place*. New York: St. Martin's Press, 1980.

Caird, G. B. *Jesus and the Jewish Nation*. London: Athlone Press, 1965.

———. *A Commentary on the Revelation of St. John the Divine*. London: Black, 1966.

———. *The Christian Hope*. London: SPCK, 1970.

———. *New Testament Theology*. Oxford: Clarendon, 1994.

Caldecott, S. "Zeal in Detachment." In *The Inner Journey: Views from the Christian Tradition*, edited by L. Kisly, 227–31. Sandpoint, ID: Morning Light Press, 2008.

Callahan, D., ed. *The Secular City Debate*. New York: Macmillan, 1966.

Callicott, J. B. "Genesis and John Muir." In *Covenant for a New Creation: Ethics, Religion and Public Policy*, edited by C. J. Casebolt and C. S. Robb, 107–40. Maryknoll, NY: Orbis, 1991.

Calvin, J. *Genesis*. Edinburgh: Banner of Truth Trust, 1975.

———. *The First Epistle of Paul to the Corinthians*. Translated by J. W. Faser. Edited by T. F. Torrance and D. W. Torrance. Calvin New Testament Commentaries 9. Grand Rapids: Eerdmans, 1996.

Campanella, T. J. *The Concrete Dragon: China's Urban Revolution and What It Means for the World*. New York: Princeton Architectural Press, 2008.

Campbell-Culver, M. *The Origin of Plants: The People and Plants That Have Shaped Britain's Garden History*. London: Eden Project Books, 2001.

Caneday, A. B. "Mark's Provocative Use of Scripture in Narration: 'He Was with the Wild Animals and Angels Ministered to Him.'" *Bulletin for Biblical Research* 9 (1999): 19–36.

Carlson, A. *Nature and Landscape: An Introduction to Environmental Aesthetics*. New York: Columbia University Press, 2009.

Carretto, C. *Letters from the Desert*. New York: Orbis, 1990.

Carroll, J. T. "Creation and Apocalypse." In Brown and McBride, *The God Who Creates*, 251–60.

Carson, D. A., P. T. O'Brien, and M. A. Seifrid, eds. *Justification and Variegated Nomism*. Vol. 1, *The Complexities of Second Temple Judaism*. Grand Rapids: Baker Academic; Tübingen: Mohr Siebeck, 2001.

Carter, J. *Palestine: Peace Not Apartheid*. New York: Simon & Schuster, 2006.

Casey, E. S. *Getting Back into Place: Toward a Renewed Understanding of the Place-World*. Bloomington and Indianapolis: Indiana University Press, 1993.

———. *The Fate of Place*. Los Angeles: University of California Press, 1998.

Casparay, G. E. *Politics and Exegesis: Origen and the Two Swords*. Los Angeles: University of California Press, 1979.

Casson, L. *Travel in the Ancient World*. Toronto: Hakkert, 1974.

Cataldi, S. L., and W. S. Hamrick, eds. *Merleau-Ponty and Environmental Philosophy*. Albany, NY: SUNY, 2007.

Caygill, H. *A Kant Dictionary*. Cambridge, MA: Blackwell, 1995.

Cayley, D., ed. *Ideas: On the Nature of Science*. Fredericton, NB: Goose Lane, 2009.

Chadwick, O. *John Cassian*. Cambridge: Cambridge University Press, 1968.

Chambers, D. *Stonyground: The Making of a Canadian Garden*. Toronto: Knopf, 1996.

Chaplin, J. *Herman Dooyeweerd: Christian Philosopher of State and Civil Society*. Notre Dame, IN: University of Notre Dame Press, 2011.

Chapman, D. W. "Locating the Gospel of Mark." *Biblical Theology Bulletin* 25 (1995): 24–36.

Charles, R. H. *A Critical and Exegetical Commentary on the Revelation of St. John*. Edinburgh: T&T Clark, 1920.

Charlesworth, A. "Contesting Places of Memory: The Case of Auschwitz." *Environment and Planning D: Society and Space* 12.5 (2010): 579–93.

Chenu, M. D. *Nature, Man, and Society in the Twelfth Century: Essays on New Theological Perspectives in the Latin West*. Edited and translated by J. Taylor and L. K. Little. Chicago: University of Chicago Press, 1968.

Chesterton, G. K. *Saint Thomas Aquinas*. New York: Doubleday, 1956.

Childs, B. S. *Exodus: A Commentary*. London: SCM, 1974.

———. *Introduction to the Old Testament as Scripture*. London: SCM, 1979.

———. *Biblical Theology of the Old and New Testaments: Theological Reflections on the Christian Bible*. Minneapolis: Fortress, 1992.

———. *Isaiah: A Commentary*. Louisville: Westminster John Knox, 2001.

Chilton, B. *The Temple of Jesus: His Sacrificial Program within a Cultural History of Sacrifice*. University Park, PA: Pennsylvania State University, 1992.

———. *Pure Kingdom: Jesus' Vision of God*. Grand Rapids: Eerdmans, 1996.

Christensen, D. L. *Deuteronomy 1–11*. Word Biblical Commentary 6. Dallas: Word Books, 1991.

———. *Deuteronomy 21:10–34:12*. Word Biblical Commentary 6B. Nashville: Nelson, 2002.

Clément, O. *The Roots of Christian Mysticism*. New York: New City Press, 1993.

Clines, D. J. A. *Job 1–20*. Word Biblical Commentary 17. Dallas: Word Books, 1989.

Coakley, S., ed. *Religion and the Body*. Cambridge: Cambridge University Press, 1997.

Collins, J. J. and P. W. Flint, eds. *The Book of Daniel: Composition and Reception*. Leiden: Brill, 2001.

Comblin, J. "La Liturgie de la Nouvelle Jérusalem (Apoc. 21:1–22:5)." *Ephemerides Theologicae Lovanienses* 29 (1953): 5–40.

Connor, T., and P. Vicente. *The Language of Doors*. New York: Artisan, 2005.

Conzelmann, H. *The Theology of Luke*. Translated by G. Buswell. New York: Harper & Row, 1960.

———. *The Theology of St. Luke*. New York: Harper & Row, 1961.

Cooper, A. *The Body in St. Maximus the Confessor*. Oxford: Oxford University Press, 2005.

Coote, R. B., and D. R. Ord. *The Bible's First History*. Philadelphia: Fortress, 1989.

Cousteau, J. *The Silent World*. New York: Harper & Brothers, 1953.

———. *The Living Sea*. New York: Harper & Row, 1963.

Cousteau, J., and S. Schiefelbein. *The Human, the Orchid, and the Octopus: Exploring* and Conserving Our Natural World. New York: Barnes & Noble, 2007.

Cox, H. The Secular City. 2nd ed. New York: MacMillan, 1966.

Craigie, P. C. The Book of Deuteronomy. Grand Rapids: Eerdmans, 1976.

———. Ugarit and the Old Testament. Grand Rapids: Eerdmans, 1983.

———. The Twelve Prophets. Edinburgh: St. Andrews Press, 1985.

Craigie, P. C., P. H. Kelley, and J. F. Drinkard Jr. Jeremiah 1–25. Word Biblical Commentary 26. Nashville: Nelson, 1991.

Cranfield, C. E. B. A Critical and Exegetical Commentary on the Epistle to the Romans. 2 vols. Edinburgh: T&T Clark, 1975.

Cresswell, T. Place: A Short Introduction. Oxford: Blackwell, 2009.

Cresswell, T., and D. Dixon, eds. Engaging Film: Geographies of Mobility and Identity. Lanham, MD: Rowman & Littlefield, 2002.

Cross, F. M. "The Tabernacle: A Study from an Archaeological and Historical Approach." Bulletin of the American Schools of Oriental Research 10 (1947): 45–68.

Crossan, J. D., and J. L. Reed. Excavating Jesus: Beneath the Stones, Behind the Texts. New York: Harper, 2001.

Crouch, D., and C. Ward. The Allotment: Its Landscape and Culture. Nottingham, UK: Five Leaves Publications, 1997.

Cullman, O. Christ and Time: The Primitive Christian Conception of Time and History. 5th ed. Philadelphia: Westminster Press, 1975.

Cunningham, L. S. "Foreword." In C. Carretto, Letters from the Desert, vii–x. New York: Orbis, 2002.

Dahl, N. A. The Crucified Messiah, and Other Essays. Minneapolis: Augsburg, 1974.

———. Studies in Paul: Theology for the Early Christian Mission. Minneapolis: Augsburg, 1977.

Dalman, G. The Words of Jesus Considered in the Light of Post-Biblical Jewish Writings and the Aramaic Language. Edinburgh: T&T Clark, 1902.

Dalrymple, W. From the Holy Mountain: A Journey in the Shadow of Byzantium. London: Flamingo, 1998.

Davids, P. H. The Letters of 2 Peter and Jude. Grand Rapids: Eerdmans, 2006.

Davies, J. A. A Royal Priesthood. New York: Continuum, 2004.

Davies, P. Exploring Chaos: A Guide to the New Science of Disorder. Edited by Nina Hall. New York: Norton, 2010.

Davies, W. D. Paul and Rabbinic Judaism: Some Rabbinic Elements in Pauline Theology. Philadelphia: Fortress, 1965.

———. The Sermon on the Mount. London: Cambridge University Press, 1966.

———. The New Creation. Philadelphia: Fortress, 1971.

———. The Gospel and the Land: Early Christianity and Jewish Territorial Doctrine. Berkeley: University of California Press, 1974.

———. Jewish and Pauline Studies. Philadelphia: Fortress, 1984.

Davies, W. D., and A. C. Allison. Matthew 1–7. Edinburgh: T&T Clark, 1988.

Davis, E. F. Scripture, Culture, and Agriculture: An Agrarian Reading of the Bible. Cambridge: Cambridge University Press, 2009.

Davis, M. City of Quartz: Excavating the Future of Los Angeles. London: Verso, 1990.

———. Planet of Slums. London: Verso, 2006.

Davis, R. D. The Heavenly Court Judgment of Revelation 4–5. New York: University Press of America, 1992.

Day, C. Places of the Soul: Architecture and Environmental Design as a Healing Art. London: Aquarian, 1990.

———. Spirit and Place: Healing Our Environment, Healing Environment. Oxford: Architectural Press, 2002.

De Blij, H. Why Geography Matters. Oxford: Oxford University Press, 2005.

———. The Power of Place: Geography, Destiny, and Globalization's Rough Landscape. Oxford: Oxford University Press, 2009.

De Caus, S. La Perspective avec La Raison des ombres et miroirs. London: Norbon, 1612.

De Certeau, M. *The Practice of Everyday Life.* Berkeley: University of California Press, 1984.

Dechow, J. F. "Origen and Early Christian Pluralism: The Context of His Eschatology." In *Origen of Alexandria: His World and His Legacy*, edited by W. L. Peterson and C. Kannengiesser, 337–56. Notre Dame, IN: University of Notre Dame Press, 1988.

De Geus, C. H. J. *Towns in Ancient Israel and in the Southern Levant.* Leuven, Belgium: Peeters, 2003.

De Gruchy, J. W. *Icons as a Means of Grace.* Wellington, South Africa: Lux Verbi.BM, 2008.

De Lubac, H. *Un témoin dans l'Eglise: Hans Urs von Balthasar, Paradoxe et Mystiere de l'Eglise.* Paris: 1967.

Derrida, J. "Point de folie—Maintenant L'Architecture." Translated by K. Linker. *AA Files* 12 (1986): sec. 13.

Descartes, R. *Meditations on First Philosophy.* Edited by M. Moriarty. Oxford: Oxford University Press, 2008.

DeWitt, C. B. *Earth-Wise: A Biblical Response to Environmental Issues.* Grand Rapids: Faith Alive, 2005.

De Young, J. C. *Jerusalem in the New Testament: The Significance of the City in the History of Redemption and in Eschatology.* Kampen: Kok, 1960.

Diamond, J. M. *Guns, Germs, and Steel: The Fates of Human Societies.* New York: Norton, 1999.

———. *Collapse: How Societies Choose to Fail or Succeed.* New York: Viking, 2005.

Dillard, A. *Pilgrim at Tinker Creek.* New York: HarperCollins, 1974.

———. *The Annie Dillard Reader.* New York: HarperCollins, 1995.

Dispenza, J. *The Way of the Traveler: Making Every Trip a Journey of Self-Discovery.* Santa Fe: John Muir Publications, 1999.

Donahue, J. R., and D. J. Harrington. *The Gospel of Mark.* Collegeville, MN: Liturgical Press, 2002.

Donnan, H., and T. M. Wilson, eds. *Border Approaches: Anthropological Perspectives on Frontiers.* Lanham, MD: University Press of America, 1994.

Donnelly, M. C. *The New England Meeting House of the Seventeenth Century.* Middletown, CT: Wesleyan University Press, 1968.

Doody, J. *Augustine and Politics.* Lanham, MD: Lexington Books, 2005.

Dooyeweerd, H. *A New Critique of Theoretical Thought.* 4 vols. Jordan Station, ON: Paideia, 1984.

Dorsey, D. A. *The Roads and Highways of Ancient Israel.* Baltimore: Johns Hopkins University Press, 1991.

Dougherty, J. *The Fivesquare City: The City in the Religious Imagination.* Notre Dame, IN: University of Notre Dame Press, 1980.

Douglas, M. *Purity and Danger: An Analysis of the Concepts of Pollution and Taboo.* London: Ark Paperbacks, 1984.

———. *Leviticus as Literature.* Oxford and New York: Oxford University Press, 1999.

Drengson, A., and D. Taylor. *Wild Foresting: Practising Nature's Wisdom.* Gabriola Island, BC: New Society Publishers, 2009.

Dubos, R. *Reason Awake: Science for Man.* New York: Columbia University Press, 1970.

———. "Franciscan Conservation versus Benedictine Stewardship." In R. J. Berry, *Environmental Stewardship*, 56–62.

Dugan, P. L., gen. ed. *Guide to Wetlands: An Illustrated Guide to the Ecology and Conservation of the World's Wetlands.* New York: Firefly Books, 2009.

Dumas, A. *Dietrich Bonhoeffer, Theologian of Reality.* Translated by R. McAfee Brown. New York: Macmillan, 1971.

Dumbrell, W. J. *Covenant and Creation.* Exeter: Paternoster, 1984.

———. *The End of the Beginning: Revelation 21–22 and the Old Testament.* Grand Rapids: Baker Books, 1985.

Dunn, J. D. G. *Romans 1–8.* Word Biblical Commentary 38A. Nashville: Nelson, 1988.

———. *Romans 9–16.* Word Biblical Commentary 38B. Nashville: Nelson, 1988.

———. *The Theology of Paul the Apostle.* Grand Rapids: Eerdmans, 1988.

Dunnhill, J. *Covenant and Sacrifice in the Letter to the Hebrews.* Cambridge: Cambridge University Press, 1998.

Dupré, L. *Passage to Modernity: An Essay in the Hermeneutics of Nature and Culture.* New Haven: Yale University Press, 1993.

Durham, J. I. *Exodus.* Word Biblical Commentary 3. Nashville: Nelson, 1987.

Durrell, L. *Spirit of Place: Letters and Essays on Travel.* London: Faber & Faber, 2009.

Dyas, D. "Pilgrimage, Medieval to (Post)Modern: The Journeying Goes On." *Australian Folklore* 15 (August 2000): 88–99.

Dyrness, W. A. *Reformed Theology and Visual Culture.* Cambridge: Cambridge University Press, 2004.

Easton, V. *A Pattern Garden: The Essential Elements of Garden Making.* Portland, OR: Timber Press, 2007.

Edwards, D. *Jesus and the Wisdom of God.* Maryknoll, NY: Orbis, 1995.

Elden, S. *Understanding Henry Lefebvre: Theory and the Possible.* London: Continuum, 2004.

Eliade, M. *The Forge and the Crucible: The Origins and Structure of Alchemy.* Chicago: University of Chicago Press, 1979.

Elie, P. *The Life You Save May Be Your Own: An American Pilgrimage.* New York: Farrar, Straus and Giroux, 2003.

Elitzur, Y. *Ancient Place Names in the Holy Land: Preservation and History.* Jerusalem: Hebrew University Magnes Press, 2004.

Elliott, J. H. *A Home for the Homeless: A Sociological Exegesis of 1 Peter, Its Situation and Strategy.* Philadelphia: Fortress, 1981.

———. "Temple versus Household in Luke-Acts: A Contrast in Social Institutions." In *The Social World of Luke-Acts: Models for Interpretation,* edited by J. H. Neyrey, 211–40. Peabody, MA: Hendrickson, 1991.

———. "The Epistle of James in Rhetorical and Social Scientific Perspective—Wholeness and Patterns of Replication." *Biblical Theology Bulletin* 23 (1993): 71–81.

Ellul, J. *The Meaning of the City.* Translated by Dennis Pardee. Grand Rapids: Eerdmans, 1970.

Emmerling, M. *Art of the Cross.* Salt Lake City: Ancient City Press, 2006.

Engels, D. W. *Roman Corinth: An Alternative Model for the Classical City.* Chicago: University of Chicago Press, 1990.

English, C. *The Snow Tourist: A Search for the World's Purest, Deepest Snowfall.* Berkeley: Counterpoint, 2008.

Entrikin, J. N. *The Betweenness of Place: Towards a Geography of Modernity.* Baltimore: Johns Hopkins University Press, 1991.

Escobar, A. *Territories of Difference: Place, Movements, Life, Redes.* Durham, NC: Duke University Press, 2008.

Estill, L. *Small Is Possible: Life in a Local Economy.* Gabriola Island, BC: New Society Publishers, 2008.

Evans, C. A. "Daniel in the New Testament: Visions of God's Kingdom." In Collins and Flint, *The Book of Daniel,* 490–527.

Evans, H. C., and W. D. Wixom, eds. *The Glory of Byzantium: Art and Culture of the Middle Byzantine Era, A.D. 843–1261.* New York: Metropolitan Museum of Art, 1997.

Fee, G. D. *Pauline Christology: An Exegetical-Theological Study.* Peabody, MA: Hendrickson, 2007.

Fekkes, J. *Isaiah and Prophetic Traditions in the Book of Revelation: Visionary Antecedents and Their Development.* Journal for the Study of the New Testament: Supplement Series 93. Sheffield, UK: JSOT, 1994.

Ferrera, L., and E. Visser, eds. *Canada Innovates: Sustainable Building.* Toronto: School of Design, 2006.

Feuerbach, L. *The Essence of Christianity.* New York: Harper & Row, 1957.

Filler, M. "Maman's Boy." *New York Review of Books,* April 30 (2009): 33–36. http://www.nybooks.com/articles/archives/2009/apr/30/mamans-boy/

Finnes, J. *Aquinas: Moral, Political, and Legal Theory.* Oxford: Oxford University Press, 1998.

Flannery, T. *The Weather Makers: How Man Is Changing the Climate and What It Means for Life on Earth.* New York: Atlantic Monthly, 2005.

Flusser, D., and R. S. Notley. *The Sage from Galilee: Rediscovering Jesus' Genius.* Grand Rapids: Eerdmans, 2007.

Foltz, B. V. *Inhabiting the Earth: Heidegger, Environmental Ethics, and the Metaphysics of Nature.* New York: Humanity Books, 1995.

Foltz, B. V., and R. Frodeman, eds. *Rethinking Nature: Essays in Environmental Philosophy.* Indianapolis: Indiana University Press, 2004.

Ford, M. *Beyond the Modern University: Toward a Constructive Post-Modern University.* Westport, CT: Praeger, 2002.

Fortna, R. T. "Theological Use of Locale in the Fourth Gospel." *Anglican Theological Review* 3 (1974): 58–95.

Foucault, M. *The Foucault Reader.* Edited by P. Rabinow. New York: Pantheon, 1984.

Fox, M. *The Coming of the Cosmic Christ: The Healing of Mother Earth and the Birth of a Global Renaissance.* San Francisco: Harper & Row, 1988.

France, R. T. *Matthew.* Grand Rapids: Eerdmans, 1985.

———. *The Gospel of Mark: A Commentary on the Greek Text.* Grand Rapids: Eerdmans, 2002.

Fraser, F. *Shack Chic: Art and Innovation in South African Shack-Lands.* Cape Town, South Africa: Quivertree Publications, 2002.

Freedman, D. N. *The Nine Commandments: Uncovering a Hidden Pattern of Crime and Punishment in the Hebrew Bible.* New York: Doubleday, 2000.

Fretheim, T. E. *Jeremiah.* Macon, GA: Smyth & Helwys, 2002.

———. *God and World in the Old Testament.* Nashville: Abingdon, 2005.

Freyne, S. *Jesus, a Jewish Galilean: A New Reading of the Jesus-Story.* London: T&T Clark, 2004.

Frick, F. S. *The City in Ancient Israel.* Missoula, MT: Scholars Press, 1977.

Frisch, A. "Structure and Its Significance: The Narrative of Solomon's Reign (1 Kings 1–12:24)." *Journal for the Study of the Old Testament* 51 (1991): 3–14.

Frugoni, C. *A Day in a Medieval City.* Chicago: University of Chicago Press, 2005.

Funkenstein, A. *Theology and the Scientific Imagination: From the Middle Ages to the Seventeenth Century.* Princeton: Princeton University Press, 1986.

Garfield, S. *The Error World: An Affair with Stamps.* Boston: Houghton Mifflin, 2009.

Gassendi, P. *Opera Omnia.* 6 Vols. Stuttgart-Bad Cannstatt: Friedrich Frommann Verlag, 1964.

Gatta, J. *Making Nature Sacred: Literature, Religion, and Environment from the Puritans to the Present.* Oxford: Oxford University Press, 2004.

Geddes, P. *City Development: A Study of Parks, Gardens and Culture Institutes.* Edinburgh: Geddes and Co., 1904.

Geertz, C. *The Interpretation of Cultures: Selected Essays.* New York: Basic Books, 1973.

George, M. K. *Israel's Tabernacle as Social Space.* Atlanta: Society of Biblical Literature, 2009.

Geyrhalter, N., director. *Our Daily Bread.* DVD. New York: Icarus Films, 2005.

Gibson, A. *Text and Tablet.* Aldershot, UK: Ashgate, 2000.

Gibson, J. B. "Jesus' Wilderness Temptation according to Mark." *Journal for the Study of the New Testament* 53 (1994): 6–9.

Gibson, J. W. *A Reenchanted World: The Quest for a New Kinship with Nature.* New York: Metropolitan Books, 2009.

Giddens, A. *Central Problems in Social Theory.* Cambridge: Cambridge University Press, 1979.

———. *Modernity and Self-Identity: Self and Society in the Late Modern Age.* Cambridge, UK: Polity, 1991.

Gill, D. W. "City, Biblical Theology of." In G. W. Bromiley, *The International Standard Bible Encyclopedia,* 1:713–15.

Gilpin, L. *The Hocus-Pocus of the Universe.* New York: Doubleday and Company, 1977.

Gilson, E. *The Christian Philosophy of St. Thomas Aquinas.* New York: Random House, 1956.

Girouard, M. *Cities and People: A Social and Architectural History*. New Haven and London: Yale University Press, 1985.

Glotfelty, C., and H. Fromm, eds. *The Ecocriticism Reader: Landmarks in Literary Ecology*. Athens, GA: University of Georgia Press, 1996.

Goheen, M. W., and C. G. Bartholomew. *Living at the Crossroads: An Introduction to Christian Worldview*. Grand Rapids: Baker Academic, 2008.

Goldingay, J. E. *Daniel*. Word Biblical Commentary 30. Dallas: Word Books, 1987.

———. *Theological Diversity and the Authority of the Old Testament*. Grand Rapids: Eerdmans, 1987.

Goldsworthy, G. *The Lamb and the Lion: The Gospel in Revelation*. Nashville: Nelson, 1985.

Gollner, A. L. *The Fruit Hunters*. New York: Simon & Schuster, 2008.

Goodenough, E. R. *The Theology of Justin Martyr: An Investigation into the Conceptions of Early Christian Literature and Its Hellenistic and Judaistic Influences*. Amsterdam: Philo Press, 1968.

Gordon, R. P. *Holy Land, Holy City*. Cumbria, UK: Paternoster, 2004.

Gore, A. *Earth in the Balance: Ecology and the Human Spirit*. New York: Rodale, 2006.

Gorman, F. H., Jr. *The Ideology of Ritual: Space, Time and Status in the Priestly Theology*. Sheffield, UK: JSOT Press, 1990.

Gorringe, T. J. "Sacraments." In *The Religion of the Incarnation: Anglican Essays in Commemoration of Lux Mundi*, edited by R. Morgan, 158–71. Bristol: Bristol Classical Press, 1989.

———. *A Theology of the Built Environment: Justice, Empowerment, Redemption*. Cambridge: Cambridge University Press, 2002.

Goudzwaard, B., and H. de Lange. *Beyond Poverty and Affluence: Towards a Canadian Economy of Care*. Translated and edited by M. R. Vander Vennen. Toronto: University of Toronto Press, 1995.

Gould, P., and R. White. *Mental Maps*. New York: Routledge, 1992.

Graham, W. F. *The Constructive Revolutionary: John Calvin and His Socio-Economic Impact*. Richmond: John Knox Press, 1971.

Grant, E. *Much Ado about Nothing: Theories of Space and Vacuum from the Middle Ages to the Scientific Revolution*. Cambridge: Cambridge University Press, 1981.

———. *The Foundations of Modern Science in the Middle Ages*. Cambridge: Cambridge University Press, 1996.

———. *God and Reason in the Middle Ages*. Cambridge: Cambridge University Press, 2001.

———. *Science and Religion: 400 B.C. to A.D. 1550: From Aristotle to Copernicus*. Westport, CT: Greenwood, 2004.

Grant, M. *From Alexander to Cleopatra: The Hellenistic World*. London: Weidenfeld & Nicolson, 1982.

Grayston, K. *The Johannine Epistles*. Grand Rapids: Eerdmans, 1984.

Gregory, R., R. Johnston, G. Pratt, H. Watts, and S. Whatmore, eds. *The Dictionary of Human Geography*. 5th ed. Oxford: Wiley-Blackwell, 2007.

Grillmeier, A. *Christ in Christian Tradition: From the Apostolic Age to Chalcedon (451)*. Translated by J. S. Bowden. London: A. R. Mowbray, 1965.

Green, M. *2 Peter and Jude*. 5th ed. Leicester, UK: Inter-Varsity, 1977.

Greenberg, M. "Idealism and Practicality in Numbers 35:4–5 and Ezekiel 48." *Journal of the American Oriental Society* 88 (1968): 59–66.

Greenberg, S. *The Infinite in Giordano Bruno*. New York: King's Crown Press, 1950.

Greene, B. *The Fabric of the Cosmos: Space, Time, and the Texture of Reality*. New York: Vintage, 2004.

Greenham, J. P., T. Larsen, and S. R. Spencer. *The Sermon on the Mount through the Centuries*. Grand Rapids: Brazos, 2007.

Greenman, J. P. "John R. W. Stott." In Greenman, Larsen, Spencer, *Sermon on the Mount*, 245–80.

Greenman, J. P., T. Larsen, and S. R. Spencer, eds. *The Sermon on the Mount through the Centuries*. Grand Rapids: Brazos, 2007.

Greer, R. A. "Translation and Introduction." In *Origen* (selections). New York: Paulist Press, 1979.

Gregor, B., and J. Zimmermann, eds. *Bonhoeffer and Continental Thought: Cruciform Philosophy*. Bloomington and Indianapolis: Indiana University Press, 2009.

Gregory, R., R. Johnston, G. Pratt, H. Watts, and S. Whatmore, eds. *The Dictionary of Human Geography*. 5th ed. Oxford: Wiley-Blackwell, 2007.

Greijdanus, S. *De openbaring des Heeren aan Johannes: Opnieuw uit grondtekst vertaald en verklaard*. Kampen: Kok, 1965.

Gribbin, M., and J. Gribbin. *Flower Hunters*. Oxford: Oxford University Press, 2008.

Grubbs, M. A., ed. *Conversations with Wendell Berry*. Jackson: University Press of Mississippi, 2007.

Gundry, R. H. *Matthew: A Commentary on His Literary and Theological Art*. Grand Rapids: Eerdmans, 1982.

Gunkel, H. *Genesis*. 9th ed. Göttingen, Germany: Vandenhoeck & Ruprecht, 1977.

———. *Folktale in the Old Testament*. Sheffield, UK: Almond, 1987.

Günther, H. W. *Der Nah- und Enderwartungshorizont in der Apokalypse des heiligen Johannes*. Forschung zur Bibel 41. Würtzburg: Echter, 1980.

Gunton, C. E. *Christ and Creation*. Grand Rapids: Eerdmans and Carlisle: Paternoster, 1993.

———. *The One, the Three, and the Many: God, Creation, and the Culture of Modernity*. Cambridge: Cambridge University Press, 1993.

Guroian, V. *Inheriting Paradise: Meditations on Gardening*. Grand Rapids: Eerdmans, 1999.

Gussow, J. D. *This Organic Life: Confessions of a Suburban Homesteader*. White River Junction, VT: Chelsea Green Publishing, 2002.

Gutiérrez, G. *A Theology of Liberation: History, Politics, and Salvation*. London: SCM, 1974.

Habel, N. C. *The Land Is Mine: Six Biblical Land Ideologies*. Minneapolis: Fortress, 1995.

———. "Geophany: The Earth Story in Genesis 1." In Habel and Wurst, *The Earth Story in Genesis*, 34–48.

Habel, N. C., and S. Wurst, eds. *The Earth Story in Genesis*. The Earth Bible 2. Sheffield, UK: Sheffield Academic Press, 2000.

Hacking, Ian. *Mad Travelers: Reflections on the Reality of Transient Mental Illnesses*. Charlottesville, VA: University Press of Virginia, 1998.

Hahn, S. W. "Kinship by Covenant: A Biblical Theological Study of Covenant Types and Texts in the Old and New Testaments." PhD diss., University of Michigan, 1995.

———. *Kinship by Covenant*. New Haven: Yale University Press, 2009.

Hahne, H. A. *The Corruption and Redemption of Creation: Nature in Romans 8:19–22 and Jewish Apocalyptic Literature*. New York: T&T Clark, 2006.

Hall, E. T. *The Hidden Dimension*. New York: Anchor Books, 1990.

Hall, P. G. *Cities of Tomorrow: An Intellectual History of Urban Planning and Design in the Twentieth Century*. Malden, MA: Blackwell, 1996.

Halweil, B. *Eat Here: Reclaiming Homegrown Pleasures in a Global Supermarket*. New York: Norton, 2004.

Hamann, J. G. *Writings on Philosophy and Language*. Translated and edited by K. Haynes. Cambridge: Cambridge University Press, 2007.

Hamilton, L. M. *Deeply Rooted: Unconventional Farmers in the Age of Agribusiness*. Berkeley: Counterpoint, 2009.

Hamilton, V. P. *The Book of Genesis, Chapters 1–17*. Grand Rapids: Eerdmans, 1990.

Hammarskjöld, D. *Markings*. Translated by W. H. Auden and L. Sjöberg. London: Faber and Faber, 1964.

Haran, M. *Temples and Temple-Service in Ancient Israel*. Oxford: Clarendon, 1978.

Harnack, A. von. *What Is Christianity?* Translated by T. B. Sanders. New York: Harper & Brothers, 1957.

Harrington, D. J. "Jude and 2 Peter." In *1 Peter, Jude and 2 Peter*, edited by D. J. Harrington, 161–314. Collegeville, MN: Liturgical Press, 2003.

Harrington, W. J. *Revelation*. Sacra Pagina. Collegeville, MN: Liturgical Press, 1993.

Harris, M. *Grave Matters: A Journey through the Modern Funeral Industry to a Natural Way of Burial*. New York: Scribner, 2007.

Harris, M. J. *Colossians and Philemon*. Grand Rapids: Eerdmans, 1991.

Harris, R. *Unplanned Suburbs: Toronto's American Tragedy, 1900–1950*. Baltimore: Johns Hopkins University Press, 1996.

———. *Creeping Conformity: How Canada Became Suburban, 1900–1960*. Toronto: University of Toronto Press, 2004.

Harrison, R. P. *Gardens: An Essay on the Human Condition*. Chicago: University of Chicago Press, 2010.

Harrisville, R. A. *The Concept of Newness in the New Testament*. Minneapolis: Augsburg, 1960.

Hart-Davis, D. *Audubon's Elephant: The Story of John James Audubon's Struggle to Publish "The Birds of America."* London: Phoenix, 2004.

Harvey, D. *The Condition of Postmodernity*. Oxford: Blackwell, 1989.

———. *Justice, Nature and the Geography of Difference*. Oxford: Blackwell, 1996.

———. *Spaces of Global Capitalism: Towards a Theory of Uneven Geographical Development*. London: Verso, 2006.

Harwood, D. *Love for Animals and How It Developed in Great Britain*. Lewiston, NY: Edwin Mellon, 2002.

Hasler, R. A. *Surprises around the Bend*. Minneapolis: Augsburg, 2008.

Hayden, D. *The Power of Place: Urban Landscapes as Public History*. Cambridge, MA: MIT Press, 1995.

Haynes, "Introduction." In Hamann, *Writings on Philosophy and Language*, x–xxv.

Hays, R. B. *Echoes of Scripture in the Letters of Paul*. New Haven: Yale University Press, 1989.

Heidegger, M. *Hebel der Hausfreund*. Pfullingen, Germany: Neske, 1957.

———. "Building. Dwelling. Thinking." In *Basic Writings*, 2nd ed., edited by David Farrell Krell, 343–63. London: Routledge, 1993.

Heinrich, B. *The Trees in My Forest*. New York: Ecco, 1997.

Hemer, C. J. *The Letters to the Seven Churches of Asia in Their Social Setting*. Sheffield, UK: JSOT Press, 1986.

Hengel, M. *Between Jesus and Paul: Studies in the Earliest History of Christianity*. London: SCM, 1983.

———. *The Pre-Christian Paul*. London: SCM, 1991.

Hennessey, L. R. "The Place of Saints and Sinners after Death." In *Origen of Alexandria: His World and Legacy*, edited by C. Kannengiesser and W. Peterson, 295–312. Notre Dame, IN: University of Notre Dame Press, 1988.

Herriot, T. *Jacob's Wound: A Search for the Spirit of Wilderness*. Toronto: McClelland & Stewart, 2004.

———. *Grass, Sky, Song: Promise and Peril in the World of Grassland Birds*. New York: HarperCollins, 2009.

Heschel, A. J. *The Prophets*. New York: HarperCollins, 2007.

Hessel, D. T. ed. *After Nature's Revolt: Eco-Justice and Theology*. Minneapolis: Fortress, 1992.

Hiebert, T. *The Yahwist's Landscape: Nature and Religion in Early Israel*. New York: Oxford University Press, 1996.

Hill, A. E. "The Ebal Ceremony as Hebrew Land Grant?" *Journal of the Evangelical Theological Society* 31/4 (December 1988): 399–406.

Hill, D. *The Gospel of Matthew*. Grand Rapids: Eerdmans, 1972.

Hillel, D. *The Natural History of the Bible: An Environmental Exploration of the Hebrew Scriptures*. New York: Columbia University Press, 2006.

Hilliard, A., and B. J. Bailey. *Living Stones Pilgrimage: With the Christians of the Holy Land*. London: Cassell, 1999.

Hock, R. F. *The Social Context of Paul's Ministry: Tentmaking and Apostleship*. Philadelphia: Fortress, 1980.

Hoffmeier, J. K. *Israel in Egypt: The Evidence for the Authenticity of the Exodus Tradition*. Oxford: Oxford University Press, 1999.

Hollenbach, P. W. "John the Baptist." In *Anchor Bible Dictionary*, edited by D. N. Freedman, 3:887–99. New York: Doubleday, 1992.

Holloway, L., and P. Hubbard. *People and Place: The Extraordinary Geographies of Everyday Life*. Harlow, UK: Prentice-Hall, 2001.

Homan, M. M. *To Your Tents, O Israel: The Terminology, Function, Form, and Symbolism of Tents in the Hebrew Bible and the Ancient Near East*. Leiden: Brill, 2002.

Honore, C. *In Praise of Slowness*. San Francisco: HarperCollins, 2004.

Hooker, R. *Works*. Arranged by John Keble. 3rd ed. Oxford: n.p., 1855.

Hooks, B. *Belonging: A Culture of Place*. New York: Routledge, 2009.

Hooper, B. *Time to Stand and Stare: A Life of W. H. Davies: Poet and Super-Tramp*. London: Peter Owen, 2004.

Hopkins, G. M. *Poems*. London: Humphrey Milford, 1918. www.bartleby.com/122/.

———. *Hopkins: Poems and Prose*. London: David Campbell, 1995.

Hoppe, R. *Der theologische Hintergrund des Jakobusbriefes*. Forschung zure Bibel 28. Würzburg: Echter, 1977.

Horne, B. "The Sacramental Use of Material Things." In *The Oil of Gladness: Anointing in the Christian Tradition*, edited by M. Dudley and G. Rowell, 7–18. London: SPCK, 1993.

Horsfall, T. *Rhythms of Grace*. Eastbourne, UK: Kingsway Publications, 2004.

Hubbard, D. A. *Joel and Amos*. Leicester, UK: Inter-Varsity, 1989.

Hurst, L. D. *The Epistle to the Hebrews*. Cambridge: Cambridge University Press, 1990.

Huxley, J. *Bird Watching and Bird Behaviour*. London: Chatto and Windus, 1934.

Hyde, L. *The Gift*. New York: Random House, 2007.

Inge, J. *A Christian Theology of Place*. Aldershot, UK: Ashgate, 2003.

Ingraffia, B. D. *Postmodern Theory and Biblical Theology*. Cambridge: Cambridge University Press, 1995.

Irenaeus, *Against Heresies*. http://www.newadvent.org/fathers/0103514.htm.

Isaacs, M. E. *Sacred Space: An Approach to the Theology of the Epistle to the Hebrews*. Sheffield: Sheffield Academic Press, 1992.

Jacob, B. *Das Erste Buch der Tora Genesis*. Newark: Ktav, 1934.

Jacobs, J. *The Death and Life of Great American Cities*. New York: Vintage Books, 1989.

Jacobsen, R. *The Living Shore: Rediscovering a Lost World*. New York: Bloomsbury, 2009.

Janzen, J. G. *Abraham and All the Families of the Earth: A Commentary on Genesis 12–50*. Grand Rapids: Eerdmans, 1993.

Japhet, S. *I & II Chronicles: A Commentary*. Louisville, KY: Westminster John Knox, 1993.

Jenkins, E. *Falling into Place: The Story of Modern South African Names*. Claremont, South Africa: David Philip, 2007.

Jenkins, P. *The Lost History of Christianity*. New York: HarperOne, 2008.

Jenson, R. W. *Essays in Theology of Culture*. Grand Rapids: Eerdmans, 1995.

———. "God, Space, and Architecture." In Jenson, *Essays in Theology of Culture*, 9–15.

Jeremias, J. *Theophanie*. Neukirchen-Vluyn, Germany: Neukirchener Verlagsgesellschaft, 1965.

———. *New Testament Theology*. Vol. 1, *The Proclamation of Jesus*. London: SCM, 1975.

Jervis, L. A., ed. *Gospel in Paul: Studies on Corinthians, Galatians and Romans for Richard N. Longenecker*. Sheffield, UK: Sheffield Academic Press, 1994.

Johnson, E. A., and M. W. Klemens, eds. *Nature in Fragments: The Legacy of Sprawl*. New York: Columbia University Press, 2004.

Johnson, E. E., and D. M. Hay, eds. *Pauline Theology: Looking Back, Pressing On*. Atlanta: Scholars Press, 1997.

Johnson, L. T. "The Use of Leviticus in the Letter of James." *Journal of Biblical Literature* 101 (1982): 391–401.

Johnson, R. W. *Going outside the Camp: The Sociological Function of the Levitical Critique in the Epistle to the Hebrews.* Sheffield, UK: Sheffield Academic Press, 2001.

Jonas, H. *The Gnostic Problem: The Message of an Alien God.* Rev. ed. Boston: Beacon Press, 1958.

Joosten, J. *People and Land in the Holiness Code.* Cologne, Germany: Brill, 1996.

Jordan, J. B. *Through New Eyes: Developing a Biblical View of the World.* Eugene, OR: Wipf & Stock, 1988.

Josephus, F. *The Works of Flavius Josephus: Comprising the Antiquities of the Jews, A History of the Jewish Wars, and Life of Flavius Josephus Written by Himself.* Philadelphia: McKay, 1896.

Josipovici, G. *The Book of God: A Response to the Bible.* New Haven and London: Yale University Press, 1988.

Kant, I. *Religion within the Limits of Reason Alone.* Translated by T. M. Greene. New York: Harper & Row, 1960.

———. *Critique of Pure Reason.* Translated by S. Pluhar. Indianapolis and Cambridge: Hackett, 1996.

———. *Theoretical Philosophy 1755–1770.* Edited by David Walford. Cambridge: Cambridge University Press, 2002.

———. *Metaphysical Foundations of Natural Science.* Edited by Michael Friedman. Cambridge: Cambridge University Press, 2004.

Kapuściński, R. *The Shadow of the Sun.* London: Penguin, 2001.

Käsemann, E. *Perspectives on Paul.* Philadelphia: Fortress, 1971.

———. *Commentary on Romans.* Translated by G. W. Bromiley. London: SCM, 1980.

———. *The Wandering of the People of God: An Investigation of the Letter to the Hebrews.* Translated by R. A. Harrisville and I. L. Sangberg. Minneapolis: Augsburg, 1984.

Kass, L. R. *The Hungry Soul: Eating and the Perfecting of Our Nature.* New York: Free Press, 1994.

———. *The Beginning of Wisdom: Reading Genesis.* New York: Free Press, 2003.

Katz, P. *The New Urbanism: Toward an Architecture of Community.* New York: McGraw-Hill, 1994.

Kaufman, G. "A Problem for Theology: The Concept of Nature." *Harvard Theological Review* 65, no. 3 (July 1972): 337–66.

Kearney, P. J. "Creation and Liturgy: The P Redaction of Ex 25–40." *Zeitschrift für die alttestamentliche Wissenschaft* 89 (1977): 375–78.

Kearney, R. *Strangers, Gods and Monsters: Interpreting Otherness.* New York: Routledge, 2003.

Keen, S. *Gabriel Marcel.* Richmond: John Knox, 1967.

Keener, C. S. *A Commentary on the Gospel of Matthew.* Grand Rapids: Eerdmans, 1999.

Keil, C. F. *Manual of Biblical Archaeology.* 2 vols. Edinburgh: T&T Clark, 1887–88.

Kelber, W. *The Kingdom in Mark: A New Place and a New Time.* Philadelphia: Fortress, 1974.

Kelly, J. N. D. *Golden Mouth: The Story of John Chrysostom, Ascetic, Preacher, Bishop.* Grand Rapids: Baker Academic, 1995.

Kereszty, R. A. *Wedding Feast of the Lamb: Eucharistic Theology from a Historical, Biblical, and Systematic Perspective.* Chicago: Hillenbrand Books, 2004.

Kidder, T. *House.* Boston: Mariner, 1985.

Kiddle, M., with M. K. Ross. *The Revelation of St. John.* Moffat New Testament Commentary. London: Hodder and Stoughton, 1940.

Kierkegaard, S. *Fear and Trembling, Repetition.* Vol. 6 of *Kierkegaard's Writings.* Edited and Translated by H. V. Hong and E. H. Hong. New Jersey: Princeton University Press, 1983.

Klassen, W. *The New Way of Jesus: Essays Presented to Howard Charles.* Newton, KS: Faith and Life Press, 1980.

Klein, R. W. *1 Samuel.* Word Biblical Commentary 10. Nashville: Nelson, 1983.

Klingbeil, G. A. *Bridging the Gap: Ritual and Ritual Texts in the Bible.* Winona Lake, IN: Eisenbrauns, 2007.

Knight, G. W. *The Pastoral Epistles: A Commentary on the Greek Text*. Grand Rapids: Eerdmans, 1992.

Koditschek, T. *Class Formation and Urban-Industrial Society*. Cambridge: Cambridge University Press, 1990.

Kotkin, J. *The City: A Global History*. New York: Modern Library, 2005.

Koyre, A. *From the Closed World to the Infinite Universe*. Baltimore: Johns Hopkins University Press, 1957.

Kraft, H. *Die offenbarung des Johannes*. Handbuch zum Neuen Testament 16a. Tübingen: Mohr, 1974.

Kraybill, J. N. *Imperial Cult and the Commerce in John's Apocalypse*. Sheffield, UK: Sheffield Academic Press, 2008.

Krey, P. D. W. *Nicholas of Lyra's Apocalypse*. Kalamazoo, MI: Medieval Institute Publications, 1997.

Kunstler, J. H. *The Geography of Nowhere*. New York: Simon & Schuster, 1993.

―――. *Home from Nowhere*. New York: Simon & Schuster, 1996.

Kuntz, J. K. *The Self-Revelation of God*. Philadelphia: Westminster Press, 1967.

Ladd, G. E. *Jesus and the Kingdom: The Eschatology of Biblical Realism*. New York: Harper & Row, 1964.

―――. *A Commentary on the Revelation of John*. Grand Rapids: Eerdmans, 1972.

―――. *The Presence of the Future: The Eschatology of Biblical Realism*. Grand Rapids: Eerdmans, 1974.

Lane, B. C. *The Solace of Fierce Landscapes: Exploring Desert and Mountain Spirituality*. New York: Oxford University Press, 1998.

―――. "Spirituality as the Performance of Desire: Calvin on the World as a Theatre of God's Glory." *Spiritus: A Journal of Christian Spirituality* 1 (2001): 1–30.

Lane, W. L. *The Gospel of Mark*. Grand Rapids: Eerdmans, 1974.

―――. *Hebrews 1–8*. Word Biblical Commentary 47A. Dallas: Word, 1991.

―――. *Hebrews 9–13*. Word Biblical Commentary 47B. Dallas: Word, 1991.

Lang, U. M. *Turning Towards the Lord: Orientation in Liturgical Prayer*. San Francisco: Ignatius, 2004.

Langer, S. K. *Philosophy in a New Key: A Study in the Symbolism of Reason, Rite, and Art*. New York: New American Library, 1951.

Lathrop, G. W. *Holy Ground: A Liturgical Cosmology*. Minneapolis: Fortress, 2003.

―――. *Holy People: A Liturgical Ecclesiology*. Minneapolis: Fortress, 2006.

Laufer, P. *The Dangerous World of Butterflies: The Startling Subculture of Criminals, Collectors, and Conservationists*. Guilford, CT: Lyons Press, 2009.

Lawson, L. J. *City Bountiful: A Century of Community Gardening in America*. Los Angeles: University of California Press, 2005.

Layton, J. *Homelessness: How to End the National Crisis*. Toronto: Penguin, 2008.

Le Corbusier. *Toward an Architecture*. Translation by J. Goodman. Los Angeles: Getty Research Institute, 2007.

Lee, K N. "An Urbanizing World." In *State of the World 2007: Our Urban Future*, edited by L. Starke, 3–25. New York: W. W. Norton, 2007.

Leibniz, G. von. *Philosophical Papers and Letters*. Edited by L. Loemker. Chicago: University of Chicago Press, 1956.

Leithart, P. *1 & 2 Kings*. Brazos Theological Commentary. Grand Rapids: Brazos, 2006.

Leopold, A. *A Sand County Almanac*. New York: Ballantine Books, 1970.

Levenson, J. D. *The Hebrew Bible, the Old Testament, and Historical Criticism*. Louisville: Westminster John Knox, 1993.

Levinas, E. *Totality and Infinity*. Pittsburgh: Duquesne University Press, 1969.

―――. *Christ's Fulfillment of Torah and Temple: Salvation according to Thomas Aquinas*. Notre Dame, IN: University of Notre Dame Press, 2008.

Lewis, C. S. *English Literature in the Sixteenth Century*. Oxford: Clarendon, 1954.

―――. *The Discarded Image: An Introduction to Medieval and Renaissance Literature*. Cambridge: Cambridge University Press, 1964.

———. *Studies in Words*. Cambridge: Cambridge University Press, 1967.

L'Hour, J. "Yahweh Elohim." *Revue Biblique* 81 (1974): 524–56.

Lightfoot, R. H. *Locality and Doctrine in the Gospels*. London: Hodder and Stoughton, 1938.

Lilburne, G. R. *A Sense of Place: A Christian Theology of the Land*. Nashville: Abingdon, 1989.

Lincoln, A. T. *Paradise Now and Not Yet: Studies in the Role of the Heavenly Dimension in Paul's Thought with Special Reference to His Eschatology*. Cambridge: Cambridge University Press, 1981.

———. *Hebrews: A Guide*. London: T&T Clark, 2006.

Lindberg, C. *Beyond Charity: Reformation Initiatives for the Poor*. Minneapolis: Fortress, 1993.

Little, D. *Religion, Order, and Law: A Study in Pre-Revolutionary England*. New York: Harper & Row, 1969.

Lock, R., and P. Quantrill. *Zulu Victory: The Epic of Isandlwana and the Cover-Up*. Johannesburg, South Africa: Jonathan Ball, 2002.

Locke, J. *An Essay Concerning Human Understanding*. Edited by P. H. Nidditch. Oxford: Clarendon, 1975.

Lohfink, G. *Jesus and Community*. New York: Paulist Press, 1984.

Lohfink, N. *Theology of the Pentateuch*. Minneapolis: Fortress, 1994.

Lopez, B. *Arctic Dreams: Imagination and Desire in a Northern Landscape*. New York and Toronto: Bantam, 2006.

———, ed. *Home Ground: Language for an American Landscape*. San Antonio: Trinity University Press, 2006.

Lorinc, J. *The New City*. Toronto: Penguin, 2006.

Losch, R. R. *The Uttermost Part of the Earth: A Guide to Places in the Bible*. Grand Rapids: Eerdmans, 2005.

Löser, W. *Im Geiste des Origenes: Hans Urs von Balthasar als Interpret der Theologie der Kirchenväter*. Frankfurter Theologishe Studien 23. Frankfurt: Joseph Knecht, 1976.

Louth, A. *Maximus the Confessor*. New York: Routledge, 1996.

———. "The Body in Western Catholic Christianity." In *Religion and the Body*, edited by S. Coakley, 111–30. Cambridge: Cambridge University Press, 1997.

Lovejoy, A. *The Great Chain of Being: A Study of the History of an Idea*. New York: Harper & Brothers, 1936.

Lucretius. *De Rerum Natura*. Translated by W. E. Leonard. Boston: E. P. Dutton, 1916.

Lundin, R., ed. *There before Us: Religion, Literature, and Culture from Emerson to Wendell Berry*. Grand Rapids: Eerdmans, 2007.

———. *Believing Again: Doubt and Faith in a Secular Age*. Grand Rapids: Eerdmans, 2009.

Luther, M. "Psalms 1." *A Complete Commentary of the First Twenty-two Psalms*. London: T. Bensley, 1826.

———. *Dr. Martin Luther's Samentliche Schriften*. St. Louis: Concordia, 1880.

———. *Luther's Works*. 55 vols. St. Louis: Concordia, 1955–86.

———. *Lectures on Romans*. London: SCM, 1961.

Lutwak, L. *The Role of Place in Literature*. Syracuse: Syracuse University Press, 1984.

Luz, U. *Matthew 1–7: A Commentary*. Minneapolis: Augsburg, 1989.

———. *Matthäus 8–17*. Evangelisch-katholischer Kommentar zum Neuen Testament. Zürich: Neukirchen-Vluyn; Benziger: Neukirchener Verlag, 1990.

Lynch, K. *The Image of the City*. Boston: Joint Center for Urban Studies, 1960.

Lyon, D. *Jesus in Disneyland: Religion in Postmodern Times*. Cambridge, UK: Polity, 2000.

Lytle, M. H. *The Gentle Subversive*. Oxford: Oxford University Press, 2007.

MacDonald, M. N., ed. *Experiences of Place*. Cambridge, MA: Harvard University Press, 2003.

MacDonald, N. *Not Bread Alone: The Uses of Food in the Old Testament*. Oxford: Oxford University Press, 2008.

Macfarlane, C. D. "Transfiguration as the Heart of Christian Life: The Theology of Thomas Traherne (1637?–1674) with Special Reference to 'The Kingdom of God' and Other Recently Discovered Manuscripts." PhD diss., University College Chichester, 2004.

Macfarlane, R. *The Wild Places*. London: Granta Books, 2007.

MacIntyre, A. *After Virtue*. 2nd ed. Notre Dame, IN: University of Notre Dame Press, 1984.

———. *Three Rival Versions of Moral Enquiry: Encyclopaedia, Genealogy, and Tradition*. Notre Dame, IN: University of Notre Dame Press, 1990.

Mackay, J. A. *The World of Classic Stamps, 1840–1870*. New York: G. P. Putnam's Sons, 1972.

Maisels, C. K. *The Emergence of Civilization: From Hunting and Gathering to Agriculture, Cities, and the State in the Near East*. New York: Routledge, 1990.

Malbon, E. S. *Narrative Space and Mythic Meaning in Mark*. San Francisco: Harper & Row, 1986.

Malherbe, A. J. *Paul and Popular Philosophers*. Minneapolis: Fortress, 1989.

Malina, B. J. *The New Jerusalem in the Revelation of John: The City as Symbol of Life with God*. Collegeville, MN: Liturgical Press, 2000.

Malina, B. J., and J. H. Neyrey. *Portraits of Paul: An Archaeology of Ancient Personality*. Louisville: Westminster John Knox, 1996.

Malina, B. J., and J. J. Pilch. *Social-Science Commentary on the Book of Revelation*. Minneapolis: Fortress, 2000.

Malpas, J. E. *Place and Experience: A Philosophical Topography*. Cambridge: Cambridge University Press, 1999.

———. *Heidegger's Topology: Being, Place, World*. Cambridge, MA: MIT Press, 2006.

Mango, C. A. *The Art of the Byzantine Empire, 312–1453: Sources and Documents*. Englewood Cliffs, NJ: Prentice-Hall, 1972.

Marcel, G. *Tragic Wisdom and Beyond*. Evanston, IL: Northwestern University Press, 1973.

Marcus, J. "Entering into the Kingly Power of God." *Journal of Biblical Literature* 107 (1998): 663–75.

Marshall, B. D. *Trinity and Truth*. Cambridge Studies in Christian Doctrine. Cambridge: Cambridge University Press, 2000.

Martin, R. P. *James*. Word Biblical Commentary 48. Waco: Word Books, 1988.

———. *Nature's Web: Rethinking Our Place on Earth*. New York: M. E. Sharp, 1992.

Matek, O. *The Bible through Stamps*. New York: Ktav, 1974.

Mathewson, D. *A New Heaven and a New Earth: The Meaning and Function of the Old Testament in Revelation 21:1–22:5*. Sheffield, UK: Sheffield Academic Press, 2003.

Matsen, B. *Jacques Cousteau: The Sea King*. New York: Pantheon, 2009.

Mauser, U. W. *Christ in the Wilderness*. London: SCM, 1963.

May, G. G. *The Wisdom of Wilderness*. San Francisco: HarperCollins, 2006.

Mays, J. L. *Psalms*. Louisville: Westminster John Knox, 1989.

———. "The Language of the Reign of God." *Interpretation* 47, no. 2 (1993): 117–26.

Mazar, A. *Archaeology of the Land of the Bible*. New York: Doubleday, 1985.

McBride, S. D. "Divine Protocol: Genesis 1:1–2:3 as Prologue to the Pentateuch." In Brown and McBride, *The God Who Creates*, 3–41.

McCann, J. C. *A Theological Introduction to the Book of Psalms: The Psalms as Torah*. Nashville: Abingdon, 1993.

McCarthy, C. *Deuteronomy*. Stuttgart, Germany: Deutsche Bibelgesellschaft, 2007.

McConville, J. G. *Deuteronomy*. Leicester, UK: Inter-Varsity, 2002.

———. *God and Earthly Power: An Old Testament Political Theology*. London: T&T Clark, 2006.

McConville, J. G., and S. N. Williams. *Joshua*. Grand Rapids: Eerdmans, 2010.

McCorquodale, C. *The History of Interior Design*. Oxford: Phaidon, 1983.

McFague, S. *A New Climate for Theology*. Minneapolis: Fortress, 2008.

McGrade, A. S. *The Political Thought of William of Ockham: Personal and Institutional Principles.* Cambridge: Cambridge University Press, 1974.

McGrath, A. *The Genesis of Doctrine.* Oxford: Blackwell, 1990.

McKane, W. *Studies in the Patriarchal Narratives.* Edinburgh: Handsel, 1979.

McKelvey, R. J. *The New Temple: The Church in the New Testament.* Oxford: Oxford University Press, 1969.

McKibben, B. *The End of Nature.* New York: Random House, 2006.

———. *Deep Economy: The Wealth of Communities and the Durable Future.* New York: Times Books/Henry Holt & Company, 2007.

———. *Hope, Human and Wild: True Stories of Living Lightly on the Earth.* Minneapolis: Milkweed, 2007.

———. *Pieces from an Active Life: The Bill McKibben Reader.* New York: Henry Holt & Company, 2008.

———. "Will Evangelicals Help Save the Earth?" In McKibben, *Pieces from an Active Life: The Bill McKibben Reader,* 226–34.

———. *Eaarth: Making A Life on a Tough Planet.* Toronto: Knopf, 2010.

McNamee, T. *Alice Waters and Chez Panisse: The Romantic, Impractical, often Eccentric, Ultimately Brilliant Making of a Food Revolution.* New York: Penguin, 2007.

Meeks, W. A. *The Moral World of the First Christians.* Philadelphia: Westminster, 1986.

———. *The First Urban Christians: The Social World of the Apostle Paul.* 2nd ed. New Haven: Yale University Press, 2003.

Mendell, H. "*Topoi* on *Topos*: The Development of Aristotle's Concept of Place." *Phronesis* 32, no. 1 (1987): 206–31.

Merleau-Ponty, M. *Phenomenology of Perception.* Translated by C. Smith. New York: Humanities Press, 1962.

Merton, T. *The Wisdom of the Desert.* New York: New Directions, 1960.

———. *A Search for Solitude: Pursuing the Monk's True Life.* Edited by L. S. Cunningham. Vol. 3 of *The Journals of Thomas Merton, 1952–1960.* New York: HarperCollins, 1997.

Mettinger, T. N. D. *Solomonic State Officials: A Study of the Civil Government Officials of the Israelite Monarchy.* Copenhagen: Gleerup, 1971.

Metzger, P. L. *The Word of Christ and the World of Culture: Sacred and Secular through the Theology of Karl Barth.* Grand Rapids: Eerdmans, 2003.

Meyer, B. *The Aims of Jesus.* London: SCM, 1979.

———. *The Early Christians: Their World Mission and Self-Discovery.* Wilmington, DE: Michael Glazier, 1986.

———. *Christus Faber: The Master Builder and the House of God.* Allison Park, PA: Pickwick, 1992.

Meyers, C. "Temple, Jerusalem." In *Anchor Bible Dictionary,* edited by D. N. Freedman, 6:350–69. New York: Doubleday, 1992.

Meyrowitz, J. *No Sense of Place: The Impact of Electronic Media on Social Behavior.* New York: Oxford University Press, 1985.

M'Gonigle, M., and J. Starke. *Planet U: Sustaining the World, Reinventing the University.* Gabriola Island, BC: New Society Publishers, 2006.

Michaels, J. R. *Servant and Son: Jesus in Parable and Gospel.* Atlanta: John Knox, 1981.

———. *1 Peter.* Word Biblical Commentary 49. Nashville: Nelson, 1988.

Michel, O. *Der brief an die Römer.* Göttingen: Vandenhoeck & Ruprecht, 1963.

Midkiff, K. *The Meat You Eat.* New York: St. Martin's Press, 2004.

Miles, M. *Augustine on the Body.* Missoula, MT: Scholars Press, 1979.

Milgrom, J. *Leviticus: A Book of Ritual and Ethics.* Minneapolis: Fortress, 2004.

Millard, A. R., and D. J. Wiseman. *Essays on the Patriarchal Narratives.* Leicester, UK: Inter-Varsity, 1980.

Miller, D. L. *Lewis Mumford: A Life.* Pittsburgh: University of Pittsburgh Press, 1989.

Miller, P. D. *Interpreting the Psalms.* Philadelphia: Fortress, 1986.

———. *The Way of the Lord.* Tübingen, Germany: Mohr Siebeck, 2004.

———. *The Way of the Lord: Essays in Old Testament Theology.* Grand Rapids: Eerdmans, 2007.

Minear, P. S. *I Saw a New Earth: An Introduction to the Visions of Apocalypse.* Cleveland: Corpus Books, 1968.

———. *New Testament Apocalyptic.* Nashville: Abingdon, 1981.

———. *Christians and the New Creation: Genesis Motifs in the New Testament.* Louisville: Westminster John Knox, 1994.

Mitchell, D. *The Right to the City: Social Justice and the Fight for the Public Space.* New York: Guilford Press, 2003.

Mitford, J. *The American Way of Death Revisited.* New York: Vintage, 1998.

Moberly, R. W. L. *The Bible, Theology, and Faith: A Study of Abraham and Jesus.* Cambridge: Cambridge University Press, 2000.

Moessner, D. P. "The 'Script' of the Scriptures in Acts: Suffering as God's 'Plan' (Boulh) for the World for the 'Release of Sins.'" In *History, Literature, and Society in the Book of Acts,* edited by B. Witherington III, 218–50. Cambridge: Cambridge University Press, 1996.

Möller, K. *A Prophet in Debate: The Rhetoric of Persuasion in the Book of Amos.* Sheffield: Sheffield Academic Press, 2003.

Moltmann, J. *A Broad Place: An Autobiography.* Minneapolis: Fortress, 2008.

Moltmann, J., and C. Rivuzumwami, eds. *Wo ist Gott? Gottes—Lebensräume.* Dresden, Germany: Neukirchener Verlag, 2002.

Montefiore, H. W. *The Epistle to the Hebrews.* Black's New Testament Commentaries. London: A&C Black, 1964.

Moo, D. J. *The Letter of James.* Grand Rapids: Eerdmans, 2000.

Moors, S. "The Decapolis: City Territories, Villages and *Bouleutai.*" In *After the Past: Essays in Ancient History in Honor of H. W. Plecket,* edited by W. Jongman and M. Kleijwegt, 157–207. Leiden: Brill, 2002.

Morris, L. *The First and Second Epistles to the Thessalonians.* Grand Rapids: Eerdmans, 1959.

Morton, M., and Balmori, D. *Transitory Gardens, Uprooted Lives.* New Haven and London: Yale University Press, 1995.

Morton, R. S. *One upon the Throne and the Lamb: A Tradition Historical/Theological Analysis of Revelation 4–5.* New York: Peter Lang, 2007.

Moses, J. *The Desert: An Anthology for Lent.* Norwich, UK: Canterbury Press, 1997.

Moule, C. F. D. *The Origins of Christology.* Cambridge: Cambridge University Press, 1977.

Moxnes, H. "Placing Jesus of Nazareth: Toward a Theory of Place in the Study of the Historical Jesus." In *Text and Artifact in the Religions of Mediterranean Antiquity: Essays in Honor of Peter Richardson,* edited by D. M. Wilson, 158–75. Waterloo, ON: Wilfred Laurier University Press, 2000.

———. "The Construction of Galilee as a Place for the Historical Jesus: Part 1." *Biblical Theology Bulletin* 31 (2001): 26–37.

———. "The Construction of Galilee as a Place for the Historical Jesus: Part 2." *Biblical Theology Bulletin* 31 (2001): 64–77.

———. "Kingdom Takes Place: Transformations of Place and Power in the Kingdom of God in the Gospel of Luke." In *Social Scientific Methods for Interpreting the Bible: Essays by the Context Group in Honor of Bruce J. Malina,* edited by J. J. Pilch, 176–209. Leiden: Brill, 2001.

———. *Putting Jesus in His Place: A Radical Vision of Household and Kingdom.* Louisville: Westminster John Knox, 2003.

Moyise, S. *The Old Testament in the Book of Revelation.* Sheffield, UK: Sheffield Academic Press, 1995.

———, ed. *Studies in the Book of Revelation.* New York: T&T Clark, 2001.

Muilenburg, J. *The Way of Israel: Biblical Faith and Ethics.* New York: Harper & Row, 1961.

Müller, U. B. *Die Offenbarung des Johannes.* Gütersloh: Gerd Mohn, 1984.

Mumford, L. *Technics and Civilization*. New York: Harcourt, Brace and Company, 1934.

———. *The Myth of the Machine: Technics and Human Development*. New York: Harcourt, Brace & World, 1966.

———. *The City in History*. New York: Harcourt, 1989.

———. "What Is a City?" In *The City Reader*, edited by R. LeGates and F. Stout, 183–88. New York: Routledge, 1996.

Muraoka, T. *Emphatic Words and Structures in Biblical Hebrew*. Jerusalem: Magnes; Leiden: Brill, 1985.

Murphy, T. J. *Pocket Dictionary for the Study of Biblical Hebrew*. Downers Grove, IL: InterVarsity, 2003.

Murray, M. J. *Taming the Disorderly City*. Ithaca, NY: Cornell University Press, 2008.

Myers, A. C. "City." In Bromiley, *The International Standard Bible Encyclopedia*, 1:705–13.

Mynott, J. *Birdscapes: Birds in Our Imagination and Experience*. Princeton: Princeton University Press, 2009.

Nabokov, V. *Speak, Memory*. New York: Random House, 1999.

Nash, J. A. *Ecological Integrity and Christian Responsibility*. Nashville: Abingdon, 1991.

Naugle, D. K. *Worldview: The History of a Concept*. Grand Rapids: Eerdmans, 2002.

Neill, S. C., and N. T. Wright. *The Interpretation of the New Testament: 1861–1986*. Oxford: Oxford University Press, 1988.

Nelson, R. S. *Hagia Sophia, 1850–1950: Holy Wisdom Modern Monument*. Chicago: University of Chicago Press, 2010.

Newbigin, L. *Sign of the Kingdom*. Grand Rapids: Eerdmans, 1980.

———. *The Light Has Come: An Exposition of the Fourth Gospel*. Grand Rapids: Eerdmans, 1982.

———. *The Gospel in a Pluralist Society*. Grand Rapids: Eerdmans, 1989.

Newman, J. H. *An Essay on the Development of Christian Doctrine. The Edition of 1845*. London: Penguin, 1973.

Newsom, C. A. "Common Ground: An Ecological Reading of Genesis 2–3." In Habel and Wurst, *The Earth Story in Genesis*, 60–72.

Neyrey, J. H., ed. *The Social World of Luke-Acts: Models for Interpretation*. Peabody, MA: Hendrickson, 1991.

———. "Spaces and Places, Whence and Whither, Homes and Rooms: 'Territoriality' in the Fourth Gospel." *Biblical Theology Bulletin* 32 (2002): 60–74.

Niditch, S. "Ezekiel 40–48 in a Visionary Context." *Catholic Biblical Quarterly* 48 (1986): 208–24.

Niebuhr, H. R. *Christ and Culture*. New York: Harper Colophon, 1951.

Nolland, J. *Luke 18:35–24:53*. Word Biblical Commentary 35C. Waco: Word, 1993.

Noort, E. "Gan-Eden in the Context of the Mythology of the Hebrew Bible." In *Paradise Interpreted: Representations of Biblical Paradise in Judaism and Christianity*, edited by G. P. Luttikhuizen, 21–36. Leiden: Brill, 1999.

Norber-Schulz, C. *Genius Loci: Towards a Phenomenology of Architecture*. New York: Rizzoli, 1979.

Normile, D. "Conservation Takes a Front Seat as University Builds New Campus." *Science* 16 (July 2004): 329–31.

Norris, K. *Dakota: A Spiritual Geography*. Boston: Houghton Mifflin, 1993.

North, R. A. E. *The Death of British Agriculture: The Wanton Destruction of an Industry*. London: Duckworth, 2001.

Northcott, M. S. *A Moral Climate: The Ethics of Global Warming*. New York: Orbis, 2007.

O'Brien, J., and W. Major. *In the Beginning: Creation Myths from Ancient Mesopotamia, Israel and Greece*. Atlanta: American Scholars Press, 1982.

O'Connor, K. M. *Lamentations and the Tears of the World*. New York: Orbis, 2002.

O'Donovan, O. *Resurrection and Moral Order: An Outline for Evangelical Ethics*. Leicester, UK: Inter-Varsity, 1986.

———. "The Loss of a Sense of Place." *Irish Theological Quarterly* 55 (1989): 39–58.

———. *The Desire of the Nations: Rediscovering the Roots of Political Theology*. Cambridge: Cambridge University Press, 1996.

O'Dowd, R. *The Wisdom of Torah: Epistemology in Deuteronomy and the Wisdom Literature*. Göttingen, Germany: Vandenhoeck & Ruprecht, 2010.

Oelschlaeger, M., ed. *The Wilderness Condition: Essays on Environment and Civilization*. San Francisco: Sierra Club Books, 1992.

Oldenburg, R. *The Great Good Place*. New York: Marlowe & Company, 1999.

———. *Celebrating the Third Place: Inspiring Ideas about the 'Great Good Places' at the Heart of Our Communities*. New York: Marlowe & Company, 2001.

Ollenburger, B. C. *Zion, the City of the Great King: A Theological Symbol of the Jerusalem Cult*. Sheffield, UK: JSOT Press, 1987.

Olson, D. T. *The Death of the Old and the Birth of the New: The Framework of the Book of Numbers and the Pentateuch*. Chico, CA: Scholars Press, 1985.

O'Meara, D. J. "The Hierarchical Ordering of Reality in Plotinus." *The Cambridge Companion to Plotinus*, edited by L. P. Gerson, 66–81. Cambridge: Cambridge University Press, 1996.

O'Neill, J. C. "The Kingdom of God." *Novum Testamentum* 35 (2008): 130–41.

Origen. *Against Celsus*. In *Ante-Nicene Fathers*, vol. 4, *Fathers of the Third Century*, 395–669. Translated by F. Crombie. Edinburgh: T&T Clark, 1885.

———. *The Commentary of Origen on S. John's Gospel*. Translated by A. Menzies. Cambridge: Cambridge University Press, 1896.

———. *Homilies on Jeremiah*. Translated by J. C. Smith. Washington, DC: Catholic University of America Press, 1998.

Ott, W. "A New Look at the Concept of the Kingdom of God." *Notes on Translation* 2 (March 1984): 2–81.

Packer, J. I. "Foreword: Why We Need the Puritans." In Ryken, *Worldly Saints*, ix–xvi.

Page, H. R. "Boundaries: A Case Study Using the Biblical Book of Judges." *Research in the Social Scientific Study of Religion* 10 (1999): 37–55.

Page, R. *The Education of a Gardener*. New York: NYRB Classics, 2007.

Paige, H. W. "Leave If You Can." In Vitek and Jackson, *Rooted in the Land*, 11–13.

Palmer, Joy A., ed. *Fifty Key Thinkers on the Environment*. New York: Routledge, 2001.

Pao, D. W. *Acts and the Isaianic New Exodus*. Grand Rapids: Baker Academic, 2002.

Parez, C. H. "The Seven Letters and the Rest of the Apocalypse." *Journal of Theological Studies* XII(2) (1911): 284–86.

Paton, A. *Cry, The Beloved Country*. New York: Charles Scribner's Sons, 1948.

———. *Towards the Mountain: An Autobiography*. New York: Penguin, 1980.

Patrick, D. "The Kingdom of God in the Old Testament." In Willis, *The Kingdom of God in 20th Century Interpretation*, 67–79.

Patrologia graeca. Edited by J.-P. Migne. 162 vols. Paris, 1857–1886.

Payton, J. R., Jr. *Light from the Christian East: An Introduction to the Orthodox Tradition*. Downers Grove, IL: IVP Academic, 2007.

Pennington, J. *Heaven and Earth in the Gospel of Matthew*. Leiden: Brill, 2007.

Petersen, N. R. *Rediscovering Paul: Philemon and the Sociology of Paul's Narrative World*. Philadelphia: Fortress, 1985.

Peterson, D. L. *Hebrews and Perfection: An Examination of the Concept of Perfection in the 'Epistle to the Hebrews.'* Cambridge: Cambridge University Press, 1982.

Peterson, E. H. *The Contemplative Pastor: Returning to the Art of Spiritual Direction*. Grand Rapids: Eerdmans, 1980.

———. *Working the Angles: The Shape of Pastoral Integrity*. Grand Rapids: Eerdmans, 1987.

———. *Under the Unpredictable Plant: An Exploration in Vocational Holiness*. Grand Rapids: Eerdmans, 1994.

———. *The Wisdom of Each Other: A Conversation Between Friends*. Grand Rapids: Zondervan, 1998.

Phelps, N. *The Longest Struggle: Animal Advocacy from Pythagoras to PETA*. New York: Lantern Books, 2007.

Phillips, A. *Ancient Israel's Criminal Law: A New Approach to the Decalogue*. Oxford: Blackwell, 1970.

Pieper, J. *Scholasticism: Personalities and Problems in Medieval Philosophy*. South Bend, IN: St. Augustine's Press, 2001.

Pitkanen, P. *Central Sanctuary and Centralization of Worship in Ancient Israel*. Piscataway, NJ: Gorgias Press, 2003.

Plato. *Plato: Complete Works*. Edited by J. M. Cooper. Indianapolis: Hackett, 1997.

Pleins, J. D. *The Social Visions of the Hebrew Bible: A Theological Introduction*. Louisville: Westminster John Knox, 2001.

Plummer, A. *The Gospel according to St. Luke*. Edinburgh: T&T Clark, 1922.

Pohl, A. *Offenbarung des Johannes Erklärt*. Edited by A. Pohl and G. Meier. Wuppertal Studienbibel. Saarbrücken: Verlag, 1969.

Polanyi, M. *Personal Knowledge: Towards a Post-Critical Philosophy*. Chicago: University of Chicago Press, 1962.

Polkinghorne, J. *The Faith of a Physicist: Reflections of a Bottom-Up Thinker*. Minneapolis: Fortress, 1995.

Pollan, M. *Second Nature: A Gardener's Education*. New York: Grove Press, 1991.

———. *A Place of My Own: The Education of an Amateur Builder*. New York: Random House, 1997.

———. *The Omnivore's Dilemma: A Natural History of Four Meals*. New York: Penguin, 2006.

———. *In Defense of Food*. New York: Penguin, 2008.

Poole, R. *Earthrise: How Man First Saw the Earth*. New Haven: Yale University Press, 2008.

Postgate, J. N. "In Search of the First Empires." *Bulletin of the American Schools of Oriental Research* 293 (February 1994): 1–13.

Postman, N. *The Disappearance of Childhood*. New York: Delacorte Press, 1982.

Praz, M. *An Illustrated History of Interior Decoration from Pompeii to Art Nouveau*. New York: Thames & Hudson, 1981.

Pretor-Pinney, G. *The Cloudspotter's Guide: The Science, History and Culture of Clouds*. New York: Berkeley Publishing Group, 2006.

Prigent, P. "Une trace de liturgie judéo-chrétienne dans le chapitre XXI de l'Apocalypse de Jean." *Recherches de science religieuse* 60 (1972): 163–72.

Pronzato, A. *Meditations on the Sand*. New York: Alba House, 1983.

Provan, I. W. *1 and 2 Kings*. Peabody, MA: Hendrickson, 1995.

———. *1 & 2 Kings*. Sheffield, UK: Sheffield Academic Press, 1997.

Putnam, R. D. *Bowling Alone: The Collapse and Revival of American Community*. New York: Simon & Schuster, 2000.

Putnam, T. "Beyond the Modern Home: Shifting the Parameters of Residence." In *Mapping the Futures: Local Cultures, Global Change*, edited by J. Bird et al., 150–65. New York: Routledge, 1993.

Rad, G. von. *The Theology of Israel's Historical Traditions*. Edinburgh: Oliver & Boyd, 1962.

———. *Genesis: A Commentary*. Translated by J. Marks. London: SCM, 1972.

———. *Old Testament Theology: The Theology of Israel's Historical Tradition*. Vol 1. Translated by D. M. G. Stalker. New York: Harper, 1985.

———. *Wisdom in Israel*. New York: Continuum, 1993.

Räisänen, H. *Paul and the Law*. Tübingen, Germany: Mohr, 1983.

Ramsay, W. M. *The Letters to the Seven Churches of Asia and Their Place in the Plan of the Apocalypse*. New York: A. C. Armstrong, 1904.

Randall, C. "Structuring Protestant Scriptural Space in Sixteenth Century Catholic France." *Sixteenth Century Journal* 25, no. 2 (1994): 341–53.

Rappaport, R. A. *Ritual and Religion in the Making of Humanity*. Cambridge: Cambridge University Press, 2001.

Räpple, E. M. *The Metaphor of the City in the Apocalypse of John*. New York: Peter Lang, 2004.

Rasmussen, L. "Eco-Justice: Church and Community Together." In *Earth Habitat: Eco-Injustice and the Church's Response*, edited by D. Hessel and L. Rasmussen, 1–20. Minneapolis: Augsburg Fortress, 2001.

Ratzinger, J. *The Spirit of Liturgy*. San Francisco: Ignatius Press, 2000.

———. *Jesus of Nazareth*. New York: Doubleday, 2007.

Ratzinger, J., with Vittorio Messori. *The Ratzinger Report: An Exclusive Interview on the State of the Church*. Translated by S. Attanasio and G. Harrison. San Francisco: Ignatius Press, 1985.

Reader, J. *Cities*. London: William Heineman, 2004.

Redekop, C., ed. *Creation and Environment: An Anabaptist Perspective on the World*. Baltimore: Johns Hopkins University Press, 2000.

Register, R. *Ecocities: Rebuilding Cities in Balance with Nature*. Gabriola Island, BC: New Society Publishers, 2006.

Relph, E. "Geographical Experiences and Being-in-the-World: The Phenomenological Origins of Geography." In *Dwelling, Place, and Experience: Towards a Phenomenology of Person and World*, edited by D. Seamon and R. Mugerauer, 15–31. Dordrecht: Nijhof, 1985.

Renz, T. *The Rhetorical Function of the Book of Ezekiel*. Leiden: Brill, 1999.

Reymond, P. *L'eau, sa vie, et sa signification dans l'ancien testament*. Supplements to Vetus Testamentum, vol. 6. Leiden: Brill, 1958.

Riches, J. K. *Conflicting Mythologies: Identity Formation in the Gospels of Mark and Matthew*. Edinburgh: T&T Clark, 2000.

Ridderbos, H. *When the Time Had Fully Come: Studies in New Testament Theology*. St. Catharines, ON: Paideia Press, 1957.

———. *Paul and Jesus: Origin and General Character of Paul's Preaching of Christ*. Translated by D. H. Freeman. Grand Rapids: Baker, 1958.

———. *The Coming of the Kingdom*. Translated by H. de Jongste. Edited by R. O. Zorn. St. Catharines, ON: Paideia Press, 1962.

———. "The Church and the Kingdom of God." *International Reformed Bulletin* 27 (October 1966): 8–18.

———. *Paul: An Outline of His Theology*. Translated by J. R. de Witt. Grand Rapids: Eerdmans, 1975.

———. *The Gospel of John: A Theological Commentary*. Translated by J. Vriend. Grand Rapids: Eerdmans, 1997.

Ridderbos, J. *Deuteronomy*. Grand Rapids: Zondervan, 1984.

Riesner, R. "Bethany beyond the Jordan (John 1:28): Topography, Theology and History in the Fourth Gospel." *Tyndale Bulletin* 38 (1987): 29–63.

Rist, J. M. *Epicurus: An Introduction*. Cambridge: Cambridge University Press, 1972.

———. *The Stoics*. Berkeley: University of California Press, 1978.

Rittner, C., and J. K. Roth, ed. *Memory Offended: The Auschwitz Convent Controversy*. New York: Praeger, 1991.

Robinson, M. *Gilead*. New York: Farrar, Straus, and Giroux, 2004.

———. *The Death of Adam: Essays on Modern Thought*. New York: Picador, 2005.

———. *Home*. Toronto: HarperCollins, 2008.

Roof, W. C. "Religious Borderlands: Challenges for Future Study." *Journal of the Scientific Study of Religion* 37, no. 1 (March 1998): 1–14.

Rosen, R. *The Life of the Skies: Birding at the End of Nature*. New York: Farrar, Straus & Giroux, 2008.

Ross, D. *Aristotle*. London: Methuen, 1964.

Ross, W. D., ed and translator. *Aristotle's Physics*. Oxford: Oxford University Press, 1963.

Rossing, B. R. *The Choice between Two Cities: Whore, Bride and Empire in the Apocalypse*. Harrisburg, PA: Trinity Press International, 1999.

Rowe, R. D. *God's Kingdom and God's Son: The Background to Mark's Christology from Concepts of Kingship in the Psalms*. Leiden: Brill, 2002.

Roy, R. *Earth-Sheltered Houses*. Gabriola Island, BC: New Society Publishers, 2006.

Rubin, C. *How to Get Your Lawn off Grass*. Madeira Park, BC: Harbour, 2002.

Rudwick, M. J. S. *Bursting the Limits of Time: The Reconstruction of Geohistory in the Age of Revolution*. Chicago: University of Chicago Press, 2005.

Rybczynski, W. *Home: A Short History of an Idea*. New York: Penguin, 1987.

———. *City Life*. New York: Simon & Schuster, 1995.

———. *The Perfect House*. New York: Scribner, 2002.

———. *Last Harvest*. New York: Scribner, 2007.

Ryken, L. *Worldly Saints: The Puritans as They Really Were*. Grand Rapids: Zondervan, 1986.

Rykwert, J. *The Seduction of Place: The History and Future of the City*. New York: Vintage Books, 2000.

Saalschütz, J. L. *Das Mosaische Recht*. Berlin: Carl Heymann, 1846.

Sack, R. D. *Homo Geographicus: A Framework for Action, Awareness, and Moral Concern*. Baltimore: Johns Hopkins University Press, 1997.

Safina, C. *Song for the Blue Ocean*. New York: Henry Holt & Company, 1997.

Sandbach, F. H. *The Stoics*. London: Chatto & Windus, 1975.

Sanders, E. P. *Paul and Palestinian Judaism: A Comparison of Patterns of Religion*. Philadelphia: Fortress, 1977.

———. *Paul, the Law, and the Jewish People*. Philadelphia: Fortress, 1983.

Sanders, E. P., A. I. Baumgarten, and A. Mendelson, eds. *Jewish and Christian Self-Definition: Aspects of Judaism in the Graeco-Roman Period*. London: SCM, 1981.

Santmire, H. P. *Brother Earth: Nature, God and Ecology in Time of Crisis*. New York: Nelson, 1970.

———. *The Travail of Nature: The Ambiguous Ecological Promise of Christian Theology*. Minneapolis: Fortress, 1985.

———. *Nature Reborn: The Ecological and Cosmic Promise of Christian Theology*. Minneapolis: Fortress, 2000.

———. *Ritualizing Nature: Renewing Christian Liturgy in a Time of Crisis*. Minneapolis: Fortress, 2008.

Sardar, Z. *Postmodernism and the Other*. London: Pluto Press, 1998.

Saul, J. R. *The Collapse of Globalism*. Toronto: Penguin, 2005.

Schaeffer, E. *Hidden Art*. Wheaton, IL: Tyndale House, 1971.

———. *What Is a Family?* Crowborough, East Sussex: Highland Books, 1975.

Schama, S. *Landscape and Memory*. New York: Vintage, 1995.

Schmemann, A. *For the Life of the World: Sacraments and Orthodoxy*. Crestwood, NY: St. Vladimir's Seminary Press, 1973.

Schmidt, K. L. "Jerusalem als Urbild und Abbild." *Eranos-Jahrbuch* 18 (1950): 207–48.

Schoenauer, N. *6,000 Years of Housing*. New York: Norton, 2000.

Schweitzer, A. *Geschichte der Paulinische Forschung von der Reformation bis auf die Gegenwart*. Tubingen: Mohr, 1912.

———. *Paul and His Interpreters: A Critical History*. New York: Schocken, 1964.

Scobie, C. H. H. *John the Baptist*. London: SCM, 1964.

———. "Johannine Geography." *Sciences Religieuses/Studies in Religion* 11.1 (1982): 77–84.

Scott, A. *Origen and the Life of Stars: A History of an Idea*. Oxford: Clarendon, 1991.

Scott, A. J., and E. W. Soja, eds. *The City: Los Angeles and Urban Theory at the End of the Twentieth Century*. Los Angeles: University of California Press, 1996.

Scott, J. M. *Paul and the Nations: The Old Testament and Jewish Background of Paul's Mission to the Nations with Special Reference to the Destination of Galatians*. Tübingen, Germany: Mohr, 1995.

Scott, P. *A Political Theology of Nature*. Cambridge: Cambridge University Press, 2003.

Scully, M. *Dominion: The Power of Man, the Suffering of Animals, and the Call to Mercy*. New York: St. Martin's Press, 2002.

Seamon, D. *A Geography of the Lifeworld: Movement, Rest and Encounter*. New York: St. Martin's Press, 1979.

Seerveld, C. *Rainbows for the Fallen World: Aesthetic Life and Artistic Task*. Toronto: Tuppence Press, 1980.

———. "Dooyeweerd's Idea of 'Historical Development': Christian Respect for Cultural Diversity." *Westminster Theological Journal* 58 (1996): 41–61.

———. "Cities as a Place for Public Artwork: A Global Approach." In *The Gospel and Globalization: Exploring the Religious Roots of a Globalized World*, edited by M. W. Goheen and E. G. Glanville, 299–324. Vancouver: Regent College Publishing, 2009.

Seitz, C. R. *Word without End: The Old Testament as Abiding Theological Witness*. Grand Rapids: Eerdmans, 1998.

Selwyn, E. G. *The First Epistle of St. Peter*. London: Macmillan, 1947.

———. "Eschatology in 1 Peter." In *The Background of the New Testament and Its Eschatology: Studies in Honor of C. H. Dodd*, edited by D. Daube and W. D. Davies, 394–401. Cambridge: Cambridge University Press, 1954.

Senior, D. "1 Peter." In *1 Peter, Jude and 2 Peter*, edited by D. J. Harrington, 3–158. Collegeville, MN: Liturgical Press, 2003.

Senior, D., and C. Stuhlmueller. *The Biblical Foundations for Mission*. New York: Orbis Books, 1983.

Seow, C. L. *Ecclesiastes*. Anchor Bible 18C. New York: Doubleday, 1997.

Sharr, A. *Heidegger's Hut*. Cambridge, MA: MIT Press, 2006.

Shevelow, K. *For the Love of Animals: The Rise of the Animal Protection Movement*. New York: Henry Holt & Company, 2008.

Shuman, M. H. *The Small-Mart Revolution: How Local Businesses Are Beating the Global Competition*. San Francisco: Berrett-Koehler, 2006.

Silentiarius, P. "Descr. S. Sophiae." In Mango, *Art of the Byzantine Empire*, 80–91.

———. "Descr. ambonis v. 50ff." In Mango, *Art of the Byzantine Empire*, 91–96.

Simkins, R. A. *Creator & Creation: Nature in the Worldview of Ancient Israel*. Peabody, MA: Hendrickson, 2008.

Skillen, J. R. *The Nation's Largest Landlord: The Bureau of Land Management in the American West*. Lawrence, KS: University of Kansas Press, 2009.

Sleeman, M. *Geography and the Ascension Narrative in Acts*. Cambridge: Cambridge University Press, 2009.

Smalley, S. S. *1, 2, 3 John*. Word Biblical Commentary 51. Nashville: Nelson, 1984.

Smith, C., and J. F. O'Connor. *Building the Kingdom: Giannozzo Manetti on the Material and Spiritual Edifice*. Tempe, AZ: Arizona Center for Medieval and Renaissance Studies, 2006.

Smith, J. Z. *To Take Place: Toward Theory in Ritual*. Chicago: University of Chicago Press, 1987.

Smith, M. A. F., J. Whiteleg, and N. J. Williams. *Greening the Built Environment*. London: Earthscan, 1998.

Smith, M. S. *The Pilgrimage Pattern in Exodus*. Sheffield, UK: Sheffield Academic Press, 1997.

Smith, N. K. "Crisis in Jerusalem." In *The Chicago Tribune Tower Competition: Late Entries*, edited by S. Cohen and S. Tigerman, 2:109. New York: Rizzoli Press, 1980.

Snell, C., and T. Callahan. *Building Green*. New York: Lark Books, 2005.

Snodgrass, K. *Stories with Intent: A Comprehensive Guide to the Parables of Jesus*. Grand Rapids: Eerdmans, 2008.

Snyder, G. *A Place of Space*. Berkeley: Counterpoint, 1995.

Soja, E. W. *Postmetropolis: Critical Studies of Cities and Regions*. Oxford: Blackwell, 2000.

Soley, L. C. *Leasing the Ivory Tower: The Corporate Takeover of Academia*. Boston: South End Press, 1995.

Solnit, R. *Wanderlust: A History of Walking*. New York: Penguin, 2000.

———. "Detroit Arcadia: Exploring the Post-American Landscape." *Harper's Magazine* (July 2007): 113–24.

Solomon, S. *Water: The Epic Struggle for Wealth, Power, and Civilization*. New York: HarperCollins, 2010.

Speiser, E. A. "'People' and 'Nation' of Israel." *Journal of Biblical Literature* 79 (1960): 157–63.

Spencer, R. W., P. K. Driessen, and E. C. Beisner. "An Examination of the Scientific, Ethical and Theological Implications of Climate Change Policy." http://www.cornwallalliance.org/articles/read/an-examination-of-the-scientific-ethical-and-theological-implications-of-climate-change-policy/

Spykman, G. J. *Reformational Theology: A New Paradigm for Doing Dogmatics*. Grand Rapids: Eerdmans, 1992.

Stahl, J. *Street Art*. Bonn, Germany: H. F. Ullmann, 2008.

Stamm, J. J., with M. E. Andrew. *The Ten Commandments in Recent Research*. Translated by M. E. Andrew. 2nd ed. London: SCM, 1970.

Starke, L., ed. *2007 State of the World: Our Urban Future*. New York: Norton, 2007.

Steinmetz, D. *From Father to Son: Kinship, Conflict, and Continuity in Genesis*. Grand Rapids: Eerdmans, 1991.

Stevenson, K. R. *Visions of Transformation: The Territorial Rhetoric of Ezekiel 40–48*. Atlanta: Scholars Press, 1996.

Steves, R. *Travel as a Political Act*. New York: Nation Books, 2009.

Stewart, A. *Flower Confidential*. Chapel Hill, NC: Algonquin Books, 2008.

Stocks, C. *Forgotten Fruits*. New York: Random House, 2008.

Strauss, L. "On the Interpretation of Genesis." *L'Homme* XXI, no. 1 (January–March 1981): 5–20.

Sumption, J. *Pilgrimage*. London: Faber and Faber, 1975.

Suzuki, D., and A. Grady. *Tree: A Life Story*. Toronto: GreyStone, 2004.

Swartley, W. M. "The Structural Function of the Term 'Way' (*Hodos*) in Mark's Gospel." In *The New Way of Jesus: Essays Presented to Howard Charles*, edited by W. Klassen, 73–86. Newton, KS: Faith and Life Press, 1980.

Talbert, C. H. *Ephesians and Colossians*. Grand Rapids: Baker Academic, 2007.

Tamez, E. *The Scandalous Message of James: Faith without Works Is Dead*. New York: Crossroad, 1992.

Tan, K. H. *The Zion Traditions and the Aims of Jesus*. Cambridge: Cambridge University Press, 1997.

Taylor, B. *An Altar in the World: A Geography of Faith*. New York: HarperCollins, 2009.

Taylor, C. *Sources of the Self: The Making of the Modern Identity*. Cambridge, MA: Harvard University Press, 1992.

Temple, W. *Nature, Man and God*. London: Macmillan, 1934.

Terpstra, J. *Falling into Place*. Kentville, Nova Scotia: Gaspereau Press, 2002.

Terrien, S. *The Elusive Presence: Toward a New Biblical Theology*. San Francisco: Harper & Row, 1978.

Thiselton, A. C. *The First Epistle to the Corinthians*. Grand Rapids: Eerdmans, 2000.

———. *The Living Paul: An Introduction to the Apostle's Life and Thought*. Downers Grove, IL: InterVarsity, 2009.

Thomas Aquinas. *Summa Theologica*. 5 vols. Notre Dame: Ave Maria Press, 1948.

———. *Political Writings*. Edited by R. W. Dyson. *Cambridge Texts in the History of Politial Thought*. Cambridge: Cambridge University Press, 2002.

———. *On Kingship: To the King of Cyprus*. Toronto: Pontifical Institute of Medieval Studies, 1967.

Thomas, K. *Man and the Natural World: Changing Attitudes in England, 1500–1800*. London: Oxford University Press, 1983.

Thompson, J. W. *The Beginnings of Christian Philosophy: The Epistle to the Hebrews*. Washington, DC: Catholic Biblical Association of America, 1982.

Thompson, L. L. "The Literary Unity of the Book of Revelation." In *Mappings of the Biblical Terrain: The Bible as Text*, edited by V. L. Tollers and J. Maier, 347–63.

Lewisburg, PA: Bucknell University Press, 1990.

Thoreau, H. D. *Wild Apples, and Other Natural History Essays*. Edited by William Rossi. Athens, GA: University of Georgia Press, 2002.

———. *Walden*. New Haven: Yale University Press, 2004.

Thornton, P. *Authentic Decor: The Domestic Interior, 1620–1920*. London: Weidenfeld & Nicolson, 1984.

Thurnberg, L. *Microcosm and Mediator: The Theological Anthropology of Maximus the Confessor*. Chicago: Open Court, 1995.

Tillich, P. *The New Being*. New York: Charles Scribner's Sons, 1955.

———. *Theology of Culture*. Edited by R. C. Kimball. London: Oxford University Press, 1959.

Tjørhom, O. *Embodied Faith: Reflections on a Materialist Spirituality*. Grand Rapids: Eerdmans, 2009.

Tollers, V. L. *Mappings of the Biblical Terrain: The Bible as Text*. Lewisburg, PA: Bucknell University Press, 1990.

Torchia, O. P. N. *Creatio Ex Nihilo and the Theology of St. Augustine: The Anti-Manichaean Polemic and Beyond*. New York: Peter Lang, 1999.

Torrance, T. F. *The Apocalypse Today*. London: James Clarke, 1960.

———. *Space, Time, and Incarnation*. Edinburgh: T&T Clark, 1997.

———. *Christian Theology and Scientific Culture*. Eugene, OR: Wipf & Stock, 1998.

Trigg, R. *The Shaping of Man: Philosophical Aspects of Sociobiology*. New York: Schocken, 1982.

Trilling, W. *Das wahre Israel: Studien zur Theologie des Matthäus-Evangeliums*. Munich: Kosel, 1964.

Trites, A. A. *The New Testament Concept of Witness*. Cambridge: Cambridge University Press, 1977.

Troeltsch, E. *The Social Teaching of the Christian Churches*. 2 vols. Translated by O. Wyon. New York and Evanston: Harper & Row, 1960.

Tsuji, M. *Glaube zwischen Vollkomenheit und Verweltlichung: Eine Untersuching zur literarischen Gestalt und zur inhaltlichen Kohärenz des Jakobsbriefes*. Wissenschaftliche Untersuchungen zum Neuen Testament 2/93. Tübingen: Mohr Siebeck, 1997.

Tudge, C. *The Tree*. New York: Three Rivers Press, 2005.

Tuplin, C. *Achaemenid Studies*. Stuttgart, Germany: Franz Steiner Verlag, 1996.

Turner, F. *Spirit of Place: The Making of an American Literary Landscape*. San Francisco: Sierra Club Books, 1989.

Turner, V. *Dramas, Fields, and Metaphors*. Ithaca, NY: Cornell University Press, 1974.

———. *The Ritual Process: Structure and Anti-Structure*. Ithaca, NY: Cornell University Press, 1974.

Tzamalikos, P. *Origen: Cosmology and Ontology of Time*. Leiden: Brill, 2006.

———. *Origen: Philosophy of History and Eschatology*. Leiden: Brill, 2007.

Ulmer, G. "Electronic Monumentality." *Nomad* 1992.

United States Catholic Conference. *Catechism of the Catholic Church*. New York: Doubleday, 1994.

Van Gennep, A. *The Rites of Passage*. New York: Routledge, 2004.

Van Kooten, G. H., ed. *The Creation of Heaven and Earth: Re-Interpretation of Genesis in the Context of Judaism, Ancient Philosophy, Christianity, and Modern Physics*. Leiden: Brill, 2005.

Van Leeuwen, R. C. "Wealth and Poverty: System and Contradiction in Proverbs." *Hebrew Studies* 33 (1992): 25–36.

———. "The Book of Proverbs." In vol. 5 of *The New Interpreter's Bible*, 17–264. Nashville: Abingdon, 1997.

Van Noy, R. *Surveying the Interior: Literary Cartographers and the Sense of Place*. Las Vegas: University of Nevada Press, 2003.

Van Selms, A. "Build, Building." In Bromiley, *The International Standard Bible Encyclopedia*, 553–55.

Van Zuylen, G. *Paradise on Earth: The Gardens of Western Europe*. New York: Harry N. Abrams, 1994.

Vavarek, T. "The Church Building and the Paschal Mystery." *The Journal of Sacred Architecture* 5 (Spring 2001). Available online at http://www.sacredarchitecture.org/articles/the_church_building_and_participation_in_the_paschal_mystery/

Veldhuis, N. *Religion, Literature, and Scholarship: The Sumerian Composition* Nanše *and the Birds*. Leiden: Brill/Styx, 2004.

Vicente, P., and T. Connor. *The Language of Doors*. New York: Artisan, 2005.

Visser, M. *The Geometry of Love: Space, Time, Mystery and Meaning in an Ordinary Church*. Toronto: HarperCollins, 2000.

Vitale, P., and A. Saralegui. *The Divine Home: Living with Spiritual Objects*. New York: Clarkson Potter, 2008.

Vitek, W., and W. Jackson, eds. *Rooted in the Land: Essays on Community and Place*. New Haven: Yale University Press, 1996.

Vögtle, A. *Das Neue Testament und die Zukunft des Kosmos*. Düsseldorf: Patmos, 1970.

Vriezen, T. C. *An Outline of Old Testament Theology*. Oxford: Blackwell, 1958.

Wainwright, G., and K. B. Westerfield-Tucker, eds. *The Oxford History of Christian Worship*. Oxford: Oxford University Press, 2006.

Walker-Jones, A. *The Green Psalter: Resources for an Ecological Spirituality*. Minneapolis: Fortress, 2009.

Wallace, R. N. "Rest for the Earth? Another Look at Genesis 2:1–3." In Habel and Wurst, *The Earth Story in Genesis*, 49–59.

Wallis, G. "Die Stadt in der Überlieferung der Genesis." *Zeitschrift für die alttestamentliche Wissenschaft* 78 (1966): 133–48.

Walser, R. *The Assistant*. New York: New Directions, 2007.

Waltke, B. K. *A Commentary on Micah*. Grand Rapids: Eerdmans, 2007.

Walton, J. H., V. H. Matthews, and M. Chavalas. *The IVP Bible Background Commentary: Old Testament*. Downers Grove, IL: InterVarsity, 2000.

Wanamaker, C. A. *The Epistle to the Thessalonians*. Grand Rapids: Eerdmans, 1990.

Ward, G. *Cities of God*. London: Routledge, 2000.

Watkins, P., and J. Stockland. *Winged Wonders: A Celebration of Birds in History*. New York: BlueBridge, 2005.

Watson, F. *Paul and the Hermeneutics of Faith*. London and New York: T&T Clark, 2004.

Watts, J. D. W. *Isaiah 1–33*. Word Biblical Commentary 24. Nashville: Nelson, 2005.

Watts, R. E. *Isaiah's New Exodus in Mark*. Grand Rapids: Baker Academic, 1997.

Wazana, N. "Water Division in Border Agreements." *State Archives of Assyria Bulletin*, vol. 10 (1996): 55–66.

———. "From Dan to Beer-Sheba and from the Wilderness to the Sea: Literal and Literary Images of the Promised Land in the Bible." In *Experiences of Place*, edited by M. N. MacDonald, 45–85. Cambridge, MA: Harvard University Press, 2003.

———. *All the Boundaries of the Land: The Promised Land in Biblical Thought in Light of the Ancient Near East*. Jerusalem: Bialik, 2007. Hebrew.

Webb, R. L. *John the Baptizer and Prophet: A Socio-Historical Study*. Sheffield, UK: Sheffield Academic Press, 1991.

Weber, M. *Gesammelte Aufsätze zur Religionssoziologie*. Tübingen, Germany: Mohr, 1921.

———. *The Protestant Ethic and the Spirit of Capitalism*. Translated by T. Parsons. New York: Routledge, 1992.

Weber, N. F. *Le Corbusier: A Life*. New York: Knopf, 2008.

Weinandy, T. G., D. A. Keating, and J. P. Yocum, eds. *Aquinas on Doctrine: A Critical Introduction*. New York: T&T Clark, 2004.

Weinfeld, M. "The Covenant of Grant in Old Testament and Ancient Near East." *Journal of the American Oriental Society* 90 (1970): 184–203.

———. *The Promise of the Land: The Inheritance of the Land of Canaan by the*

Israelites. Berkeley: University of California Press, 1993.

———. "The Covenantal Aspect of the Promise of the Land to Israel," in Weinfeld, *The Promise of the Land*, 222–64.

Welch, J. *Spiritual Pilgrims: Carl Jung and Teresa of Avila*. New York: Paulist Press, 1982.

Wells, C. *Sailing from Byzantium: How a Lost Empire Shaped the World*. New York: Random House, 2007.

Wenell, K. J. *Jesus and Land: Sacred and Social Space in Second Temple Judaism*. Edinburgh: T&T Clark, 2007.

Wenham, D. "The Kingdom of God and Daniel." *Expository Times* 98 (1987): 132–34.

———. *Paul: Follower of Jesus or Founder of Christianity?* Grand Rapids: Eerdmans, 1995.

Wenham, G. J. "The Structure and Date of Deuteronomy." PhD diss., University of London, 1970.

———. *The Book of Leviticus*. Grand Rapids: Eerdmans, 1979.

———. *Numbers*. Leicester, UK: Inter-Varsity, 1981.

———. "Sanctuary Symbolism in the Garden of Eden Story." *Proceedings of the 9th World Congress of Jewish Studies* 9 (1986): 19–25.

———. *Genesis 1–15*. Word Biblical Commentary 1. Waco: Word Books, 1987.

———. *Genesis 16–50*. Word Biblical Commentary 2. Dallas: Word Books, 1994.

Wenham, J. W. *The Goodness of God*. Downers Grove, IL: InterVarsity, 1974.

Westcott, B. F. *The Epistle to the Hebrews*. London: Macmillan, 1889.

Westerholm, S. *Israel's Law and the Church's Faith: Paul and His Recent Interpreters*. Grand Rapids: Eerdmans, 1988.

Westermann, C. *Blessing in the Bible and the Life of the Church*. Philadelphia: Fortress, 1978.

———. *Genesis 1–11*. Minneapolis: Augsburg, 1984.

White, L. "The Historical Roots of Our Ecological Crisis." *Science* 155 (1967): 1203–7.

———. *Machine Ex Deo: Essays in the Dynamics of Western Culture*. Cambridge, MA: MIT Press, 1968.

Whitehead, A. N. *The Concept of Nature*. Cambridge: Cambridge University Press, 1920.

———. *Science and the Modern World*. Cambridge: Cambridge University Press, 1926.

———. *Process and Reality: An Essay in Cosmology*. New York: Humanities Press, 1929.

Whyte, W. H. *The Last Landscape*. New York: Doubleday, 1968.

Wilder, A. N. "Preface." In Willis, *The Kingdom of God in 20th Century Interpretation*, vii–x.

Wilken, R. L. *The Land Called Holy: Palestine in Christian History and Thought*. New Haven: Yale University Press, 1992.

———. *The Spirit of Early Christian Thought*. New Haven: Yale University Press, 2003.

Wilkenhauser, A. *Offenbarung des Johannes*. Regensburger Neues Testament. Regensburg: Pustet, 1959.

William of Ockham. *A Short Discourse on Tyrannical Government: Over Things Divine and Human, but Especially over the Empire and Those Subject to the Empire, Usurped by Some Who Are Called Highest Pontiffs*. Cambridge: Cambridge University Press, 1992.

Williams, R. *Culture and Materialism: Selected Essays*. London: Verso, 1980.

Williamson, H. G. M. *Ezra/Nehemiah*. Word Biblical Commentary 16. Nashville: Nelson, 1985.

Willis, W., ed. *The Kingdom of God in 20th Century Interpretation*. Peabody, MA: Hendrickson, 1987.

Wilson, R. R. "Creation and New Creation: The Role of Creation Imagery in the Book of Daniel." In Brown and McBride, *The God Who Creates*, 292–310.

Winchester, S. *The Map That Changed the World: William Smith and the Birth of Modern Geology*. New York: HarperCollins, 2001.

Wink, W. *John the Baptist in the Gospel Tradition*. Cambridge: Cambridge University Press, 1968.

Winter, B. *Seek the Welfare of the City: Christians as Benefactors and Citizens.* Grand Rapids: Eerdmans, 1994.

Wirzba, N. *The Paradise of God: Renewing Religion in an Ecological Age.* Oxford: Oxford University Press, 2003.

Wiseman, D. J. "Abraham Reassessed." In *Essays on the Patriarchal Narratives*, edited by A. R. Millard and D. J. Wiseman, 139–56. Leicester, UK: Inter-Varsity, 1980.

———. *1 and 2 Kings: An Introduction and Commentary.* Tyndale Old Testament Commentaries. Downers Grove, IL: Inter-Varsity, 1993.

———. "Babylonia and Assyria, Religion of." In vol. 1 of *International Standard Bible Encyclopedia*, edited by G. W. Bromiley, 384–402.

Witherington, B., III. *History, Literature, and Society in the Book of Acts.* Cambridge: Cambridge University Press, 1996.

Witte, J. J. *The Reformation of Rights: Law, Religion, and Human Rights in Early Modern Calvinism.* Cambridge: Cambridge University Press, 2007.

Woginrich, J. *Made from Scratch: Discovering the Pleasures of a Handmade Life.* North Adams, MA: Storey, 2008.

Wolfe, T. *I Am Charlotte Simmons.* London: Jonathan Cape, 2004.

Wolters, A. M. *Creation Regained.* Grand Rapids: Eerdmans, 1985.

———. "Worldview and Textual Criticism in 2 Peter 3:10." *Westminster Theological Journal* 49 (1987): 405–13.

———. "Creation, Worldview and Foundations." Unpublished paper, 1997.

———. *The Song of the Valiant Woman: Studies in the Interpretation of Proverbs 31:10–31.* Carlisle: Paternoster, 2001.

Wolterstorff, N. *On Universals: An Essay in Ontology.* Chicago: University of Chicago Press, 1970.

———. *Art in Action.* Grand Rapids: Eerdmans, 1980.

———. *Until Justice and Peace Embrace.* Grand Rapids: Eerdmans, 1983.

Wright, C. J. H. *Living as the People of God.* Downers Grove, IL: InterVarsity, 1984.

———. *God's People in God's Land: Family, Land, and Property in the Old Testament.* Grand Rapids: Eerdmans, 1990.

———. *Deuteronomy.* Peabody, MA: Hendrickson, 1996.

———. *The Mission of God: Unlocking the Bible's Grand Narrative.* Downers Grove, IL: IVP Academic, 2006.

Wright, N. T. "Jesus Is Coming—Plant a Tree!" In *The Green Bible*, 72–85. San Francisco: HarperOne, 1989.

———. *The Climax of the Covenant: Christ and the Law in Pauline Theology.* Minneapolis: Fortress, 1991.

———. *The New Testament and the People of God.* Minneapolis: Fortress, 1992.

———. *Jesus and the Victory of God.* London: SPCK, 1996.

———. *What Saint Paul Really Said: Was Paul of Tarsus the Real Founder of Christianity?* Grand Rapids: Eerdmans, 1997.

———. *The Way of the Lord.* London: Triangle, 1999.

———. "Romans." In vol. 10 of *The New Interpreter's Bible*, edited by L. E. Keck, 393–770. Nashville, Abingdon, 2002.

———. *The Resurrection of the Son of God.* London: SPCK, 2003.

———. *Hebrews for Everyone.* London: SPCK, 2004.

Wright, W. J. *Martin Luther's Understanding of God's Two Kingdoms: A Response to the Challenge of Skepticism.* Grand Rapids: Baker Academic, 2010.

Wurst, Shirley. "'Beloved, Come Back to Me': Ground's Theme Song in Gen. 3?" In Habel and Wurst, *Earth Story in Genesis*, 87–104.

Yarnold, S. J. E. *Cyril of Jerusalem.* New York: Routledge, 2000.

Young, J. E. *The Texture of Memory: Holocaust Memorials and Meaning.* New Haven: Yale University Press, 1993.

Zahrnt, H. *The Question of God: Protestant Theology in the Twentieth Century.* London: Collins, 1969.

Zencey, E. "The Rootless Professors." In Vitek and Jackson, *Rooted in the Land*, 15–19.

Ziesler, J. A. *Pauline Christianity*. Oxford: Oxford University Press, 1990.

Zimmerli, W. *The Old Testament and the World*. London: SPCK, 1976.

Zimmerman, M. E. *Contesting Earth's Future: Radical Ecology and Postmodernity*. Los Angeles: University of California Press, 1994.

Zmijewski, J. "Christliche 'Vollkommenheit': Erwägungen zur Theologie des Jakobusbriefes." *Studien zum Neuen Testament und seiner Umwelt* 5 (1980): 50–78.

Zornberg, A. G. *The Particulars of Rapture: Reflections on Exodus*. New York: Doubleday, 2001.

Zylstra, B. "Preface." In H. E. Runner, *The Relation of the Bible to Learning*, 9–34. Jordan Station, ON: Paideia, 1982.

Scripture Index

89   81n19
93–99   81n19
95   144
95:4–7   144
96:2   102
102:26–27   144
103:19   96
104:12   20n50
104:17   20n50
118   81n19
120–34   66
121:2   66
122   81, 303
122:4   303
124:8   66
125–26   81
128–29   81
132–134   81
134:3   66
145:11–13   96
148:10   20n50

Proverbs

1–9   88
2:21   88
3:10   88
3:18   161n96
3:33   88
8   87
8:1–5   88
8:15–16   88n54
8:27–31   87
20:4   36n15
31   88, 89
31:14   89
31:14–15   89
31:16   89
31:21   89
31:26   89
31:30   89

Ecclesiastes

2:4–6   269
12:4   20n51

Isaiah

1   84
1–39   85n37
1:21   85
1:27   84
2:1–4   85
11:6–9   106
13–23   85
19:18–19   85
19:18–24   85

19:20   85
19:24–25   85
31:5   20n50
33:11   154n59
33:12   154n59
34:4   145
40–55   114
40–66   85n37
40:3   103
40:9   102
42:1   104
49:10   161n96
52:7   102
55:1   161n96
55:10–11   111
55:10–13   111
55:12–13   111
58:6   107
61   107
61:1   102
61:1–2   107
61:2   107
61:11   107
64:1   104, 105
64:2   105
65   85
65:17   160
65:17–18   86
65:17–66:24   86
65:25   106
66   85
66:1   145
66:18–23   86

Jeremiah

3:14   84
4:6   84
4:25   20n51
5:24   27
9:10   20n51
12:4   20n51
31   141, 142
31:31–34   144
51:44   85n37

Ezekiel

10   84
17:22–23   112
17:23   20n50
28:13–20   161
31:6   20n50
32:27   13
34   13
34:4   13
34:25–31   103
34:31   13

36:35   268
40–48   84, 86
40:2   86, 161
43   86, 163
43:7   86
43:12   86
45:1–8   87
45:8   108
47–48   46, 87
47:1–12   161n96
47:12   161n96
47:13   108
47:22   87

Daniel

2   96
2–7   96, 101
2:38   20n50
4:10–12   112
4:21   20n50
7   96, 114, 115
7:12–14   109

Hosea

2:18   20n50
4:3   20n51
5:14   83n30
11:10   83n30
13:7   83n30

Joel

2:1   84
2:15   84
3:16   83n30, 84

Amos

1:1   82
1:2   83, 84
1:2–2:16   82
2:9–16   65
2:13   83
3:15   35n14
4:2–3   82
4:13   83
5:8–9   83
6:7   82
7:14   83n29
8:1–2   35n14
9:5–6   83
9:11–15   84
9:12   84

Obadiah

17   84
21   84

Jonah

1:9   84
2:4   84
2:7   84

Micah

1:2   84
3:10   84
3:12   84
4   84
4:1   85n37
4:1–5   85n36
4:7   84

Nahum

1:5   84

Habakkuk

2:14   84
2:20   84

Zephaniah

1:3   20n51
1:18   154n59
3:5   84
3:9   84
3:19   84

Haggai

1–2   84
2:6   147

Zechariah

2:12   84
2:13   84
8:3   84
9–14   114
12:6   154n59
14:8   161n96

Malachi

4:1   154n59

New Testament

Matthew

1:1   102
1:23   101
3:15   105
5   91
5:3   107

Subject Index

Printed and bound by CPI Group (UK) Ltd, Croydon, CR0 4YY

13/04/2025

14656456-0004